TOMORROW'S CRIMINALS

Tomorrow's Criminals
The Development of Child Delinquency and Effective Interventions

Edited by

ROLF LOEBER
N. WIM SLOT
PETER H. VAN DER LAAN
MACHTELD HOEVE

ASHGATE

Published by
Ashgate Publishing Limited
Wey Court East
Union Road
Farnham
Surrey GU9 7PT
England

Ashgate Publishing Company
Suite 420
101 Cherry Street
Burlington, VT 05401-4405
USA

www.ashgate.com

British Library Cataloguing in Publication Data
Tomorrow's criminals : the development of child delinquency
and effective interventions
1. Juvenile delinquency 2. Juvenile delinquency -
Prevention
I. Loeber, Rolf
364.3'6

Library of Congress Cataloging-in-Publication Data
Tomorrow's criminals : the development of child delinquency and effective interventions / by Rolf Loeber ... [et al.].
p. cm.
Includes bibliographical references and index.
ISBN 978-0-7546-7151-0
1. Juvenile delinquency--Netherlands. 2. Juvenile delinquency--Prevention--Netherlands. 3. Crime prevention--Research--Netherlands. I. Loeber, Rolf.

HV9125.3.A5T66 2008
364.3609492--dc22

2008009814

ISBN 978 0 7546 7151 0

Mixed Sources
Product group from well-managed forests and other controlled sources
www.fsc.org Cert no. SA-COC-1565
© 1996 Forest Stewardship Council
FSC

Printed and bound in Great Britain by
MPG Books Ltd, Bodmin, Cornwall.

Contents

List of Figures

List of Tables

List of Contributors

Channa M.W. Al, Drs., is a PhD candidate at the University of Amsterdam. Her research focuses on the effectiveness of intensive in-home crisis intervention for families. She received her Master's degree in social psychology at the VU University Amsterdam. c.al@uva.nl.

Rob Allen, PhD, is Director of the International Centre for Prison Studies at King's College London. Rob was a member of the Youth Justice Board for England and Wales between 1998 and 2006. His research interests include youth justice, alternatives to prison, and public attitudes to punishment, as well as the links between criminal and social policy. rob.allen@kcl.ac.uk.

Leena K. Augimeri, PhD, is the Director of Program Development and the Centre for Children Committing Offences at the Child Development Institute (CDI) in Toronto, Canada, and Adjunct Professor and Sessional Lecturer, University of Toronto. As a scientist-practitioner, Leena has spent over twenty years developing a comprehensive model for young children in conflict with the law that encompasses police-community protocols, gender-sensitive clinical interventions (she is a co-founder/developer of the SNAP™ Model) and clinical risk assessment tools such as the EARL-20B. augimeri@childdevelop.ca.

Leonieke Boendermaker, PhD, is senior research officer at the Netherlands Youth Institute (NJi). Her research interests focus on interventions for youth, with special interest on young offenders and (secure) residential care. l.boendermaker@nji.nl.

Jan J. van Busschbach, PhD, works as Associated Professor at the Department for Medical Psychology and Psychotherapy of the Erasmus University Medical Centre and the Vierspong Institute for Studies on Personality Disorders (VISPD) of the Psychotherapeutic Centre 'De Viersprong'. His main research topics are the economic evaluation of psychotherapy in personality disorder and the relation between coping and health-related quality of life. jan.busschbach@deviersprong.net.

Jaap E. Doek, PhD, is Emeritus Professor Family and Children's Law at the VU University Amsterdam and chairperson of the UN Committee on the Rights of the Child (2001–07). His research interests include international children's rights in general, and juvenile justice in particular. jaapedoek@cs.com.

Lieke van Domburgh, Drs., is Researcher at the Department of Child and Adolescent Psychiatry, VU University Medical Centre Amsterdam. Her research interests are the development of very young official offenders, such as children with police encounters below the age of 12. l.vandomburgh@debascule.com.

Andrea G. Donker, PhD, is Assistant Professor at the Department of Criminology of the University of Leiden, the Netherlands. After studying cognitive psychology and medical biology at the University of Amsterdam, she wrote a thesis on the development of antisocial behaviour at the Netherlands Institute for the Study of Crime and Law Enforcement. Her research interests include developmental criminology, bio-criminology and psychology and law. a.g.donker@law.leidenuniv.nl.

Theo A.H. Doreleijers, MD, PhD, is head of the Department of Child and Adolescent Psychiatry, VU University Medical Centre Amsterdam, and training professor at de Bascule. His research interests are disruptive behaviour disorders and forensic child and adolescent psychiatry. t.doreleijers@debascule.com.

Paola Ferrante, BA, Researcher I for the Centre for Children Committing Offences and Residential Worker at the Child Development Institute (CDI) in Toronto, Canada. Paola currently works as a clinician with antisocial children. Her interests include the intersection of children's mental health and education, specifically, how childhood factors promote academic success and social competence. ferrante_paola@yahoo.com.

Machteld Hoeve, Drs., is a Research Associate and Lecturer at the Department of Educational Sciences of the University of Amsterdam. She wrote a thesis on the relationship between parenting and juvenile delinquency at the Netherlands Institute for the Study of Crime and Law Enforcement. Her research interests include the development of juvenile delinquency, environmental influences such as family processes, and girls' delinquent behaviour. m.hoeve@uva.nl.

Lucres Jansen, PhD, is Senior Researcher at the Department of Child and Adolescent Psychiatry of the VU University Medical Centre Amsterdam. Her main research interest includes the neurobiology of psychiatric disorders, with main focus on stress and adaptation. l.nauta@debascule.com.

Harry Jonkman, Drs., is Senior Researcher at the Netherlands Youth Institute (NJi). His work focuses on social and cognitive development, the development of problem behaviour and the prevention of mental health and behaviour problems among children and adolescents. He is intervention specialist on family, school and community programmes. He is also programme leader of Communities that Care Netherlands. h.jonkman@nji.nl.

Christopher Koegl, MA, and PhD Candidate, Cambridge University, is the Project Manager of the Centre for Children Committing Offences (CCCO) at Child Development Institute, Toronto, Canada. His current research focus is the assessment of childhood, family and community risk factors that predict future antisocial behaviour and health service use in young children, health systems and continuity of care, and clinical approaches for at-risk children and their families. koegl@childdevelop.ca.

Hans M. Koot, PhD, is Professor of Developmental Psychology and Developmental Psychopathology at the VU University Amsterdam. His research interests regard mechanisms of emotional and behavioural development and psychopathology in children and adolescents. jm.koot@psy.vu.nl.

Peter H. van der Laan, PhD, is Senior Researcher at the NSCR in Leiden and Professor of Social and Educational Care at the University of Amsterdam, the Netherlands. His research activities concentrate on juvenile delinquency and antisocial behaviour, and the working and impact of youth care in general and juvenile justice in particular. PvanderLaan@nscr.nl.

Francien Lamers-Winkelman, PhD, is Professor at the Faculty of Psychology and Pedagogy of the VU University Amsterdam. Her research interests are child (sexual) abuse and neglect, family violence and other forms of traumatisation of children. Next to that, she is the coordinator of the Children's and Youth Trauma Centre in Haarlem, the Netherlands. f.lamers@psy.vu.nl.

Pol A.C. van Lier, PhD, is Associate Professor at the Department of Developmental Psychology, VU University Amsterdam. His research focus is on understanding the causes of individual differences in children's (behavioural and emotional) development. This research focus is carried out through several longitudinal and experimental studies, spanning the period from infancy, to childhood, and adolescence. pac.van.lier@psy.vu.nl.

Rolf Loeber, PhD, is Distinguished Professor of Psychiatry, and Professor of Psychology and Epidemiology, University of Pittsburgh, Pittsburgh, PA, USA, and Professor of Juvenile Delinquency and Social Development, Vrije University, Amsterdam, the Netherlands. He is author of *Child Delinquents* (2001), *Serious and Violent Juvenile Offenders* (1998) and *Ernstige en Gewelddadige Jeugdcriminaliteit* (2001). loeberr@upmc.edu.

Ton Mooij, PhD, is Professor for Educational Technology at Open University of The Netherlands (Heerlen) and a manager for educational research and innovation at ITS, Radboud University Nijmegen. His interests concern educational and ICT conditions to improve prosocial, cognitive and organisational aspects of learning with pupils, teachers, schools and wider school environments. t.mooij@its.kun.nl.

Anna Neumann, Drs., is a PhD Candidate at the Department of Developmental Psychology of the VU University Amsterdam. Her research interests are the social and emotional aspects of the development of aggression. a.neumann@psy.vu.nl.

Jaap Oosterlaan, PhD, is Professor of Clinical Neuropsychology at the VU University Amsterdam. His main research interests are neuropsychological dysfunctions in children with disruptive behaviour disorders as well as acquired and congenital disorders in the central nervous system. j.oosterlaan@psy.vu.nl.

Bert Prinsen, MSc, is Senior Researcher at the Netherlands Youth Institute (NJi). He is especially interested in prevention and parenting support. b.prinsen@nji.nl.

Peter Prinzie, PhD, is Associate Professor at the University of Utrecht. His research interests are the predictive effects of negative parenting behaviour and parent and child personality characteristics on the development of externalising and internalising problem behaviour in children. p.prinzie@fss.uu.nl.

Nicola Slater, NNEB, is a Coordinator-Trainer for the Centre for Children Committing Offences – the national division of the Child Development Institute, in Ontario, Canada. She currently provides training and consultation to SNAP™ licensed sites throughout Canada and Europe, and has trained and supported hundreds of professionals in the implementation and delivery of the SNAP™ Model. ccco@childdevelop.ca.

Wim Slot, PhD, is Professor at the VU University Amsterdam and Director of PI Research in Duivendrecht, the Netherlands. His research interests are child protection and juvenile delinquency. nw.slot@psy.bu.nl.

Djøra I. Soeteman, Drs., is working as a researcher at the Viersprong Institute for Studies on Personality Disorders (VISPD) in Halsteren and is, as a PhD student, connected to the Department of Medical Psychology and Psychotherapy of the Erasmus Medical Center in Rotterdam. Her research interests are the economic evaluation of psychotherapy in personality disorders and intervention programmes for child delinquents. djora.soeteman@deviersprong.nl.

Geert Jan J. M. Stams, PhD, is Associate Professor of Forensic Orthopedagogy at the Department of Social and Behavioural Sciences, University of Amsterdam. Research interests include moral development, moral education, juvenile delinquency, psychosocial development (for example, attachment relationships), and effectiveness of child and youth care. g.j.j.m.stams@uva.nl.

Robert R. R. J. M. Vermeiren, MD, PhD, is Professor of Child and Adolescent Psychiatry at Leiden University Medical Center-Curium in Leiden and Professor of Forensic Youth Psychiatry at the VU University Medical Center Amsterdam. His main research interests relate to public mental health issues aiming at an optimisation of diagnostic assessment of children in primary care settings, and to the neuro-biological correlates of psychopathology and antisocial behaviour. r.r.j.m.vermeiren@curium.nl.

Margaret Walsh, BA, and MA Candidate of Sociology and Gender Equity Studies at the University of Toronto, works as a Research Coordinator for the Child Development Institute. Her research interests include the effect of gender stereotypes on academic performance, classroom interactions and gender-specific risk assessment. She is currently coordinating a multi-phase evaluation of the SNAP™ Girls Connection – a gender-specific programme for antisocial girls. walsh@childdevelop.ca.

Karin Wittebrood, PhD, is Senior Researcher at the Social and Cultural Planning Office in The Hague. Her research interests are on criminal victimisation and fear of crime, the impact of the social context on these issues and the effectiveness of policy measures to reduce (fear of) crime. k.wittebrood@scp.nl.

Tom A. van Yperen, PhD, is head of the Knowledge Centre of the Netherlands Youth Institute (NJi) and special Professor of Research and Development of Effective Youth Care at Utrecht University. Most of his work concerns the effectiveness of prevention and intervention programmes for children, adolescents, parents and teachers. He is the initiator of the Dutch database for Effective Youth Interventions and the related website <www.jeugdinterventies.nl and t.vanyperen@nji.nl>.

Foreword

It is a pleasure to welcome this book as a great contribution to knowledge about child delinquents (that is, those who commit offences under age 12). This book should enormously increase the visibility and accessibility of Dutch research for an international audience. I am sure that many English-speaking scholars will be very impressed to discover the wide range of interesting studies that have been conducted in the Netherlands. In addition to its major focus on Dutch research, the book also contains some discussions of European research, policy and practice. Almost the only other English-language collection of Dutch criminological research was *Crime and Justice in the Netherlands* (2007) edited by Michael Tonry and Catrien Bijleveld, although there have been special issues of major international journals devoted to Dutch research (for example, *Journal of Quantitative Criminology*, vol. 8, no. 1, 1992).

Rolf Loeber should be warmly congratulated for his excellent work as a catalyst in bringing together previously isolated Dutch researchers to address key problems in criminological research. A very important product of these efforts was *Serious and Violent Juvenile Delinquency in the Netherlands* (2001), edited by Rolf Loeber, Wim Slot and Joseph Sergeant, a great contribution to knowledge about serious and violent juvenile offenders, which was inspired by the American volume edited by Rolf Loeber and myself (1998). Unfortunately for English-speaking scholars, this volume was published in Dutch, thereby limiting its international visibility and accessibility. Happily, *Tomorrow's Criminals* is published in English and hence can be appreciated more widely. It was inspired by the American volume on *Child Delinquents* edited by Rolf Loeber and myself (2001). All four volumes are based on the work of study groups of scholars who met on several occasions to discuss their chapters. In my opinion, this is the best method for producing a high-quality, path-breaking edited book.

Child delinquents are extremely important, but remarkably neglected in all countries. This is very surprising because it has been known for many years that an early onset of delinquency tends to predict a long and serious criminal career (see, for example, Loeber & Farrington, 2000). Most research on delinquency focuses on the teenage years when it is in full flow, and similarly, most intervention resources are targeted on these years. This book argues convincingly that more research and interventions should be targeted on the pre-teenage years. This argument applies to the Netherlands and many other countries.

Tomorrow's Criminals is squarely in the tradition of developmental criminology, which focuses on the development of delinquency, risk and promotive factors, and the effects of life events on the course of development (for example, Farrington, 2003a). This book provides important new information and analyses on biological, individual, family, peer, school and neighbourhood risk factors. In addition, it contains important reviews of screening tools and risk-focused prevention methods. All countries should invest in early prevention techniques designed to tackle key risk factors, in order to save children from a life of crime (see Farrington & Welsh, 2007).

In the Netherlands, as in many European countries, evaluation research rarely conforms to the highest standards of methodological quality (for example, Farrington, 2003b). Similarly, cost-benefit analyses of the effectiveness of interventions are generally lacking. These considerations lead to clear-cut research recommendations. Just as more prospective longitudinal studies are needed, so are more randomised experiments to evaluate the effectiveness of prevention and intervention methods (for example, Farrington & Welsh, 2005). And more cost-benefit analyses are needed, since they are especially influential for policymakers. In addition, more research is needed on screening tools to identify children at risk.

Rolf Loeber, Wim Slot, Peter H. van der Laan, and Machteld Hoeve break new ground in presenting Dutch and international research on the explanation and prevention of child delinquency. I hope very much that their book will be widely read and widely cited by the international community of criminological scholars.

David P. Farrington
Professor of Psychological Criminology
Cambridge University

Part I
The Problem

Chapter 1

Child Delinquents and Tomorrow's Serious Delinquents: Key Questions Addressed in This Volume

Rolf Loeber, Wim Slot, Peter H. van der Laan and Machteld Hoeve

'Show me the child at seven, and I will tell you what his/her future will be' (Fergusson, Horwood & Ridder, 2005a, 2005b) is a saying that has the appearance of accuracy but remains highly speculative. On the one hand, we know that some young children exhibit problem behaviours at a young age and later begin to commit crime. Thousands of young boys first show their disruptive behaviours and delinquency prior to age 7 and thousands more will have initiated these behaviours by the end of elementary school (*basisschool* in the Netherlands). The extent to which young children with problem behaviours at a young age will become tomorrow's chronic offenders has enormous implications for society. Can the criminal victimisation of thousands of innocent persons be prevented? Is a life of crime with its accompanying risks of poor education, unemployment and unstable survival skills inevitable for children who exhibit problem behaviours at a young age? Or can early criminogenic processes be moulded to produce long-term prosocial rather than delinquent outcomes? This volume addresses these and many other issues that are relevant to preventive interventions and treatment.

Definitions

In this volume two categories of children are of greatest concern: *children who show persistent disruptive behaviour* and *child delinquents* (those children who start delinquency prior to age 12). Table 1.1, see over, provides definitions of these and other key terms used throughout.

The Purpose of this Volume

The primary goal of this volume is to present basic empirical knowledge about the development, causes and consequences of child delinquency and disruptive behaviours in children. The secondary goal is to identify successful preventive interventions and treatments. It also serves as a platform for demonstrating where there are currently critical gaps in this knowledge. The volume is written for informed lay people, scholars and programme staff working with children.

Table 1.1 Key terms used in this volume

Attention-Deficit/ Hyperactivity Disorder (ADHD)	Persistent pattern of inattention and/or hyperactivity-impulsivity that is more frequent and severe than is typically observed in individuals at a comparable level of development (American Psychiatric Association, 1994).
Child delinquents	Child delinquents are defined as those youth who commit delinquent acts before age 12. Most child delinquents commit minor to moderately serious forms of delinquency and only a minority will commit serious acts. Since Dutch youngsters under age 12 cannot be criminally prosecuted, the term 'child delinquent' or 'very young offender' does not have a legal basis.
Chronic offenders	Chronic offenders are individuals who commit frequent serious offences over long periods of time. Researchers are not in full agreement about the minimum frequency and the time period required which classifies an individual as a chronic offender, and this may also vary depending on whether official records or self-reported delinquency is considered (Loeber & Farrington, 1998; Piquero, Farrington & Blumstein, 2007).
Conduct Disorder (CD)	Repetitive and persistent pattern of behaviour in which the basic rights of others or major age-appropriate societal norms or rules are violated and causes significant impairment in social, academic, or occupational functioning (American Psychiatric Association, 1994).
Disruptive behaviours	We define 'disruptive behaviours' (sometimes also called 'externalising problem behaviours' or 'problem behaviours')[a] as a persistent pattern of negativistic, disobedient, or hostile behaviour toward peers and adults, and behaviours such as truancy, aggression, running away from home, and underage drinking (American Psychiatric Association, 1994; Loeber et al., 2001). Hence, disruptive children are those who show persistent disruptive behaviour.[b] The majority of these behaviours do not concern the breaking of criminal laws and never lead to police contact. However, child problem behaviour is important in that child delinquents often display such behaviour and this can be a stepping-stone to delinquency (Loeber et al., 1993; Loeber & Farrington, 2001).
Externalising problem behaviours	See *Disruptive behaviours*.
Internalising problem behaviours	Internalising problem behaviours are emotional problems such as anxiety and depression.
Oppositional Defiant Disorder (ODD)	Recurrent pattern of negativistic, defiant, disobedient and hostile behaviour toward authority figures that persists for at least six months (American Psychiatric Association, 1994).
Promotive factors	Factors in the child, family, peer group, school, or neighbourhood associated with: (a) a low probability of disruptive or delinquent behavior in the general population of young people; and/or (b) desistance from disruptive and delinquent behaviour in populations of juvenile with such problem behaviours.

Risk factors	Factors in the child, family, peer group, school, or neighbourhood associated with an increased probability of disruptive or delinquent behaviour in youth.
Serious delinquency	Serious delinquency includes violent acts and several forms of serious property crime, including breaking-and-entering, fire-setting, theft over €100, drug-dealing and extortion.
Violence	Violence is a sub-category of delinquent acts and includes aggravated assault, rape, robbery and homicide.

Notes: [a]The choice of terms largely depended on the measurement instruments used by researchers in their studies of children. [b]We eschewed the use of the term 'antisocial children' for two reasons. We wanted to avoid unnecessary labelling of children as antisocial when in fact they were going through age-normative disruptive behaviour. Secondly, most indexes of 'antisocial' behaviour also include behaviours that do not inflict harm on others (such as disobedience and frequent arguing).

Preliminaries to this Volume

The current volume is much inspired by our earlier report, *Ernstige en Gewelddadige Jeugddelinquentie: Omvang, Oorzaken, en Interventies* [Serious and violent juvenile delinquency: prevalence, causes, and interventions], edited by Loeber, Slot and Sergeant (2001). This report was the result of almost four years of work by an interdisciplinary group of thirty-three Dutch experts in the field of serious and violent juvenile delinquency, chaired by Rolf Loeber. The study group was funded by the Nationaal Fonds voor de Geestelijke Volksgezondheid (NFGV). The volume was welcomed enthusiastically by Dutch policymakers, researchers and juvenile justice officials, and is now in its second edition. Recently, we published an update of this report in which the same group of experts describe the latest developments in the study of juvenile delinquency in the Netherlands (Loeber & Slot, 2007). However, the report, as well as the update, only occasionally touched on the need to better understand child delinquency, its causes, courses and consequences.

Earlier, Rolf Loeber and David P. Farrington and thirty-seven experts in child development and criminology reported on child delinquency to the Office of Juvenile Justice and Delinquency Prevention of the US Department of Justice in Washington, DC, which resulted in one volume (*Child Delinquents: Development, Intervention and Service Needs*) for North American readership (Loeber & Farrington, 2001) and four bulletins (Burns et al., 2003; Loeber, Farrington & Petechuk, 2003; Snyder et al., 2003; Wasserman et al., 2003; see <www.ojjdp.ncjrs.org>).

One of the key conclusions of the US report was that most very serious offenders display early-onset delinquency and acting-out behaviours, often starting before age 13, and that a proportion of child delinquents (but not all) are at risk to become tomorrow's serious criminals. Longitudinal studies, especially from the United States (US), Canada, and the United Kingdom (UK) – but also the Netherlands (Blokland & Nieuwbeerta, 2006; Tonry & Bijleveld, 2007a) – indicate that most child delinquents have a history of non-delinquent disruptive behaviours that tend to start in the preschool years. Although very young delinquents raise much concern in the Netherlands (*Nota Kalsbeek*, Kalsbeek, 2003), prior to the publication of this volume little was known about young offenders and the magnitude of the problem they pose to society.

The present volume deals with child delinquency in the Netherlands and several other European countries, and has the enormous advantage of drawing on the expertise of thirty-two scholars who were responsible for writing state-of-the art chapters. It also differs from the earlier report on serious delinquency in the Netherlands (Loeber, Slot & Sergeant, 2001) in that it is written in English and has a broader orientation toward delinquency in European countries rather than in the Netherlands alone.

The Dutch Study Group on Child Delinquents

The leadership of the study group was in the hands of Rolf Loeber, N. Wim Slot, Peter H. van der Laan and Machteld Hoeve. They received much logistical support at an early stage from Manon van Riet, and later editorial assistance from Elizabeth King (in the UK), Ariena van Poppel (NSCR, Leiden, Netherlands), and Jenn Wilson (Life History Studies Program, Pittsburgh, PA, USA).

Members of the study group are the primary authors of the respective chapters in this volume and include: Rob Allen, Jaap E. Doek, Machteld Hoeve, Harrie Jonkman, Hans M. Koot, Francien Lamers-Winkelman, Rolf Loeber, Ton Mooij, Peter Prinzie, Djøra Souteman, Lieke van Domburgh, Peter H. van der Laan, Pol A.C. van Lier and Tom van Yperen. Several of the primary authors received support from colleagues in the writing of the chapters, and the latter group includes: Channa Al, Leonieke Boendermakers, Theo Doreleijers, Andrea Donker, Lucres M. Jansen, Marjolein Luman, Anna Neumann, Jaap Oosterlaan, Bert Prinsen, Geert Jan Stams, Magda Stouthamer-Loeber, Karin Wittebrood, Jan J.V. van Busschbach, Robert Vermeiren, and Karin Wittebrood. In addition, this volume contains a valuable appendix that highlights the operation of one of the best-researched programmes for child delinquency in the world in Toronto (Canada) (see Appendix 1 by Christopher J. Koegl and colleagues).

The following are key questions pertaining to child delinquents that are addressed in this volume.

What are Some Common Myths about Disruptive and Delinquent Child Behaviour?

Examples of common (and sometimes contradictory) myths pertaining to disruptive and delinquent child behaviours are:

- There is a new and more serious 'breed' of children who become delinquent at a young age.
- Today's child delinquents are destined to become tomorrow's 'hard core' or chronic offenders.
- Most disruptive and delinquent children will 'grow out' of their problem behaviour.

- We can accurately tell which preschoolers will become child delinquents and, subsequently, serious and violent juvenile offenders.
- Many early problem behaviours are relatively harmless and, therefore, can be safely ignored.
- The implementation of harsh sanctions in the juvenile justice system (incarceration in a detention centre or correctional facility) is effective in reducing child delinquency.
- Going soft on crime by advocating prevention is a waste of resources.

Although several of these statements may have intuitive appeal, this book serves to undermine and correct these myths (see summary in Chapter 16).

Why Focus on Disruptive Children and Child Delinquents?

Why do we emphasise the study of and interventions for disruptive and delinquent children? Figure 1.1 sketches the developmental link between persistent disruptive child behaviour, child delinquency, and serious and violent offences in adolescence and adulthood. The story-line embedded in the figure is as follows. Only a small proportion of children below age 12 show persistent disruptive behaviours. Some disruptive children (called 'child delinquents' in Figure 1.1) will start committing delinquent acts. Child delinquents have a two to three times higher likelihood of becoming violent, serious and chronic offenders, and have longer delinquency careers (Loeber & Farrington, 2001; Loeber et al., 2001, 2008). This sequence is repeated for each new generation of youth. Viewed retrospectively, the majority of eventual chronic serious offenders in adolescence and adulthood are former child delinquents. Research shows that chronic offenders (sometimes called *de harde kern* [hard core] in Dutch; Beke & Kleiman, 1993; Ferwerda, Jakobs & Beke, 2006; Meeus et al., 2001) are responsible for about half of all crime, including serious property crime and violence (Loeber & Farrington, 1998; Meeus et al., 2001; Piquero et al., 2007; Wolfgang, Figlio & Sellin, 1972). Thus, a proportion of disruptive children and child delinquents become tomorrow's chronic, serious and violent offenders.

The developmental linkage between disruptive children, child delinquents, chronic, serious and violent offenders and the large amount of crime that they commit has two major implications for interventions. The interventions can be compared to the principle of supply and demand in economics, which describes market relations between prospective sellers' supply of goods and buyers' demand for goods. Delinquency is part of a different supply-and-demand chain, with disruptive children and child delinquents supplying the future population of chronic, serious and violent offenders, which, once recognised in the justice system, demands the application of justice to satisfy, reimburse and protect victims and society in general.

Interventions can take place on either the supply or on the demand side of delinquency. On the demand side, the conventional type of intervention (aside from diversion) is through the penal system of applying judicial sanctions to the chronic, serious and violent offenders through court hearings, trials, sentencing, probation, incarceration, parole, and so on. We know from longitudinal studies that in many cases the judicial system very often identifies these offenders at a late stage of their

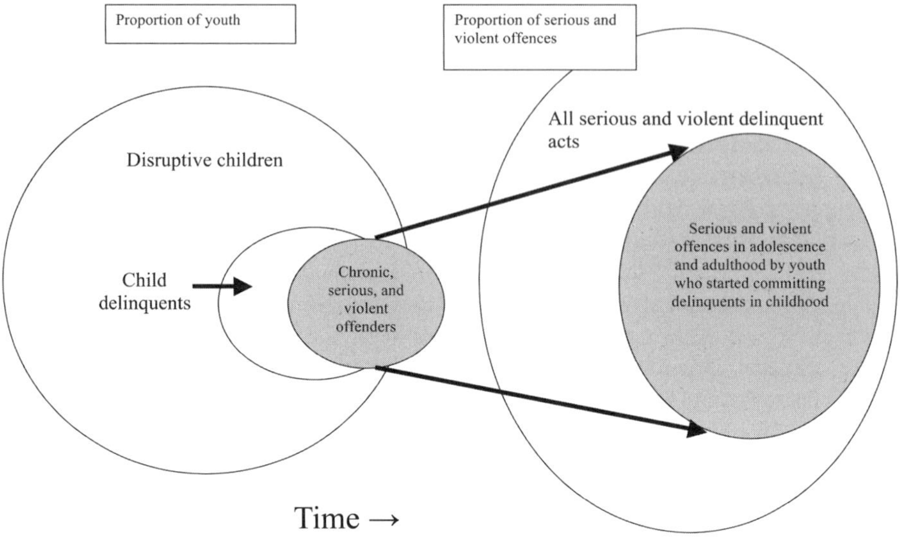

Figure 1.1 A small proportion of delinquents are responsible for about half of all crime

delinquency career, when their delinquency has led to years of victimisation of others (Farrington et al., 2007; Loeber & Farrington, 2001).

The other type of intervention is based on a source-directed strategy and aims to cut off the 'supply' of future chronic, serious and violent offenders. This strategy is often obliquely called 'delinquency prevention'. We argue that that there is a place for the prevention of delinquent acts, but that the highest priority is the prevention of the *emergence* of chronic, serious and violent offenders in society because of their large contribution to the overall level of crime in society. *Hence, the reduction of child delinquents in the general population can be expected to reduce the supply of chronic, serious and violent offenders and is most likely to take a large cut out of serious and violent crime for future generations of youth.* Thus, the prevention of child delinquency is one of the best ways to reduce serious and violent offences for years to come.

How Common are Child Delinquents and Disruptive Children?

Chapters 2 and 3 address how common child delinquents and children with disruptive behaviour are in the Dutch population. Chapter 2 shows how common child delinquency is in the US and in the Netherlands when figures are based on self-reports (of importance because many adults may not be aware of the delinquent acts) or on police reports. This chapter also addresses Dutch government policy changes pertaining to child delinquency over the past few decades, what we know about the proportion of child delinquents identified by the police, and how this has changed over the past years. Police officers have some freedom in deciding which delinquent children to refer to their parents, or which children should be referred to the 'Stop' programme, which is an intervention programme specifically designed for child delinquents. However, the effectiveness of this programme in curtailing children's risk of becoming tomorrow's serious and chronic offenders is still uncertain.

The question of how widespread are disruptive behaviours and child delinquency can also be addressed through information collected from parents and teachers. Chapter 3 reviews this information and also considers what percentage of child delinquents has other problem behaviours (such as attention-deficit hyperactivity problems, oppositional behaviours, and internalising problem behaviours such as anxiety and depression) that may affect their delinquent activity. The prevalence of child delinquency and the disruptive behaviours that child delinquents display can vary from population to population and is highest in special populations. This chapter contains information on newly collected and as yet unpublished data. Aside from reporting on a general population sample, it also shows the degree to which disruptive behaviours (and co-morbid or co-occurring problems) are present in special samples, such as children referred to special day care, in an outpatient sample, and in an intellectually disabled sample.

How Important are Ethnic and Cultural Factors?

Certain but not all minorities are over-represented in the justice system and in institutions for delinquent youth (Huizinga et al., 2006; Junger, Wittebrood & Timman, 2001; Loeber & Farrington, 2004). The reasons for this over-representation are many and include racial discrimination, selective arrest and intake in the justice system, and a higher exposure by minority youth to risk factors associated with disruptive behaviour and delinquency. Given the considerable continuity between child disruptive behaviours and delinquency during adolescence, one might expect a similar over-representation in minority children. Chapters 3 and 11 review the current evidence of ethnic and cultural differences in children's disruptive behaviours.

How Important are Gender Differences?

Boys compared to girls show more disruptive behaviours at a young age and more serious forms of delinquency in adolescence and early adulthood (Moffitt et al., 2001). A small group of disruptive girls emerges during childhood (Loeber, Pardini et al., 2007). Early onset of conduct problems prior to adolescence predicts later chronic delinquency in girls as well as in boys (Loeber & Farrington, 2001). However, girls' disruptive behaviours tend to emerge more during adolescence. Delinquency in girls is a risk factor for suicide attempts during adolescence (Thompson et al., 2006; see also Wasserman et al., 2006). Adolescent girls with CD or a major depressive disorder are at risk of becoming teenage mothers. These young mothers often have poor parenting skills, and their offspring in turn are at heightened risk for developing externalising problem behaviours and depression (for example, Cassidy et al., 1996; Conseur et al., 1997). Conduct problems in girls and boys are also costly in terms of the service delivery systems. Delinquent girls in the justice system, compared to delinquent boys, have more co-morbid psychiatric disorders (Teplin et al., 2006; Wasserman et al., 2005), and require additional mental health services. Discussions of these and other gender differences can be found throughout this volume, but especially in Chapters 2 to 4, 7, and Appendix 1.

Are There Developmental Pathways to Serious Delinquency?

The development of serious and chronic delinquency is not a random process, but in most young people evolves over time in an orderly fashion along developmental pathways. Young individuals can be on one or more of three developmental pathways. A first pathway, the Overt Pathway, consists of the development of overt, confrontational disruptive acts in three steps or stages. The other two developmental pathways – the Covert Pathway and the Authority Conflict Pathway – have each several steps that increase in severity with development. Developmental pathways from persistent minor disruptive behaviours to serious delinquency are described in Chapter 9.

The identification of pathways is important for several reasons. Pathways help us to better understand developmental markers in youths who are at highest risk of escalating from minor to more serious problem behaviours. This knowledge has great implications for preventive interventions and treatments (see below), specifically in curtailing or stopping individuals' progression from persistent minor forms of disruptive behaviours to the most serious forms of delinquency.

What are the Negative Consequences of Early Delinquent Careers for Juvenile Delinquents?

Aside from the infliction of harm on others by child delinquents there are many negative consequences of early-onset delinquency that can affect the quality of life of the offenders themselves. These negative consequences have been listed by Loeber and Farrington (2001, pp. 8–10) and are mentioned in Chapters 3–5, 8 and 9, and summarised in Chapter 16.

What are Correlates and Causes of Disruptive and Delinquent Child Behaviour?

In general, risk factors for disruptive behaviours and delinquency – as approximations of causes – reside in the individual child, the family, the peer group, the school, and probably the neighbourhood in which the child lives. The various chapters that follow indicate the extent to which children at a young age are exposed to specific risk factors in the domains of individual-level influences (Chapter 5), family influences (Chapter 6), and peer influences (Chapter 7), in two types of contexts: school influences (Chapter 8), and neighbourhood influences (mentioned in Chapters 3 and 16). The cumulative impact of the factors and contexts with development is reviewed in Chapter 9.

What are Promotive Factors that Protect against Disruptive Behaviour and Delinquency?

Chapter 9 also describes the impact of promotive factors that predict and explain why some young people have a low probability of later persistent disruptive behaviour or serious delinquency, and why some desist from persistent disruptive behaviour and/or serious delinquency. Thus, promotive factors differ from risk factors in that they are positive factors which explain prosocial behaviours of youth in the general population and explain desistance from delinquency and/or disruptive behaviour among disruptive and delinquent youth. Research indicates that promotive factors can buffer the impact of risk factors and for that reason are of great interest and relevance for preventive and treatment interventions (see Chapter 9).

One of the most consistent findings across studies on delinquency in different countries is the age-crime curve, which has the shape of an inverted 'U' (Farrington, 1986; Tremblay & Nagin, 2005; Laub & Sampson, 2003). The age-crime curve shows that the prevalence of offenders is low in late childhood and early adolescence, peaks in middle to late adolescence and decreases subsequently. The age-crime curve tells part of the story of when individuals tend to decrease their delinquency, which to some extent occurs during late adolescence and early adulthood. However, the question is raised as to what extent the age-crime curve, including the age of desistance, applies to child delinquents. On the one hand, we know that child delinquents compared to later-onset offenders have a two to three times higher likelihood of becoming serious and violent offenders. This means that early-onset offenders have a lower probability of desistance, including during late adolescence and early adulthood when many other youth desist from delinquency. It is often not recognised, however, that a proportion of child delinquents already desist during early adolescence, and that some advances have been made in the prediction of which child delinquents will do so (for details, see Chapter 9).

Few studies have addressed the question of whether promotive factors associated with a low likelihood of delinquency (and associated with the development of prosocial behaviours) operate throughout childhood and adolescence, or whether they are particularly relevant in certain phases of development. Chapter 9 examines whether promotive factors are particularly strong in childhood, and appear to wane or decrease subsequently when risk factors become the stronger forces. Knowledge of promotive factors can be relevant to interventions. For instance, is it practical to advance promotive factors in the elementary school years, rather than waiting to introduce them during the secondary school years?

What is the Role of Victimisation?

We review three types of victimisation: child maltreatment (child abuse and neglect), children's witnessing of violence between parents (Chapter 4), and exposure to bullying in school (Chapter 8). Each of these factors is related to later delinquency, disruptive behaviours and mental health problems in children. Chapter 4 also considers the extent to which victimised children are referred to treatment agencies and whether or not interventions focus on the child's problems resulting from victimisation.

How Early can Child Delinquents be Identified and What are the Early Warning Signs?

Some researchers have argued that we need to identify during the preschool years or in early childhood those who run the risk of later becoming serious and chronic delinquents (Moffitt, 1993). The question of how this can best be done and the current limitations of early identification are discussed in Chapters 10 and 16.

What Are Effective Screening Methods?

Screening instrument help to identify children who are at most risk of persistent disruptive behaviour and/or child delinquency and serve to channel rare therapeutic resources to children at highest risk. Typically, screening instruments are based on knowledge of child problem behaviours and known risk factors. Some child problem behaviours – such as disobedience, stubbornness and temper tantrums – are somewhat age-normative in childhood, but other behaviours are not (Loeber & Farrington, 2001). It is crucial to include in screening instruments examples of age-atypical behaviours because their identification can serve as a 'red flag' for the presence of persistent rather than transient deviant development. Since minor disruptive behaviours can constitute a stepping-stone to serious delinquency, information about such behaviours is a crucial element in screening instruments.

There are several screening instruments available for teachers and mental health workers that are promising and that have been used to identify the more serious cases among child delinquents and children with disruptive behaviours (see Chapters 8 and 10, and Appendix 1).

What are Relevant Judicial and Legal Interventions?

Since children below age 12 in the Netherlands cannot be held criminally responsible for their delinquent acts, they therefore cannot be prosecuted, processed in the criminal court, or receive criminal sanctions (for more details, see Chapter 14).[1] The fact is, however, that there are children below age 12 who are actually committing delinquent acts, some of which are brought to the attention of the police.

The question needs to be raised whether the minimum age of criminal responsibility needs to stay the same, to be lowered, or increased. Another important question is whether the police should be one of the 'gatekeepers' to identify child delinquents. Several avenues are open to the police to deal with child delinquents. The police may refer parents of young children to voluntary care and support agencies, and in more

1 For juveniles aged 12 to 17, separate rules and regulations apply. At age 18, criminal cases are dealt with according to adult penal law. Under specific conditions, 16- and 17-year-olds can be referred to adult court, just as 18–20-year-olds can be dealt with according to juvenile penal law.

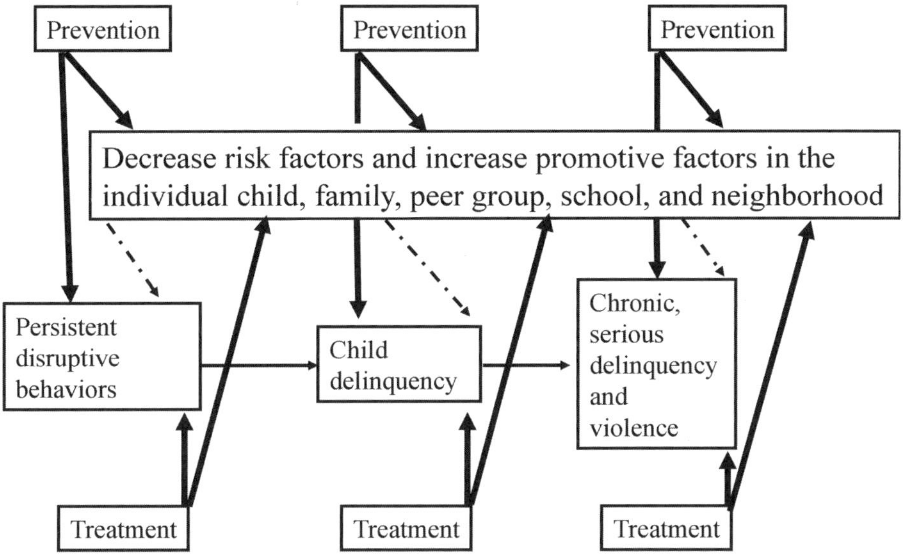

Figure 1.2 Prevention and treatment of persistent disruptive behaviours, child delinquency, and chronic, serious delinquency and violence in the context of risk and promotive factors

Note: Thin arrows depict escalation in problem behaviours from childhood to adolescence. Dotted arrows show the influence of risk and promotive factors on these problem behaviours. Bold arrows indicate foci of preventative and treatment interventions.

serious cases to formally notify the Council of Child Care and Protection (*Raad voor de Kinderbescherming*). In the administration of the Council, these cases are not registered as 'penal cases' but as 'complaint or protection cases'. How frequently police make these referrals is discussed in Chapter 2.

What are Effective Preventive Interventions for Disruptive Child Behaviours and Child Delinquency? What are Effective Treatments for Disruptive Child Behaviours and Child Delinquency? Are Interventions for Child Delinquents Taking Place Sufficiently Early?

How can we best envision interventions to prevent or treat disruptive child behaviours, child delinquency and serious delinquency and violence? Figure 1.2 (adapted from Loeber and Farrington, 2001) schematically shows the interrelations between: (a) the development of problem behaviours from persistent disruptive behaviours first, to child delinquency, and second, to serious and violent juvenile delinquency (the thin horizontal arrows in Figure 1.2); (b) the relationship between these problem behaviours and risk and promotive factors in the individual, family, peer group, school and neighbourhood (the dotted arrows in Figure 1.2).

Preventive interventions (the bold arrows pointing downward in Figure 1.2) can be aimed, first of all, at the prevention of persistent disruptive behaviours in children in general; second, at the prevention of child delinquency, particularly among persistent disruptive children, and third, at the prevention of serious and violent juvenile delinquency, particularly among known child delinquents. There are three major objectives of preventive interventions: a) prevent the emergence of disruptive and delinquent child behaviours; b) reduce the presence of individual, family, peer group, school and neighbourhood risk factors to which children can be exposed, and c) increase the presence of promotive factors that enhance children's prosocial behaviours. Relevant preventive interventions are reviewed in Chapter 11.

Figure 1.2 also shows treatment interventions that can focus on persistent disruptive behaviours, child delinquency, or serious and violent juvenile delinquency (represented by the bold arrows in Figure 1.2 pointing upward). Treatment interventions, similar to preventive interventions, can be aimed at a reduction of child problem behaviours *and* a reduction of risk factors in each domain of the individual child, family, peer group, school and neighbourhood. At the same time, ideally, treatment interventions should also be able to enhance promotive factors in each of the domains associated with prosocial behaviours instead of child delinquency. Relevant preventive interventions are reviewed in Chapter 12. In addition, in Chapter 15, Allen reviewed European programmes aimed at child delinquents. Finally, the Appendix 1 highlights one of the best-researched programmes for disruptive children and delinquents, developed in Canada.

The best evaluations for preventive and treatment interventions assign participants to an experimental and a control group. In such experiments, the best assignment of participants is done randomly, thereby evenly spreading other influential factors across the two groups. Quasi-experimental evaluations consist of a less stringent evaluation design in which experimental and control group participants are matched on criteria such as age, socioeconomic background, and so on. Chapters 11 and 12 indicate the range of evaluation studies that have been done in the Netherlands. While this range is very restricted, several evaluation studies are currently underway. A summary of whether interventions take place sufficiently early is reserved until Chapter 16.

Are there Treatments that Can Do Wrong?

One would like to believe that all treatments are effective in reducing disruptive and delinquent child behaviours. However, not only are some treatments ineffective, they may have the opposite effect and stimulate disruptive and aggressive child behaviours. Evidence for treatments that have adverse effects is reviewed in Chapters 5 and 7.

For Which Problems (Other than Delinquency) Do Disruptive and Delinquent Children Require Services?

Children with persistent disruptive behaviours often display other problems as well and, consequently, can be considered multi-problem youth. Prominent co-occurring problems are early substance use, ADHD symptoms, internalising problem behaviours (particularly depressed mood), peer rejection, and educational problems such as academic underachievement, repeating grade(s), and truancy. The co-occurring problems may aggravate disruptive and delinquent child behaviours and often complicate the implementation of interventions. Chapters 3–5, 8 and 9 review the evidence for these co-occurring problems.

Do Services Need to be Integrated?

Child delinquents usually are dealt with by a great variety of agencies, including the police, child welfare and protection agencies, schools, mental health clinics, and occasionally the juvenile courts. Each of these agencies, usually with the best intentions, attempts to enhance positive outcomes for child delinquents, but to our knowledge there is a paucity of published reports on the effectiveness of integrated interventions with this population. Because many child delinquents are multi-problem individuals, it is crucial to have *optimal integration* of these services with the juvenile justice system, which is rare. This volume highlights programmes that have achieved a successful integration of services for child delinquents (see Appendix 1).

What are the Monetary Costs of Crime and the Cost-Benefit Ratio of Interventions?

The monetary cost of a life of crime, not to mention the human cost, is very high. Cohen (1998) calculated that in the US the cost of a single high-risk youth engaging in four years of delinquency as a juvenile and ten years as an adult ranged from $1.7 to $2.3 million (in 1997 dollars). Given that many of these high-rate offenders start their delinquent and disruptive careers early in life, we can safely assume that the cost to society of child delinquents is considerable. Welsh et al. (2008) were the first to examine the costs of self-reported delinquency between ages 7 and 17. Juvenile delinquency by inner-city young men caused a substantial burden of harm on citizens in US society through victim costs, with the estimate ranging from a low of $89 million to a high of $110 million. Most of the costs of delinquency to victims is caused by violence (the costs associated with property offences is much lower). The costs incurred by early-onset offenders were much higher than those of later-onset offenders, while chronic offenders (those accounting for half of all self-reported offences), compared to other offenders, caused five to eight times higher than average victim costs. These figures do not include the cost of agencies working with at-risk or delinquent youth, or the cost of incarceration and other special services (briefly reviewed in Chapter 16). We are not aware that victim costs have been quantified in the Netherlands or in other European countries.

Another major issue is the cost of programmes to reduce crime. There are three types of economic issues that are relevant here: the economic net benefits of prevention and treatment programmes, the cost benefits of intervention programmes, and the relative cost to taxpayers of different types of interventions. In the first category, Chapter 13 shows that in the US effective programmes for juvenile offenders may have net benefits (benefits minus costs) ranging from $1,900 to $31,200 per youth. In comparison, non-effective programmes had negative 'benefits' range from -$408 to -$12,478 per youth. In the second category, cost-benefit studies demonstrate that for each dollar or euro spent on intervention, there is a benefit of so many more dollars or euros in future savings for society (see Chapter 13). In the third category, the key question for taxpayers is whether their money is well spent, and whether to reduce crime, it is more advantageous to spend tax money on incarceration or on alternatives such as delinquency prevention programmes (see Chapter 16).

Why Do International Rights and Standards Apply to Children?

Child delinquents, like other children, need protection under the law, and fall under United Nations (UN) regulations governing the rights of children (see Chapter 14). In addition, child delinquents because of their young age often have special needs that are not necessarily applicable to older offenders. Child delinquents are often of less than average intelligence, have a poor understanding of official – including court – procedures, and have general immaturity (Geraghty, 1997). Thus, child delinquents often are cognitively less mature and are in different stages of learning right from wrong. For these reasons, we emphasise that compared to older delinquents, child delinquents have special needs. For instance, child delinquents need to be assessed for their intellectual competence before being processed through different child agencies and, if applicable, the juvenile justice system. Ideally, child delinquents need to have an advocate, especially in the case of the absence or impairment of the parents. This makes it all the more important to approach child delinquents from a human rights perspective, which is illustrated in Chapter 14.

It should also be recognised that child delinquents need protection in different ways, such as protection from maltreatment by their guardians (Chapter 4), but also protection from the negative and criminogenic influence of older delinquent youth in institutions or in delinquency programmes outside of institutions (Chapter 7).

What are High-Priority Recommendations for Research?

Chapters in this volume systematically review the state of the art of research on the course and causes of disruptive and delinquent child behaviours, and preventive and treatment interventions. There are many gaps in knowledge that require research efforts to address. These gaps are discussed throughout this volume but especially in Chapter 16.

What Kinds of Annual National or Regional Surveys are Needed?

Disruptive and delinquent child behaviours in society are not constant over time. The only way that policymakers can identify whether secular changes in disruptive and delinquent child behaviours take place is to undertake yearly national or regional surveys (secular change meaning an increase or decrease in the national or regional prevalence of child behaviours over several years). Such surveys are also essential to gauge whether taxpayers' money used to prevent or deal with juvenile delinquency has an impact on broad strata of society. Annual surveys that include information about the prevalence of risk and promotive factors are also ideal to identify concentrations of specific forms of disadvantage, which in turn, can form the focus of interventions for specific regions or neighbourhoods. These aspects of surveys are reviewed in Chapter 16.

What Information is Relevant to Policy?

The evidence presented in this volume has many implications for national, provincial and local decision- and policymakers. These implications are summarised in Chapter 16.

We hope that this volume will be useful to policymakers, but also to scholars and practitioners in the Netherlands and other European countries. We also hope that this volume will widely advance their knowledge of child delinquency and ultimately help to prevent or remedy it so that children prone to delinquency can be helped to lead productive and satisfying lives, and more people can enjoy their lives without being victimised by juvenile delinquents.

Part II
Manifestations

Chapter 2

Child Delinquency as Seen by Children, the Police and the Justice System

Peter H. van der Laan, Lieke van Domburgh and Machteld Hoeve

Until a decade ago, politicians, local authorities, academics and the media paid little attention to children under age 12 who commit crimes. Since then, however, policymakers and researchers have paid greater attention to very young offenders. This chapter describes the recent history of studies on child delinquency in the Netherlands addressed in policy papers, public statements and research. We are particularly interested in children who come into contact with the police and the justice system because of their disruptive behaviour or delinquency. Unfortunately, few data and statistics are available, but where possible information about prevalence and developmental trends of child delinquency is presented irrespective of whether contact with the police took place.

Child Delinquency in the US

In his contribution to *Child Delinquents* (Loeber & Farrington, 2001), Snyder (2001) presented trends and figures on young children and delinquency in the US. Numbers of arrested children under age 13 were small compared to older juveniles but significant in total numbers. Nationwide, over 250,000 children younger than age 13 entered the justice system in 1997. Some 42,000 (17%) were under age 10. It was estimated that 1% of all 7–13-year-olds in the US (23 million) had some sort of contact with the juvenile justice system. Of these, 75% were boys and 24% were girls. Over a quarter (27%) of these children had been arrested for larceny-theft, while other offence categories included simple assault (12%), vandalism (10%), disorderly conduct (8%), burglary (6%), and running away from home (6%).[1] In 1997, arrests of young children made up 9% of all juvenile arrests. Between 1988 and 1997, the number of juvenile arrests increased by 35%, but for very young juveniles by only 6%. In the same period, the nature of crimes for which these children were arrested changed considerably: property crimes went down while violent crimes increased by 45%.[2]

---

1 In the United States, running away is a status offence. In the Dutch context, running away from home is not considered an offence, nor is non-compliance with curfews or underage drinking.

2 Between 1988 and 1997, about six hundred children under age 12 were involved in murder cases.

About eight out of ten young children arrested were referred to juvenile court. Twelve per cent of court cases involved children under age 10. Between 1988 and 1997, the number of cases dealt with by juvenile courts increased by 33%. In 1997, 60% of the cases referred to court were handled informally, with the children being dismissed or voluntarily put on probation. For older juveniles, this proportion was smaller (46% for 13- and 14-year-olds, and 40% for 15-year-olds or older). Adjudication followed in about half of the cases for which a court hearing was petitioned. Adjudication resulted in residential (detention and/or correctional) placement in an institution (19%); probation (64%); other dispositions (14%) and dismissals (3%). Girls were less often petitioned and adjudicated and non-white children more often.

The Census of Juveniles in Residential Placement revealed that on a single day in October 1997, 2,200 children under age 13, of whom 70% were 12-year-olds, were in a detention or correctional facility for juveniles, that is, 2% of the daily population in these institutions. The average length of stay for children awaiting adjudication was 23 days. Young children committed to an institution by the court spent on average four months in such a facility.

Age of Criminal Responsibility and Child Delinquency in the Netherlands

Unlike the US, very little police or other data is available on child delinquency in the Netherlands. Insights in trends and developments are completely lacking. This is primarily the result of legal age limits. Criminal responsibility for young people in the Netherlands starts at age 12. For juveniles aged 12–17, separate rules and regulations apply (De Jonge & Van der Linden, 2004). At age 18, criminal cases are dealt with according to adult penal law. Under specific conditions, 16- and 17-year-olds can be referred to adult court and 18–20-year-olds can be dealt with according to juvenile penal law. In the past, the lower age of criminal responsibility has varied from zero – that is, children of all ages could be held criminally responsible – to 12. Since 1965, it has been set at 12. Under that age, it is thought that children are not yet fully developed morally to bear responsibility for their behaviour. The principle of guilt does not apply to them since guilt is related to responsibility (Bol, 1991). Therefore, children under age 12 cannot be held criminally responsible and thus no penal intervention or sanction can be imposed. This of course does not mean that young children do not commit acts that according to law are considered delinquent or criminal. Nor does it imply that no formal or official reaction to disruptive behaviours and delinquency is possible. However, a side-effect to this is that such behaviours are not necessarily registered as delinquent or criminal. Police and other crime statistics only cover suspects and/or arrestees aged 12 years and older. It is difficult to obtain reliable and valid data regarding prevalence and trends of delinquency of young children.

Before the early 1990s, child delinquency in the Netherlands was not considered a problem and received little media or policy attention. This has since changed. There are two reasons for this, the first being the tragic event in England in 1993 when two 10-year-old boys killed 3-year-old Jamie Bulger (Thomas, 1993). The

Bulger case sparked long and intense discussions in many countries, including the Netherlands (see also Weijers, 2000). The question was raised whether such cases had ever happened or were ever likely to happen in the Netherlands.[3] Some people suggested that perhaps the age limit for criminal responsibility should be lowered to age 10, or even be abolished.

The second reason for the change stemmed from a better understanding of the need to attend to young children and their disruptive behaviours or delinquency, through what we now call 'developmental and life-course criminology' (Farrington, 2003). Longitudinal studies such as the Cambridge Study in Delinquent Development, the Pittsburgh Youth Study, the National Youth Study, the Rochester Youth Development Study, the Dunedin Study and others have contributed enormously to our knowledge of risk factors for the development of criminal and otherwise problematic careers (Kalb, Farrington & Loeber, 2001). Certainly, persistent disruptive behaviour at a young age is such a risk factor. From a prevention perspective, there is a need to deal with such behaviours rather than ignoring them or considering them as not serious. A study commissioned by the Dutch Ministry of Justice (Junger-Tas, 1996) greatly accelerated the examination of risk factors and young children (and their families). This was further supported by another study, also commissioned by the Ministry of Justice, which surveyed evidence for risk factors in the Dutch context (Ferwerda et al., 1996). Even though this was a retrospective study and may have overestimated the strength of correlations between specific risk factors and criminal careers, aggressive and other forms of disruptive behaviours at a (very) young age were ranked among the strongest risk factors.

By the mid-1990s, the first policy papers addressing delinquent children appeared. They were prepared in reaction to the report of the Van Montfrans Committee, which was set up by the Minister of Justice to give advice on how to deal with juvenile delinquency. The committee's final report, *Met de neus op de feiten* (Facing the facts), mentioned the concerns raised by the police and the judiciary about an increasing number of delinquent young children (Van Montfrans Committee, 1994). The committee explained that it was not able to provide evidence for this trend but nevertheless wanted to stress the importance of the reports they had received. The committee believed that more thorough research into this issue was warranted.

Dutch Research in the 1990s

In response to suggestions of the Van Montfrans Committee, the Research and Documentation Centre (WODC) of the Ministry of Justice conducted two research projects in order to shed more light on the phenomenon of child delinquency.

Police information databases in the cities of Amsterdam, Haarlem and Alphen aan den Rijn in 1994 and 1995 were scanned for those contacts between police officers and young children aged 7–11, who had committed delinquent acts (Grapendaal et al.,

3 Aside from a single murder committed by a 10-year-old girl almost a century ago, no serious violent acts by young children appear to have occurred in the Netherlands. In 1998, however, two 10-year-old boys caused the death of a young girl. The court imposed a (civil) supervision order and the boys were temporarily placed in a children's home.

1996). In all three cities, less than 1% of the children were registered by the police for delinquency. In 1995, 199 children were registered in Amsterdam, fifty-seven children in Haarlem and twenty-seven in Alphen aan den Rijn (see Table 2.1). About half of these children were 11 years old; a very few of them were aged 7 or 8. In Amsterdam, most children were taken to the police station for shoplifting or other forms of theft. In Haarlem and Alphen aan de Rijn, it was either shoplifting or vandalism.

Table 2.1 Police contacts with children aged 7–11 in Amsterdam, Haarlem and Alphen aan den Rijn (1994–95)

	1994	1995
	N (%)	N (%)
Amsterdam	172 (0.5)	199 (0.6)
Haarlem	62 (0.8)	57 (0.8)
Alphen aan den Rijn	20 (0.3)	27 (0.4)

Source: WODC (Grapendaal et al., 1996).

In addition to looking at the number of contacts between the police and young children, thirty-five interviews were held with officers of the police, the Council of Child Care and Protection, and Halt bureaus,[4] teachers of primary schools, juvenile judges, doctors at advice centres and school attendance officers.

On the basis of police data, it was not possible to draw conclusions regarding child delinquency trends or the reliability of such data. But interviewees did not consider the issue of child delinquency a structural or serious problem. They had not noticed an increase, nor did they believe that the police had come across more young children than their databases revealed. In their view, child delinquency should be seen primarily as a pedagogical or social problem and not as a justice or security problem and dealt with accordingly. Respondents were convinced that even though no penal reaction is possible, most of the cases known to the police were reported to the Council of Child Care and Protection. It is up to the Council then to decide whether a social inquiry report should be made up and eventually a protection measure should be requested from the court. From a few case studies, it was learned that this happens occasionally but informants could not tell how often.

The WODC also decided to expand its biannual self-report delinquency survey of 12–17-year-olds to include both 8–11-year-olds and 18–24-year-olds (Van der Laan et al., 1997). Using the same format but adjusting the wording of the questionnaire to be suitable for young children, a group of seven hundred children was asked about behaviour that 'is not allowed'. Table 2.2 presents the outcomes of the 1994 survey for the three age groups.

---

4 The Halt programme is a diversion programme for youngsters arrested for shoplifting, vandalism and other minor offences. Instead of filing a report with the public prosecutor, the police can refer young offenders to Halt. At Halt, they carry out work for the benefit of victims or the community for a maximum of twenty hours.

Table 2.2 Self-reported delinquency by children, adolescents and young adults during 'last year' (in %) (1994)

Age	8–11 (N=699)	12–17 (N=1,096)	18–24 (N=1,572)
Fare-dodging	2.0	15.7	20.3
Graffiti	1.7	10.1	1.3
Harassment	19.60	14.1	8.3
Vandalism	6.4	9.1	6.4
Shoplifting	1.4	7.0	3.3
Arson	6.4	4.3	1.1
Receiving stolen goods	0.5	4.2	8.7
Bicycle theft	0.9	1.3	5.0
Assault	2.6	2.7	1.9
Burglary	0.8	1.6	0.3
Theft from phone box or automated machine	0.8	1.1	0.2
Theft at school	3.7	7.2	5.6
Threatening to extort money	0	0.3	0.1
Combination of offences*	26.9	37.8	36.1

Source: WODC (Van der Laan et al., 1997). Note: *Fare dodging, graffiti, harassment, vandalism, shoplifting, arson, receiving stolen goods, bicycle theft, assault and burglary/illegal entry.

Within the age group of 8–11-year-olds, delinquent acts were predominantly reported by 11-year-olds and to a lesser extent by 10-year-olds. Very few 8- and 9-year-olds reported delinquent acts. Furthermore, three times as many boys as girls reported having done things 'that are not allowed'. Not surprisingly, fewer children compared to adolescents and young adults reported having committed delinquent acts. However, harassment and arson were reported by relatively more children, in particular by 8-year-olds, and assault and theft at school at more or less the same level. Authors believed that in particular young children probably perceive harassment, arson and assault differently than older children. In order to respond sincerely to the questionnaire, the children may have included relatively innocent forms of harassment, arson and assault in their reports. Children often know that teasing, nagging, fighting in the schoolyard, and setting bonfires, as innocent as such acts may appear, are not allowed in school or elsewhere. The authors and practitioners and policymakers who were asked to comment on the outcomes, suggested that in most cases this kind of behaviour perhaps is not as worrisome as, for instance, theft at school, which was reported by almost 4% of the children. The youngest age category (8–10-year-olds) reported being caught by an adult for a delinquent act far more often than did adolescents and young adults, but the children reported that they rarely were caught by the police.

It is clear from these reports that some young children are involved in delinquency. But because of the small numbers, many researchers were not convinced that crime prevention policies need to be developed to focus specifically and exclusively on young children. However, taking into account that little is known about child delinquency, they recommended including young children in future self-report studies so that trends in young offending would become more easily discernible.

Policy Developments in the Late 1990s

The most important policy development regarding children committing delinquent acts dates back to the late 1990s when in reaction to the Van Montfrans report and the outcomes of the WODC surveys, the then-State Secretary of Justice issued a memo on children and crime (*Notitie Kinderen en Criminaliteit*, 1997). The memo states that child delinquency does not seem to be a large-scale phenomenon but occurs regularly. With the absence of a possible penal response, and the available civil dispositions not being considered adequate, a new prevention programme, the so-called 'Stop' programme was presented (see also Chapters 11 and 12). The Stop programme shows similarities and differences with the Halt programme. Similar to the procedures for Halt, police officers can refer children under age 12 to Stop. At Stop, the children are required to perform a series of pedagogically sound activities. Stop differs from Halt in its intensity – children are expected to attend the Stop programme for a maximum of ten hours, and children can only be referred to Stop with the written consent of the parent. In 1999, the first Stop programmes were set up in a few police districts. In 2001, Stop was rolled out nationally. In 1999, the Council of Prosecutors-General (*College van Procureurs-Generaal*) issued an official circular with instructions for the police about the conditions under which young children can be referred to Stop.

The 1997 memo on children and crime was followed in 1998 by a letter from the State Secretary of Justice in which she formally announced that youth crime policies in the future would not only formally apply to 12–23-year-olds but to children under age 12 as well. The letter also mentions the Stop reaction, and provides directions to the police on how to handle cases involving young children: the police must issue a warning to the child and to notify the parents; if necessary, the police must refer to care and support agencies in the case of a first offender if the offence is not of a violent nature and no other risk factors in terms of child abuse, lack of social competencies, truancy, addiction problems or psychological problems are present; if the offence is more serious, or the child has been previously registered in a police database, and/or is known to the Council of Child Care and Protection, and if one or more of the above mentioned risk factors is present, a warning to the child can be issued, the parents must be informed, and the Council of Child Care and Protection must be notified; warnings to children should be given in the presence of the parents.

Further Research on Child Delinquents

In 2003, 229 children under age 12 appeared in the police database for incidents of delinquency in Amsterdam (Kroon, 2005). This was 15% more than found in 1995 (Grapendaal et al., 1996), but included young offenders, young victims, and young witnesses and bystanders. Further analysis of a sample of 126 children with two or more incidents of various kinds showed that 13% of the children were considered offenders, 47% victims, and 36% either witnesses or bystanders. The mean age of child delinquents was 11.64 years, considerably older than victims (9.55) or witnesses (9.29).

Van Domburgh studied children under age 12 who were registered for the first time during the period 2000–01 in three rural and urban police regions (Van Domburgh, 2006; Van Domburgh et al., submitted). The study included 350 children, of whom 83% were male and ranged in age from 5 to 12. Children were registered for property damage or vandalism (32%), theft (27%), mischief (24%) and violence (17%).

All known studies using police registrations were primarily of an explorative nature, focusing on the prevalence of child delinquency in a specific year or period. They did not explore developmental aspects of misbehaviour. The studies were not set up to describe trends in offending over time. Nevertheless, the studies demonstrated that young children are caught and registered by the police for delinquent acts. The mere existence of the Stop programme may have caused the police to pay more attention to the phenomenon of child delinquency and it is likely to have resulted in an increased identification of child delinquents. Absolute numbers, however, remain relatively small and registrations and databases are incomplete and also flawed. Several authors point out that children are sometimes wrongfully regarded as witnesses or victims and not as offenders (Grapendaal et al., 1996; Kroon, 2005; Van Domburgh, 2006). This agrees with the possibility that official police data underestimate the involvement of young children in crime and delinquency (Ferwerda et al., 1996).

Since the 1980s, self-report studies on crime and delinquency are believed to be helpful and reliable complements to official data because self-reports shed light on delinquent acts either unknown to the police and justice authorities or not officially registered (Junger-Tas & Haen-Marshall, 1999), particularly as it applies to young delinquent children (see the 1994 WODC trial survey of 8–11-year-olds above). More recently three self-report studies were carried out in which children under age 12 participated.

In the early 2000s, a longitudinal study called TRAILS was started in the northern part of the Netherlands (Soepboer, Veenstra & Verhulst, 2006). TRAILS stands for Tracking Adolescents' Individual Lives Survey. In this longitudinal study of psychological health and social development, around 2,200 children are followed up to the age of 25. At the first wave (their last year of primary education) they were ages 10–12 (mean age 11.09). A second wave followed two to three years later. Aggressive behaviours and delinquency were measured by collecting information from children, parents and teachers using the Youth Self Report (YSR), the Child Behaviour Checklist (CBCL) and the Teacher's Report Form (TRF). For the measurement of disruptive behaviours, the Antisocial Behaviour Questionnaire (ASBQ) was also used. In general, the prevalence of aggression and delinquency was small, though higher for boys than for girls. Also, slightly more aggression than delinquency was reported. Children reported lower levels than their parents or teachers. Differences between the first and second wave were small. Children and teachers reported a small increase in delinquency and aggression over time, while parents reported less delinquency and aggression over time. Almost two-thirds of the children showed no disruptive behaviour at all; 21% displayed some disruptive behaviour at both wave 1 and 2. Few children (3%) were considered desisters (reports of disruptive behaviours at the first wave but not at the second). A group of similar size (3%) was not delinquent at wave 1 but started to show some disruptive behaviour at wave 2 (starters). A group of serious persisters (9%) showed serious disruptive behaviours at both waves. No information was available about the extent to which children had come into contact with the police or other agencies.

In 2002 and 2003, the Sociaal Cultureel Planbureau (SCP) and the Nederlandse Organisatie voor Toegepast Natuurwetenschappelijk Onderzoek (TNO) conducted research among almost 4,800 children aged 1–12, of which 1,350 were in the age range of 8–12 (Zeijl et al., 2005). Through youth health care professionals (doctors and nurses), parents and children aged 8–12 were asked to fill in questionnaires (including CBCL) on family and parenting, education, free time and psychosocial development. According to health professionals, 23% of the 8–12-year-old boys and 18% of the girls suffered from light to serious psychosocial problems, and 31% and 17% respectively showed externalising problem behaviour. According to the parents, 6% of both boys and girls showed externalising problem behaviour.

The children filled in a delinquency questionnaire (see Table 2.3). About 55% of the children reported no delinquent acts. Only a few children reported serious delinquent acts such as theft and vandalism. Aggressive behaviour towards other people was reported more often, in particular having a row with a teacher and threatening to beat someone up. Boys reported more delinquency than girls. Few girls, but 5% of the boys, mentioned being questioned by the police because of their behaviour. It is not known whether this resulted in any further official action.

Table 2.3 Self-reported delinquency by children aged 8–12 during the previous twelve months (in %) (2002–03)

	Boys (N=488)	Girls (N=525)
Shoplifting	3	3
Theft at school from fellow students	5	2
Theft at home	5	3
Burglary	2	0
Threatening someone to extort money	4	2
Graffiti	5	2
Damaging property	4	0.4
Arson	3	2
Frightening someone with a knife	6	3
Row with teacher	18	11
Verbally abusing teacher	6	2
Hitting parents	5	6
Threatening to beat up someone	28	14
Beating up someone	5	0.4
Questioned by the police	5	0.4
At least one of the above	55	37

Source: SCP/TNO (Zeijl et al., 2005).

Table 2.4 Prevalence of offences in previous twelve months (in %)

	10–11 years (N=337)	12–13 years (N=384)	14–15 years (N=378)	16–17 years (N=362)
Vehicle damaged	0.8	1.1	1.6	3.1
House damaged	0.3	0.9	1.4	2.2
Public transport damaged	0.0	1.6	1.9	2.2
Something else damaged	1.0	3.9	8.1	5.8
Graffiti	3.3	8.9	16.1	12.4
Cursing because of skin colour	8.5	8.4	12.9	15.0
Called someone gay	0.7	3.3	6.9	4.4
Changed price tags	3.3	4.3	7.5	6.9
Shoplifted < €10	3.8	6.4	7.7	4.2
Shoplifted > € 10	0.0	0.0	1.5	0.3
Theft at school or work	6.9	10.2	17.1	13.4
Theft of bicycle or moped	0.0	0.5	2.4	5.5
Pickpocketed	0.7	0.0	1.3	0.3
Theft from car	0.4	0.7	0.7	1.8
Received stolen goods	0.1	2.3	9.0	8.8
Sold stolen goods	0.0	0.4	4.1	3.6
Theft from vehicle	0.0	0.0	0.0	0.0
Burglary	0.0	1.7	0.8	0.8
Frightened someone	4.3	8.0	16.6	12.8
Hit someone, not wounded	9.0	14.1	19.3	16.7
Hit someone, wounded	6.2	6.4	10.9	11.7
Threatened to extort money	0.2	0.0	0.0	0.3
Used violence to extort money	0.0	0.0	0.0	0.0
Wounding with a weapon	0.0	0.7	0.7	0.7
Involuntary sex	0.0	0.0	0.1	1.3
Carryied a weapon	0.0	4.3	5.5	6.1
Sold soft drugs	0.0	0.0	2.1	4.9
Sold party drugs	0.3	0.0	0.0	1.4
Sold hard drugs	0.0	0.0	0.0	0.0
Spread Internet viruses	0.0	1.5	3.1	1.4
Bullied or nagged via the Internet	2.0	4.4	7.6	8.0
Fare-dodged	3.2	9.1	21.5	31.0
Set off fireworks	21.3	40.0	48.9	41.8
Any or more of the above	33.3	55.0	66.4	66.3

Source: WODC (Van der Laan & Blom, 2006).

The third self-report study concerns a survey in 2005 (Van der Laan & Blom, 2006). Compared to the assessments of TRAILS and the SCP/TNO studies, it contained a much more extensive list of delinquency behaviours. As with earlier WODC self-report studies, this survey concentrated on 12–17-year-olds, but this time 10–11-year-olds were also included (see Table 2.4). The questionnaire was newly developed, which means that comparisons with the 1994 survey cannot be made. However, comparisons made with regard to 12–17-year-olds in the 2005 survey showed similar outcomes, that is, fewer young children reporting delinquent acts.

The prevalence of offences clearly increased with age. For almost all offences the 10–11-year-olds scored lowest on most forms of delinquent acts. The exceptions were: setting off fireworks, hitting someone, and cursing someone because of skin colour, which were reported most often by 10–11-year-olds. Their prevalence is still limited in comparison to the older children. Young children were not involved, yet, in common forms of property crimes such as theft and burglary. But some of them reported theft at school (6.9%), minor shoplifting (3.8%), and changing price tags (3.3%). Violence was limited to verbal violence (cursing) (8.5%), hitting someone (9.0%), physically wounding (6.2%), and threatening (4.3%). Graffiti (3.3%) and fare dodging (3.2%) occurred occasionally, but at a much lower level than for older youths and younger children. For 12–17-year-olds, on average twice as many boys as girls reported offences. Theft at school, however, was reported by 6.9% for both 10–11-year-old boys and girls. In general, respondents to the survey considered it unlikely that they would be caught for delinquent acts. No information was available about children being reported to the police for their delinquency.

In summary, self-report surveys, compared to official police data, show higher prevalence rates of delinquent acts by young children. The actual percentages differ from study to study, largely as a result of differences in definition and operationalisation of delinquency behaviours. In general, the prevalence of delinquency was low and was limited mainly to 10–11-year-olds. Hardly any younger children reported delinquent acts. But even children in the 10–11 age groups were somewhat involved in delinquency, while certainly much less than older juveniles.

Since most surveys are conducted once and/or cross-sectionally, they provide no insight as to increases or decreases over time. Thus, we cannot conclude whether young children today are more involved in delinquency than in the past. On the other hand, since the self-report surveys have collected data not only on delinquency but also include questions on a range of personal characteristics and risk and sometimes promotive factors, we now know more than previously about the links between delinquency and risk factors in various domains.

Formal Reactions to Child Delinquency

We mentioned before that the minimum age of criminal responsibility in the Netherlands is 12. This does not imply that judicial responses to delinquency in younger children are absent. The police may refer parents of young children to voluntary care and support agencies, and in more serious cases, they are legally required to notify the Council of Child Care and Protection (*Raad voor de*

Kinderbescherming). In addition, as mentioned, the police can refer children to the Stop programme.

There appears to be no data showing how often the police refer young children to voluntary care and support agencies, and whether or not parents follow up this advice. The police do not keep records of such referrals, and agencies do not seem to report the backgrounds of referrals in their caseload. On the other hand, the police have to notify the Council of Child Care and Protection when a minor (child under age 18) has committed an offence for which an official police report is filed with the prosecutor's office. The Council registers these notifications as 'penal cases'. In 2006 over 31,000 of such penal cases were dealt with, but 'penal cases' do not concern children under age 12 (Jaarbericht, 2006, 2007). The police are required also to inform the Council in cases of children committing a more serious offence even though an official report is not presented to the public prosecutor. In the administration of the Council, these cases are not registered as 'penal cases' but as 'complaint or protection cases'. In 2005, the Council of Child Care and Protection performed further social enquiries in over 7,300 protection cases that were brought to its attention in which young children were involved. In only 0.4% of these enquiries was punishable behaviour of the child mentioned as the core problem. In 4% of the cases, it was about behaviour that was difficult to handle. Figures for 2006 were about the same.

Social enquiries may result in a request by the Council to the court for a child protection measure, such as a supervision order. About 1,500 supervision orders were imposed on children aged 6–11 each year. However, from the Council's data information system it is not possible to identify the number of child protection measures as a direct or indirect reaction to cases in which delinquency of a child was the main reason to inform the Council of Child Care and Protection. Child protection measures are carried out by the regional Youth Care Bureau (*Bureau Jeugdzorg*). But the Youth Care Bureau's information system does not reveal information about the exact reason for a measure and, therefore, the bureaus do not know how often the measure is a response to serious disruptive behaviours or child delinquency.

The best-known and best-documented formal response to child delinquency in the Netherlands is the Stop programme. The Stop initiative has led to new research on child delinquency, including several evaluations and new analyses of police data (Kroon, 2005; Van Domburgh, 2006). The Stop programme in the police district Haaglanden was the first one to be evaluated (Van den Hoogen-Saleh, 2000). Between February 1999 and January 2000 the police questioned 531 children on 613 occasions. Of this group, 83% were boys and 17% girls, and their mean age was 9.2. They were questioned for shoplifting (25%), vandalism (25%), theft (16%), mischief (13%), arson (7%), and fireworks (7%). Half (261) of the 531 children were referred to Stop, mainly for shoplifting (29%), vandalism (29%), theft (14%) and fireworks (11%). Thus, the Stop initiative had an impact on police operations and reporting activities. Compared to 1998, the number of young children questioned tripled from 143 to 531, probably the result of increased attention given to child delinquents and the possibility of referral to Stop.

The first national evaluation of the Stop programme was published in 2000 (Slump et al., 2000). Between May 1999 and May 2000, 1,717 children under age 12 were referred to fifty-three operational Stop programmes (Table 2.5). The Stop programme in the police district of Haaglanden received most referrals (14%), twice as many as in the police district of Amsterdam-Amstelland. Most of the children in this evaluation were boys (88%): 51% were 11-year-olds, 26% 10-year-olds, and 14% 9-year-olds. Shoplifting (27%), vandalism (19%), fireworks (16%), and mischief (11%) make up almost three-quarters of all referrals. The majority of children (75%) completed the Stop programme successfully. In 17% of the initial police referrals, parents refused their consent. The number of referrals to Stop increased from about 1,784 in 2000 to about 2,070 in 2005 and then went down to about 1,950 in 2006 (see Table 2.5) (Eggen & Van der Heide, 2006; Jaarbericht Halt-sector, 2006, 2007). The number of referrals does not seem to represent a clear secular trend.

Table 2.5 Referrals of children to Stop (2000–05)

Year	Number of referrals
2000	1,784
2001	1,639
2002	1,962
2003	2,304
2004	2,167
2005	1,948
2006	2,069

Source: CBS/WODC (Eggen & Van der Heide, 2006).

Child Delinquents and the Law

We observed that each year several thousand children who have committed delinquent acts come into contact with the police. Over two thousand of them are referred to the Stop programme. If the ratio between questioning young children on the one hand and referring them to Stop on the other is the same as it is in the police district of Haaglanden a couple of years ago, then we may conclude that today somewhere between four and five thousand young children get into trouble with the law. Around 15% of these children are registered by the police on more than one occasion, which indicates that recidivism is not an exceptional phenomenon for this age category. It seems fair to estimate that at least three-quarters of these children are aged 10 and 11, with the numbers of 7- and 8-year-olds being in all likelihood very small. In the absence of reliable and valid statistics however, we cannot identify what trend has taken place over the recent past.

Judging from self-reports, it appears that young children are caught more often than older youngsters. However, we can expect that the numbers who are known to the police are less than the number of young children committing delinquent acts. Self-report surveys in which young children have participated show different prevalence rates of delinquent acts as a result of different definitions and constructs. However, if we consider the latest self-report study by the WODC (Van der Laan & Blom, 2006) for 10- and 11-year-olds, we can estimate some prevalence rates.

According to the WODC study, one-third of the 10–11-year-olds admitted one or more delinquent acts. Taking into account that the total population of 10- and 11-year-olds in the Netherlands amounts to 395,000, we estimate the number of delinquent children at 131,000. Even though this is by far not as large as the number of 12–17-year-olds admitting delinquent acts, it is still an impressively large number. Undoubtedly the prevalence is higher when non-serious acts, such as setting off fireworks, are included. However, the absolute numbers remain high even if delinquency is restricted to more serious or traditional delinquent acts such as theft at school, shoplifting, changing price tags and graffiti. Theft at school is committed by over 27,000 children, and changing price tags, shoplifting and graffiti by about 13,000 children. Aggressive behaviours such as hitting, threatening, harassment and several forms of verbal aggression are not uncommon for tens of thousands of 10- and 11-year-olds. According to the TRAILS study (Soepboer, Veenstra & Verhulst, 2006), some of them may desist within a few years, whereas others will start to show these behaviours, and many of them will continue to show these behaviours for at least several years.

Information is scarce regarding formal reactions by the police to known child delinquency. The number of formal (that is, in the presence of parents) or informal police warnings is probably at least twice as high as the number of Stop referrals, but we are not certain of this. The same is true for other actions such as referrals to voluntary care or supervision orders. Nor can we say anything about the impact of such action in terms of preventing the reoccurrence of the unwanted behaviour. Thus far, no outcome evaluations have been carried out on child delinquents in the Netherlands.

Conclusions

Relatively little is known about child delinquency and police contacts with children under age 12. The few analyses of police data and self-report studies suggest a small but substantial number of children showing aggressive behaviours and having committed delinquent acts. Whether this is increasing or decreasing over the years remains unclear. Compared to older juveniles, delinquency by young children is certainly less prevalent and of a less serious nature. For this reason and because of limited culpability at this young age, it does not seem justified to apply the same intrusive penal interventions that older juveniles receive. Due to age limits and legal arrangements, this is not current practice but other formal interventions of a less penal and more pedagogical nature are usually imposed. Whether they are effective in terms of preventing delinquent children from becoming tomorrow's serious offenders is not known. Referrals to Stop or supervision orders imposed in response to child delinquency have not yet been evaluated in terms of recidivism risk. The same is true for prevention and family support programmes that are introduced for families with children at risk of serious psychosocial problems (see Chapter 11 and Appendix 1).

Elsewhere we have indicated the serious limitations of much of the Dutch delinquency evaluation research and this situation constitutes an important reason for the lack of knowledge concerning the performance, effectiveness and outcomes of preventive and remedial programmes for serious and violent juvenile delinquents (Loeber & Slot, 2007). These shortcomings undermine the validity of research outcomes. Methodological failings include the absence of control or comparison groups; problems regarding the matching of criteria for control groups; small numbers of participants in programmes and outcome studies; different definitions and interpretations of effects and recidivism that hamper comparison; short-term evaluations, and gaps in knowledge of the nature, fidelity and content of the intervention.

We have reason to believe that such shortcomings also affect outcome studies of programmes for young children. Therefore, similar suggestions for future research regarding young children can be made. Some of these suggestions relate to the object of the research; others concern the nature and quality of the research. First of all, there is a need for greater transparency in the Dutch system of childcare and protection and in the way the police and the judiciary respond to child delinquency. Which children, and for what reasons, are they referring to these organisations, and what decisions are being made about them? Only scattered and unreliable information and assumptions are available, creating many gaps in our knowledge. Secondly, we know little about the content and efficacy of prevention efforts through police and judicial interventions. Outcome evaluations are rare and seldom properly (that is, experimentally) conducted. In addition, much needed cost-benefit evaluations are not available. The current situation is typified by selective and incidental evaluations. This implies that the quality of evaluation studies needs improvement. Designs should achieve a score of at least three but preferably four or five on the Scientific Methods Scale (Farrington, 2003). Research on outcomes should implement at least quasi-experimental designs, though ideally they should be based on randomised controlled designs. Standardisation of reoffending measures is an indispensable requirement. Furthermore, the nature, content and method of interventions should be extensively described, and the fidelity of implementation should be monitored and secured. In this respect, there is certainly a need for sound process and implementation evaluations. Thorough descriptions of intervention programmes also clarify how interventions are dictated by theoretical considerations. This is important, since well-conceived and elaborated theories can considerably increase the effectiveness and efficacy of interventions (Andrews & Bonta, 2003). Many interventions in the Netherlands lack such a theoretical basis. For the same reason, assessments are needed of risk and promotive factors that young children and their families are exposed to and that are known to influence children's development of serious psychosocial problems and future criminal careers. The same is true for assessing the risk that problems reappear in the near future. Prevention strategies that address these risk and promotive factors associated with recidivism are a worthwhile and cost-effective investment for society. Advances towards evidence-based practice apply to all age groups of youth at risk of serious delinquency but can best start with child delinquents.

Chapter 3

Child Delinquency as Seen By Parents, Teachers and Psychiatrists

Machteld Hoeve, Andrea G. Donker, Channa Al, Peter H. van der Laan, Anna Neumann, Karin Wittebrood and Hans M. Koot

Serious delinquent acts are often preceded by problem behaviours – particularly disruptive behaviours – in childhood. Longitudinal studies have shown that children who exhibit persistent disruptive behaviours early in life have an increased risk of becoming delinquent. For example, Patterson and Yoerger (1997, 2002) observed that such children display long-lasting patterns of disruptive behaviours and delinquency. Loeber, Stouthamer-Loeber and Green (1991) found that compared to non-problem children, preschool problem children were twice as likely to become delinquent. Furthermore, studies have shown that early aggression predicts later delinquency (Loeber & Dishion, 1983). In addition, Farrington (1991) found that adults convicted of a violent crime had been significantly more aggressive at ages 8 to 10. The link between early problem behaviours and later delinquency has also been found in Dutch studies. In particular, a strong association has been found between childhood problem behaviours and adult violence (Donker et al., 2003).

Two influential theoretical models incorporate the notion that disruptive children have an elevated risk of later delinquency compared to non-disruptive children. In her Dual Taxonomy Model, Moffitt (1993) distinguished between life-course persistent delinquents (who start early in life exhibiting problem behaviours and go on to engage in delinquency and crime throughout their lives) and adolescent-limited delinquents (who start committing crimes in adolescence, and who have a far better chance of desisting from crime when they enter adulthood). The second model is the Loeber (1996) developmental model, which is described in Chapters 1 and 9 of this volume. This model includes three pathways, each of which is characterised by less serious problem behaviours in childhood, followed by more serious forms of delinquency in adolescence.

In this chapter, we address the prevalence of problem behaviours in children as reported by parents and teachers and according to psychiatric diagnoses. Our main focus is on externalising problem behaviours such as minor delinquency, aggression, disobedience and cruelty to others. Emotional or internalising problem behaviours, such as depression and anxiety, are only occasionally addressed.

Our purpose is to answer the following questions:

- How prevalent are problem behaviours in Dutch children under age 12?
- What are the differences in prevalence rates between informants?

- Does the prevalence of problem behaviours vary by gender, age, ethnicity and neighbourhood characteristics?

We start with reviewing previous Dutch research and present new analyses on prevalence figures in four different Dutch samples: a general Dutch sample, and three specific high-risk groups of Dutch children. Subsequently, we discuss differences between parents' and teachers' reports of problem behaviours. Next, we examine whether prevalence figures are different for boys and girls and whether they vary with age and neighbourhood characteristics. Finally, we present our findings on the prevalence of serious and cumulative problems in children.

Past Research

In the past, Dutch scholars have focused primarily on a broad range of problem behaviours in children based on the Child Behaviour Checklist completed by parents (Verhulst, Van der Ende & Koot, 1996), and the Teacher's Report Form completed by parents (Verhulst, Van der Ende, & Koot 1997).[1] An additional source has been psychiatric diagnoses, completed by psychiatrists or researchers, following DSM-IV criteria (American Psychiatric Association, 1994) to identify children with serious clinical problems.[2] Prevalence rates of child problem behaviours tend to differ across studies due to several factors that include the definition of problem behaviour, characteristics of the sample, and different research methods. The definition of problem behaviour is a normative concept dependent on subjective societal norms in a particular time period (Van der Ploeg, 2000), whereas prevalence rates of problem behaviours are based on subjective interpretations by informants. Different opinions may exist on the degree of seriousness of the behaviour. Reviewing the international literature, Van der Ploeg (2000) concluded that the prevalence of internalising and externalising problem behaviours in children in general ranges from 2% to 35%.

1 These questionnaires measure problem behaviour of children and adolescents reported by parents (CBCL) and teachers (TRF). They are standardised measures of emotional and behavioural problems in children and adolescents reported by parents for the previous six months and by teachers for two months. The questionnaires include eight syndrome-scales: Withdrawn, Somatic complaints, Anxious/depressed, Social problems, Thought problems, Delinquent behaviour and Aggressive behaviour, and two broad-band scales of syndromes: Internalising (consisting of the Withdrawn, Somatic complaints, and Anxious/depressed scales) and Externalising (consisting of the Delinquent behaviour and Aggressive behaviour scales). A Total problem score covers all syndromes, summing up the individual item scores. The items of the Delinquency, Aggression, and Attention Problems scales are shown in the tables in this chapter.

2 The DSM-IV is a classification system of mental disorders which is used by practitioners and researchers and lists three distinct syndromes that reflect persistent patterns of disruptive behaviour: Conduct Disorder (CD) characterised by antisocial and norm-violating behaviour, Oppositional Defiant Disorder (ODD), characterised by disobedient, defiant and hostile behaviour, and Attention-deficit/Hyperactivity Disorder (ADHD) characterised by inattentive and hyperactive behaviour (American Psychiatric Association, 1994).

In the Netherlands, different prevalence rates have been reported depending on the type of problem behaviour. For example, in a general Dutch sample, parents reported by means of the CBCL, high rates of oppositional behaviours, including temper tantrums, disobedience, sulking and teasing (83% for 4–7-year-olds and 73% for 8–11-year-olds), while covert destructive behaviours such as stealing, lying and vandalism in ages 4–7 was reported by 22% of the parents and in ages 8–11 by 17% (Donker et al., 2004). Aggression was prevalent in about one-third of the boys, and status violations in about 20–25% of the boys.

Van Lier et al. (2003) examined disruptive behaviours in 7-year-old children from two large cities in the Netherlands (Amsterdam and Rotterdam), using parent CBCL-scores on items that reflect the DSM-IV criteria for Conduct Disorder (CD), Oppositional Defiant Disorder (ODD), and Attention-Deficit/Hyperactivity Disorder (ADHD). The prevalence of children scoring somewhat true or often true on CD items ranged from 3% for being cruel to animals to 23% for swearing or obscene language. Prevalence rates of ODD ranged from 16% for being disobedient at school to 60% for arguing a lot. The prevalence of ADHD problems ranged from 32% for being unusually loud to 51% for not being able to sit still and being restless or hyperactive (Van Lier et al., 2003).

Prevalence rates of problem behaviours also differ among specific groups of children. For example, mentally disabled children have significantly higher levels of all kinds of problem behaviours than children without intellectual disability (De Ruiter et al., 2007; Dekker et al., 2002). Within a group of trainable children (IQ 30–60), aggression was more prevalent than in a general population sample (Dekker et al., 2002). In particular, delinquency was more common in educable children (IQ 60–80). For example, attacking people and fire-setting was reported over three times more in the group of children with an intellectual disability than in the general sample; vandalism was reported over four times more; stealing outside the home and being cruel to animals was reported five times more, and threatening people seven times more (Dekker et al., 2002). Furthermore, some differences were reported between ethnic groups, which we discuss later.

Although the popular Dutch media often cites a general increase in the prevalence of aggression and delinquency in children, few findings exist to support such a claim. For example, by comparison of several cohorts of different ages, Stanger et al. (1997) found some evidence suggesting that aggressive child behaviours have increased. However, Verhulst, Van der Ende and Rietbergen (1997) did not find an increase in problem behaviours in the 1980s and early 1990s, but trends of the last decade remain to be studied (Sytema et al., 2006). In a study of contacts between children and youth mental health services, Sytema et al. (2006) found relatively the same number of contacts in a one-year period: 2.1% (boys 2.9%, girls 1.2%) in 2001, and 2.3% (boys 3.1%, girls 1.3%) in 2002, suggesting that no increase has taken place in more recent years as well.

How Many Children have the Most Serious Problems?

Van der Ploeg (2000) focused on different levels of severity in problem behaviours and suggested that about 15% of Dutch children show some problem behaviours, about 10% have minor problems, and 5% show serious problem behaviour. Sytema et al. (2006) concluded that 7% of children and adolescents (aged 6–19) had serious problems and are in need of professional help. In addition, about 10–15% of the children and adolescents were at risk of serious internalising and externalising problem behaviours.

Compared to these estimates, Dutch research findings indicate higher proportions of children showing serious problem behaviours, with 17–20% of the children scoring in the deviant range. For example, Dekker et al. (2002) found that about 18% of the children from a general population sample showed serious internalising or externalising problem behaviours, scoring in the borderline/clinical range on the Total problems scale of the CBCL. Twenty per cent (parent reported) and 17% (teacher reported) of a general practice population (ages 4–11) had deviant scores on the Total problems CBCL-scale (Zwaanswijk et al., 2005). About 18% of 7-year-old children from a school sample were classified in a high disruptive behaviour class characterised by high levels of ODD and ADHD and medium levels of CD (Van Lier et al., 2003).

Prevalence figures for specific serious problems and syndromes vary. Deviant scores on delinquency and aggression were found in 5% (delinquency) and almost 6% (aggression) of the sample. About 16–18% of the children had deviant scores on externalising problem behaviours (Dekker et al., 2002; Oldehinkel et al., 2004; Zwaanswijk et al., 2005). The prevalence of deviant externalising scores in girls was 10% and in boys 21%, not using gender-specific percentile scores (Oldehinkel et al., 2004). In a survey of 9–10-year-old children living in a large city in the Netherlands (Rotterdam), the following prevalence rates of externalising scores in the deviant range were found: aggression was reported by 20% of the boys and 6% of the girls, and delinquency was reported by 9% of the boys and 2% of the girls (Jansen, Van Berkel, & Veelen-Dieleman, 2003). Parents reported deviant externalising problem behaviours in 13% of the children and teachers reported these problems in 22% of the boys and 6% of the girls. Two per cent of the children had scores on internalising and externalising problem behaviours within the clinical range reported by all three informants.

Children with seriously disruptive behaviours have also been identified using person-oriented methods, classifying children based on their problem scores at one point in time or over several years. Using longitudinal statistical methods, Bongers et al. (2004) identified several groups of children following different trajectories of externalising problem behaviours. Most children (71%) showed very little aggression during childhood, while a small group of children (8%) showed persistent high levels of aggression. Similarly, a large group of children (75%) showed no or very low levels of property violations. The two highest trajectories consisted of a small group of children showing high persistent (5%) and extremely high persistent (0.3%) behaviours such as being cruel to animals, stealing, vandalism and lying. Half of the children did not engage in status violations such as running away from home or truancy. In general, this type of problem behaviour was relatively rare during childhood. The number of status violations rose from low to medium levels in childhood to medium to high levels in adolescence. The most problematic group showing the most status violations escalating in adolescence consisted of 1% of the sample. Oppositional behaviours characterised by disobedience, stubbornness, teasing and temper tantrums was much more prevalent compared to other externalising problem behaviours. Only 7% of the children showed hardly any oppositional behaviour, while most children followed a decreasing trajectory with medium levels of oppositional behaviours. A small group (6%) showed increasing (low to medium) levels of this type of problem behaviour over time. In addition, 7% of the sample showed persistent problematic high-level oppositional behaviour.

Children with Disruptive Behaviour Disorders

Studies on psychiatric disorders found different prevalence rates of disruptive disorders such as CD, ODD, and ADHD, varying from 10% to 25%. These variations may be due to differences in diagnostic and sampling methods. For example, Zwirs et al. (2007) found 25% of the children ages 6–10 living in low socioeconomic status (SES) inner-city neighbourhoods in the Netherlands qualified for a disruptive disorder diagnosis. Nine per cent of the children had an externalising disorder with a functional impairment. ADHD was the most prevalent disorder (19% and 7% including impairment), followed by ODD (11% and 4% including impairment). CD was rare with 3% of the children diagnosed and 2% having impairment. Van Lier et al. (2003) found that about 10% of 7-year-old elementary-school children scored within the clinical range of the CBCL-DSM-IV scales (65 out of 636 children).

Co-morbidity

Co-morbidity, that is, the co-occurrence of different problems or syndromes, has been found relatively frequently in children. The co-occurrence of CD and ODD with ADHD was found to be more prevalent in younger than older children (Loeber & Keenan, 1994). Van Lier et al. (2003) found some evidence to suggest that high levels of co-morbidity exist between syndromes of disruptive behaviour (that is, CD, ODD, and ADHD) in 7-year-olds. They identified three categories of children with externalising problem behaviours: one category included all three syndromes (18%), a category consisting of ODD and ADHD (50%), and a category with very low levels of externalising problem behaviours (32%). The three syndromes of CD, ODD and ADHD were highly correlated and the classification of the children revealed that no category consisted of one specific syndrome only (Van Lier et al., 2003). About 70% of the children in the category characterised by CD, ODD and ADHD had externalising problem scores in the borderline and clinical range. Males and children of low socioeconomic status had higher probabilities for being classified in this category. Problem behaviours in the borderline or clinical range of the externalising problem behaviour scale were far less prevalent among the children in the other two categories: 15% among the category with ODD and ADHD problems and only 1% among the children with low levels of externalising problem behaviours.

Verhulst and Van der Ende (1993) also reported an overlap between the majority of problem behaviour scales of the CBCL, showing co-morbidity between various disruptive behaviours. In a study on pre-adolescents (ages 10–12), co-occurring deviant rates of internalising and externalising scores were found in almost 6% of the children, whereas 20% had either only internalising or only externalising problem behaviour (10% each; Oldehinkel et al., 2004). Nearly 7% of the boys and 5% of the girls showed deviant scores of both internalising and externalising problem behaviours. Furthermore, children with deviant scores on these dimensions suffered more often from additional problems such as physical disorders, school problems, and having parents with mental health problems (Zwaanswijk et al., 2005).

Recent Findings

We will now present new information on four distinct Dutch samples: a general population sample and three specific population samples. The general population sample is a representative Dutch sample. The three specific samples include a day-care sample, an outpatient sample, and a mentally-disabled sample. We present the delinquency and aggressive behaviour CBCL-scales of 1218 children aged 8–11. Data were collected in 2002 and 2003 by the Netherlands Institute for Social Research/SCP (*Sociaal Cultureel Planbureau* in Dutch) and the TNO Quality of Life division of the research institute TNO.[3] Details on the sample have been presented by Zeijl et al. (2005).

The day-care sample was obtained from ninety-two day-care centres (Boddaert centres) from 1994 to 1998. These centres provided after-school day-care for 1365 boys and 478 girls aged 4–11 who were referred for guidance and treatment, mainly for disruptive problems. Parents were asked to complete a CBCL upon referral of the child. The outpatient sample was recruited from 1988 to 1989 from five mental health institutions in the Rotterdam region (Verhulst et al., 1996; Verhulst, Van der Ende & Koot, 1997). Data were gathered on 2004 children aged 4–18 referred to one of these institutions. For this chapter, we used the data of children aged 4–11 (*N*=1422). The intellectually disabled sample was obtained from special schools for trainable and educable children in the Dutch province of Zuid-Holland. The main criterion to enter a school for trainable child was an IQ between 30 and 60 (moderate to mild ID), and an IQ of about 60–80 (mild to borderline ID) to enter a school for educable children. In this chapter, we used data from 537 children aged 6–11. Data were gathered in 1996. Details of this sample are described in Dekker et al. (2002).

Table 3.1 presents the prevalence of externalising problem behaviours for the general population sample based on two of the CBCL syndrome-scales of delinquency and aggression.[4] The prevalence rates in the general sample are the lowest (comparison between Table 3.1 and Tables 3.2, 3.3 and 3.4).[5] Some externalising problem behaviours were quite common among the children in the general sample. For example, over half of the children argued too much, sometimes or often, and bragged or boasted. Almost half of the children demanded a lot of attention and

3 The project was financed by the SCP, the Ministry of Health, Welfare and Sport (Ministerie van VWS).

4 The delinquency scale includes some externalising, non-delinquent behaviours, for which juveniles typically are not arrested.

5 Teacher reports and figures on attention problems in the general sample were not available.

Table 3.1 Prevalence of delinquent and aggressive behaviours, by gender, in the general population sample, ages 8–11 (based on parent reports – CBCL)

	% Boys (*N*= 592)	% Girls (*N*= 626)
Delinquent behaviour		
Doesn't feel guilty after misbehaving	20.7	20.1
Hangs around with children who get in trouble	13.5	7.3
Lying or cheating	19.8	15.7
Prefers being with older kids	22.3	15.9
Sets fires	1.2	0.3
Steals at home	1.7	0.7
Steals outside home	0.7	0.3
Swearing or obscene language	27.8	16.8
Thinks about sex too much	3.7	1.5
Truancy, skips school	0.5	0
Uses alcohol or drugs	0	0
Vandalism	1	0
Aggressive behaviour		
Argues a lot	57.2	59.3
Bragging, boasting	56.4	28.1
Cruel to animals	3.1	2.9
Cruelty, bullying, or meanness to others	13.4	9.3
Demands a lot of attention	45.0	43.3
Destroys their own things	7.1	3.5
Destroys things belonging to others	5.1	4.0
Disobedient at home	47.7	39.4
Disobedient at school	31.1	13.8
Easily jealous	31.7	34.8
Gets in many fights	17.8	6.0
Physically attacks people	2.8	1.8
Screams a lot	26.2	26.4
Shows off, clowns around	31.9	17.6
Stubborn (sullen or irritable)	44.1	41.9
Sudden changes in mood (or feelings)	19.4	19.6
Talks too much	32.0	37.8
Teases a lot	13.8	9.4
Has Temper tantrums or a hot temper	24.4	20.3
Threatens people	1.7	0.7
Unusually loud	17.5	11.0

Source: SCP/TNO-PG (2002–03). *Note*: The prevalence rate is the proportion of children who scored 'sometimes or somewhat true' (1) or 'often or very true' (2). The parent reports concern the previous two months.

Table 3.2 Prevalence of delinquent and aggressive behaviours, and attention problems, by gender, for the day-care sample, ages 4–11 (based on parent reports – CBCL)

	% Boys (*N*= 1365)	% Girls (*N*= 478)
Delinquent behaviour		
Doesn't feel guilty after misbehaving	72.5	66.7
Hangs around with children who get in trouble	38.9	22.6
Lying or cheating	71.4	74.5
Prefers being with older kids	52.7	50.0
Runs away from home	16.9	12.6
Sets fires	24.3	5.6
Steals at home	25.8	21.3
Steals outside home	18.7	14.9
Swears or uses obscene language	71.0	60.3
Thinks about sex too much	14.5	14.4
Truancy, skips school	4.2	3.3
Uses alcohol or drugs	1.2	0.8
Vandalism	30.1	13.6
Aggressive behaviour		
Argues a lot	95.2	93.1
Bragging, boasting	84.5	63.4
Cruelty, bullying, or meanness to others	66.6	56.7
Demands a lot of attention	93.2	91.6
Destroys their own things	58.5	44.4
Destroys things belonging to others	52.1	37.2
Disobedient at home	91.4	90.0
Disobedient at school	71.6	56.3
Easily jealous	72.2	79.7
Gets in many fights	73.7	42.7
Physically attacks people	53.1	30.8
Screams a lot	73.8	74.7
Showing off, clowning	80.2	77.2
Stubborn (sullen or irritable)	88.0	87.4
Sudden changes in mood (or feelings)	73.0	69.5
Talks too much	72.8	72.0
Teases a lot	80.7	69.9
Has temper tantrums or a hot temper	82.2	74.3
Threatens people	25.2	13.8
Unusually loud	81.3	74.3
Attention problems		
Acts too young	53.2	52.1
Can't concentrate	91.9	88.9
Can't sit still	91.9	83.5

Table 3.2 continued

Confused	35.0	33.7
Daydreams	49.6	52.9
Impulsive	85.2	75.5
Nervous, tense	73.6	75.5
Nervous movements	45.6	36.2
Poor schoolwork	44.9	43.7
Clumsy	54.5	47.3
Hums, stares blankly	30.0	31.6

Note: The prevalence rate is the proportion of children who scored 'sometimes or somewhat true' (1) or 'often or very true'

were disobedient at home. In contrast, according to the parents, none of the children used alcohol or drugs and only 1% engaged in vandalism. Furthermore, threatening people, fire-setting and stealing were very uncommon.

Parent reports of externalising problem behaviours were much more prevalent for children in the day-care sample (Table 3.2) than in the general population sample (Table 3.1). For example, 70% of the day-care boys compared to 20% of the boys in the general sample did not feel guilty after misbehaving, and lied or cheated. Destroying things belonging to others and physically attacking people were prevalent in half of the day-care boys, and a quarter of day-care boys sometimes set fires, while these behaviours – at most 5% – were very uncommon in the general sample. Aggressive behaviours were also highly prevalent in the day-care sample with almost all aggressive symptoms apparent in at least half of the children. Threatening people was the least prevalent: only 25% of the boys and 14% of the girls showed this behaviour. According to parents, almost all children in the day-care sample (that is, over 90%) sometimes argued a lot, demanded a lot of attention and were disobedient at home. Over 90% of the boys had attention problems such as not being able to concentrate and being overactive. Rates of delinquency were generally smaller than rates of aggressive behaviours and attention problems. As in the general sample, truancy, skipping school and using alcohol or drugs were relatively uncommon.

Children in the outpatient sample (Table 3.3) also showed more externalising and attention problems than children from the general sample, although prevalence rates tended to be somewhat lower than those of the day-care sample. Based on parent ratings, the highest prevalence rates (over 80% of the boys) were found in arguing a lot, demanding a lot of attention, being not able to concentrate and being overactive. Many girls also showed these behaviours, with prevalence rates ranging from 67% for being overactive to 82% for demanding a lot of attention. Similar to the other samples, most forms of delinquency were less prevalent than aggressive behaviours and attention problems. The majority of delinquent acts were committed by less than 20% of the children. Relatively many children did not feel guilty after misbehaving (54% boys, 45% girls), lied or cheated (44% boys, 39% girls), and preferred being with older kids (41% boys, 36% girls).

Children with an intellectual disability (Table 3.4) showed more problem behaviours than children from the general population sample, but scored clearly

Table 3.3 Prevalence of delinquent and aggressive behaviours, and attention problems, by gender, in the outpatient sample, ages 4–11 (based on parent reports – CBCL, and teacher reports – TRF)

	Parent reports		*Teacher reports*	
	% Boys (*N*=944)	% Girls (*N*=478)	% Boys (*N*=848)	% Girls (*N*=417)
Delinquent behaviour				
Doesn't feel guilty after misbehaving	53.8	44.8	46.7	28.8
Hangs around with children who get in trouble	16.7	11.3	21.2	13.9
Lying or cheating	43.6	38.5	30.9	20.1
Prefers being with older kids	40.7	36.2	18.6	13.2
Runs away from home	7.3	3.2	-	-
Sets fires	13.7	1.9	-	-
Steals at home	11.2	8.4	-	-
Steals outside home	9.4	6.1	9.1	7.0
Swears or uses obscene language	39.7	27.4	25.8	10.8
Thinks about sex too much	6.6	7.3	-	-
Truancy, skips school	2.5	3.6	3.9	3.8
Uses alcohol or drugs	.2	0	.6	.5
Vandalism	13.6	5.6	-	-
Tardy to school or class	-	-	9.9	11.5
Aggressive behaviour				
Argues a lot	81.9	77.0	55.4	35.7
Bragging, boasting	65.9	30.3	51.7	18.0
Cruelty, bullying, or meanness to others	42.3	28.5	38.8	18.7
Demands a lot of attention	85.1	81.8	67.1	55.2

Destroys their own things	39.3	20.9	18.8	6.5
Destroys things belonging to others	28.8	18.0	23.0	8.4
Disobedient at home	74.5	65.1	-	-
Disobedient at school	45.8	28.5	44.9	23.5
Easily jealous	62.5	69.0	30.8	34.1
Gets in many fights	45.3	18.8	45.3	16.3
Physically attacks people	34.9	17.2	33.6	13.2
Screams a lot	56.5	52.3	36.3	17.7
Showing off, clowning	62.3	43.7	51.2	23.0
Stubborn (sullen or irritable)	73.5	73.6	46.0	38.1
Sudden changes in mood (or feelings)	59.1	60.7	41.3	35.0
Talks too much	55.6	49.0	47.6	34.3
Teases a lot	58.9	41.2	47.2	21.3
Has temper tantrums or a hot temper	66.4	53.1	33.8	19.4
Threatens people	8.9	4.0	13.8	4.8
Unusually loud	68.2	48.7	47.9	26.1
Defiant	-	-	42.3	26.9
Disturbs other pupils	-	-	61.9	36.0
Talks out of turn	-	-	59.1	40.5
Disrupts class discipline	-	-	40.8	19.2
Explosive, unpredictable behaviour	-	-	43.0	23.7
Easily frustrated	-	-	42.8	30.2
Attention problems				
Acts too young	47.5	39.5	49.5	40.0
Can't concentrate	81.1	71.1	75.7	63.5

Table 3.3 continued

Can't sit still	82.9	66.7	65.6	42.9
Confused	38.1	35.1	50.6	34.1
Daydreams	50.3	48.5	57.5	53.2
Impulsive	70.0	49.6	62.3	38.1
Nervous, tense	71.4	70.3	69.9	58.0
Nervous movements	33.9	27.6	-	-
Poor schoolwork	42.5	30.8	52.1	40.0
Clumsy	47.6	33.7	48.6	27.8
Hums, stares blankly	28.0	28.2	39.2	35.7
Odd noises	-	-	46.7	19.2
Fails to finish	-	-	58.1	42.2
Fidgets	-	-	49.9	31.2
Difficulty with directions	-	-	62.7	43.4
Difficulty learning	-	-	57.0	48.0
Apathetic	-	-	49.2	34.8
Messy work	-	-	70.6	46.8
Inattentive	-	-	71.5	56.1
Underachieving	-	-	52.7	35.0
Fails to carry out tasks	-	-	46.0	28.1

Note: The prevalence rate is the proportion of children who scored 'sometimes or somewhat true' (1) or 'often or very true' (2). Parent reports concern the past six months and teacher reports concern the previous two months.

Table 3.4 Prevalence of delinquent and aggressive behaviours, and attention problems, by gender, in an intellectually disabled sample, ages 6–11 (based on parent reports – CBCL, and teacher reports – TRF)

	Parent reports		*Teacher reports*	
	% Boys ($N = 320$)	% Girls ($N = 217$)	% Boys ($N = 234$)	% Girls ($N = 170$)
Delinquent behaviour				
Doesn't feel guilty after misbehaving	39.4	34.1	36.8	24.1
Hangs around with children who get in trouble	13.4	6.0	20.1	9.4
Lying or cheating	23.4	27.6	29.5	21.8
Prefers being with older kids	28.4	27.2	20.5	16.5
Runs away from home	6.3	4.6	-	-
Sets fires	7.2	1.8	-	-
Steals at home	5.3	4.6	-	-
Steals outside home	2.5	4.6	6.4	4.7
Swears or uses obscene language	34.4	28.6	20.9	14.7
Thinks about sex too much	3.4	4.1	-	-
Truancy, skips school	.9	.9	2.6	3.5
Uses alcohol or drugs	0	0	1.3	1.2
Vandalism	6.9	3.7	-	-
Tardy to school or class	-	-	6.8	8.2
Aggressive behaviour				
Argues a lot	59.1	61.8	51.3	41.2
Bragging, boasting	48.4	27.2	52.2	26.5
Cruelty, bullying, or meanness to others	24.4	15.7	33.3	18.2
Demands a lot of attention	70.9	70.0	58.1	45.9

Table 3.4 continued

Destroys their own things	28.4	15.2	7.7	6.5
Destroys things belonging to others	22.8	10.1	15.4	8.8
Disobedient at home	56.6	50.7	-	-
Disobedient at school	39.7	27.2	47.4	23.5
Easily jealous	42.8	47.0	25.6	31.2
Gets in many fights	28.8	13.8	38.5	11.8
Physically attacks people	18.8	13.4	35.5	12.4
Screams a lot	36.3	32.3	23.9	14.7
Showing off, clowning	46.3	34.6	47.0	24.7
Stubborn (sullen or irritable)	64.4	59.4	51.7	42.9
Sudden changes in mood (or feelings)	40.0	30.9	25.2	25.9
Talks too much	41.9	45.6	42.7	34.7
Teases a lot	36.9	30.0	41.5	23.5
Temper tantrums or hot temper	53.1	39.2	24.8	15.9
Threatens people	6.3	2.8	14.1	4.1
Unusually loud	46.3	39.2	37.6	22.4
Defiant	-	-	48.3	32.9
Disturbs other pupils	-	-	55.1	36.5
Talks out of turn	-	-	59.4	44.7
Disrupts class discipline	-	-	47.0	31.2
Explosive, unpredictable behaviour	-	-	34.6	17.1
Easily frustrated	-	-	32.5	27.1

Attention problems				
Acts too young	72.2	68.2	70.1	69.4
Can't concentrate	87.5	78.8	77.8	72.9
Can't sit still	70.9	57.1	53.4	32.4
Confused	16.3	12.9	24.4	20.0
Daydreams	39.1	40.6	49.1	45.3
Impulsive	57.2	50.2	60.7	43.5
Nervous, tense	48.4	49.8	49.6	47.1
Nervous movements	25.6	15.7	-	-
Poor schoolwork	30.0	27.6	51.7	46.5
Clumsy	46.3	42.4	50.0	41.2
Hums, stares blankly	25.0	15.7	30.8	34.1
Odd noises	-	-	32.1	46.5
Fails to finish	-	-	56.4	41.2
Fidgets	-	-	52.6	35.3
Difficulty with directions	-	-	62.0	52.4
Difficulty learning	-	-	89.3	91.2
Apathetic	-	-	38.0	31.2
Messy work	-	-	53.8	42.9
Inattentive	-	-	73.9	61.2
Underachieving	-	-	27.8	18.8
Fails to carry out tasks	-	-	32.9	22.4

Note: The prevalence rate is the proportion of children who scored 'sometimes or somewhat true' (1) or 'often or very true' (2). Parent reports concern the past six months and teacher reports concern the previous two months.

Table 3.5 Percentage of children scoring within the clinical range in three specific Dutch high-risk samples for aggression, delinquency and attention problems (based on parent reports – CBCL)

	Day-care sample		*Outpatient sample*		*Intellectually disabled sample*	
	% Boys	% Girls	% Boys	% Girls	% Boys	% Girls
Aggression	7.4	22.6	1.0	5.9	0.3	1.8
Delinquency	44.2	51.5	18.6	17.6	8.4	10.1
Attention problems	12.0	16.3	8.9	11.7	7.5	7.8

lower than the day-care children (Table 3.2) and slightly lower than outpatient children (Table 3.3). However, intellectually disabled children acted too young for their age more often than the other samples and, not surprisingly, according to teacher reports these children had more difficulties with learning. The highest rates in this sample were found for attention problems, such as not concentrating or sitting still. According to parents, about 70% of these children also demanded a lot of attention. In summary, authority problems such as disobedience at home or school and being stubborn were most common. Covert behaviours including fire-setting, stealing and vandalism were uncommon. Overt problem behaviours differed in prevalence: while arguing a lot was very common, physically attacking people was uncommon. More specifically, the prevalence of arguing a lot, demanding a lot of attention and being disobedient at home were most common, at least 45% in the general sample and up to at least 90% in the day-care sample. Truancy or skipping school and using drugs and alcohol were relatively uncommon in all samples. Children from the general sample were found to have the least amount of externalising problem behaviours, followed by the children with an intellectual disability and the outpatient sample, respectively. Children in the day-care sample generally showed the most problem behaviours, which is not surprising because their disruptive behaviour led to referral to this after-school guidance service. The outpatient sample consisted of children referred for the whole spectrum of problem behaviours, including children with only internalising problem behaviours. This might explain why the outpatient sample had slightly lower prevalence rates of disruptive behaviours than the day-care sample.

Children Scoring in the Clinical Range

We examined prevalence rates of children with scores in the clinical range of the narrow-band CBCL syndromes delinquency, aggression, and attention problems (Table 3.5). According to Achenbach (1991), 2% of a normative sample consisting of non-referred children have scores in the clinical range on these syndromes, indicating that these children show clinically significant deviant behaviours. We compared the above-mentioned Dutch high-risk samples with the Dutch normative data of Verhulst, Van der Ende and Koot (1996). The general population sample data were not available for these analyses.

As expected, children from the three high-risk samples showed higher rates of extreme externalising and attention problems compared to the normative sample of Verhulst and colleagues. In the day-care sample, about 7% of the boys and almost 23% of the girls showed highly aggressive behaviours, using gender-specific percentile scores. Scores within the clinical range for delinquency were 44% of the boys and 52% of the girls. Deviant attention problems were apparent in 12% of the boys and 16% of the girls.

The prevalence rates of deviant delinquency and attention problems in the outpatient sample were also higher. About 17% of the outpatient children had deviant levels of delinquency (17% in boys; 18% in girls), and 9% of the boys and 12% of the girls had deviant attention problems. The prevalence of serious aggression was lower: 1% for boys and 6% for girls.

Deviant problems in the intellectually disabled sample were only slightly more common than those in the general sample. Hardly any boys and only 2% of the girls showed highly aggressive behaviours. Prevalence rates of delinquency and attention problems were somewhat higher: 8–10% for delinquency and about 8% for attention problems. Using the same sample, Dekker et al. (2002) found that somewhat more educable children (IQ 60–80) than trainable children (IQ 30–60) had deviant delinquency scores, while trainable children had more often deviant attention problems than educable children. Prevalence rates of aggression were relatively similar across these groups.

Co-morbidity in the Special Dutch Samples

In the Dutch high-risk samples (day-care, outpatient, and intellectually disabled), deviant scores on one, two, or all three syndromes of delinquency, aggression and attention problems were as follows: of the day-care children, 36% of boys and 34% of girls were found to have a single deviant syndrome; 11% of boys and 21% of girls had two deviant syndromes and 2% of boys and 5% of girls had both deviant delinquent, aggressive and attention problems. In the outpatient sample, prevalence rates were slightly lower: 21% of boys and 20% of girls qualified for a single syndrome; 4% of boys and 5% of girls qualified for two syndromes, and 0.1% of boys and 2% of girls qualified for three syndromes. About 13% of the children with an intellectual disability had a single deviant externalising or attention syndrome and about 1% had two of these syndromes. Prevalence rates were relatively similar for boys and girls. A small proportion of children had deviant scores on all three syndromes: 0.3% of the boys versus 1% of the girls. Notably, day-care and outpatient girls had relatively higher prevalence rates than boys for two or three co-occurring deviant externalising problem behaviours. This agrees with previous findings suggesting that co-morbidity is more prevalent in disruptive girls than in boys. About half of the girls with externalising problem behaviours also showed deviant internalising problem behaviours, while both kinds of problems occurred in only one-third of the boys (Oldehinkel et al., 2004).

Differences in Parents', Teachers', and Professionals' Views of Child Problem Behaviour

Epidemiological studies on children under 12 years of age rarely include self-report measures. Instead, the informants are most commonly parents, teachers and professionals employed in youth mental health services. Zeijl et al. (2005) found a much higher prevalence of psychosocial problems in professional reports (11–28%) compared to parent reports (4–6%), but this may be because different measurement instruments and different categories of problems were used. The prevalence figures in professional reports included minor problems, whereas the parent reports only differentiated serious problem behaviours on a clinical level. In the following text, we focus on differences between parent and teacher reports.

Earlier Dutch studies on 4–11-year-olds from a general population sample showed that for the prediction of poor outcomes, teacher reports on externalising problem behaviours provided additional relevance to those of parents (Donker et al., 2004; Verhulst, Koot & Van der Ende, 1994). The authors found that parents reported all externalising child problem behaviours more often than teachers (Donker et al., 2004). The difference was most apparent for oppositional behaviours. For instance, over 80% of the parents reported oppositional behaviours, versus only 40% of the teachers for the same sample of four- to seven-year-old boys. Differences were less striking for aggressive behaviours and covert destructive behaviours such as stealing and lying (Donker et al., 2004). The highest consistency between parents and teachers was found for aggressive behaviours among eight- to 11-year-olds (r=.40; p<.01).

In the Dutch TRAILS study, the differences between parents and teachers reporting on 10–12-year-old children were much smaller (Soepboer, Veenstra & Verhulst, 2006). Based on parent reports, about 20% of the children showed aggressive behaviour and 2% committed delinquent acts, whereas teachers reported 17% and 6%, respectively. Consistency between parents and teachers measured with the Pearson correlation coefficient was .31 for aggression and .26 for delinquency scales.

Tables 3.3 and 3.4 present parent- and teacher-reported child problem behaviours based on Dutch outpatient and intellectually disabled samples. Both tables show that parents compared to teachers reported slightly more problem behaviours. For example, parents reported more often that their child had temper tantrums, demanded a lot of attention, destroyed his or her own things, and was stubborn. In contrast, teachers reported more often that the child was confused and that boys hung around with children who got into trouble. Furthermore, teachers of children with an intellectual disability reported more often that boys had stolen outside the home and were disobedient at school.

It is possible that, some of these differences may be due to the location at which the behaviour is observed. Hoffenaar and Hoeksma (2002) studied self-reported oppositional emotions and behaviours in Dutch children and found that oppositional behaviour was dependent on the context in which the behaviour occurred during interactions with parents, teachers, or peers. Children more often showed the emotional aspects of oppositional behaviours to their parents rather than teachers. Girls were more affected by the context of the behaviour than boys. While oppositionality was more pronounced in situations with teachers and peers in boys than in girls, boys and girls showed similar levels of oppositionality to parents. However, there are other differences that must be taken into account when considering different informants. For instance, parents often are able to observe their child's behaviour in more settings than teachers. On the other hand, teachers are in a better position to compare far more children than parents usually can. Furthermore, visibility is an important factor. For example, less agreement between parents and teachers was found for covert than for overt conduct problems in boys (Hoffenaar, 2004).

In summary, prevalence rates differ between informants, and consistency between informants is moderate to good. Parents appear to report more child problems – particularly for young children – than teachers. In the next section we elaborate on age and other correlates of problem behaviours.

Past Research on Gender Differences in Problem Behaviours

Previous Dutch studies show that, during childhood, boys have higher levels of problem behaviours than girls (Bongers et al., 2004; Zeijl et al., 2005). In particular, externalising problem behaviours (that is, delinquency and aggression) are more prevalent in boys (Stanger et al., 1997; Stevens et al., 2003; Zeijl et al., 2005; Zwirs et al., 2007). These findings are consistent across cultures (Crijnen, Achenbach & Verhulst, 1999; Zwirs et al., 2007). Despite this marked difference in prevalence, the shape of the developmental pathway of externalising problem behaviours over time was the same for boys and girls (Bongers et al., 2003; Stanger et al., 1997).

Sex differences in externalising problem behaviours (such as aggression and oppositional behaviour) were more pronounced in childhood than in adolescence. Differences between boys and girls usually decrease with age, with boys showing higher rates of aggression relative to girls at age 4, while levels of aggression were relatively similar at age 18 (Bongers et al., 2003; Crijnen, Bengi Arslan & Verhulst, 2000). However, more boys than girls escalate to more serious and violent delinquent acts – such as rape, robbery and homicide – during early adolescence and adulthood (Loeber & Farrington, 1998).

Bongers et al. (2004) distinguished between several developmental trajectories and found that boys were over-represented in problem trajectories showing high levels of aggression and property and status violations, while girls were more prevalent in trajectories with relatively few of these externalising problem behaviours.

Gender Differences in the Special Dutch Samples

Similar to previously-published studies, problem behaviours were more pronounced in boys than in girls in the four special Dutch samples mentioned previously, and this was particularly true for externalising problem behaviours.[6] For example, boys

6 We conducted t-tests on parent and teacher reports of delinquency, aggressive behaviour, attention problems, externalizing problems and internalizing problems to test differences between boys and girls in the day-care, outpatient and intellectually disabled samples. With regard to the general sample, similar tests were done by Zeijl et al. (2005).

had an average score of 0.27 on aggressive behaviours, while this was 0.21 for girls. Similarly, scores on the delinquency scale were higher for boys than for girls (0.09 for boys *versus* 0.06 for girls).[7] However, gender differences are not consistent: in the general population sample, boys had significantly higher rates of externalising problem behaviours than girls, according to youth mental health professionals, but not when parent ratings were considered (Zeijl et al., 2005, see also Table 3.1). In the day-care sample, boys had significantly more externalising problem behaviours than girls, but boys and girls did not differ on arguing, screaming and demanding a lot of attention, while being easily jealous and talking too much was slightly more common in girls (Table 3.2).

According to parent and teacher reports, boys from the outpatient sample had significantly more externalising problem behaviours and attention problems than girls, particularly fire-setting, fighting, being impulsive and threatening people (Table 3.3). Most externalising and attention problems were significantly more prevalent in boys with an intellectual disability (Table 3.4), although delinquency was relatively similar in boys and girls with an intellectual disability.

In summary, externalising problem behaviours tended to be more prevalent in boys than in girls (with the exception of arguing, screaming and demanding a lot of attention), and were more pronounced during childhood than adolescence.

Age, Development and Stability of Problem Behaviours

Across cultures, externalising problem behaviours tends to become more prevalent in adolescence, while levels of internalising problem behaviours tend to be higher in younger children (Crijnen et al., 1999). The increase in externalising problem behaviours is mostly due to an increase in the more covert forms of delinquency, whereas physical aggression has been found to decrease from early childhood on (Brame, Nagin & Tremblay, 2001). At the end of the second year, children tend to be most physically aggressive, but by the time these children enter kindergarten aggressive behaviours in most children has decreased (Tremblay, 2001; see also NICHD Early Child Care Research Network, 2004). In a national representative Dutch sample, Verhulst, Van der Ende and Koot (1996) found some interaction effects between age and gender. For example, higher prevalence rates of vandalism, drugs use and poor schoolwork were found in adolescent boys, while temper tantrums, getting in many fights, and being unusually loud were more prevalent in boys under age 12.

In the four Dutch samples, problem behaviours during childhood varied by age. Regarding the general sample, most externalising problem behaviours were found in 3-year-old children, comparing observations of professionals of youth health services on psychosocial behaviours in children from age 0–12 (Zeijl et al., 2005).

In the day-care sample, more young compared to older children showed aggressive problems. The same was found in teacher reports on outpatient children, but not according to parent reports, although they did report more attention problems

---

7 A table with prevalence rates of behavioural problems of children in the general population sample by individual characteristics such as gender, age, and ethnicity, and SES characteristics is available on request: <k.wittebrood@scp.nl>.

and more delinquent acts among older children. In contrast, younger children with an intellectual disability showed more attention problems than older children, but externalising problem behaviours did not significantly vary by age.

These findings concern comparisons between different children of different age groups (between-subjects) and thus, the results may be due to cohort effects. Bongers et al. (2003; 2004) examined change and stability in problem behaviours using a within-subjects design, that is, scores of behaviours were longitudinally analysed over time for the same individuals. They found that externalising problem behaviours generally decreased with age. The authors identified different trajectories for different types of externalising problem behaviours. In particular, aggression, property violations and oppositional behaviours decreased when children grew older. Minor delinquency decreased during childhood and reached the lowest rates at the transition from primary school to secondary school (age 11–12), but then increased during adolescence (Bongers et al., 2004; Stanger et al., 1997). Furthermore, status violations including running away from home, swearing, truancy and using alcohol and drugs decreased slightly until age 9 and then increased during adolescence (Bongers et al., 2004).

The rise in minor delinquency during adolescence is in line with self-report studies on adolescent delinquency and criminal career research (for example, Farrington, 1986). Moreover, during adolescence delinquent acts tend to increase in severity (Loeber et al., 2008). As others have noted, given that a decrease of delinquency during childhood may be followed by an increase during adolescence, assessing delinquency prior to adolescence is important (Stanger et al., 1997).

Bongers et al. (2004) studied trajectories for aggression, oppositional behaviour, property violations and status violations in Dutch children age 4–18. The authors identified three to six trajectory groups for each of the problem categories, with large groups showing only a few problem behaviours throughout childhood and adolescence. Over 70% of the children showed hardly any aggression or property violations and 50% showed virtually no status violations. In contrast, only 7% followed an oppositional behaviour trajectory of near zero. Some youth became deviant in childhood and outgrew these problems (about 30% within the aggression cluster and 80% within the opposition cluster), yet others persisted in serious extreme behaviour (about 5% within the property violations cluster and 7% in the opposition cluster). Bongers et al. (2004) identified two late-onset groups: a small group of children (6%) showing increasing oppositional problems during late adolescence and about 25% showing increasing levels of status violations.

Despite the differences among children in developmental trajectories of problem behaviours, studies have found notable stability of problem behaviour over time. Verhulst and Van der Ende (1992) in a longitudinal study on 4–11-year-old children reported that externalising problem behaviours were markedly stable over six years. They found stability coefficients of .65 for two years, .63 for four years and .55 for six years, $p < .001$, $N = 936$ (Verhulst & Van der Ende, 1992, p. 602). In addition, Hofstra et al. (2000) found that problem behaviour in children was significantly related to similar behaviour in young adulthood. This is remarkable given the different informants (children and parents) and the long interval of fourteen years. Not all types of problem behaviour appear equally stable. In a four-year period, overt aggression was found to be more stable than covert delinquency (Verhulst, Koot & Berden, 1990; see also Loeber et al., 2008). Externalising problem behaviour scores were significantly more stable than internalising problem behaviours in children under age 12. Furthermore, externalising problem behaviours in childhood were found to predict both internalising and externalising problem behaviours in young adulthood (Hofstra et al., 2000).

In summary, externalising problem behaviours tended to decrease when children grew older. However, developmental pathways differed depending on the type of problem. Both aggressive behaviours and delinquency during childhood decreased with age. Aggression further decreased during adolescence, while delinquency increased. Furthermore, studies uniformly report stability over time in externalising problem behaviours. Overt aggression tends to be more stable than covert forms of delinquency. Moreover, studies report heterogeneity of development among children. Many children show virtually no problems or outgrow their externalising problem behaviours. A small group of children begins to show problems during adolescence. Furthermore, a small group persists in externalising problem behaviours or shows an escalation of problem behaviours over time leading to serious property crime and violence.

Ethnicity

Several risk factors, such as low socioeconomic status, are known to put ethnic minority youngsters at risk of problem behaviours (for example, Loeber & Farrington, 2004). In the Netherlands, Turks and Moroccans are among the largest non-indigenous groups. These ethnic minority groups are over-represented in official records on arrest and conviction figures, whereas self-report studies found no or very little differences between Dutch indigenous and non-indigenous groups (Junger-Tas & Slot, 2001; Wissink, 2006). Research on differences between ethnic groups in the Netherlands is scarce. Moreover, Dutch research mainly concentrates on adolescents, relying on short self-report questionnaires (Stevens et al., 2005).[8] We found seven published papers on differences between ethnic groups of children in the Netherlands.

Relying on multiple informants including children, parents and teachers, Zwirs et al. (2007) examined psychiatric disorders in an ethnically diverse sample of children between ages 6 and 10. Prevalence figures of externalising disorders were relatively similar for Dutch (11%), Moroccan (8%), Turkish (9%) and Surinamese (6%) children (Zwirs et al., 2007). Likewise, no differences have been found between ethnic groups in mood and anxiety disorders.

However, when single informant data are used, findings differ, depending on which informant is questioned. For example, youth mental health workers observed few differences between Dutch Western and non-Western children, except for Moroccan children who had fewer psychosocial problems than Western children

8 Since data on ethnic group membership were not available, we were not able to test ethnic differences in prevalence rates in the four Dutch samples.

(Zeijl et al., 2005). In contrast, non-Western parents reported more psychosocial problems than Western parents. The researchers argue that professionals of youth mental health services may have more difficulties in identifying problems in non-Western children because of communication difficulties.

Differences have also been found between teacher and parent reports. Teacher reports noted relatively small differences between Dutch and Turkish immigrant children (Crijnen et al., 2000; Stevens et al., 2005). However, comparing reports of the same immigrant children, Turkish immigrant teachers reported more problems than Dutch teachers (Crijnen et al., 2000). In addition, Turkish parents reported more internalising and externalising problem behaviours than Dutch parents (Jansen et al., 2003; Stevens et al., 2003; 2005). In particular, anxiety and depression were more prevalent according to Turkish parents (Bengi-Arslan et al., 1997). Turkish parents reported three times more internalising problem behaviours than Western parents (Zeijl et al., 2005).

Substantial discrepancies have been found between the reports of Moroccan parents and their children's teachers. Whereas parents of Moroccan children reported similar levels of externalising problem behaviours as Dutch parents, and fewer problems than Turkish parents, the teachers reported significantly more problems for Moroccan children than for Dutch and Turkish children (Stevens et al., 2003; 2005). Teacher-reported externalising problem scores for Moroccan children were almost twice as high as those for Dutch and Turkish children and they also had more attention problems compared to the other groups.

Similar differences between informants have been found regarding boys and girls. Turkish parents reported more externalising problem behaviours for both boys and girls than Moroccan and Dutch parents, whereas teachers reported more externalising problem behaviours in Moroccan boys and girls compared to Dutch and Turkish boys and girls (Stevens et al., 2005). Furthermore, differences between ethnic groups have been found in externalising problem behaviours in girls. Antillean and Arabian parents reported more serious externalising problem behaviours in girls than parents from other ethnic groups, and Cape Verdean parents reported much more serious attention problems in girls than reported by other parents (Jansen et al., 2003).

The higher rates of externalising problem behaviours reported by Turkish immigrant parents were also found in Turkish parents living in Turkey. Bengi-Arslan et al. (1997) compared problem behaviour scores of Turkish (living in Turkey), Turkish immigrant (living in the Netherlands) and Dutch children. Turkish immigrant parents reported significantly more problems (both internalising and externalising) than Dutch parents. Comparisons of reports on Turkish children and Turkish immigrant children revealed that problem behaviours in these Turkish groups were relatively similar. Turkish children had somewhat higher rates of somatic complaints, whereas immigrant children had higher levels of withdrawal, anxiety and depression, social problems and aggressive problems, but these differences were much smaller than those between immigrant and Dutch children (Bengi-Arslan et al., 1997).

Stevens et al. (2003) offer several explanations for the discrepancies between informants from different ethnic groups. First, the findings may reflect differences in problem behaviours across the contexts of school and home. Moroccan children may show more externalising problem behaviours in school than at home, while internalising problem behaviours in Turkish children may be more visible at home than at school. Secondly, parental punishment and criticism, which is found to be rather common in Turkish culture, may result in internalising problem behaviours in Turkish children (Bengi-Arslan et al., 1997). Third, perceptual biases of teachers due to prejudices may exist: teachers may expect Moroccan children to be more problematic than other children and may therefore have a stronger focus on these behaviours in Moroccan children. Fourth, Moroccan parents may under-report negative behaviours in their children so as not to add to the negative image of Moroccan youngsters in Dutch society.

Finally, differences in opinions of informants with regard to which behaviour is problematic may result in different evaluations of behaviour. Ethnic differences in parental detection of externalising problem behaviours in children have been found in a Dutch study. Zwirs et al (2006) compared diagnoses based on parent interviews alone with best-estimate diagnoses of psychiatric disorders in children based on clinical and diagnostic interviews with children, parents and teachers. They found that Moroccan and Turkish parents detected notably fewer externalising disorders in their children than Dutch parents. Given that 61% of the children with an externalising disorder would not have been detected based on structured interviews with parents, using the parent reports was clearly not suitable. Comparing ethnic groups, higher detection rates of externalising disorders were found in Dutch parents' reports (70%), compared to Moroccan (16%), Turkish (47%), and Surinamese (36%) parents. In contrast, parental detection of the absence of any externalising disorder was better among Turkish (95%) and Moroccan (91%) parents than among Dutch (72%) and Surinamese (85%) parents (Zwirs et al., 2006). Thus, perceptual differences rather than actual differences in problem behaviours may explain at least part of the different findings (Zwirs et al., 2007).

Socioeconomic Status and Neighbourhood Characteristics

Socioeconomic status (SES) has been linked to various child problem behaviours. Children from low SES families showed higher rates of social and attention problems (Crijnen et al., 2000), aggression (Soepboer et al., 2006) and minor delinquency (Crijnen et al., 2000; Soepboer et al., 2006). In another study, lower parental education was found to be linked to higher levels of attention problems and aggressive behaviours, and SES was associated with scores on the total problem scale of the CBCL (Bengi-Arslan et al., 1997). However, Verhulst, Van der Ende, and Koot (1996) found that the explained variance of the SES effects was not larger than 1% (see also Loeber & Dishion, 1983). SES was not found to be linked with the prevalence of any psychiatric disorder in the study of Zwirs et al. (2007), although the authors note that their low SES inner-city sample may overshadow the individual levels of SES. On the other hand, Zeijl et al. (2005) found that 22% of the children who lived below the poverty line had externalising problem behaviours, compared to 4% of the children living in a family with an income above the poverty borderline. These researchers did not find an elevated risk for other indicators of SES such as unemployment or low maternal education levels.

In summary, SES is linked to externalising problem behaviours such as aggression and delinquency. However, the effects of SES on these behaviours tend to be relatively small. Living below the poverty borderline seems to have the strongest link with delinquency compared to other indicators of SES.

Conclusions

Prevalence rates of externalising problem behaviours in Dutch children vary widely. The most recent prevalence figures range from 4–6% (parent reports) to 11–28% (reports by youth mental health employees) (Zeijl et al., 2005). Symptoms such as arguing too much, bragging or boasting, and demanding a lot of attention are relatively common; over half of the children sometimes or often show this behaviour. In contrast, skipping school, using alcohol or drugs, and vandalism are very rare. About 18% of the children show deviant externalising problem behaviours. Scholars have estimated that about 5% of Dutch children have serious problems and are in need of professional care and treatment (Sytema et al., 2006; Van der Ploeg, 2000; Zeijl et al., 2005).

Compared to other countries, Dutch children generally have average scores on externalising and internalising problem behaviours (Crijnen, Achenbach & Verhulst, 1997; Crijnen et al., 1999). Dutch children, in particular girls, were found to have fewer problems than American children (Zeijl et al., 2005). Offord, Lipman and Duku (2001) found higher prevalence rates of aggression and delinquency symptoms in Canadian children than were found in the general Dutch sample. For example, stealing at home was about five times higher in Canada. More Canadian compared to Dutch children engaged in many fights. Only cruelty or meanness to others was slightly higher in Dutch children.[9]

Given that children who have more than one syndrome are at increased risk of later delinquency and disruptive behaviours, assessment and prevention efforts should focus on children with multiple problems. Furthermore, some symptoms are of considerable concern. In particular, children who have overt aggression problems are at increased risk of showing these problems later in life.

Since marked differences were found across reports of different informants, relying on multiple informants tends to improve identification of children at risk (for example, Offord et al., 2001). Furthermore, Hoffenaar (2004) suggests that the context of the child's problem behaviours, such as home or school, should be taken into account when disagreement between informants is observed. Multiple informants represent several settings/situations and such situational information is relevant to the assessment of the severity of children's externalising problem behaviours. For example, children with a cross-situational pattern of oppositional problems (for example, home-schooling) had the highest conduct problem ratings,

---

9 These comparisons concern parent reports of 8–11-year-olds. Stealing at home 5.7% (US) vs. 1.7% (Netherlands) for boys, and 5.1% (US) vs. 0.7% (Netherlands) for girls; Getting into many fights: 35.8% (US) vs. 17.8% (Netherlands) for boys, and 29.1% (US) vs. 6.0% (Netherlands) for girls; Cruelty or meanness to others: 12.4% (US) vs.13.4% (Netherlands) for boys; and 7.1% (US) vs. 9.3% (Netherlands) for girls.

followed by children with deviant school problems only. Children with deviant scores on oppositionality at home had the lowest rates of conduct problems (Hoffenaar, 2004). Further, the reliability of the informant and their personal characteristics are important (ibid.).

The occurrence and course of psychosocial problems in girls differs from those of boys. Behavioural problems were more prevalent in boys, while girls had more internalising problem behaviours such as anxiety and mood disorders (for example, Bastiaansen et al., 2004). However, similar prevalence figures of internalising psychiatric disorders were found for boys and girls during childhood (Zwirs et al., 2007).

Interestingly, with regard to *deviant* levels of externalising and attention problems, prevalence rates in girls were in general higher than those in boys. This is in accordance with previous studies from abroad that found some evidence for the 'gender-paradox' (Hipwell & Loeber, 2006; Loeber & Keenan, 1994). This pattern suggests that although boys show higher rates of externalising problem behaviours, clinically referred girls show more severe problems than boys. Comparing the prevalence rates of boys and girls in our high-risk samples (day-care and outpatient samples), we found some evidence to suggest that the 'gender-paradox' pattern also exists in the Netherlands. Clinically referred girls showed relatively more frequent severe externalising problem behaviours than boys, suggesting that girls with less severe externalising problem behaviours do not get professional care and treatment, while boys do. Moreover, among the clinically referred children, relatively more girls than boys had deviant scores on two or three behaviour syndromes (that is, delinquency, aggression and attention problems). The underlying reasons for this gender paradox and its accompanying multi-problem nature of some girls are not well understood (Hipwell & Loeber, 2006). Further study is warranted to examine to what degree this pattern occurs in the Netherlands and to investigate potential explanations.

Some Dutch research has focused on ethnic differences in child problem behaviours. Turkish children seem to have more problems than other ethnic groups. Prevalence rates of Moroccan children are inconsistent. While Moroccan parents report similar levels of problems compared to Dutch parents, teachers tend to identify more problems in Moroccan than in Dutch children. Furthermore, according to their parents, externalising problem behaviours are more prevalent in Antillean, Arabian and Cape Verdean girls. Differences in the prevalence of problem behaviours could point to the need for different prevention strategies for different ethnic groups.

Deviant children are at increased risk of deviant behaviours later in their lives. For example, 44% of the children who showed deviant externalising problem behaviours in childhood also showed these behaviours fourteen years later in young adulthood (Hofstra et al., 2000). About 70% of deviant children were identified later among the 50% of the young adults with the highest scores (Hofstra et al., 2000). Moreover, children who had several behaviour problems were at higher risk of later disruptive behaviours than children who had deviant scores on only one syndrome (Verhulst & Van der Ende, 1993). These findings show the importance of early interventions in young children with multiple serious problem behaviours.

In summary, we found that prevalence rates of externalising problem behaviours vary widely across studies. About 5–7% of Dutch children show serious externalising problem behaviours and are in need of professional help. Prevalence rates of externalising problem behaviours vary by kinds of symptoms. Authority problems, such as being disobedient at home or school and being stubborn, are relatively common. Covert behaviours including fire-setting, stealing and vandalism are rare in children. Overt behaviours differ in prevalence: while arguing a lot is very common, physically attacking people is uncommon.

Children from the general population sample had the least externalising and attention problems, followed by children with an intellectual disability and clinically referred children (outpatient sample). Children who were referred for after-school guidance and treatment (day-care sample) generally had the most symptoms; the most frequent symptoms were prevalent in over 90% of these children.

We found that parents generally reported somewhat more externalising and attention problems than teachers. In particular, parents reported more often that their child had temper tantrums, demanded a lot of attention, destroyed their own things and was stubborn. In contrast, teachers reported more often that the child was confused and that boys hung around with children who got in trouble.

Boys had more problems – particularly externalising problem behaviours – than girls. While internalising problem behaviours are more prevalent in adolescent girls, during childhood these problems are relatively similar for boys and girls. However, clinically referred girls (day-care and outpatient) had relatively more severe externalising and attention problems than boys. Externalising problem behaviours tend to decrease when children grow older. However, while aggression continues to decrease during adolescence, levels of delinquency and violence increase after childhood.

Child problem behaviours tended to be stable over time. However, some symptoms were more stable than others; in particular children showing overt aggression have an elevated risk of later problems. Moreover, stability is not complete, and many children with externalising problem behaviours tend to outgrow such problems. At this stage, we cannot predict which children will outgrow externalising problem behaviour and which children will not.

Chapter 4

Victimisation of Children

Francien Lamers-Winkelman

Research on children and delinquency points to a 'cycle of violence', where children who witness verbal – and especially physical – aggression between their parents, and children who are abused by their parents, are in danger of developing aggressive behaviours towards other children and becoming violent offenders themselves (Widom, 1992). In addition, research indicates that a minority of sexually abused children will become sexual offenders themselves, starting their criminal careers in early adolescence. According to Loeber and Farrington (2001), repeated victimisation, such as child (sexual) abuse and witnessing interparental violence, can be found in the history of an unknown proportion of cases of child delinquents. Many victims of child abuse develop serious problems which, if not treated in childhood, will extend into adulthood.

This chapter deals with victimisation of young children (12 years of age and younger) with emphasis on physical abuse and neglect, sexual abuse, emotional abuse and neglect, psychological abuse, and witnessing interparental violence (IPV). In a longitudinal study comparing individuals with substantiated cases of child maltreatment against controls, Widom and Maxfield (2001) found that abuse and neglect increased the likelihood of arrest as a juvenile by 59%, of adult criminal behaviours by 28%, and of violent crime by 30%.

Since 2004, interparental violence has been included in the categories of child maltreatment used by the Advice and Reporting Centres on Child Abuse and Neglect in the Netherlands (*AMKs* in Dutch). Research shows that 60–80% of children living with 'parents who fight' are victims of physical abuse (Appel & Holden, 1998; Holden et al., 1998; Lamers-Winkelman, 2004; O'Keefe, 1995), or are ridiculed, belittled, or humiliated (psychological abuse). Men who batter their wives, tend to be rigid, authoritarian and often are under-involved and neglectful parents (Bancroft & Silverman, 2002). A father who batters his wife undermines her authority and conveys to a child the message that physical violence is acceptable. Dutton (1992) found that many teenage and preteen children of battered women, especially boys, assault their mothers physically (also see Holden & Ritchie, 1991). Interparental violence is associated with poor parenting skills and a higher risk of intergenerational transmission of violence and abuse, problematic parent-child relationships, and substance abuse (Center for Substance Abuse Treatment, 1997; Kaufman & Zigler, 1987).

This chapter starts with an overview of the recent literature concerning the relationship between victimisation of children by a parent or other adults and disruptive child behaviours (victimisation by peers, such as bullying, will be discussed in Chapter 8). Next, we will present preliminary results of an ongoing study on sexual abuse victims and children who witness interparental violence.

Correlates of Victimisation

Child maltreatment constitutes a major societal problem all over the world, and the Netherlands is not an exception. However, child maltreatment represents an understudied area in the Netherlands. Some children suffer only one type of child abuse, but many children experience several forms of child maltreatment (Trickett, 1998; Lamers-Winkelman, Slot, Bijl & Vijlbrief, 2007). Of the substantiated cases of child maltreatment reported in 1999 in the US, 35.9% were reported for more than one form of abuse (US Department of Health and Human Services, 2001). Children who experienced multiple types of maltreatment show significantly higher levels of trauma symptomatology and self-depreciation in adulthood than child victims of single-type maltreatment (Higgins & McCabe, 2000). Maltreatment can have devastating effects on the development of children, although children differ in the ways that they are affected. Maltreated children can exhibit a large variety of internalising and externalising problem behaviours. In victims of all ages, nightmares, depression, neurotic disorders, post-traumatic stress disorder (PTSD), and aggressive and regressive behaviours are reported. Depression is the most common and long-lasting syndrome and is not limited to a specific age group (Kendall-Tackett, Williams & Finkelhor, 1993).

Mood and anxiety disorders are fairly common in maltreated children (Heim & Nemeroff, 2001). Merry, Franzcp and Andrews (1994) assessed 63.5% of ninety-five sexually-abused children (aged 4–16 years, boys and girls), referred by several agencies for axis I psychiatric diagnosis on DSM-III. They found particularly high rates of Oppositional Defiant Disorder (19.6%), PTSD (18.2%), Anxiety Disorder (30.3%), and Depressive Disorder (12.1%), with 36.4% warranting two diagnoses or more. They also found an unexpectedly high rate of Attention-Deficit/Hyperactivity Disorder (13.6%), which was twice as high as in the community sample. In a study by Deblinger, Lippmann and Steer (1996), 71% of the sexually abused children (boys and girls, age 7–13) were diagnosed with PTSD (DSM-III-R). Using an abbreviated KIDDIE-SADS-P (modified for DSM-III-R; Chambers et al., 1985), Kolko (1996) found that 61% of the physically abused children (aged 6–13 years, boys and girls) in a referred sample had an axis I psychiatric diagnosis, although only 4% met the criteria for a full diagnosis of PTSD. Further, Ackerman et al. (1998) diagnosed sexually, physically, and both sexually and physically abused girls and boys (aged 7–13) with the Diagnostic Interview for Children and Adolescents (DICA; Reich & Welner, 1988), and found that 20–58% of the children qualified for a diagnosis of PTSD. As expected, the highest percentage for PTSD diagnosis was found in children who had been both sexually and physically abused (58% for boys and 53% for girls). In the case of sexual abuse, this was 20% for boys and 35% for girls, and in the case of physical abuse, 8% for boys and 50% for girls. Researchers have found a high co-morbidity of PTSD with other psychiatric problems (De Bellis, 1997; McFarlane & Van der Kolk, 1996). Collin-Vézina and Hébert (2005) compared sixty-seven sexually-abused school-aged girls with sixty-seven non-abused girls. Thirty per cent of the abused girls were diagnosed with pathological dissociation compared to 5% of the non-abused girls, and 46% of the sexually abused girls qualified for a diagnosis of PTSD (based on the DSM-IV criteria) compared to 18% of the non-abused girls. Based on a review of published data, De Bellis (2001) concluded that the psychobiological consequences of child maltreatment can be regarded as an environmentally induced complex developmental disorder.

The manifestation of problems associated with maltreatment is partly related to the developmental stage of the child. Abused preschool children tend to exhibit fear and nightmares, post-traumatic stress symptoms, and internalising and externalising problem behaviours. Eighty per cent of the infants and young children who were abused displayed disorganised and disoriented attachment patterns. They show unpredictable alterations of approach and avoidance toward their mothers as well as other conflict behaviours such as prolonged freezing, stilling, or slowed 'underwater' movements (Lyons-Ruth, 1991). This can affect their capacity to regulate future emotional arousal. In abused children, this lack – or loss – of development of self-regulatory processes, can result in problems with self-definition. According to Van der Kolk (1996), this may lead to: 1) disturbances of the sense of self, such as sense of separateness, loss of autobiographical memories, and disturbances of body image; 2) poorly modulated affect and impulse control, including aggression against self and others, and 3) insecurity in relationships, such as distrust, suspicion, lack of intimacy, and isolation. Functioning in social settings is difficult for abused children since they tend to display angry, threatening, fearless, acting-out behaviour or meek, submissive, fearful, or incompetent behaviour (ibid.).

Delays in speech and language, especially in the area of object-relations, have been noted in maltreated children. Chronic child maltreatment is associated with a lower IQ (De Bellis et al., 1999; Trickett, McBride-Chang & Putnam, 1994), delays in language development (Carrey et al., 1995), and reading and learning delays (Kolko, 1992). Eigsti and Cicchetti (2004) compared nineteen maltreated preschool children (chronic maltreatment, onset prior to age 2) with fourteen non-maltreated children from similar socioeconomic backgrounds. They found that at age 5 maltreated children exhibited syntactic delays, produced less complex language, and had a less advanced knowledge of vocabulary than non-maltreated children. Maltreating mothers were less talkative with their children, directed fewer utterances to the children, and their utterances correlated less with child language abilities compared to the non-maltreating mothers. Eigsti and Cicchetti (2004) emphasised that these language delays can lead to emotional, social, or cognitive delays, or exacerbate existing problems. Prasad, Kramer and Ewing-Cobbs (2005) compared nineteen hospitalised, physically abused children (aged 14–77 months) with nineteen hospitalised but not physically abused children matched for age and socioeconomic status. Physically abused children scored significantly lower on measures of cognitive functioning, motor skills and language skills (also see Eckenrode, Laird & Doris, 1993). Finally, maltreatment during the toddler period, or onset of maltreatment during the toddler years, and physical abuse were associated with delay in the development of theory of mind (Cicchetti et al., 2003). In summary, child maltreatment disrupts the normal development of most children and can result in developmental delays, behavioural and emotional problems, PTSD, aggression, and delinquency at a young age. Psychiatric symptoms are fairly common in maltreated children, and a high co-morbidity of PTSD with other psychiatric problems has been found in maltreated children.

Relationships Between Victimisation and Disruptive Behaviour

Low verbal IQ, delayed language development, and problems at school have been linked to juvenile delinquency (Moffitt, 1993; Moffitt, Lynam & Silva, 1994; Seguin et al., 1995; Herrenkohl et al., 2001). Delays in language development may weaken the foundation of learning and contribute to later disruptive behaviours and child delinquency (Keenan, 2001).

In a prospective longitudinal study of 574 children (from age 5–21), Lansford and colleagues (2007) found that physical abuse in the first five years of life increased the risk for arrest in adolescence for violent, nonviolent and status offences. However, Ireland, Smith and Thornberry (2002), using data from the Rochester Youth Development Study (RYDS), found that childhood-only maltreatment did not significantly increase the risk of delinquency during adolescence. Thornberry, Ireland and Smith (2001), also using the RYDS data, found that childhood-only maltreatment was unrelated to several negative behavioural 'adaptations' in late adolescence (a finding that awaits replication). They suggest that these outcomes can be due to the fact that in the US, interventions for maltreated school-age children are available on a fairly large scale and that these interventions are often successful. However, a retrospective study, funded by the National Institute of Justice showed quite different results: 68% of adult male felons in New York state prisons had suffered physical abuse, sexual abuse, or neglect before age 12 (Weeks & Widom, 1998). Other researchers also found child maltreatment before age 12 related to delinquency in later life. Over half (59%) of male inmates (convicted for a variety of crimes) in Harris County Jail in Houston, Texas reported some form of sexual abuse before or at the age of 13 (Johnson et al., 2006). In another study, childhood maltreatment has been found in the history of sexually abusive adolescents. Although half of them lived in intact (two-parent) families (Bruinsma, 1996; Hendriks & Bijleveld, 1999), 40% were emotionally neglected, 15% physically abused, and 14% sexually abused. Van Wijk and colleagues (2001) reported that most sexually abusive adolescents grew up in 'abusive families'. The authors stressed that children growing up in abusive families are at risk of developing an attachment disorder. Because of a lack of positive attention, these children often develop other ways to satisfy their primary need for attention, such as aggressive behaviour, violence and manipulation. Van Wijk and colleagues emphasise that these children often develop a delinquent lifestyle because of their lack of social skills, low self-image and inability to conduct romantic relationships successfully.

In summary, although the above studies show very high percentages of child maltreatment in the early lives of incarcerated men and sexually abusive adolescents, it should be kept in mind that these studies are based on retrospective reports. In retrospective research, data are collected after the period of the actual abuse.

Intervening experiences and events, such as arrest and incarceration, can interfere with the accuracy of the memory of abuse. Many studies show inaccurate memory in child sexual abuse victims (Warren & McGough, 1996). Source confusion, suggestibility, the role and the bias of the interviewer, recent events that cloud childhood experiences, can all contribute to recall bias.

Snyder and colleagues (2003) reported that in the US, children younger than 13 are involved in 10% of all juvenile arrests. Nearly one-fifth of these arrests are related to sex offences and vandalism. Loeber and Farrington (2001) concluded that delinquent children between ages of 7 and 12 have a two to three times higher risk of becoming serious, violent and chronic offenders compared to adolescents who become involved in delinquency in their teens. The type of maltreatment experienced by children was found to be a relevant predictor of their subsequent offending (Stewart, Dennison & Hurren, 2005). Emotional and sexual abuse did not predict juvenile offending. In contrast, neglected and physically abused children were more likely to offend than children who had not suffered these forms of abuse.

In summary, childhood maltreatment is fairly common in the history of many adolescents and adults arrested or incarcerated for delinquent acts. It is suggested that childhood-only maltreatment is not related to several forms of negative behavioural adjustment in late adolescence. However, it is also suggested that this can be due to interventions for school-age children that are available on a fairly large scale in the US. Whether childhood-only maltreatment is also not related to negative behavioural adjustment later on in countries that do not have these interventions is not yet known.

Identification of Child Maltreatment

The identification of child maltreatment is not an easy task. Although many maltreated children develop internalising and externalising problem behaviours, these problems also can be seen in non-maltreated children from problematic but not maltreating families. A 'child maltreatment recognition profile' does not exist. While a proportion of maltreated children do not show signs of maltreatment at the time of the maltreatment, there may be long-term effects even though short-term effects are not apparent (Beitchman et al., 1991).

Physical abuse can be detected more easily than other forms of maltreatment because of unexplained bruises or bone fractures, bite marks, burn damage and other physical manifestations. A proportion of sexually abused children show inappropriate sexual behaviour toward other children and/or adults, but sexual abuse rarely leaves physical evidence. Identification of sexual abuse in children greatly depends on the willingness of the child to disclose.

Emotional neglect is the most prevalent form of child maltreatment (Office of Human Development Services, 1981, 1988; Sedlak & Broadhurst, 1996; Wolzak, 2005; Lamers-Winkelman et al., 2007). Identifiers of emotional neglect include developmental delays, lack of parental supervision, alcohol and/or drug abuse by parents, and inadequate or dirty clothing. In addition, violence between parents can be a marker for possible child abuse.

Referral Patterns of Victimised Children

It remains unclear whether children who are referred for treatment because of sexual abuse or warning signals of interparental violence are representative of children suffering similar abuse but not being referred. Are children being referred on the basis of problematic behaviours or are other factors involved? For example, referral may depend on the proximity to a treatment facility, but treatment possibilities for these children in the Netherlands are scare. If a treatment organisation is willing to intervene in the child's family, most often services will be provided to the abusers and to the families in an effort to reunite the family, but few services are provided directly to the child (Fossen, 1998; Melief, Verkuyl & Flikweert, 2000).

Nevertheless, there are exceptions and in some parts of the Netherlands child victims of sexual abuse and child witnesses of interparental violence are treated by specialised professionals. In contrast, physically-abused or emotionally-neglected children are seldom referred to a treatment facility. And if a referral is made, the treatment usually focuses on the family as a whole, without recognition that the abused and neglected child needs individual treatment as well.

A Recent Dutch Study on Victimised Children

Lamers-Winkelman (in preparation) recently collected data on sexually abused children (CSA) and children who witnessed interparental violence (IPV). The study involves several institutes in the Netherlands (*Vrouwenopvang Overijssel/Riagg Zwolle*; *Jeugdzorg Zeeland*; *Jeugdzorg Groningen*; *Kinder en Jeugdtraumacentrum Haarlem*; *Riagg Leiden*; *Jeugdzorg Twente*; *Vrouwenopvang Eindhoven*; *Riagg Zeeland*; *Riagg Deventer*; *Riagg Rotterdam*). All the children in the study had been referred to treatment because of sexual abuse and/or as witnesses of interparental violence. Data were collected at the start of a treatment programme (T 1), directly after the programme (T 2), and for some children from six to twelve months after they finished the treatment programme (T 3). The treatment programmes had an 'abuse-focused', directive approach within a cognitive-behavioural framework, and involved the non-abusing parent. For the purpose of this chapter, we will only give a broad overview, derived from the preliminary data collected at the start of the treatment. Demographic information and information on stressful and traumatic events during the lifetime of the child (Table 4.1) was collected with a questionnaire developed by Bill Friedrich at the Mayo Clinic in Cleveland, Ohio (1997).

Nearly all the arrested parents in the study were fathers but only a small portion of the arrested fathers of the sexually abused children had been arrested for sexual abuse. Most of their arrests were for drug or alcohol abuse, or other non-sexual crimes. IPV fathers were mostly arrested for violence in public (bars, street) or other (lesser) crimes, but hardly ever for violence in their homes. Slightly less than half of the sexually abused children had been abused by someone within their family. Only in a minority of the cases was the perpetrator a father or stepfather. Most perpetrators within the family were (step)brothers, uncles, grandfathers, or a 'lover' (not living in) of the mother. Parental psychiatric diagnoses (DSM-IV) mostly concerned

Table 4.1 Demographics of sexually abused children and children who witnessed or were victims of interparental violence (IPV)

	Sexually abused children N=179	Children who witnessed or were victims of IPV N=146
Mean age	8.07 (2.45)	8.53 (1.86)
Males ~ females	45% ~ 55%	54% ~ 46%
Ethnicity		
Dutch mother	91%	82%
Dutch father[a]	91%	68%
No. of traumatic life events[b]	4.9 (2.73)	7.5 (3.02)
Education above Lower vocational training (LBO)		
Mother	73%	64%
Father	55%	56%
Parent arrested[c]	24%	41%
Psychiatric diagnosis in (one of) the parents[d]	29%	53%

Note: Standard deviations shown in parentheses. a) $F(1, 279)=19.744$, $p<.001$; b) $F(1, 239)=49.758$, $p<.001$; c) $F(1,265)$, $p=.002$; d); $F(1, 182)=9.078$, $p=.003$.

depression and borderline personality for mothers, and schizophrenia, depression, borderline and antisocial personality disorder for fathers. Results from the data at Time 1 give the following picture of the children. According to their parents (CBCL-PRF), the majority of the sexually abused children who witnessed IPV showed a lot of internalising and externalising problem behaviours: 47% of the children who witnessed interparental violence scored in the clinical range of externalising problem behaviours (and 13% in the borderline range); 71% in the clinical range of internalising problem behaviours (and 10% in the borderline range), and 64% in the clinical range of Total Problems (and 12% in the borderline range). Of the sexually abused children, 63% scored in the clinical range of externalising problem behaviours (borderline range 12%); 66% in the clinical range of internalising problem behaviours (borderline range 9%), and 75% in the clinical range of Total Problems (borderline range 7%).

Contrary to our expectation, sexually abused children (SA) exhibited significantly more externalising problem behaviours than children who witnessed and/or were victims of IPV (mean score of externalising problem behaviours respectively 66.8 and 61.92; $p<.001$). Sexually abused children, compared to IPV children, also had significantly higher scores on the CBCL scales Social Problems, Thought Problems, Attention Problems, Delinquent Behaviour and Aggressive Behaviour (Table 4.2). While many parents did not want the teacher to report on the child, those teachers who completed the CBCL-TRF confirmed this pattern (56% for sexually abused children, and 58% for IPV children). Teachers reported that sexually abused children were significantly more problematic on externalising problem behaviours ($p=.03$), Total Problems ($p=.02$), and Aggressive Behaviour ($p=.03$).

Table 4.2 Mean scores on the CBCL-PRF scales for sexually abused children and children who witnessed or were victims of interparental violence (IPV)

	Sexually abused children		Child witnesses/victims of IPV	
	Girls (N=99)	Boys (N=80)	Girls (N=67)	Boys (N=79)
Anxious/depressed	66.34 (10.77)	67.22 (11.55)	70.30 (12.88)	66.09 (10.49)
Withdrawn	65.79 (10.18)	65.97 (10.53)	67.84 (9.02)	65.31 (8.87)
Somatic complaints	62.09 (11.17)	61.11 (9.59)	61.70 (9.87)	60.06 (8.86)
Social problems	64.50 (10.35)	65.06 (10.27)	63.27 (10.96)	60.00 (9.43)
Thought problems	64.24 (11.07)	67.35 (12.53)	62.42 (12.09)	61.86 (10.23)
Attention problems	64.72 (11.64)	67.70 (11.58)	64.75 (10.36)	62.21 (9.72)
Delinquent behaviour	64.09 (9.33)	65.72 (10.58)	60.45 (8.98)	60.94 (8.51)
Aggressive behaviour	65.94 (10.41)	69.64 (12.39)	62.09 (10.24)	63.81 (10.47)
Total score internalising problem behaviour	66.00 (11.81)	66.65 (10.23)	68.84 (10.93)	65.87 (10.26)
Total score externalising problem behaviour	66.07 (10.93)	67.71 (11.92)	61.45 (11.71)	62.47 (10.56)
Total problem score	68.23 (10.72)	69.76 (10.49)	67.16 (10.99)	65.42 (9.64)

Note: Standard deviations shown in parentheses.

While many parents scored their child in the clinical range on psychopathology, it seems strange that when asked to fill in whether they found the behaviours of their child problematic ('Overall, how much of a problem has this child been in your life, lately?'), only 27% of the IPV mothers answered that the child had been a problem, contrary to 56% of the mothers of sexually abused children. IPV mothers often wrote a comment in the margin: 'My child does not show problem behaviours; it is my ex-husband who is the problematic one.' Lamers-Winkelman (in preparation) did not find significant gender differences on CBCL scores of traumatised girls and boys (summed up CSA and IPV). However, in the sexually-abused-only group, boys scored significantly higher than girls on aggressive behaviours (p=.03). In the IPV-only group, girls scored higher on anxiety/depression (p=03).

Sexually abused children exhibited a range of problematic sexual behaviours. Half of them (49%) scored in the clinical range (and 24% in the borderline range) on the Child Sexual Behaviour Inventory (CSBI; Friedrich, 1997). Of the IPV victims/witnesses, 21% scored in the clinical range of the CSBI, and 30% in the borderline range (significant difference between CSA and IPV: p<.001). In the IPV group, boys showed significantly higher sexually problematic behaviours than girls (p=.001), but no gender differences were found in the sexually abused group.

The study did not find gender differences in externalising and internalising problem behaviours. The exception, however, was that sexually abused boys exhibited more aggressive behaviours, as measured with the Child Behaviour Checklist (CBCL). In summary, these results underline the need for early intervention to reduce psychopathology in affected children.

Treatment Interventions

The scale at which children are being maltreated and the increased risk for these children to develop internalising and externalising problem behaviours disorders emphasise the need to provide evidence-based treatment to help children cope with these experiences and to prevent further maladaptive development. An estimate of the Ministry of Justice (2005) is that approximately a hundred thousand children witness interparental violence each year. In the Dutch national study on the incidence and prevalence of child maltreatment, 20% of the interviewed secondary-school students (aged 12–17) reported that they had been maltreated in the last year. Thirty-seven per cent reported maltreatment at some point or during some period in their life (Lamers-Winkelman et al., 2007).

There is a dire shortage of treatment possibilities for maltreated children in the Netherlands. The number of mental health institutes offering 'abuse-focused' (and evidence-based) therapy for sexually abused children is small. Programmes for maltreated children are scarce. Verhoeven (2002) found that nine out of ten physically abused children in the Netherlands do not receive any help.

Conclusions

Fairly high percentages of sexually abused children, maltreated children, and children who witnessed interparental violence scored in the clinical range on internalising and externalising problem behaviours, especially aggressive behaviours. The combination of externalising and internalising problem behaviours is a known, strong predictor for adult antisocial behaviour.

Early detection of child maltreatment (which includes being a witness of interparental violence) is of the highest priority. Family characteristics such as antisocial parents, substance-abusing parents, parental psychopathology, poor parenting practices, physical abuse and family violence also are predictors of early onset offending (Loeber, Farrington & Petechuk, 2003; Van Lieshout et al., 2001; Deković, Janssens & Van As, 2001). Many of these risk factors apply to sexually abused children and children exposed to interparental violence. Thus child maltreatment, including children's exposure to IPV, constitutes a risk factor for the development of disruptive behaviours and depression at a young age. Combined with the family characteristics of maltreating families, this can lead to the early onset of delinquency. Although not every maltreated child becomes a serious delinquent or a violent offender, it is of the utmost importance to intervene in maltreating families.

It is particularly necessary to make interventions available to child victims. Providing services to the families to stop the violence and abuse, as well as efforts to reunite the family, are just the beginning. The internalising and externalising problem behaviours of abused children do not 'fade away' when family problems decrease and familial relations improve. Maltreated children are traumatised children and therefore need individual treatment in order to overcome their traumatic experiences.

Even though the literature addressing the link between early child maltreatment (before age 12) and the development of early-onset delinquency is somewhat inconsistent, none the less, it is essential that mental health professionals (and politicians) keep in mind that many CSA and IPV victims already have developed disruptive behaviours. The principal aim of treatment programmes focused on these young children is to prevent them becoming delinquent.

Part III
Correlates and Causes

Chapter 5

Individual Factors

Hans M. Koot, Jaap Oosterlaan, Lucres M. Jansen, Anna Neumann, Marjolein Luman and Pol A.C. van Lier

Children's disruptive behaviours result from the synergy between individual (personal) and social (environmental) factors. In this chapter, we define individual factors that result from genetic, physiological, neurological and neuropsychological, and psychosocial factors (that influence differences among children in their development, including their development of disruptive behaviours). These emotional, cognitive, physical and social characteristic factors are frequently interrelated, yet the underlying mechanism of how this occurs is not fully understood.

This chapter summarises research findings on genetic and physiological characteristics, neurological and neuropsychological functioning, psychological development and person-environment interaction as correlates and causes of disruptive child behaviours. Genetic and physiological characteristics affecting the development of disruptive behaviours involve genetic influences, physical growth and hormones. Neurological and neuropsychological functioning concerns children's brain development, the role of neuromodulators of inhibition and aggression and executive functioning. IQ and language development are also part of this subject. Finally, aspects of psychological development that are of interest include social development and emotional development. Most notably, all of these individual factors do not develop in a vacuum, but function in direct interaction with the child's environment. Person-environment interaction focuses on interactional and transactional aspects of both personal characteristics and environmental – most notably social – sources of influence.

Genetic and Physiological Characteristics

Genetics

There is a consensus among research studies that disruptive behaviour is partly genetically determined (see review by Rhee & Waldman, 2002). To date, the specific genes that are involved in the genetic predisposition to disruptive behaviours are still unknown. There are indications that certain genes are responsible for serotonergic functioning, such as the gene encoding the neurotransmitter-metabolising enzyme monoamine oxidase A (MAOA) (Craig, 2005), as well as genes responsible for dopaminergic functioning, such as the dopamine transporter gene DAT1 (Young et al., 2002). As with most behavioural traits, there is probably not a single gene that determines the development of disruptive behaviours, and instead an accumulation of the influence and interaction between several genes takes place. There may also be large differences in heritability between various types of disruptive behaviours. Especially in those who show aggressive behaviours already in childhood, genetic influences are found to be much more important than in those who do not show aggressive behaviours until adolescence. Continuity in aggressive behaviours between childhood and adolescence has also been shown to be largely genetically determined (Eley, Lichtenstein & Moffitt, 2003).

Moreover, it should be noted that gene-environment interactions play an important role in the development of disruptive behaviours (Moffitt, 2005). For example, in adoption studies, an adverse adoptive home environment has been found to interact with antisocial personalities of the biological parents in predicting increased aggression in the offspring (Cadoret et al., 1995). The term 'interaction' means that not only do genetic susceptibility and adverse influences of environmental factors add up to an increased risk of developing disruptive behaviours, but the interaction between both results in a risk that is higher than the sum of both individual risk factors. The exact mechanisms behind the interplay between genes and environment are not yet well understood. Most likely, genes that regulate arousal and stress-processing mechanisms as well as brain development are involved (Popma & Raine, 2006).

Psychophysiology

The psychophysiological factor that is most studied in relation to disruptive behaviour is autonomic activity. According to low arousal theories, patterns of low arousal are related to disruptive behaviours. The *fearlessness theory* claims that low psychophysiological arousal levels are markers of low levels of fear (Raine, 1993). According to this theory, children with low arousal levels are more likely to engage in delinquent acts, physical fights and other forms of disruptive behaviour because they do not fear the negative consequences of their aggressive actions. A second interpretation is provided by the *stimulation seeking theory* (Zuckerman, 1979) which argues that low arousal levels represent an aversive physiological state. As such, individuals with low arousal levels are motivated to seek out stimulation in order to raise their arousal levels to an optimal or normal level. In this view, engaging in disruptive behaviours constitutes a way of stimulation seeking.

Low resting heart rate, as the main parameter of autonomic arousal, is the most consistently replicated biological correlate of disruptive behaviours in children and adolescents (Lorber, 2004; Ortiz & Raine, 2004). Low basal heart rate at a young age may even have predictive value for later disruptive behaviours. Raine et al. (1997) measured autonomic functioning (heart rate) children as young as age 3 and found a relationship with aggressive behaviours at 11 years (Raine, Venables, & Mednick, 1997). This early predictive value of basal heart rate, in relation to the finding that basal heart rate is highly heritable (Boomsma & Plomin, 1986), suggests that low heart rate may be a genetically determined marker for later disruptive behaviours. However, this has never been proven by means of prospective studies including repeated measurements of heart rate.

Research findings on autonomic activity in response to a stressor appear to be somewhat less consistent. In a meta-analysis of the relationship between heart rate level and disruptive behaviours by Ortiz and Raine (2004), the effect size was almost doubled in studies assessing heart rate during a stressor, while in a meta-analysis of Lorber (2004), findings concerning heart rate reactivity in relation to aggression, psychopathy, and conduct problems were less consistent than for resting heart rate. This may partly be due to the low number of studies, as well as due to the heterogeneity of stimuli that were used. Still, from both meta-analyses (Lorber, 2004; Ortiz & Raine, 2004), a general picture emerges of decreased heart rate responsivity in children with disruptive behaviours.

In line with studies on heart rate, similar findings of a decreased level of skin conductance, another measure of autonomic activity, have been documented (Lorber, 2004). Moreover, a lower basal skin conductance level at age 10 was found to predict poor adolescent outcome at age 17 (Van Bokhoven et al., 2005).

Thus, findings show a rather consistent picture of decreased autonomic arousal in children showing disruptive behaviours, which may be a stable, or even genetically determined, marker for persistent disruptive behaviours later on in life.

Neuroendocrinology

Studies on neuroendocrine functioning in disruptive individuals have mainly focused on the Hypothalamic-Pituitary-Adrenal (HPA) axis. The HPA axis regulates the secretion of cortisol, the main stress hormone. As such, the HPA axis is of major importance for the individual's reaction and adaptation to the (social) environment and is, together with the autonomic nervous system, part of the arousal system. Therefore, research on the HPA axis also fits with the low arousal theory of disruptive behaviours.

The HPA axis has a circadian rhythm: cortisol is released in a pulsative fashion during the day, with the highest frequency in the first hour after awakening and a gradual decrease in cortisol levels during the day. As a result, measurement of basal cortisol levels is more complex than the measurement of autonomic activity. Most inconsistent results regarding basal HPA activity are due to sampling methods neglecting the circadian rhythm. The main two reliable methods that take into account the circadian rhythm of the HPA axis are the cortisol day profile (measurement of cortisol at regular intervals during a whole day) and the cortisol awakening response (CAR, measurement of cortisol directly after awakening, and thirty and sixty minutes later). Studies using these methods have shown that basal HPA activity is decreased in children showing disruptive behaviour and that the decreased activity is seen only in the early morning hours (Popma et al., 2007a; McBurnett et al., 2000; Van Goozen, Matthys, Cohen-Kettenis, Buitelaar, & Van Engeland, 2000; Gispen-de Wied et al., 1998).

Aside from persistently decreased basal cortisol levels, a decreased cortisol response to psychosocial stress has also been found in several studies (McBurnett et al., 2000). Decreased basal cortisol levels may be a trait phenomenon, since higher levels of externalising problem behaviours have been found to be consistently associated with lower cortisol attributable to trait-like sources across three years of behavioural assessment (Shirtcliff et al., 2005). Moreover, genetic influences may play a role. For example, low cortisol levels in children were related to the presence of aggressive behaviours in their fathers (Vanyukov et al., 1993). Thus decreased basal HPA activity, like decreased autonomic activity, may be a stable, or even genetically determined, marker for persistent disruptive behaviours. However, current insights suggest that basal HPA activity can also change over time as a result of environmental influences. For example, chronic stress may alter the 'set point' of HPA functioning, resulting in chronically altered basal cortisol levels or hypo-reactivity of the stress system. This idea of changing levels of homeostasis is called 'allostasis' (McEwen & Lasley, 2003). The mechanism of allostasis may also play a role in the interaction between neurobiology and environment that is thought to determine the development of disruptive behaviours.

Apart from persistently decreased cortisol levels, a decreased cortisol response to psychosocial stress has also been found in several studies (Popma et al., 2006; Van Goozen et al., 1998), while others have not found such decreases (McBurnett et al., 2005). These findings are in accordance with the fearlessness theory of disruptive behaviour, since decreased responses were found only in response to psychosocial stress and not to physical stress (Jansen et al., 1999). There are indications that findings of decreased responsiveness to stress in disruptive children may be helpful in diagnosis and treatment decisions. A study by Popma et al. (2007b) on delinquent adolescent males in a diversion project, showed that boys with a diagnosis of Oppositional Defiant Disorder (ODD) or Conduct Disorder (CD) had decreased HPA and heart rate activity as compared to delinquent boys without a psychiatric diagnosis. As for the value of neurobiological markers in treatment decisions, disruptive children with decreased cortisol stress responsivity have been found to be less responsive to treatment (Van de Wiel et al., 2004).

Sex Hormones and the Development of Puberty

Studies have found a consistent relationship between testosterone levels and aggression in young adults (Book, Starzyk & Quinsey, 2001), but this is less consistent in prepubertal boys, possibly because the relationship between testosterone and aggression does not become apparent until the onset of adolescence, a time when hormonal changes, including changes in testosterone levels, take place. This may be illustrated by the fact that an increase in disruptive behaviours usually coincides with the onset of puberty. However, one study of prepubertal boys found a relationship between aggression and a precursor of testosterone (DHEAS) (Van Goozen et al., 2000). Another possible explanation for the inconsistent findings is that the relationship between testosterone and aggression may be influenced by other (neuro)endocrinological factors. For instance, a recent study on disruptive adolescent boys reported only a relationship between testosterone and aggression if cortisol levels were low (Popma et al., 2007b).

Children who reach puberty relatively early tend to have a higher chance of developing serious and persistent disruptive behaviours (see Chapter 1). Although these studies all suggest a relationship between hormonal changes and development of disruptive behaviours, the exact role of hormonal changes in the onset of disruptive behaviours remains unclear, mainly because the role of hormonal *changes* have never been investigated in longitudinal studies (Rowe et al., 2004).

Neurocognitive Deficits

A substantial literature links neurocognitive deficits to disruptive behaviours in children and older age groups (for a review, see Blair, 2001; Moffitt, 1993). Neurocognitive impairments may be a key route through which genetic, perinatal and psychosocial influences on disruptive behaviours find expression. Studies have used both clinical and community-based samples, a great variety of neurocognitive measures, and diverse selection criteria to define groups of disruptive children. Studies have included youth diagnosed with ODD or CD; categorised as aggressive, or delinquent; or identified as having a variety of externalising problem behaviours. In addition, few studies have employed stringent controls for co-morbid conditions (Sergeant, Geurts & Oosterlaan, 2002).

There are multiple pathways to disruptive behaviours and neurocognitive deficits seem most germane for early-onset, persistent disruptive behaviours (Moffitt, 1993; Moffitt, Lynam & Silva, 1994; White et al., 1994). Neurocognitive deficiencies seem to figure most notably in children with prominent ADHD symptoms early in development (Hinshaw, Lahey & Hart, 1993; Moffitt, 1993).

We will review impairments in three domains associated with neurocognitive functioning. The three most well-established domains of neurocognitive abnormalities are (1) deficits in IQ and verbal abilities; (2) deficits in executive function, and (3) abnormal processing of reward and punishment.

IQ and Verbal Abilities

The association between low IQ and disruptive behaviours has been supported by many studies (Elmund et al., 2004; Giancola & Mezzich, 2000; see for review Hogan, 1999; Nigg & Huang-Pollock, 2002). Of the twenty-seven studies reviewed by Hogan (1999), seventeen supported a negative association between IQ and disruptive behaviours. Disruptive children on average score eight IQ points *lower* than their normal peers (Teichner & Golden, 2000; Moffitt, 1993), which constitutes a large effect. It is unclear whether low IQ is causally related to the onset of disruptive behaviours, although there are a number of studies suggesting such a causal relationship (Moffitt & Caspi, 2001; Moffitt et al., 1994; see for review Moffitt, 1993; but see Aguilaret al., 2000).

Some researchers have suggested that low verbal IQ and poor verbal intelligence rather than a global intellectual deficit, are associated with disruptive behaviours (Giancola & Mezzich, 2000; Moffitt et al., 1994; Giancola see for review, Lynam & Henry, 2001; Moffitt, 1993). Studies show that low verbal IQ or a large discrepancy between verbal and performance IQ in favour of the latter is characteristic of disruptive behaviours (see for review Hogan, 1999; Lynam & Henry, 2001; Nigg & Huang-Pollock, 2002). Low verbal IQ has been taken as evidence for a left hemispheric dysfunction. However, the understanding of the underlying mechanism linking verbal impairments to disruptive behaviours is limited (Hill, 2002). Lynam and Henry (2001) described several possible mechanisms, emphasising the role of language in prosocial processes such as delaying gratification, anticipating consequences, and linking belated, that is, non-immediate punishments with earlier transgressions. Moffitt (1993) suggested that deficits in verbal skills promote disruptive behaviours because the deficits lead to poor self-control, poor comprehension and poor communication skills evoking negative interactions.

The widespread finding of low IQ of disruptive children cannot be explained by several methodological factors, including the selection of less bright subjects, socioeconomic status, or test motivation (Lynam & Henry, 2001; Moffitt, 1993; Nigg & Huang-Pollock, 2002). Few studies, however, have examined the association between low IQ and disruptive behaviours in girls, and findings for this gender are somewhat mixed (Giancola & Mezzich, 2000; see for review Hogan, 1999). Furthermore, not all studies have found the association between IQ and disruptive behaviour to be present across different ethnic groups (Nigg & Huang-Pollock, 2002).

Researchers have reported that the IQ-disruptive behaviour link is strongest when co-morbid ADHD symptoms were not controlled (or measured), suggesting that the risk for low IQ is particularly strong for children with a combination of disruptive behaviours and ADHD symptoms (see Hogan, 1999). However, several studies show that the association between low IQ and disruptive behaviours remains when ADHD symptoms are controlled (see for review Hogan, 1999). In addition, there is evidence that the relationship between IQ and disruptive behaviours becomes stronger with increasing age (Aguilar et al., 2000; Hogan, 1999; Teichner & Golden, 2000). One possible explanation for this finding is that disruptive behaviours are associated with poor school adjustment and attendance, interfering with academic performance and thereby producing an increasing gap between disruptive youth and their normally developing peers (Hogan, 1999).

Executive Function Deficits

Executive functioning (EF) comprises a set of higher-order cognitive abilities that facilitate goal-directed behaviour and problem solving, and encompass diverse abilities including behaviour inhibition, working memory (the ability to actively combine information), planning, flexibility and the ability to creatively generate solutions for problems (Pennington & Ozonoff, 1996). Executive functioning reflects how individuals solve problems, rather than whether they have acquired knowledge of problem solving. The prefrontal cortex and its subcortical connections are the primary sites in the brain that subserve executive functioning (Eslinger, 1996).

Scientists have proposed several models of how poor executive functioning relates to disruptive behaviours. Quay (1993) argued that the fundamental deficit in CD is an overactive Behavioural Activation System in conjunction with an underactive Behavioural Inhibition System (discussed in more detail below). This leads to reward-seeking behaviour and poorly developed inhibitory abilities. Inhibitory control is thought to be fundamental for the later emergence of other aspects of executive functioning (Barkley, 1997). Moffitt (1993) distinguished between adolescent-limited and life-course persistent antisocial behaviours. Adolescent-limited antisocial behaviour was hypothesised to arise in the peer social context. In contrast, Moffitt hypothesised that life-course persistent antisocial behaviour arises from neurocognitive deficits fostering a difficult and undercontrolled temperament, which interact in a cumulative fashion with well-known 'criminogenic' environmental factors during development.

The neurocognitive deficits are thought to originate from both inherited brain abnormalities as well as prenatal and postnatal brain damage. Blair (2001) distinguished between reactive aggression, elicited by frustration and threat, and goal-directed instrumental aggression. He noted that damage to the orbitofrontal cortex can lead to reactive aggression and impaired executive functioning. Executive functioning deficits may increase the likelihood of responding on the basis of the here and now.

There is a substantial literature linking executive functioning deficits to disruptive behaviours in children. Acquired lesions to the orbitofrontal cortex have long been recognised as a source of disruptive behaviours (Blair, 2001). Numerous studies have shown that children displaying disruptive behaviours are characterised by poorly developed executive functioning (see review by Lynam & Henry, 2001; Moffitt, 1993; Morgan & Lilienfeld, 2000; Nigg & Huang-Pollock, 2002). A meta-analysis of thirty-nine studies of executive functioning deficits in various antisocial populations reported a medium to large effect size of d=.62 (Morgan & Lilienfeld, 2000). This review also reported the effect size for CD which was d=.36. Other meta-analyses focusing exclusively on children have obtained effect sizes in the medium range (Oosterlaan, Logan & Sergeant, 1998; Van Mourik, Oosterlaan & Sergeant, 2005). Longitudinal data, derived from both high-risk and non-selective samples, show that executive functioning measured as early as during preschool years predicts the onset and persistence of disruptive behaviours during childhood, adolescence and adulthood (Piquero & White, 2003; White, Bates & Buyske, 2001).

It should be noted that, although there is overlap between IQ and executive functioning, the two concepts can be distinguished. Several studies reported that impaired executive functioning was independent of IQ (Nigg & Huang-Pollock, 2002; White et al., 1994). Impaired executive functioning is also independent of gender (Giancola & Mezzich, 2000; Moffitt, 1993), socioeconomic status (Giancola & Mezzich, 2000; White et al., 1994), and in diverse ethnic samples (Piquero & White, 2003). Thus, findings on the relationship between disruptive behaviours and IQ should not be generalised to executive functioning. A key issue is the impact of co-morbid ADHD symptoms on the development of disruptive behaviours. Executive functioning impairments have been most reliably demonstrated in disruptive children who showed co-morbid ADHD symptoms (Moffitt, 1993; Pennington & Ozonoff, 1996; Toupin et al., 2000). Studies investigating the joined and separate effects of CD and ADHD have obtained mixed results (see review by Banaschewski et al., 2005), with some studies showing unique effects of ADHD, unique effects of CD, independent effects of both disorders, with some studies suggesting that the combination of both disorders carries the highest risk for executive functioning deficits (Clark, Prior & Kinsella, 2000; Oosterlaan, Scheres & Sergeant, 2005; Seguin et al., 2004; Toupin et al., 2000; see review by Banaschewski et al., 2005).

Sensitivity to Reward and Punishment

Disruptive behaviours have been related to poor self-regulation, specifically in the face of cues for reward and punishment (Quay, 1993; Newman & Wallace, 1993; Raine, 1993). When both cues are present, children with disruptive behaviours are hypothesised to focus on reward signals while ignoring signals for punishment (Newman & Wallace, 1993). This tendency has been explained in terms of an overactive Behavioural Activation System, which initiates behaviour in response to cues of reward, and an underactive Behavioural Inhibition System that produces anxiety and inhibits ongoing behaviour in the presence of non-reward or punishment (Gray, 1987).

There are several experimental studies showing that disruptive children and adolescents tend to search for reward, irrespective of changing contingency schedules and increasing punishment (Daugherty & Quay, 1991; Fonseca & Yule, 1995; Matthys et al., 1998; Shapiro et al., 1988). Task performance in disruptive groups usually was independent of impulsive behaviour (Daugherty & Quay, 1991; O'Brien & Frick, 1996; Van Bokhoven, Matthys, Van Goozen, & Van Engeland, 2005) and characterised by a rigid response style, that is inconsistent with the goal of the task. This possible 'myopia' for future consequences in disruptive children has also been demonstrated in studies that used delayed gratification (Campbell et al., 1994; Krueger, Caspi, Moffitt, White, & Stouthamer-Loeber, 1996) and decision-making paradigms (Blair, Colledge & Mitchell, 2001; Ernst et al., 2003). The decision-making studies showed that disruptive children and adolescents showed a maladaptive preference for large rewards and large losses over small rewards and small losses.

Aberrant reinforcement sensitivity in disruptive behaviours has also been related to impaired emotional reactivity (Newman & Wallace, 1993; Raine, 1993). Raine (1993) proposed that a lack of fear in children with disruptive behaviour decreases the attention to threat-related stimuli, such as punishment, and prevents passive avoidance learning. Indeed, co-morbid internalising problem behaviours (high fear levels) have been found to diminish impaired performance of disruptive children on reinforcement tasks (O'Brien & Frick, 1996).

Disruptive children's insensitivity to punishment is partly dependent on external influences such as social environment and parenting style (Dadds & Salmon, 2003). Yet, there are clear biological markers for aberrant reinforcement sensitivity. Disruptive children show impaired autonomic nervous system activity, such as reduced skin conductance responses (SCRs), and faster SCR habituation to aversive stimuli (Herpertz et al., 2003; 2001). In addition, studies show reduced SCRs and heart rate in response to rewards (Beauchaine et al., 2001; Crowell et al., 2006). Recent studies suggest that disruptive behaviours are related to structural and functional abnormalities in brain areas that are implicated in reward processing, such as the striatum and nucleus accumbens (NAcc) (Galvan et al., 2006; McAlonan et al., 2007).

In summary, children and adolescents showing disruptive behaviours differ in a number of neurocognitive respects from those who don not. These differences are in regard to deficits in IQ and verbal abilities and deficits in executive function. There is some emerging evidence for abnormal processing of reward and punishment in disruptive children. These deficits seem to be especially salient in those with early-onset and life-course persistent disruptive behaviours, and much less in those with adolescent-onset disruptive behaviours. However, in those affected, the effects of several of these deficits (low IQ, language deficits) seem to become stronger with age.

Social and Emotional Development

Social Development

Problems in social relationships, especially with parents and peers, are consistently found in studies of children with problem behaviours (also detailed in Chapters 6 and 7, this volume). Insufficient parental supervision is among the strongest predictors of delinquency (including violent offences) (e.g., Farrington, 2004; Wasserman & Seracini, 2001). Harsh or punitive parenting, physical punishment and authoritarian parenting styles have also been implicated in the development of disruptive behaviour (e.g., Farrington, 2004; Snyder et al., 2005), just as parent-child conflict, and a lack of positive parental involvement with the child predict conduct problems and delinquency (Wasserman & Seracini, 2001; Coie & Dodge, 1998).

Troublesome parent-child relationships often have their origin early in life. Although both parent and child contribute to the quality of their relationship, influences are strongest from parent to child (but see potential effects of difficult child temperament discussed below), and the earliest influences on deviant behaviours are manifested in the context of early child aggression. Several studies have shown that parental insensitivity (e.g., pointing out a child's mistakes while the child is trying to complete a puzzle) can be a precursor to child aggression (for example, NICHD, 2004b; Olson et al., 2000). For example, the NICHD study identified several aggression trajectories between ages 2 and 9. Mothers of children in the moderate- and high-aggression trajectories were less sensitive than mothers of children in the other groups. Furthermore, Olson et al. (2000) showed that positive affective mother-child exchanges were predictive of low rates of aggression in elementary school and adolescence. As toddlers, children at risk of later externalising problem behaviours were perceived as difficult and resistant to control, and relationships with their caregivers were relatively low in warmth and affective enjoyment. Further, the caregiver's perception of their toddler as emotionally unresponsive was a consistent predictor of later externalising problem behaviours, suggesting that negative maternal cognitions associated with child conduct problems may begin in toddlerhood. These predictive patterns were similar for boys and girls and, with minor exceptions, generalised across different sub-dimensions of externalising problem behaviours. In addition, several studies have shown that maternal insensitivity is related to the broader category of externalising problem behaviours (for example, Shaw, Bell & Gilliom, 2000). A second important parenting dimension is control. Several studies revealed that negative or harsh discipline (e.g., giving negative commands or spanking the child) is related to the development of aggressive behaviours and delinquency. The longitudinal effect of physical discipline on aggressive behaviours was demonstrated by Fine and colleagues (2004) in a sample of elementary school-aged children. They found a direct relationship between caregiver reports of physical discipline and later child aggression, indicating that children who received more physical discipline were more likely to show aggressive behaviours four years later. Similar results were obtained by Knutson and colleagues (2005), who found that when parents used more angry and punitive disciplinary responses, their children aged 4–8 were more likely to show high levels of aggression. More aspects of how parenting behaviours are related to child disruptive behaviours can be found in Chapter 6 of this volume.

Peer relations become increasingly important in the course of childhood and provide vital stimulation for socio-emotional development. Therefore, it is not surprising that peer problems are linked to subsequent mental health problems (Reis, Collins & Berscheid, 2000). The peer factors found to be most strongly related to aggression are peer rejection and associating with peers who are highly aggressive (for example, Vitaro & Brendgen, 2005; Van Lier et al., 2005). It is important to differentiate between proactive and reactive aggression, in that peer rejection has been linked to reactive aggression (Vitaro & Brendgen, 2005), whereas boys' friendships with aggressive peers have been linked to proactive aggression (Poulin & Boivin, 2000). Theoretically, the finding that friends are often similarly aggressive can be explained either by mutual selection processes or by processes of mutual influence (Poulin & Boivin, 2000). Poulin and Boivin (2000) found evidence for mutual selection: they reported that boys who became friends showed similar levels of proactive aggression prior to the beginning of the friendship, and that friends who were dissimilar in levels of proactive (but not reactive) aggression prior to the friendship often broke up the friendships. While no clear evidence of mutual influence was found in this study, the authors speculate that this might be due to the fact that similarity between friends was already high at the beginning of the study, and further that mutual reinforcement might have contributed to the stability of similarity in levels of proactive aggression. Studies investigating the broader concept of disruptive behaviours found clear support for mutual influence in the form of deviancy training. Patterson, Dishion and Yoerger (2000) demonstrated that their construct of deviancy training (defined as rate of reinforcement of deviancy by friends, association with deviant peers, disruptive behaviours of peers and amount of time spent with disruptive peers) mediated the link between early involvement with deviant peers and growth in new forms of disruptive behaviours and delinquency. Furthermore, Dishion (2000) showed that higher levels of deviancy training within friendships were linked to heightened levels of externalising and co-morbid externalising-internalising problem behaviours. Of course, peer relations can also have positive effects for the development of the individual. Non-deviant friends can protect against the influence of other markers of risk (Gatti & Tremblay, 2005). More details on the nature of peer processes can be found in Chapter 7 of this volume.

An important outcome of suboptimal social relationships in childhood is the ways that children think about social relations and the ways that they process social information (cf. Crick & Dodge, 1994). Multiple studies have shown that children who experience such relationships have low expectations of their relationships with significant others. In turn, those who are aggressive in the context of poor relationships have deviant attitudes concerning disruptive behaviours and often display positive expectations of disruptive behaviour. It may well be that these same cognitions carry forward into multiple antagonistic interactions and ultimately lead to a turning against the world that seems characteristic of disruptive children at prepubertal age.

Emotional Development

Many studies link children's difficult temperament to the development of disruptive behaviours (see Sanson, Hemphill & Smart, 2004). Key aspects of temperament that appear relevant in this respect are negative emotionality and low-effortful control. Temperament seems to have its greatest impact on disruptive development when other risk factors are also present, particularly poor parent-child relationship. Belsky (1997) suggested that while some children are genetically biased towards externalising problem behaviours, others may be genetically biased towards environmental reactivity, that is, they have an enhanced susceptibility to the influences of poor parental childrearing practices. Studies show that parenting characteristics such as unskilled maternal discipline (Stoolmiller, 2001), parental rejection (Lengua et al., 2000), maternal hostility (Morris et al., 2002) and punitive parenting (Paterson & Sanson, 1999) are more strongly related to externalising problem behaviours in children with a difficult temperament.

Recent research has focused on the role of emotional processes (such as anger regulation and emotional dysregulation) on normal and atypical development (Southam-Gerow & Kendall, 2001). Problems with children's emotional regulation are implicated in both internalising and externalising problem behaviours (for example, Gross, 1998), as well as in general adjustment problems (Lengua, 2002). In addition, emotional regulation plays a role in children's resilience to adverse circumstances, like poverty or divorce (for example, Buckner et al., 2003; Lengua, 2002).

Children's difficulties in their regulation of anger seem to be related to externalising problem behaviours (Gross, 1998; Lemerize & Dodge, 1993), while emotional dysregulation in general plays a role in several externalising diagnoses, such as Oppositional Defiant Disorder (ODD) and CD (Casey, 1996). Similarly, dysfunctional emotional regulation between parent and child is related to the stability of conduct problems from preschool to early school age (Cole, Teti & Zahn-Waxler, 2003). Aggression has also been linked to dysfunctional emotional regulation. Pope and Bierman (1999) noted that children who were identified as high in emotional intensity and low in behavioural regulation by Eisenberg and Fabes (1992) also fit the description of aggressive-rejected children by other researchers (Bierman, Smoot & Aumiller, 1993). Most of the studies mentioned above have been conducted with children, but in a study with 12–17-year-olds, which made use of the experience sampling method, Silk et al. (2003) also found that the intensity and lability of anger was associated with disruptive problem behaviours in adolescence.

As mentioned, researchers have made a distinction between proactive and reactive aggression (Dodge & Coie, 1987), and between physical and relational aggression (for example, Conway, 2005; Vitaro & Brendgen, 2005). Anger is a correlate of reactive, but not of proactive, aggression (Vitaro & Brendgen, 2005), and therefore it seems logical that difficulties in the regulation of anger apply to reactive but not to proactive aggression. In general, reactive aggression is impulsive in nature, characterised by high levels of bodily arousal, instability of affect and disinhibition. In contrast, proactive aggression is controlled rather than impulsive and there is evidence that proactively aggressive individuals are less likely to show unstable affect (Van Goozen, 2005). As to the distinction between physical and relational aggression, it also seems likely that more emotional control is required for relational aggression than is true for the expression of anger in relation to reactive physical aggression, but we are not aware of empirical evidence for this.

Scholars appear to agree that children's emotional regulation to some degree is modulated by social relationships (Eisenberg et al., 2003) and that emotional regulation strategies are primarily learned in the context of these social relationships (for example, John & Gross, 2004). For example, recent studies confirm the important role that parents play in their child's emotional development. Particularly, maternal instruction (Supplee, Shaw, Hailstones, & Hartman, 2004), parental warmth and the expression of positive emotion play a role in the development of their children's emotional regulation (Eisenberg et al., 2003). Further support for the parents' role in the development of emotional regulation comes from research conducted within the framework of attachment theory. A key aspect of Bowlby's original attachment theory (Bowlby, 1969) is the idea that caregiver-child exchanges early in life provide an important context within which the child learns to regulate their feelings. If the caregiver is available and responsive to the child's emotional needs, the child learns that emotions can be effectively regulated (Cooper, Shaver & Collins, 1998). A study which assessed emotional regulation and attachment styles in adolescents found that different kinds of attachment (secure, anxious-ambivalent and avoidant) can be linked to differences in the ways adolescents experience, express and regulate negative emotions (Cooper et al., 1998).

Especially in infancy and early childhood, the socially mediated co-regulation of the child's emotion is important. As children grow older, caregivers need to encourage the child's emotional autonomy in order to optimally support the child's emotional development (Southam-Gerow & Kendall, 2001). The question of which parenting styles contribute to the development of autonomous, well-functioning emotional regulation in children has not specifically been investigated, but several methods of, and mechanisms behind, the parental socialisation of emotion and emotional regulation have been proposed. For example, John and Gross (2004) have emphasised the influence of the parents' meta-emotion philosophy, that is, their feelings and thoughts about their own as well as others' emotions. Parents' acceptance of their own and others' emotions, and the discussion of emotions with their children should positively contribute to the development of children's emotional regulation abilities (see Eisenberg et al., 2003 for empirical support). Furthermore, the infant-caregiver relationship provides opportunities for the child to learn emotion regulation techniques through modelling (Southam-Gerow & Kendall, 2001), social referencing and imitation (Saarni, 1993).

It is important to keep in mind that the link between parents' socialisation of emotion and children's emotional development is reciprocal. Poor emotion regulation probably adversely impacts all social relationships (Buckner et al., 2003), just as social relationships affect emotional regulatory skills. Reciprocal, positive emotion regulation seems to be characteristic of healthy adjustment, while reciprocity of anger is associated with both the origin (Herrenkohl & Russo, 2001; Ramsden & Hubbard, 2002) and stability of children's conduct problems and aggressive behaviours from childhood to adolescence (Cole et al., 2003).

Gene-Environment Interactions

We mentioned that individual child characteristics, including disruptive behaviour, partly originate from the social context in which the child develops. Behavioural problems are thought to stem from both social environmental and genetic influences, and gene-environment interactions (GxE). Indeed, a multitude of environmental influences have been associated with both the infancy antecedents of externalising problem behaviours and externalising problem behaviours themselves later in life (see also Chapter 9, this volume). During pregnancy, such environmental influences are tobacco use (Brennan, Grekin, Mortensen, & Mednick, 2002; Fergusson, Woodward & Horwood, 1998), alcohol use (Olson et al., 1997), substance use (Fried, 1996; Fried, Watkinson & Gray, 1998, 2003), maternal mental health problems (Killingsworth Rini et al., 1999; Tremblay et al., 2004), parental antisocial behaviour (Tremblay et al., 2004), stress (Huizink, Mulder & Buitelaar, 2004; Huizink et al., 2003), low social support, teenage pregnancy (Jaffee et al., 2001; Nagin & Tremblay, 2001; Tremblay et al., 2004), low education and low SES (Tremblay et al., 2004). Many of these risk factors co-occur in about 10% of the population. Risk factors after birth include ineffective parental responses (Feehan et al., 1991; Patterson et al., 1992; Reid, Patterson & Loeber, 1982; Shaw et al., 2003), parental psychopathology (Barling, MacEwen & Nolte, 1993), parental antisocial traits (Bardone et al., 1998), family-break-up (Japel et al., 1999) and single parenthood (Jaffee et al., 2001). In addition to environmental influences, heritability is an important factor in the development of problem behaviours. For instance, meta-analyses of over a hundred twin and adoption samples found that genes account for approximately 40–50% of the population variance in externalising problem behaviours (Miles & Carey, 1997; Rhee & Waldman, 2002).

Although genes and environment may independently influence behaviours, their interaction with the environment (GxE) (Kendler & Eaves, 1986) is thought to have an important role in the onset and course of externalising problem behaviours. Gene-environment interactions postulate that adverse environmental factors may pose a risk depending upon genetic susceptibility. Several studies have used genetic informative samples to study whether the expression of disruptive behaviours and delinquency depended upon the children's genetic susceptibility and exposure to adverse environmental factors. For example, some studies found that the probability of externalising problem behaviours is highest when genetically vulnerable children experience adverse familial conditions such as, for example, harsh parenting (Button et al., 2005; Jaffee et al., 2005; O'Connor et al., 2003; Riggins-Caspers et al., 2003) or negative peer influences (Van Lier et al., 2007).

The findings on gene-environment interactions should be interpreted with caution. First, environmental risk variables tend to occur in concert rather than singly.

For instance, most findings on gene-environment interactions have been based on childhood maltreatment as an environmental risk factor. However, maltreatment may serve as an index of range of adverse familial conditions, including mothers who use substances during pregnancy (Smith & Testa, 2002), antisocial parents (Walsh et al., 2002), and low SES (Dodge et al., 1994), each of which has also been associated with externalising problem behaviours in the offspring. As a consequence, the importance of the interaction between gene(s) and any single environmental risk factor on the development of externalising problem behaviours can easily be overestimated. Secondly, environmental risk variables may be entangled with genetic risk variables (gene-environment correlations; rGE). For instance, prenatal smoking and harsh parenting have been associated with externalising problem behaviours in the offspring. However, both these risk variables are more frequently found among antisocial parents (passive rGE; Bardone et al., 1998; Walsh et al., 2002). Moreover, active heritability may account for the association because both prenatal smoking and harsh parenting, and the children's externalising problem behaviours may be the result of some genetic characteristics of the parent. If this is the case, then the apparent interaction between the adverse environment and the child's genetic makeup is in fact a correlate of the genetic liability of the child because of the common link between children's genetic risk and the environmental risk variable with the parental genetic liability. Consequently, the interaction between genetic liability and socio-familial environmental factors may actually be either over- or under-estimated because of these gene-environment correlations (which may act as confounding factors). For instance, Maughan and colleagues (2004) have shown that the association between prenatal smoking and CD in the offspring was, by and large, accounted for by correlated environmental (antisocial parents, low SES) and genetic risk for conduct problems.

Third, although results on gene-environment interactions based on candidate genes (Caspi et al., 2002, 2003, 2005; Huang et al., 2004) make it attractive to turn to molecular genetics, caution is required. Traits such as externalising problem behaviours represent complex phenotypes, and their aetiology is likely the result from multiple rather than single DNA variants interacting with environmental factors (Plomin & Crabbe, 2000). A variety of genes with small effect sizes are most probably involved in externalising problem behaviours (Plomin & Asbury, 2005). It is therefore not surprising that many findings on direct or gene-environment influences of candidate genes predicting psychopathology have not been replicated (Pérusse & Gendrau, 2005).

Finally, most authors assume that studies show that environmental risk factors, through gene-environment interactions, lead to children's problem behaviours. However, prior problem behaviours may cause parents to employ harsh parenting practices (that is, maltreatment may take place as a consequence of problem behaviours). Therefore, researchers need to follow up prenatal samples so that they can establish whether environmental risk factors preceded the onset of problem behaviours. Because the onset of externalising problem behaviours for a category of children lies within the first two years (Archer & Côte, 2005; Tremblay et al., 2004; Van Zeijl et al., 2006), studying genetic and environmental influences in relation to externalising problem behaviours among very young children may be particularly important to understand the development of externalising problem behaviours.

Conclusions

Decreased autonomic arousal, as indicated by heart rate and skin conductance, both in resting conditions and under stress may be a stable, even genetically determined, marker for persistent disruptive behaviours and development. This is mirrored by a similar relationship between low neuroendocrine levels (HPA activity/cortisol level) and disruptive behaviours. In contrast, the role of sex hormones (testosterone) and of (early) pubertal hormonal changes in the development of disruptive child behaviours remains unclear.

Neurocognitive deficits seem more germane to early-onset than late-onset disruptive behaviours. Low IQ, low verbal IQ and a large discrepancy between verbal and performance IQ are related to disruptive behaviours, especially when in combination with ADHD symptoms. Executive functioning, most notably inhibitory control, is related to and predicts the onset and persistence of disruptive behaviours from early preschool onwards. Deficits in executive functioning are related to lesions in the orbitofrontal cortex, and their associations with disruptive behaviours are most consistent among children with co-morbid ADHD symptoms. When disruptive children are presented with cues for reward and punishment, they tend to focus on reward signals while ignoring signals for punishment. These tendencies are associated with poor self-regulation.

Negative parent-child and child-peer relationships are closely linked to the development of children's disruptive behaviours. Lack of positive parental involvement and poor supervision, harsh or punitive parenting, and parent-child conflict are predictive of child disruptive behaviours from early childhood onward. Peer rejection and association with deviant peers are predictive of child aggression through mutual selection of aggressive friends and subsequent deviancy training.

Difficult temperament in children, including negative emotionality and low-effortful control, is related to disruptive child behaviours, especially in the context of poor parent-child relationships. Similarly, children's poor regulation of anger is related to externalising problem behaviours, most notably aggression. Children's emotional regulation strategies are strongly related to parents' childrearing practices and parents' emotional development.

Disruptive behaviours are partly genetically-determined, most likely by the cumulative and interactive effects of several specific genes, most notably in those already starting disruptive behaviours early in life. In this influence, gene-environment interactions play an important role. Although not well studied yet, genes and environment may influence the development of disruptive and delinquent child behaviours independently, but also through their interaction, in which adverse environmental factors may pose a risk depending upon genetic susceptibility. There is some evidence that externalising problem behaviours are increased when genetically vulnerable children are exposed to adverse familial or peer influences.

Chapter 6

Family Processes and Parent and Child Personality Characteristics

Peter Prinzie, Geert Jan Stams and Machteld Hoeve

Research on disruptive behaviours in children is prolific and the literature is voluminous and complex (Connor, 2002). Empirical studies have yielded a multitude of single-family factors that are significantly related to disruptive child behaviours (reviewed by Coie & Dodge, 1998). In order to classify the large numbers of etiological factors, Dishion, French and Patterson (1995) have presented a comprehensive conceptual framework. They distinguish intra-individual factors (for example, gender, genetic influences, temperament), relationship processes (parenting practices, parent psychopathology, peer influences), behavioural settings (neighbourhood settings, schools), and community contexts (employment resources, mass media).

From the literature on etiological factors (Deković, Janssens & Van As, 2003; Dishion et al., 1995; Loeber & Farrington, 1997), it is clear that environmental factors play a significant role in the onset and course of disruptive behaviours. Within this category, parent-child interaction and determinants of the parenting process take a prominent place. The study of the relationship between parenting and behavioural outcomes has been on the agenda of socialisation researchers for several decades (Patterson & Fisher, 2002). This relationship may be conceptualised from different theoretical perspectives, for instance: the psychoanalytic, the ethological, the social learning, or the parent-child attachment perspective. According to Rubin, Stewart and Chen (1995), the conceptualisations may differ in the perspective taken to define and describe the parent-child relationship, but they do agree on placing 'a primary responsibility on parental attributes and behaviours, as well as on the quality of the parent-child relationship' (p. 260).

In this chapter, we focus on the parent-child relationship and on the proximal determinants of the parenting process, that is, child and parent personality characteristics. We first provide a short overview of the literature on family factors and delinquency in general. Next, we will focus on family processes that operate in childhood. Although Dutch family studies with young children are scarce, we provide interesting findings from recent empirical studies.

Family Factors, Disruptive Child Behaviours and Delinquency

Researchers have shown a wide interest in the relationship between family characteristics and disruptive and delinquent child behaviours. Studies agree that there is a relationship between disruptive and delinquent child behaviours and various family factors, such as lack of supervision, harsh punishment and weak attachment (Loeber & Dishion, 1983; Loeber & Stouthamer-Loeber, 1986; Wasserman & Seracini, 2001). The majority of these studies concentrated on adolescents rather than on children. A key reason for the focus on this age group is the peak in the age-crime curve, occurring around age 18 and indicating that adolescents are responsible for a large percentage of delinquent acts (Farrington, 1986). Reviews that analysed studies of predictors from different domains, including family factors, have found that next to offence history family factors were among the best predictors of recidivism compared to other domains, such as criminal history, socioeconomic status and personal distress (Cottle, Lee & Heilbrun, 2001; Gendreau, Little & Goggin, 1996). To be more specific, lack of supervision, over-protection, weak family relationships, rejection and inconsistency in discipline had the strongest link with delinquency (Hoeve et al., submitted). Research indicated that these parenting variables have stronger associations with delinquency, compared to structural variables such as family socioeconomic status (SES), single-parent families, parental stress and depression, and large family size (for example, Glueck & Glueck, 1950; Loeber & Stouthamer-Loeber, 1986; Nye, 1958; Sampson & Laub, 1993; Van Voorhis et al., 1988; Wells & Rankin, 1988). Therefore, our focus in this chapter is on parenting factors and more proximal factors such as parental and child personality characteristics.

The empirical findings are largely in accordance with some of the most important theoretical perspectives on the aetiology of delinquency. According to Hirschi (1969), families with strong affective family ties are less likely to have delinquent children than families with weak affective family ties. When juveniles are closely attached to their parents, they are more likely to comply with the normative expectations of their parents, which may protect them against norm-trespassing impulses. Quality of attachment functions as 'indirect parental control', that is, compliance with social limits set by laws, norms, rules and societal expectations, and is fostered by strong child-parent attachments and not by parental disciplining (Burton, Cullen, Evans, & al., 1995; Cernkovich & Giordano, 1987; Rankin & Wells, 1990; Rosen, 1985; Wells & Rankin, 1988). Delinquency will increase if attachment to parents is weakened. In one meta-analysis, Hoeve and colleagues (submitted), found a strong association between lack of attachment and delinquency, as evident from police and justice records. Given that self-report measures tend to reflect less serious delinquency and official records cover more serious crimes (Babinski, Hartsough & Lambert, 2001; Maxfield, Weiler & Widom, 2000), the aforementioned finding suggests that poor attachment is particularly associated with more serious delinquency.

Another important perspective is a socialisation theory that distinguishes between two childrearing dimensions, namely, parental support and control (Maccoby & Martin, 1983). Support is defined as warmth, affection and responsiveness. Control is best defined as parental pressure for children to think, feel or behave in desired ways. By combining these dimensions, the following parenting styles can be identified: authoritative parenting (high on both control and support), authoritarian parenting (high on control and low on support), permissiveness (low on control and high on support), and neglectful parenting (low on both control and support) (Baumrind, 1971; Maccoby & Martin, 1983). It is widely assumed that an authoritative style promotes positive child adjustment. The remaining styles, permissiveness and neglect, in particular, are thought to result in negative child adjustment. Several studies have found a substantial association between child abuse and problem behaviours (Coie & Dodge, 1998, for the effects of child abuse; see also Chapter 4, this volume). In particular, studies show that neglectful parenting increases the probability of delinquency in the offspring (Maccoby & Martin, 1983; Steinberg et al., 1994).

The foregoing findings apply particularly to adolescents. However, research on family factors and disruptive behaviours in younger children is as important. Moffitt and Caspi (2001), showed that life-course-persistent delinquent behaviour, which originates early in life, was associated with weak family bonds, which was not true for adolescence-limited delinquent behaviour, which begins around puberty. In a meta-analysis of parenting and delinquency, which included studies of both adolescents and children, Hoeve et al. (submitted), found that the age of the participants moderated the association between delinquency and parenting characteristics, such as affection and harsh punishment. The effect size for the relationship between affection and delinquency was relatively large for younger children, while the effect size for the relationship between harsh punishment and delinquency was relatively small for younger children. Thus, the link between some parenting characteristics and delinquency is different for young children compared to adolescents.

Relation between Parenting Practices and Disruptive Child Behaviour

The literature offers ample evidence that there is a substantial relationship between dysfunctional parenting practices and the development of disruptive behaviours in children (Dishion et al, 1995; Maccoby & Martin, 1983; Patterson, 1982; Patterson, Reid & Dishion, 1992; Rothbaum & Weisz, 1994). According to these studies, negative (that is, harsh, authoritarian) discipline by parents is correlated with disruptive behaviours in children. A comprehensive model of inept parental disciplinary practices that is very influential in the field is Patterson's 'coercive family process' theory (Patterson, 1982; Patterson et al., 1992; Reid, Patterson & Snyder, 2002). According to Patterson (2002), negative parenting practices are the proximal mechanism for the development of disruptive child behaviours.

From a social learning perspective and based on extensive observational data of moment-by-moment parent-child interactions in clinic families, Patterson elucidated how parents and children change each other's behaviour over time (Patterson, 1982; Patterson et al., 1992). In his coercion theory, Patterson (1982; 2002) describes a multi-step family process called *coercion training* that commonly occurs in families of aggressive boys and that consists of escape-conditioning contingencies. The first step is an aversive intrusion of the parent. Typically, the intrusions are minor ones. For example, a mother simply scolds a child for not doing his homework. The second step involves a counterattack by the child, through arguing, yelling, whining, shouting, or complaining about the parent's directive. The third step, the parent's response to the child's coercive attempt, is crucial. When the parent does not enforce the directive, the child is rewarded for his coercive behaviours. The danger of this step lies in the behavioural trap inherent in negative reinforcement. The trap is that coercion is functional in the short run but leads to maladaptive long-term outcomes. In the short run, a coercive response effectively terminates conflict. In the long run, the likelihood of coercive behaviours in subsequent conflicts is increased. At the fourth step, the child terminates the counterattack, and the parent is reinforced for her or his backing off. In this way, both parent and child reinforce each other in the use of coercive tactics. These reinforcements increase the probability that the coercive exchange will be repeated in future interactions. Not only will the exchange be repeated, as the interaction chains increase in length and hostility, it may also escalate (Dishion & Patterson, 1997; Patterson, 1982, 2002; Patterson et al., 1992). In the long term, coercive training can lead to poor social skills and academic deficits in children.

Further, Patterson and colleagues described in very general terms how parenting practices control the contingent parent-child interactions (Patterson, 2002; Patterson et al., 1992; Snyder, 1995). A strong association was found between harsh, capricious and inconsistent parental discipline, parental monitoring and disruptive child behaviours (Patterson et al., 1992). According to this model, the impact of contextual variables such as social disadvantage (Conger et al., 1994), divorce (Forgatch, Patterson, & Skinner, 1988), parental stress (Conger, Patterson & Ge, 1995), parental depression (Bank et al., 1993), parental antisocial behaviour (Patterson & Dishion, 1988) and of children's characteristics on child adjustment is mediated by the impact of parenting practices (Dishion & Patterson, 1997; Reid & Patterson, 1989). However, in contrast to the contextual variables, the impact of the more proximal variables (that is, parental and child personality characteristics) has not yet been empirically studied.

Recently, a longitudinal study by Prinzie (2002) revealed associations between negative parenting and child externalising problem behaviours in a population-based sample that included boys and girls. At Time 1, the total sample consisted of 674 Belgian families with a child of elementary school age. Four different birth cohorts were followed: 4-year-old children (cohort 1), 5-year-old children (cohort 2), 6-year-old children (cohort 3), and 7-year-old children (cohort 4). Assessments were made yearly, over a three-year period. There were 337 boys (M=5 years, 10 months; SD=1.12 years) and 337 girls (M=5 years, 10 months; SD=1.15 years). Parents of 609 children (90%) participated in the study at Time 2, and parents of 588 children (87%) participated in the study at Time 3. Correlational and longitudinal analyses corroborated the link between inept parenting and externalising problem behaviours. Consistent with Patterson's coercion model, negative and coercive discipline were directly related to children's externalising problem behaviours (Prinzie et al., 2003; 2004).

Further, a multivariate latent growth analysis indicated that parenting behaviour was differentially related to children's aggressive and delinquent problem behaviours (Prinzie, Onghena & Hellinckx, 2006). Coercion was significantly related to aggressive behaviours, but not to delinquency. Higher scores on coercion were related to higher initial levels and a slower decrease of aggressive behaviours. In addition, high scores on overreactivity were associated with higher initial levels of aggressive and delinquent problem behaviours. The stronger association between harsh discipline and aggressive problem behaviours is consistent with Patterson's coercion model (Patterson, 1982; Patterson et al., 1992). Overreactive and coercive parenting behaviour might lead to inconsistent behavioural contingencies, a capricious and unpredictable environment, and a parent's decreased sense of control. This in turn might increase the likelihood of aggressive problem behaviours. As described in the coercion theory of Patterson (Patterson et al., 1992), the negative reinforcement of externalising problem behaviours may increase the frequency, the intensity and the duration of these problem behaviours.

Thus, dysfunctional parenting practices were related to the initial level of delinquency, but not to changes in delinquency, which suggests that harsh disciplinary practises are partly responsible for the onset of delinquency, but not for its persistence. Previous studies found that the persistence of delinquency is more environmentally influenced, for instance, by delinquent peer affiliation and the use of social mimicry or attempts to gain peer-group respect (for the impact of peers see also Eley, Lichtenstein & Moffitt, 2003; see also Chapter 7, this volume). Richman, Stevenson and Graham (1982) observed that family factors, measured when children were 3 years old, had an influence on the development of problem behaviours five years later, but not on the outcome of problem behaviours once established.

These findings are in agreement with those of Hoeve and colleagues (submitted), who found stronger short-term than long-term associations regarding support, rejection and conflict, suggesting that these family characteristics influence the child's behaviour more immediately. The time-limited effect of parenting indicates that changes in growth rates are sensitive to ongoing changes in the family environment, or to the introduction to and changes in other environments (for example, school settings). In addition, in the Dunedin Study, variables other than parenting practices (such as neurocognitive deficits, callousness, impulsivity and hyperactivity) had a stronger predictive effect (Moffitt & Caspi, 2001).

An important finding is that no gender differences were found in the relationship between coercive parenting and the developmental trajectory of aggressive behaviours. Eddy, Leve and Fagot (2001) reported that similar coercion processes apply to both boys and girls. Overreactivity on the other hand was more strongly related to initial levels of delinquency in boys compared to girls. In their meta-analysis, Rothbaum and Weisz (1994) found that in preadolescence the association between parenting and delinquency, but not aggression, was stronger in boys compared to girls. Lytton and Romney's (1991) meta-analysis of differential parental socialisation revealed that in Western countries physical punishment was more often used with boys than with girls. Physical punishment, in turn, was found to be associated with higher levels of delinquency (Gershoff, 2002).

Likewise, many similarities were found among different ethnic groups with regard to reported parenting, parent-child relations and disruptive behaviours (Deković, Wissink & Meijer, 2004; Wissink, Deković & Meijer, 2006). In addition, links between parenting and parent-child relations were similar to some extent. However, some differences between ethnic groups have been found. For example, restrictive control had a stronger link to delinquency in Moroccan and Turkish youngsters compared to other ethnic groups in the Netherlands (Wissink et al., 2006). It should be noted that these findings were found for adolescents and should be replicated with child problem behaviour outcomes.

In summary, these findings highlight the association between negative parenting and externalising problem behaviours in boys and girls and in different ethnic groups. However, the most important finding is that dysfunctional parenting behaviours were differentially related to children's aggressive and delinquent problem behaviours.

Relation Between Child Personality Traits and Disruptive Child Behaviour

Transactional models emphasise that parenting not only influences children's adjustment, but that child characteristics also affect parenting and adjustment (Lytton, 1990; Sameroff, 2000). The modern understanding that children make important contributions to their social interactions has two roots. The first study on temperament was done by Thomas and Chess (1977) and their colleagues. Introducing the concept of 'goodness-of-fit', the authors stressed how important it is that individual temperament is geared to the environment. That is, if the child's temperament is in harmony with environmental expectations, the child is expected to develop positively. Rothbart and Bates (1998) also emphasised that the expression of temperament depends on the environment. There is goodness-of-fit when the child's capacities, motivations and temperament are sufficiently adequate to master the demands, expectations and opportunities of their environment (Moffitt, 2005).

The second root is Bell's reconceptualisation of socialisation as a mutually interactive process, with both child and caregiver seeking to redirect, reduce, stimulate, or intensify the behaviour of the other (Bell, 1968, 1974; Bell & Chapman, 1986). These insights together have led to the recognition that children differ in such qualities as responsiveness to parents' soothing strategies, capacity to control their own emotional responses, and capacity to bring pleasure or distress to their parents. In theory, temperament does not result in problem behaviours by itself; it does so only in conjunction with a particular environment. However, few empirical studies give detailed models of developmental interplay between specific temperamental characteristics and environment.

The complex interplay between child temperament, environment and problem behaviours is especially highlighted in a series of Dutch studies conducted by Paulussen-Hoogeboom and colleagues (in press). They show in their meta-analysis that both the strength and direction of the relationship between child negative emotionality and parental behaviour varies as a function of the child's age, environmental risk (SES, and ethnic minority background) and parenting dimension; that is, support and restrictive or inductive control. For example, a relatively strong and negative relationship was found between child negative emotionality and supportive parenting in low SES families, whereas a weak and positive relationship was found in high SES families. The latter finding was replicated in a recent observational study by Paulussen-Hoogeboom, Stams, and colleagues (2008), who found in a Dutch sample of families from higher socioeconomic backgrounds that perceived child negative emotionality was positively associated with supportive parenting, that is, maternal sensitive responsiveness. In a cross-sectional study, Paulussen-Hoogeboom, Stams, Hermanns, Peetsma and Van den Wittenboer (2006) found that the relations between perceived child negative emotionality and parent reports of both internalising and externalising problem behaviours were partially mediated by the mother's authoritative parenting style. Interestingly, when confirmatory factor analysis was used to decontaminate measures assessing temperament and problem behaviours from item-content overlap, the association between negative emotionality and internalising problem behaviours was found to be fully mediated by authoritative parenting. Finally, results of a multilevel study showed that perceived parental control mediated the relationship between child negative emotionality and authoritative parenting (Paulussen-Hoogeboom, Stams, Hermanns, Peetsma, & Hoffenaar, 2006).

Several studies have examined childhood temperament in relationship to the broader concept of externalising problem behaviours, which includes conduct problems, aggression and oppositional behaviours, as well as hyperactive and impulsive behaviours (see also Chapter 5, this volume). Negative emotionality, high unmanageability, poor self-regulation, impulsivity and callousness emerge as relevant, early temperamental correlates (review by Rothbart & Bates, 1998; Sanson & Prior, 1999). These temperament characteristics have been shown to be heritable (Plomin et al., 1993). In Moffitt's (1993) taxonomy of antisocial behaviour, personality traits play a pivotal role in the aetiology of life-course persistent antisocial behaviours. Most of these studies have considered direct linear effects where the contribution of a particular temperament trait to the development of an adjustment pattern is investigated. However, the integration of the various results is hindered by conceptual differences accompanied by assessment differences (see Paulussen-Hoogeboom et al., 2007).

With regard to personality traits in children, considerable progress has been made over the past decade toward the development of a more generally accepted taxonomy (Caspi, 1998; Shiner & Caspi, 2003). There is a growing consensus that children's individual differences can be described in terms of the Big Five personality traits observed in adults (Shiner & Caspi, 2003). These factors have traditionally been numbered and labelled as follows: (I) Extraversion (or Surgency, Positive Affectivity), (II) Agreeableness (vs. Antagonism), (III) Conscientiousness (or Constraint Dependability), (IV) Emotional Stability (vs. Neuroticism or Negative Affectivity) and (V) Openness to Experience (or Intellect, Culture) (see Caspi, 1998). An advantage of the Big Five categorisation is that it serves as a framework to conduct systematic research and that it provides an integration of the diversity of individual personality measures (McCrae & Costa, 1996).

Only a few studies have investigated relations between the five factor dimensions and adjustment behaviour. John and colleagues (1994) suggested that personality traits in young adolescents are differentially implicated in the expression of psychopathology, providing evidence for the discriminatory power of the Big Five. Externalising problem behaviours were more prevalent among boys with high scores on extraversion and low scores on agreeableness and conscientiousness. Krueger and colleagues (1996) have linked externalising problem behaviours to lower scores on conscientiousness and agreeableness. Research in criminology showed that greater delinquent participation was associated with a personality configuration characterised by high negative emotionality and weak constraint in different countries, different age cohorts, across gender and across race (Caspi et al., 1994).

Personality-environment interactions have figured especially in theories of development and in diathesis theories of psychopathology, but they have seldom been examined in empirical work (Moffitt, 2005). Using a cross-sectional design, Prinzie et al. (2003) reported that parenting and children's personality characteristics have both *additive* and *interactive* effects on children's adjustment. Dysfunctional parenting disciplines and children's personality were *directly* related to children's externalising problem behaviours. Consistent with previous studies (Huey & Weisz, 1997; John et al., 1994; Rothbart & Bates, 1998), high levels of extraversion, low levels of conscientiousness, but especially low levels of agreeableness, predicted higher levels of externalising problem behaviours in children. This pattern of personality scores is similar to that found by Robins, John and Caspi (1994) in adolescents. Ego under-control is primarily expressed in energetic yet antagonistic and undependable behaviour that reflects high extraversion, low agreeableness and low conscientiousness. The recurrent noncompliant and coercive behaviours of children with low scores on agreeableness may evoke permissive or negative reactions from parents, resulting in higher initial levels of externalising problem behaviours (Patterson et al., 1992). Agreeableness encompasses the lower-order trait 'dominance', representing the child's ability to act cooperatively and competitively to secure desirable outcomes (Hawley, 1999). Children who are egocentric and dominant in interactions may have more conflict with siblings and/or peers.

The most important finding, however, was that significant interaction effects were found, which indicated that some parenting effects may depend on child personality characteristics or vice versa (Prinzie et al., 2003). In the mother ratings as well as in the father ratings, child agreeableness moderated the relationship between overreactivity and externalising problem behaviours. Overreactivity was more strongly related to externalising problem behaviours for children with low scores on agreeableness than those who were more agreeable and sociable.

Evidence for the dynamic interplay between child and parent characteristics is also found in behaviour genetic studies using adoption designs. These studies are extremely powerful in showing the contribution of environmental influences on children's development relative to genetic influences (Plomin & DeFries, 1985). It should be noted, however, that most adoption studies underestimate the true contribution of environmental factors, since the comparison is restricted to subjects living under relatively similar circumstances (Stoolmiller, 1999; Loehlin & Horn 2000). Nevertheless, adoption studies can provide direct evidence for the independent effects of family environment and heredity that are always confounded in intact nuclear families (Fulker, DeFries & Plomin, 1988). It has even been suggested that correlations between specific measures of parental treatment (childrearing practices) and children's characteristics are not interpretable when based on biological relatives reared together (Bouchard & McGue, 2003).

Stams, Juffer and Van IJzendoorn (2002) prospectively followed from infancy to middle childhood a group of 146 internationally adopted children who were not genetically related to their adoptive parents; Stams and colleagues found that maternal sensitive responsiveness and quality of child-parent attachment relationships strongly predicted children's development at age 7, even after controlling for child temperament, parental characteristics and current circumstances. The study design, however, could not account for genetic influences from child to parent, that is, evocative gene-environment correlations. Notably, Ge et al. (1996) and O'Connor and colleagues (1998) showed that psychopathology and substance abuse disorder in the birth parents were associated with problem behaviours in the adopted children, which subsequently impacted on parenting behaviour of the adoptive parents.

In a recent overview of personality differences in children, Shiner and Caspi (2003) described six processes through which childhood individual differences put children at risk of psychopathology. First, *learning processes* may explain why specific personality characteristics may lead to difficulties in learning to inhibit behaviours when faced with potential rewards. As O'Brien and Frick (1996) have documented, children with conduct disorder are especially sensitive to signals of reward, but they are rather insensitive to punishing stimuli. According to Gray's (1987) psychobiological model of personality, individual differences in sensitivity to reward and punishment may lead to different learned reactions to objectively identical social reinforcements. A child with a high score on agreeableness, who is punished for performing an undesirable act, may be more likely to inhibit future performance of the act because memory of the aversive consequence overrides the immediate reward of performing the act. For children with low scores on agreeableness, potential punishment is less likely to inhibit undesirable behaviours.

Secondly, children with low scores on agreeableness may also evoke negative reactions from parents. Anderson, Lytton and Romney (1986) were among the first to provide a convincing test of child evocative effects. When interacting with children with conduct disorder, mothers of normal boys became significantly more averse than when they were observed with their own child. These findings point to *environmental elicitation* in which children's genetically-influenced personality traits evoke coercive parenting behaviours.

A third possible mechanism is *environmental construal*, that is, children's personality characteristics may influence how environmental experiences are construed. Children with low scores on emotional stability may often misperceive the intentions of others. It is plausible that such children seek less information about social situations and are more likely to assume hostile intent on the part of other persons (Coie & Dodge, 1998).

Related to the process of environmental construal are *social comparison processes* in which personality characteristics shape the way individuals evaluate themselves in relationship to others. Hughes, Cavell and Grossman (1997) reported that children with externalising problem behaviours overestimate their social competence relative to others.

A fifth process, *environmental selection*, may be seen in the ways by which some children 'select' situations that can subsequently reinforce particular behaviours. For example, children with a low score on benevolence are more likely to form ties to delinquent peers who in turn encourage their disruptive behaviours (Wright et al., 2001).

Finally, through *environmental manipulation* an individual's personality alters and shapes the environment. For example, dominant children not only perceive greater interpersonal conflict in their environment, but also attempt to resolve conflict with destructive tactics (Jensen-Campbell & Graziano, 2001).

In summary, studies indicate that children differ in risks for developing externalising problem behaviours in the presence of dysfunctional parenting practices (Rutter, 2002). These moderating effects suggest that integrating the effects of children's individual differences with parenting effects can improve our understanding of the development of externalising problem behaviours. This integration may also have important implications for intervention programmes or parent training programmes (Johnson & Sheeber, 1999; Sheeber & McDevitt, 1998). It is crucial that such programmes are conceptually based on a goodness-of-fit model, which assumes that optimal child development is determined by the degree to which the demands of the environment are congruent with the child's personality characteristics.

Relationship between Parent Personality Traits and Disruptive Child Behaviour

Although parent personality characteristics have a place in most ecological models of child development (Belsky, 1984), the exact nature of that influence is a challenging issue that continues to stimulate controversy (Collins et al., 2000; Maccoby, 1992). In his process model of parenting, Belsky (1984) explicitly proposed that parents' personalities influence their parenting practices and children's developmental outcomes. However, until now, surprisingly few empirical investigations systematically explored which personality characteristics are primarily involved, and to what extent these characteristics influence parenting or child development (for a review, see Belsky & Barends, 2002). Personality characteristics may influence parenting and through parenting, child development. In addition, however, behavioural genetic studies have reported that personality is, in part, heritable (for example, Goldsmith et al., 1994; Jang et al., 1998). This means that parent and child characteristics may be linked due to shared genes and biological dispositions above and beyond the influence of negative parenting (see also Chapter 5, this volume).

Using the Five Factor Model, Prinzie et al. (2005) examined the extent to which mothers' and fathers' personality characteristics were related to overreactive, lax and coercive parenting and children's externalising problem behaviours. Path analysis indicated that negative parenting practices and parents' personality characteristics operate together to predict children's externalising problem behaviours. Consistent with past research (Patterson & Dishion, 1988; Patterson et al., 1992), parent personality traits were *indirectly* related to children's externalising problem behaviours. Their effect was partly mediated by negative parenting practices. The factor of Emotional Stability was negatively related to all negative parenting variables. The factors Agreeableness and Autonomy were negatively related to overreactivity and laxness, and Extraversion was negatively related to laxness. These results fit very well with other empirical research. Mothers who score high on negative emotionality express more negative affects in interactions with their children (Kochanska, Clark & Goldman, 1997). Because they are liable to becoming tense and distressed, they are more likely to resort to power assertion. Research has amply documented that maternal anger, sadness and other negative affects expressed in interactions with children, predicted children's problem behaviours and poor internalisation of parental rules (Belsky, Crnic & Woodworth, 1995). Kochanska, Clark & Goldman (1997) also reported that disagreeableness interfered with adaptive parenting. Mothers with low scores on agreeableness were more affectively negative and less positive with their children. They used more verbal power and were less responsive and warm. The negative association between agreeableness and overreactivity confirms Patterson's clinical impression that hostile interchanges occur more in clinic-referred families compared to families not referred to clinics (Patterson, 1982).

Parent personality traits also contributed *directly* to children's externalising problem behaviours. For the mother ratings, as well as for the father ratings, the personality dimensions of emotional stability and children's conscientiousness were negatively related, while autonomy was positively related to children's externalising problem behaviours. Also, previous studies showed that parental autonomy or openness was related to child sensation-seeking (Zuckerman, 1991). According to Frick and colleagues (Frick et al., 1995), sensation-seeking can promote disruptive child behaviours. Along that line, impulsivity observed as early as age 3 can foretell alcohol dependence and criminal behaviour in early adulthood (Caspi et al., 1996).

Parents with low scores on emotional stability have difficulties in coping with daily interpersonal stressors. This may result in more confrontations and hostile interactions between them and their children (Gunthert, Cohen & Armeli, 1999). Externalising problem behaviours in children may be an imitation of parents' explosive reactions (Brook, Whiteman & Zheng, 2002). Another possibility is that children with the same inherited personality characteristics as their parents have a propensity to engage in more interactions that are hostile and are at risk in developing externalising problem behaviours. Nigg and Hinshaw (1998) reported that higher rates of overt disruptive behaviours in boys with ADHD were associated primarily with maternal characteristics such as higher neuroticism and lower conscientiousness.

Conclusion and Future Directions

Studies agree that disruptive child behaviours are the result of complex person-environment interactions in which parents' childrearing practices play a key role. Research indicates that parenting variables (lack of supervision, overprotection, weak family relationships, rejection and inconsistency in discipline) have stronger associations with disruptive and delinquent child behaviours compared to structural variables such as single-parent families, working mothers and large families. However, the effects of parenting on children's disruptive behaviours partly depend on child personality characteristics. This means that the child is an active participant in the parenting process. Integrating child and parent personality characteristics within parenting models can improve the understanding of the aetiology of disruptive and externalising child problem behaviours and hence are likely to improve intervention programmes.

It is important that intervention programmes are conceptually based on a goodness-of-fit model, which assumes that the degree to which the demands of the social environment (that is, parent behaviour) are congruent with the child's personality characteristics determines optimal child development. Findings with regard to the persistence of externalising problem behaviours indicate that a wait-and-see policy cannot be justified. This highlights the importance of early prevention and intervention and may stimulate the development of effective programmes (see further Chapters 11 and 12, this volume).

Chapter 7

Peer Relationships and the Development of Externalising Problem Behaviour

Pol A.C. van Lier and Hans M. Koot

The association between children's peer relations and psychopathology has received persistent attention in the last decade from researchers throughout the world. For every child's development, peer relations are of immense importance. Peer relations provide a context in which the developing child can acquire and rehearse social skills, learn to self-regulate, to solve interpersonal conflicts, and to discover social roles, norms, and processes involved in interpersonal relationships (Rubin, Bukowski & Parker, 1998). Unfortunately, not all peer relationships are beneficial to the child. In fact, numerous studies have demonstrated the potentially hazardous influence of peer relations on child development. This chapter focuses on how relations with peers contribute to the development of childhood disruptive and aggressive behaviours.

Peer Relationships and Externalising Problem Behaviours

Children's externalising problem behavioural acts are hypothesised to stem from genetic or biological vulnerabilities, which are exacerbated by troublesome environmental influences (Miles & Carey, 1997; Moffitt, 1993; Rhee & Waldman, 2002). In the preschool years, much attention has been paid to troublesome (social) interactions with parents, expressed as harsh parenting style and as defiant behaviours of the child. With the transition to elementary school, the domains of risk expand. While social risk factors for a troublesome development prior to this period are primarily found in the interaction between the parents/caretakers and the child, after the transition to school, such social interactions expand with the addition of classmates and friends. Typically, research on the influence of peers has focused on two different but equally important processes through which peer relations contribute to maladjustment. First, peers may evoke aggressive behaviours in children because they reject them, which may accentuate the externalising problem behaviours of the child. The second process is the selective affiliation of children, where children who are at risk of developing externalising problem behaviours affiliate with aggressive peers. The resulting learning from – and reinforcement of – deviant behaviours may result in increases in the child's externalising problem behaviours.

Peer Rejection

As early as when children move beyond the scope of the parental home and start interacting with peers, children start to evaluate their peers' behaviour. As a consequence of this evaluation, approximately 5–10% of children experience chronic rejection by peers (Boivin & Vitaro, 1995). Although peer acceptance is mostly defined in terms of a child's social status (popular, rejected) and typically assessed through sociometric techniques, rejection covers a wide variety of behaviours. These behaviours range from covert rejection behaviours, such as excluding the child from social interaction and preventing a child having access to peer networks, to more overt behaviours, such as various forms of aggression directed at the child, expressing moral disapproval of the child, and gossiping, tale-telling, or saying hurtful things about the rejected child to others in the presence of the child (Asher, Rose & Gabriel, 2001). The experience of peer rejection has been related to many negative consequences for the child, including early-onset conduct problems (Miller-Johnson et al., 2002) and delinquency (Coie, Terry, Lenox et al., 1995; Miller-Johnson et al., 1999) and also internalising problem behaviours (Rubin et al., 1998).

It is, however, incorrect to assume that rejected children are merely the passive victims of the larger peer group. In fact, there is an abundance of research linking aggressive child behaviours to peer rejection (Brendgen et al., 2001; Coie & Dodge, 1998; Rubin et al., 1998; Van Lier & Crijnen, 2005; Van Lier et al., 2005). For instance, Van Lier et al. (2005) found that all of the children who followed a stable-high trajectory of disruptive behaviours from age 7 to age 10 experienced peer rejection. In contrast, of those who followed a low disruptive trajectory, only 1% experienced peer rejection in this period. Similarly, Brendgen et al. (2001) found that aggressive behaviours in childhood predicted chronic low peer acceptance. The directional effect between aggressive behaviours and peer rejection was explored in a series of experimental playgroup studies (Coie & Kupersmidt, 1983; Dodge, 1983). In these studies, unacquainted boys were observed on their emerging peer status. The results demonstrated that boys' verbal and physical aggressive acts preceded the emergence of peer rejection, suggesting a directional effect of aggressive acts leading to rejection by mainstream peers. These findings thus not only link peer rejection to children's externalising problem behaviours, they also suggest that peer rejection is the social consequence of externalising problem behaviours exhibited by children.

The fact that the initial peer rejection is best viewed as the consequence of early externalising problem behaviours in children, does not imply that peer rejection is not related to further increases in problem behaviours. In fact, once a child experiences rejection by peers, it is at risk of successive peer rejection experiences and increases in aggressive behaviours. For instance, Miller-Johnson et al. (2002) reported that low sociometric scores in first and second grade predicted grade four conduct problems. This predictive association was found while controlling for first-grade attention-hyperactivity and aggression, demonstrating the independent role of peer rejection in the prediction of conduct problems. Similarly, Keiley et al., (2000) demonstrated that children who were rejected in kindergarten showed either stable-high or increasing levels of externalising problem behaviours in later school years. Moreover, Dodge et al. (2003) demonstrated that rejection in kindergarten predicted successive rejection experiences. Each of these successive rejection experiences was uniquely associated with subsequent growth in aggression, but only for those who were already high on aggression in kindergarten. These results thus suggest that once rejected, children are at risk of undergoing a process of continued poor relations with peers and stable-high or increasing levels of externalising problem behaviours. The findings from these studies also suggest that such a development is observed particularly among those children who already had elevated levels of externalising problem behaviours at the time of rejection.

Possible Mechanisms of the Contribution of Peer Rejection to Externalising Problem Behaviours

A number of processes may explain the association between peer relations and the development of externalising problem behaviours. The first regards psychological processes in the rejected child. Rejected children's social information processing may be altered in that these children are more likely to make hostile attributions about their peers' behaviour. Moreover, rejected children may have low expectancy to achieve positive outcomes (Dodge et al., 2003; Rabiner & Coie, 1989). For instance, Dodge et al. (2003) found that the predictive association between early childhood rejection and later aggressive behaviours was, in part, accounted for by the rejected children's tendency to generate aggressive responses to ambiguous situations and to have low perceived self-efficacy in achieving positive outcomes.

Another pathway concerns exchanges with peers. Interactions between peers and rejected children are likely to result in mutual coercive exchanges, which may maintain or increase the level of externalising problem behaviours of the rejected child (Miller-Johnson et al., 2002; Snyder et al., 2004). For instance, Snyder et al. (2004) reported that the longitudinal link between kindergarten children's impulsiveness-inattention and conduct problems two years later was mediated by peer rejection and coercive exchanges with peers.

A third pathway is the reduction of opportunities for rejected children to interact with normative peers and to learn normative behaviour from them. Rather, because of the resentment and suspicion that may rise because of the feeling of being rejected by non-deviant peers (Dodge, 1993), rejected children are 'pushed' towards other, possibly also rejected, children who are likely to have a similar behavioural repertoire. This process is known as 'affiliation with deviant peers'. Because affiliation with deviant children has received great attention in research on peer influences on the development of externalising problem behaviours, it will be discussed in detail below.

Affiliation with Deviant Peers

Despite the fact that rejection and exclusion from peer groups is observed among especially aggressive children, these children do affiliate with others. However, similar to prosocial children who affiliate with other prosocial children (and reject aggressive children), aggressive children tend to affiliate with each other (Boivin & Vitaro, 1995). This process of homophily with respect to aggressive behaviours is observed already in young children (Estell et al., 2002; Farver, 1996; Snyder, Horsch & Childs, 1997). For instance, Farver (1996) found that members of teacher-rated cliques were moderately similar in aggression, as rated by independent observers. Similarly, Snyder et al., (1997) found that 4- and 5-year-old children select friends who are similar in aggression. That is, of those who were regarded as aggressive, 50% of their friends were also aggressive. Of those who were regarded as non-aggressive, only 12% of their friends were regarded as aggressive. Longitudinal evidence of selective affiliation has also been provided. For instance, using samples of Dutch children followed from age 7 to 10, and French-Canadian children followed from age 9 to 12, Van Lier et al. (2005b) identified children who developed along distinct disruptive behaviour trajectories. In both samples, approximately 10% followed a high and deviant disruptive behaviour trajectory. Children in this trajectory affiliated with friends whose disruptive behaviours increased with age. These increases in the level of aggression of their friends were not matched by children who followed any of the other developmental trajectories. Thus, aggressive children do affiliate with other children, but their affiliation seems to be aimed at selecting other similarly aggressive friends.

Given that aggressive children tend to affiliate with aggressive friends, the question then becomes whether the behavioural characteristics of these friends matter in the development of the child's externalising problem behaviours. There is strong evidence they do. In addition to studying the selection of friends among preschoolers, Snyder et al. (1997) also studied the relationship between the amount of time these children spent with aggressive friends and change in their aggression from baseline levels over a three-month interval. They found increases in observed and teacher-rated aggressive behaviours among children who spent much time with aggressive friends. In contrast, children who spent little time with aggressive peers showed decreases in aggression over the follow-up period. Similarly, Vitaro and colleagues (1997) found that the level of delinquency at age 13 increased only if moderately aggressive boys at age 11 and 12 affiliated with aggressive friends. It is important to note that the apparent influence of aggressive children is not limited to their friends. Studies have also demonstrated that children tend to be pulled to the mean level of aggressiveness that is present in the group to which they belong. For instance, tracking elementary school children in homogeneous classrooms with respect to aggressive behaviours may increase aggressive behaviours in these children (Kellam et al., 1998; Warren et al., 2005). Similarly, highly aggressive children who participated in a small group intervention study showed decreases of such behaviours to the group mean level (Boxer et al., 2005). However, in the same study, a reverse pattern was found for initially non-aggressive children who became more aggressive, up to the level of the group's aggregate. Regardless of whether the effect is limited to friends, or to larger peer groups, these results show that children's own level of externalising problem behaviours is, in part, related to the level of externalising problem behaviours of their peers.

Deviancy Training

Now that we have established that affiliation with deviant peers matters, the question becomes what mechanism may account for the pathway through which this affiliation results in disruptive outcomes. Work by Dishion and others provides an answer (Dishion, Andrews & Crosby, 1995; Dishion et al., 1996). These authors analysed the topics and responses of 206 adolescent male friendship dyads during 25-minute conversations. They found that social reinforcement (positive affect, gesture) was strongly associated with the conversation topic. Among non-deviant dyads, social reinforcement followed normative conversation. In contrast, among deviant dyads, social reinforcement was most observed following rule-breaking conversation. Moreover, the authors found a strong association between the nature of the conversation during these laboratory sessions and increased rates of delinquency (Dishion et al., 1996) and tobacco, marijuana, and alcohol use (Dishion et al., 1995).

This process, called 'deviancy training', has received substantial empirical support since these initial studies. For instance, Patterson, Dishion and Yoerger (2000) showed that the association between involvement with deviant peers by age 10, and growth in arrests, substance use, and sexual intercourse from age 10 to age 18 was mediated by deviancy training at age 14. In addition, deviancy training has been held responsible for undermining intervention effects. For instance, Mager and colleagues (2005) reported unfavourable post-intervention externalising problem behaviour scores among initially low disruptive adolescents who were assigned to mixed groups (comprising adolescents who were high and adolescents who were low on conduct problems). Mediation analyses showed that the deviancy training that occurred in this group accounted for these unfavourable outcomes. Other intervention study findings substantiate that deviancy training is not only related to poor development, but also undermines intervention outcomes (Boxer et al., 2005; Cho, Hallfors & Sanchez, 2005; Dodge, Dishion & Lansford, 2006). In other words, it is not the affiliation with deviant friends *per se*, but the consequent learning of and reinforcement for deviant behaviours that shapes a child's own behaviour. Such reinforcement can be found at multiple levels. First, the friendship itself may be seen as reinforcing. Secondly, reciprocating deviant talk could be highly reinforcing, and third, positive reactions to deviant behaviours could serve as powerful reinforcement for such behaviour.

Thus, we have so far demonstrated that both peer rejection and affiliation with deviant peers may contribute to the development of externalising problem behaviours. We have also discussed the possible mechanisms through which rejection and selective affiliation may exacerbate externalising problem behaviours. In the following sections of this chapter, we will focus on moderators of the influence of peer processes in the development of externalising problem behaviours.

Moderators of Peer Contextual Risk Variables on Externalising Problem Behaviours

Rejection as the Moderator of Affiliation

Patterson, DeBaryshe and Ramsey (1989) proposed a model in which peer rejection and affiliation with deviant friends mediate the link between early childhood disruptiveness and later externalising problem behaviours in a sequential manner.

Studies that explored peer rejection and affiliation, and deviant peer affiliation longitudinally, found mixed results. For instance, Laird and colleagues (2001) found that peer rejection and deviant peer affiliation were correlated processes. However, because peer rejection but not affiliation with deviant peers predicted later externalising problem behaviours, the authors concluded that these processes may represent different pathways to externalising outcomes. In contrast, support for the sequential process between rejection and affiliation was found by Vitaro, Pedersen and Brendgen (2007), who reported that initial childhood disruptive behaviours resulted in rejection by peers, which in turn led to affiliation with deviant friends, resulting in violence in adolescence.

Age and Gender

Chronological age has been explored as a moderator of the influence of peer contextual risk variables. There is some evidence that the correlation between peer rejection and aggressive behaviours diminishes with age (Sandstrom & Coie, 1999). Furthermore, the link between peer rejection and later disruptive behaviours may depend on children's ages, so that younger children are more susceptible to the adverse effects of peer rejection than older children (McDougal et al., 2001).

With respect to age and the susceptibility to influences resulting from affiliation and deviancy training, no clear empirical data are present. It is reasonable to assume that because younger children are more closely monitored, these influences may be stronger among adolescents.

When regarding the child's gender, it has been found repeatedly that apart from early childhood (see Tremblay et al., 2004), girls exhibit lower levels of disruptive behaviours than boys (for example, Archer & Côte, 2005; Blokland, Nagin & Nieuwbeerta, 2005; Bongers et al., 2003, 2004; NICHD Early Child Care Research Network, 2004; Shaw, Lacourse & Nagin, 2005). Because girls affiliate with girls during childhood (Maccoby, 1998), it seems reasonable to assume that they are at lower risk for experiencing peer rejection and to affiliate with deviant disruptive peers. Two competing patterns may account for gender differences in the influence of peer environmental risk variables on the development of disruptive behaviours and delinquency. The first is that boys are more under the influence of peers in their development of externalising problem behaviours. Since boys exhibit higher levels of disruptive behaviours and delinquency, they are, stereotypically, more exposed to aggressive and delinquent acts than girls. However, the opposite may also be true. Because females are less exposed to aggressive and delinquent acts than boys, the relative influence may be larger for them than for males because aggression and externalising problem behaviours are an expected part of the social interactions and daily lives of males, but not of females.

Support for the hypothesis that boys are more under the influence of peers was found by Van Lier et al. (2005b). The authors found that peer rejection and affiliation with deviant peers was observed most among children who followed a high disruptive behaviour developmental trajectory in childhood. This trajectory was exclusively followed by males, suggesting that boys in particular are at risk of negative peer influences. Moreover, in the same study, a gender specific peer influence was found.

Only a minority of the females followed an intermediate disruptive behaviour trajectory, which was the most deviant disruptive behaviour trajectory for them. Compared to males in this trajectory, females affiliated with peers who were rated less disruptive, but were equally likely to experience peer rejection and equally high on delinquency as their male counterparts in this trajectory. This suggests that relative to males, females' pathways to delinquency were more influenced by peer rejection and less by deviant peer influences.

These findings were partly substantiated by the report of Hanish and colleagues (2005) among preschool and kindergarten children. These authors reported that children's observed activity level was predictive of externalising peer exposure for boys, but not for girls, suggesting that problem behaviours in boys are more predictive of association with externalising peers than for girls. However, the authors also studied the *effect* of exposure to externalising peers in boys and girls. The results showed that exposure to deviant peers predicted equally well aggressive behaviour in boys and in girls. However, exposure to externalising peers also predicted hyperactivity and anxiety among girls, but not among boys. Therefore, the gender of a child seems to moderate the likelihood of affiliating with deviant peers and encountering deviancy training.

Level of Externalising Problem Behaviours; Deviant versus (Relatively) Normative Developmental Trajectories

There is some evidence that the role of peer risk variables differs depending upon the level of externalising problem behaviours and, possibly related to this, the developmental trajectory that a child follows. A developmental trajectory assumes that children will follow distinct developmental courses. The causes of both onset and course of the behaviour in children in each of the developmental trajectories may be different. In this regard, an influential theory of antisocial behaviour is the life-course-persistent vs. adolescent-onset theory (Moffitt, 1993; Patterson & Yoerger, 1997). According to this theory, life-course-persistent antisocial behaviour originates early in life through minor neurological deficits and temperamental problems. When children grow older, the domain of environmental risk expands to poor relationships with peers and teachers and affiliation with deviant peers. In contrast, adolescent-onset antisocial behaviour is thought to emerge along with puberty, when previously well-functioning children are exposed to increased social and environmental risk factors, especially negative peer influences (Loeber & Stouthamer Loeber, 1998; Moffitt, 1993; Patterson & Yoerger, 1997). Therefore, affiliations with deviant peers seem to play a role in both developmental courses. However, while peer influences may play a crucial role in behavioural development of children who follow the adolescent-increasing path of antisocial behaviour, the onset – and possibly even the development – of antisocial behaviour may not be driven primarily by peer contextual risk variables in early-onset children.

There is a great deal of evidence, indeed, that suggests the early-onset, life-course persistent pathway is primarily caused by factors other than peer influences, such as temperamental, neuro-developmental, and family adversity risk factors (Arseneault et al. 2002, 2000; Jeglum-Bartusch et al., 1997; Moffitt & Caspi, 2001), and genetic influences (Lyons et al., 1995; Taylor, Iacono & McGue, 2000; Van der Valk et al., 1998). There is also evidence that the role of peers for children who follow the early-onset path is limited, but that peers are the primary force behind adolescent-increasing antisocial behaviours (Gatti et al., 2005; Van Lier, Vitaro & Wanner, in press; Vitaro et al., 1997). For instance, Vitaro et al. (1997) found that delinquency at age 13 was facilitated by affiliation with deviant friends for boys who were moderately aggressive in preadolescence but not for highly aggressive boys. The authors argued that the moderate trajectory of aggressive behaviours may correspond to a late onset, whereas the high trajectory may correspond to an early onset. Similarly, Van Lier, Vitaro and Wanner (in press) studied whether the level of disruptive behaviours of peers, over time, matched the level of this behaviour in children who followed a chronically high and adolescent-increasing trajectory from age 10 to 15. The authors found that children on the chronically high disruptive path affiliated with increasingly disruptive children with time. However, the level of disruptive behaviours of their friends was always lower than their own disruptive behaviours. Moreover, although they affiliated with increasingly deviant friends, their own level of deviancy did not increase. In contrast to early-onset children, the increase in disruptive behaviours of children on the adolescent-onset path was *preceded* by an increase in disruptive behaviours of their friends.

Parent-Child Interaction

Parental monitoring has been found to moderate the link between deviant peer affiliation and the development of child externalising problem behaviours. For instance, Galambos, Barker and Almeida (2003) studied whether behavioural control, psychological control and parental support moderated the influence of deviant peers on the development of externalising problem behaviours in early adolescence. The authors reported that in general, deviant peer affiliation resulted in increases in externalising problem behaviours with age. However, among children whose parents had higher levels of behavioural control, the influence of deviant peer affiliation was moderated in that it resulted in decreases in the growth of externalising problem behaviours. Although not specifically aimed at externalising problem behaviours, a number of Dutch studies explored how parent-child interaction influences child-peer interaction (Dekovic & Meeus, 1997; Meeus, Oosterwegel & Vollebergh, 2002). For instance, Dekovic and Meeus (1997) found that warm and supportive parenting increases a child's feelings of self-worth, which in turn positively affected the involvement with, and quality of, peer relations.

Peer Processes and Externalising Problem Behaviours: Research in the Netherlands

When reviewing the findings of the influence of peer processes on the development of externalising problem behaviours, one cannot be blind to the fact that the vast majority of research is conducted in North America. This raises the question whether the knowledge base of peer influence is applicable to the Dutch situation. There are a number of reasons to assume that peer processes may be differently associated with the development of children's problem behaviours in the Netherlands. First, comparisons of parent-reported aggressive behaviours between nine cultures showed that the Netherlands had significantly lower aggressive behaviour scores than the Omni cultural mean, whereas the aggression scores in the US were significantly higher (Crijnen, Achenbach & Verhulst, 1999). This difference in the level of aggressive behaviours could be accounted for by differences in peer processes with regard to externalising problem behaviours between these two cultures. Secondly, class compositions are relatively stable over the kindergarten and elementary school grades in the Netherlands; that is, children remain more or less in the same peer group throughout elementary school, whereas class compositions in North America often change from year to year. Such differences in peer group stability could influence the impact of peer processes. For instance, the influence of peer rejection can be more entrenched in the Netherlands because rejected children generally remain for a longer period with the peer group that rejected the child. Changing class composition would provide the opportunity for rejected children to avoid rejection once they enter the new peer group. Especially prolonged rejection experiences were found to be linked to increases in externalising problem behaviours. This would suggest that the influence of peers would be stronger in the Netherlands than in North America, which may contradict the reported lower levels of aggression.

There is, however, evidence to suggest that despite the cultural differences, the influence of peer rejection and affiliation with deviant peers on the development of externalising problem behaviours is more or less similar in the Netherlands as compared to North America. For instance, a number of classroom-based studies in the Netherlands produced sociometric data, which found clear links between rejection/dislikability and externalising problem behaviours (Van Lier & Crijnen, 2005; Veenstra et al., 2005). In addition, Van Lier and colleagues (2005) studied the longitudinal link between rejection, affiliation with deviant friends and the development of disruptive behaviours in Dutch and Canadian samples. In the Canadian sample, class compositions were not stable. Perhaps because of this, the probability of experiencing peer rejection for children who followed a high and increasingly deviant disruptive behaviour trajectory was lower than in the Dutch sample. However, in both samples, peer rejection was observed far more among highly deviant children. Moreover, in both samples, children on the deviant trajectory affiliated with increasingly deviant friends with respect to externalising problem behaviours. Although we cannot rule out cultural differences in the link between peer rejection and selective affiliation on the one hand, and the development of externalising problem behaviours on the other, it is clear that as in North America, both these processes are linked to the development of externalising problem behaviours in Dutch children.

To fully understand the influence of peer processes on the development of externalising problem behaviours, future research in the Netherlands should focus on a number of issues. Such research should be directed at establishing a causal link between peer processes and the development of child problem behaviours, and should be directed at identifying the conditions, or moderators, through which, or for whom, peer processes are most influential. It is important to note that these two topics are not mutually exclusive. By adopting specific research designs, *both* these topics can be very effectively combined. In the following section, we will review future key areas and research designs that should be adopted, and highlight promising Dutch research directed towards them.

The Need for Research Designs that Focus on Causal Links

Despite the findings that peer processes are associated with the development of child problem behaviours, it remains unclear whether peer processes are causally linked to such problem development. According to the *Causal* model, rejection by normative peers and/or deviant friends plays a causal role in aggression development and related problems, such as delinquency and drug use (Elliott, Huizinga & Ageton, 1985; Patterson et al., 1989). These peer experiences could either mediate the link between early personal or socio-familial risk factors and later externalised problems, or contribute an additive effect of their own. However, conclusions on a causal role of peer processes in externalising problem behaviours may be premature because of: (1) the correlated nature of negative peer influences with other environmental risk variables within the school, neighbourhood and home context (Deater-Deckard, Dodge, Bates & Pettit, 1998; Dekovic, 1999); or because: (2) personal variables, such as the genetic likelihood of developing externalising problem behaviours may account for the association. That is, children's genes may influence the risks they encounter, or friends' behavioural characteristics may not predict the disruptive behaviour outcomes above and beyond genetic influences. This is in line with the *Incidental* or *Selection* model, which proclaims that early childhood disruptive behaviours lead independently to prolonged aggression behaviours and delinquency. According to this model, aggressive children will experience peer rejection and/or association with deviant peers, but these processes are seen as a consequence of deviant behaviours, not as the cause (Coie et al., 1995a; Gottfredson & Hirschi, 1990). A relationship between these variables can exist, but this relationship is viewed as spurious and attributable to a common link with the same third variable (that is, disruptiveness).

To arrive at causal inferences on the link between risk variables and outcomes, three research designs have been suggested (Rutter et al., 2001):

1. longitudinal models of within-individual change, in which each individual serves as their own control (that is, does the affiliation with deviant friends increase externalising problem behaviours above and beyond other experiences?);
2. randomised treatment experiments to test whether reductions in the manifestation of the risk variable are linked to the changes in the manifestation of the outcome (that is, are reductions in disruptive behaviours as a result of intervention linked to reductions in peer rejection and/or affiliation with non-deviant children?), and
3. behavioural-genetic designs to control for the genetic basis of problem behaviours and gene-environment interplay.

It is important to notice that none of these designs alone can provide decisive proof of causation, but aggregate findings from several of these sources can make a strong case.

Within-Individual Change Studies

With regard to the role of peer rejection, there is some evidence that the experience of peer rejection adds to the level of externalising problem behaviours above and beyond control variables. As mentioned earlier, the experience of peer rejection in the first grade predicted increased levels of Attention-Deficit/Hyperactivity Disorder (ADHD) symptoms and proactive and reactive aggression in the third and fourth grade, even when controlling for first-graders' levels of ADHD and aggression (Miller-Johnson et al., 2002). In addition, Miller-Johnson et al. (1999) and Dodge et al. (2003) reported that the combination of aggression *and* rejection only predicted the most serious forms of externalising problem behaviours in childhood and early adolescence. In fact, Dodge et al. (2003) reported that each successive rejection experience was uniquely associated with increases in aggression among those who were already high on aggression in kindergarten.

Some studies also focused on the *temporal* relationship between affiliation with deviant friends and increases in externalising problem behaviours. For instance, Lacourse and colleagues (2003) identified distinct probability groups for gang affiliation (as an index for affiliation with severely disruptive peers). The authors found that affiliation with gangs preceded the increase in delinquent acts. Moreover, leaving delinquent peer groups was associated with decreases in the individual's violence. In addition, Gatti et al. (2005) studied the influence of gang membership on the level of delinquency in adolescents followed annually from age 14 to 16. The authors distinguished 'transient' gang members (that is, adolescents who were a gang member at some point in the studied period, but not at each assessment) from adolescents who never joined a gang in the studied period. They reported increased delinquency scores among transient gang members when they were part of the gang. When these transient adolescents were not members of a gang, their level of delinquency was similar to those adolescents who never joined gangs. More importantly, the increased levels of delinquency were associated with gang membership *and* peer delinquency above and beyond personal and environmental control variables. Taken together, there is some evidence on the specific role of peer processes in the development of increasing externalising problem behaviours. However, evidence is incomplete and lacking for (early) childhood in particular (see Boivin, Vitaro & Poulin, 2005). Moreover, to study this, longitudinal research is needed where repeated assessments of both peer processes and outcomes are included. However, a number of methodological issues need to be considered when adopting this approach. First, because in an observational study both the mediators (peer rejection, deviant peer affiliation) and outcomes (aggression) are not controlled/manipulated (for example, through intervention), both these variables may cause each other, making it impossible to disentangle them. One way to overcome this problem would be to assess peer variables and outcome measures at each data wave on at least two occasions. This would enable the use of a bi-directional (or cross-lagged) model that could aid in teasing out whether changes in peer acceptance/deviant peer affiliation mediate the changes in aggression, or whether peer processes simply co-occur but are not related to changes in aggression over time. The second issue is more difficult to overcome. This pertains to the possibility of missing important mediators (Howe, Reiss & Yuh, 2002). Omitted mediator(s) may share considerable variance with the study mediator (that is, peers) and the distal outcome (for example, delinquency). Hence, links between the latter variables may well be spurious. For instance, deviant peer affiliation may be linked to poor parenting practices, as shown previously. Therefore, when adopting the within-individual difference design, it is preferable to have longitudinal studies with repeated assessments of peer processes and outcomes, and a full family design in which the child together with friends and family members are included. Although not directed at children, project RADAR (Research of Adolescents' Development and Relationships) is a Dutch longitudinal study on the development of children that includes assessments of both child-friends interaction, and parent-child and sibling-child interaction, in order to study the role of, and the changes within, the social network. Another project that aims to understand behaviour development in adolescence and incorporates measurements of both parent-child and peer-child interactions is Tracking Adolescents' Individual Lives Survey (TRAILS).

Experimental Studies

The advantage of experimental studies is that intervention can be aimed at the manipulation of the outcome variable (aggression) or be directed at the manipulations of the hypothesised causal risk variable (peer rejection/affiliation with deviant peers). When studied in a randomised controlled setting, experimental studies are potentially very powerful in studying the role of peers in the development of externalising problem behaviours. According to the *Causal* model, a preventive intervention aimed at reducing early disruptive behaviours is successful only when it first fosters social acceptance by the normative peer group and/or associations with non-deviant friends. If peer processes are found to mediate the reductions in aggressive behaviours, due to intervention, it can be concluded that peer processes are indeed a necessary and sufficient element in the developmental chain leading to (reduced) aggression and related problems. Partial mediation would suggest that they are necessary but not sufficient elements. However, if the experiment fails to impact peer processes, or if changes in peer processes do not mediate the reductions in aggression in the child, this would provide evidence for the *Incidental* model.

A number of randomised intervention studies have explored the mediating relationship between indices of peer contextual risk variables and changes in externalising problem behaviours. For instance, Bierman et al. (2002) found lower levels of third-grade teacher-rated oppositional and aggressive behaviours in intervention children in the Fast Track intervention study (Conduct Problems Prevention Research Group, 1992) compared to controls. These decreases in oppositional and aggressive behaviours mediated the positive effect of the intervention on fourth-grade social preference scores. Similarly, the reduced risk for conduct disorder (Vitaro et al., 1999) and delinquency (Vitaro, Brendgen &

Tremblay, 2001) at age 13, as observed among males in the Montreal experimental study (Tremblay et al., 1991), were, among other variables, mediated by their lower probability to affiliate with deviant peers at age 10–12.

With regard to Dutch research, Van Lier, Vuijk and Crijnen (2005) studied the impact of the intervention called *Taakspel* (based on the Good Behaviour Game; Dolan et al., 1989) on developmental trajectories of disruptive behaviours from age 7 to age 11. The authors found that intervention children who started on a high–disruptive behaviour trajectory – 10% of all children – had large decreases in problem behaviours due to intervention. These decreases in disruptive behaviours coincided with an increased tendency over time to select non-deviant peers as their friends. Moreover, compared to their control group counterparts, the probability of being rejected at age 10 was reduced by 47% (75% of the high-disruptive control group children received a rejected status at age 10 compared to 40% of the intervention children who started off on the high-disruptive trajectory).

Although the above-mentioned programmes were experimental studies, they did not specifically aim to manipulate peer processes, however, thus making it difficult to confirm that reductions in problem behaviours were truly the result of improved peer relations, or alternatively, that the resulting improved peer relations were due to the reductions in aggressive behaviours. Moreover, these studies cannot confirm that the reductions in aggression did not result from other processes yet to be studied (see Howe et al., 2002). A more direct test for peer processes being causally linked with externalising problem behaviours would be to actively manipulate the processes themselves. For instance, rejected children could be made aware of their social status and their bias in encoding and interpreting social situations. They could be trained in social skills and helped in building self-esteem to initiate contact with prosocial peers. Non-rejected peers could also be made aware of their rejecting behaviours and be supported in having an open mind to the rejected child, especially when the rejected child is helped in improving their behaviour, social skills and information processing.

A second option is to make peers co-therapists. One possibility is to train children in conflict skills and have them mediate conflict situations on the playground, which in one study was shown to be effective (Cunningham et al., 1998). Another approach is to facilitate interaction between aggressive children and those prosocial peers with whom they usually do not associate by forming them into dyads or groups. Aggressive children could then learn the social skills and prosocial norms of the low aggressive peers and receive positive reinforcement for social instead of deviant behaviours.

One potential problem when focusing on specific mechanisms is that the intervention may not be effective. That is, when only one mechanism is manipulated, this may be ineffective in reducing externalising problem behaviours. Moreover, there is the risk of iatrogenic effects. A number of recent studies that matched aggressive with non-aggressive peers in an effort to break the cycle of selective affiliation found that initially non-aggressive children adopted the deviant behaviours of the aggressive children (Boxer et al., 2005; Cho et al., 2005; Dishion, McCord & Poulin, 1999; Dishion, Poulin & Burraston, 2001; Lavallee, Bierman & Nix, 2005; Mager et al., 2005). A recent overview of the effectiveness of peer-group counselling programmes targeting aggression and violence concluded that deviant peer effects reduce the overall effectiveness of programmes and may even result in net adverse effects (Dodge et al., 2006). And although the findings of these studies may be supportive of a causal connection between peer processes, it also shows that these peer processes operate in ways not yet well understood (Dishion & Dodge, 2005).

From the above-mentioned studies, it is clear – and painfully illustrated by the reported iatrogenic effects – that we do not know enough about the mechanism through which peer influences operate. Despite this, experimental studies remain potentially very promising, if effort is made to control the possible negative effects. A number of Dutch intervention projects that included assessments of peer processes are currently being conducted, although to our knowledge no randomised control trial (RCT) is aimed at specifically manipulating peer processes. However, one programme, project *Spelregels*, is a longitudinal study on the impact of both a classroom-based intervention, the Good Behaviour Game, and a parent management training programme, *Opvoeden & Zo*, with children followed from age 6 onward. In this project, repeated assessments of peer processes and possible moderating variables are included. Another project focuses on social-emotional development by using a classroom-based intervention (the PATHS curriculum) among elementary school children aged 5–10 at the start of the project, who will then be followed for two years. In addition to measures of social-emotional development, peer processes are assessed, which will enable study of the interplay between these processes.

Peer Processes in Genetic Informative Samples

It is important to study the role of peer contextual risk variables while controlling for the genetic likelihood to develop externalising problem behaviours. It is well established that a large percentage of the population variance in the development of externalising problem behaviours is accounted for by genetic influence. In fact, the high heritability in children's externalising problem behaviours has been found repeatedly (see Rhee & Waldman, 2002 for a review). It has also been found in Dutch twins (Bartels et al., 2004; Ligthart et al., 2005; Van der Valk et al., 2003, 1998). This genetic influence is even more prevalent among children who are at high risk for developing persistent externalising problem behaviours (Lyons et al., 1995; Taylor et al., 2000; Van der Valk et al., 1998), the group which is hypothesised to be most exposed to negative peer processes. Consequently, peer contextual risk variables may not contribute to the development of externalising problem behaviours *above and beyond* genetic influences, or, alternatively, peer contextual risk variables may be under the control of genes. Such findings would undermine the causal model and instead suggest that, at a minimum, part of the association is accounted for by personal variables. There is some evidence for this. The genetic influence in children's externalising problem behaviours has been found to shape also the environment these children encounter because 'environmental' risk variables (that is, peer processes) have been found to be – in part – under the control of genes (gene-environment correlation). Studies in adolescent (Manke et al., 1995; Pike et al., 2000; Rose, 2002) and adult twin samples (Rushton & Bons, 2005), for instance, found higher similarities between monozygotic friends' characteristics than dizygotic friends' characteristics. This suggests that friends' characteristics are – in part – linked to a person's genetic makeup. If this is the case, then the seemingly independent influence of deviant friends on a child's development of externalising problem behaviours may in fact be a correlate of the same genes that account for the development of externalising problem behaviours in the child.

Little research has been directed at the role of combined genetic and peer environmental influences on the development of disruptive behaviours in children, none of which has been conducted on Dutch samples. However, two recent studies (Bullock, Deater-Deckard & Leve, 2006; Van Lier et al., 2006) looked at the gene-environmental ecology of friends' aggressive behaviours in a sample of twins. In the study by Bullock et al. (2006) which focused on 6–14-year-old twins, there was a moderate heritability estimate for teacher-rated deviant peer affiliation, but not for the externalising problem behaviours of the friends of the twins, as rated by both teachers and independent observers. In the study by Van Lier and colleagues (2006) among kindergarten twins, a modest heritability estimate was found for teacher- and peer-rated friends' physical aggressive behaviours. In this last study, it was also found that both genetic influences and friends' aggressiveness independently predicted kindergarten children's physical aggression. This study therefore provided the first evidence that friends' aggression adds uniquely to the prediction of males' physical aggressive behaviours while controlling for these children's genetic likelihood for aggression.

Although there is a good tradition of studying the gene-environmental ecology of externalising problem behaviours in the Netherlands, especially through the Netherlands Twin Register (Boomsma et al., 2002), to our knowledge no studies have been directed at incorporating peer contextual influences in genetic informative Dutch samples. This is much needed however, because our knowledge of a possible causal role of peer influences on the development of problem behaviours will remain incomplete if we do not account for the genetic influences on the development of such problems.

Focus on Moderators and Mechanisms

The rather disappointing iatrogenic effects found in some recent prevention studies are a very clear illustration that more research is needed to better understand the role of peer risk variables in the aetiology of externalising problem behaviours. Such research should focus on the interplay between rejection and affiliation, age and gender differences, and the mechanism through which peer contextual risk factors result in externalising problem behaviours. These studies on moderators and mediators should aim at the interplay between peer influence and their interaction with other moderating variables, and on the interplay between moderating and mediating variables.

Age and Gender

A field that is almost totally ignored is peer influences in early childhood (Boivin, Vitaro & Poulin, 2005). However, some studies that started in kindergarten samples demonstrated that peer influences begin to operate early (Estell et al., 2002; Snyder et al., 1997). Aggressive behaviours are frequently observed in preschool children (NICHD Early Child Care Research Network, 2004; Tremblay et al., 2004), which may indicate that the consequences of this behaviour may also emerge early. Because later peer interactions are likely to be perceived and processed in light of earlier experiences, knowledge about when peer processes start to operate is needed.

With regard to gender and the influence of peers on the development of child problem behaviours, it is important to note that most studies have focused on male forms of problem behaviours as outcomes. As Hartup (2005) suggested, girls may be more influential with girls than boys when feminine norms and behaviours are involved, while the reverse occurs when masculine norms and behaviours are involved. For instance, girls have been found to engage in relational forms of aggression (for example, gossiping, excluding peers from group activities, and so on), whereas boys mainly engage in physical aggression, especially in childhood (Crick, 1997; Crick, Casas & Mosher, 1997). Because research on peer processes in aggression development has mainly concentrated on male forms of aggression, it may well be that (differences in) the findings with regard to females result from this gender bias.

Multiple Levels of Friendship

Apart from dyadic friendships with – possibly – multiple friends, children are also involved in small groups of friends and larger peer groups such as classrooms. Each of these levels of friendship can influence a child's behaviour, possibly in different ways. For instance, in the Utrecht Social Development Project, Van den Oord and Rispens (1999) showed that lower levels of teacher-reported aggression existed where many of the children in classes indicated they liked to play with each other, and in classes where children have 'access' to many other children, either through direct friendship choices or via friendship networks. Such class processes may depend upon moderating variables. For instance, as shown previously, the engagement in many friendship cliques may depend upon the quality of parent-child interaction, as shown by Dekovic & Meeus (1997), illustrating that multiple moderating courses should be studied to fully understand peer processes.

Genetic Influences

Apart from controlling for genetic traits when studying peer influences, it is important to note that genetic background may also moderate the influence of peer contextual variables in predicting externalising outcomes (gene-environment interaction). Support for Gene x Environment (GxE) in the development of externalising problem behaviours has been found for family-contextual risk variables (for example, maltreatment by parents; Caspi et al., 2002; Jaffee et al., 2005). The study by Van Lier et al. (2006) also explored whether the genetic influences on children's development of aggressive behaviours moderated their susceptibility to friends' aggressive behaviours. Indeed, it was found that kindergarten children's physical aggression was increased most when genetically vulnerable children interact with aggressive friends, providing the first evidence that the influence of peers on the development of aggressive behaviours in part depends upon genetic factors.

In addition to the sex of the child, and possibly the outcome studied (note that physical aggression is especially observed among boys), age may also be of influence. Because it has been found that the selection of friends may in part come under the control of genes in late childhood, adolescence and adulthood (that is, gene-environment correlation: rGE), it is uncertain whether interactions between genetic background and the influences of deviant friends remain a predictor of the child's aggressive behaviours. It is possible that the interaction between genetic liability and the influences of friends in early childhood (GxE) may direct already vulnerable children to more actively select friends whose behaviour resembles their own (rGE; that is, the GxE experiences in early childhood may cause rGE later in life). Therefore, as stated earlier, knowledge about the role of peer processes in aggression development will remain incomplete if the genetic likelihood of children to develop aggression and the interplay with peer processes is not taken into account. It also seems important to address the possible moderating role of age, and also of environmental variables such as parental monitoring, while studying this issue. It is, however, important to note that the same is true for research on the gene-environmental ecology of externalising problem behaviours. The influence of genes on externalising problem behaviours can be a direct effect (that is, genes causing problem behaviours), or the effect of an interaction between genes and environmental influences (that is, genetic liability X deviant friend affiliations, as shown above). Therefore, both phenomena need to be accounted for; that is, from a perspective of studying the gene-environmental ecology of externalising problem behaviours, as well as from a perspective of understanding the influence of peers on its development.

Conclusions

Much is already known about peer relationships as potential risk factors for the development of externalising problem behaviours. However, far more longitudinal research is needed to effectively prevent peer risk variables influencing this development. As mentioned earlier, such studies should incorporate experimental components, preferably components that target specific risk variables in randomised controlled settings, while carefully monitoring possible iatrogenic effects. In addition, peer influences should be studied, taking into account genetic factors. When feasible, such studies should incorporate as many of the moderating variables as possible. These studies should start early in life to establish when peer contextual risks are starting to operate and how they influence children's further development, including the selection of friends. Such studies should include measures on the social context of the child – which includes parents and possibly siblings – in addition to peers, friends and friendship networks. These friends are not necessarily part of the classroom, as is the focus of most current studies, but may represent influences from a wider context. For instance, attending unstructured recreation centres, in which young people were exposed to externalising peers, has been related to increases in externalising problem behaviours (Mahoney, Stattin & Magnusson, 2001). Moreover, such studies should include measures of possible mediating variables, such as deviancy training between peers or coercion and rejecting behaviours. The results of these studies will provide much-needed insight into the precise role of peers in the development of externalising problem behaviours and the conditions under which these processes operate. This insight can then be used to develop intervention programmes that use peers more effectively as intervention agents or intervention targets in our effort to prevent the further development of externalising problem behaviours and their many related serious negative consequences.

Chapter 8

Bullying in Primary School

Ton Mooij

In 1982, several Norwegian students committed suicide as a result of exposure to bullying over long periods of time. One result of this tragedy was the initiation of a nationwide campaign against bullying and victimisation (Olweus, 1984). Parents, teachers, school officials and individuals involved with national policy in many countries became interested in bullying as a serious form of disruptive behaviours. In several countries, research was carried out to provide more information on bullying and its effects on those being bullied in and around schools (American Psychological Association, 1993; Haselager & Van Lieshout, 1992; Van Lieshout, Haselager & Liebrand, 1992; Olweus, 1987; Roland, 1989; Smith & Sharp, 1994).

In this chapter, I will focus on the bullying of and by Dutch students below age 13. The first questions to be answered are what is 'bullying', and how can it be distinguished from other types of disruptive behaviours? The answer to these questions are given by means of conceptual definitions, based on empirical research and the use of precise instrumentation to measure relevant bullying behaviours. Secondly, how common is bullying and being bullied among students aged 4–12 in preschools and primary schools? As in other countries, there is some good information available about bullying in the Netherlands (see Chapter 7, this volume). Usually, research consists of descriptive statistics of bullying and victimisation and their relationships to variables such as other persons, classrooms and schools (for example, Lane, 1989; Stevens, de Bourdeaudhuij & Van Oost, 2000).

Third, what are the characteristics or variables that function either as correlates or as causes of bullying behaviour? Many risk and promotive factors may be relevant and are mentioned in intervention research to reduce bullying (Olweus, 1991, 1993; Sharp & Smith, 1993). The final, and probably most important question, focuses on systemic or sustainable prevention of bullying behaviour. In a review of Dutch youth health-intervention programmes, Hermanns, Öry and Schrijvers (2005) were negative about the available programmes and proposed the implementation of effective programmes from the US that concentrated on at-risk youth. In this chapter, however, I will sketch a somewhat different and more optimistic picture of systemic multilevel prevention in preschool and primary schools in the Netherlands. I will suggest substantive collaboration between educational practitioners and youth health and other community staff to assist parents and children in the effective prevention of bullying.

Concepts of Bullying and Being Bullied

Bullying denotes aggressive behaviour that is characterised by individuals' wilful and conscious desire to hurt and place another person under stress (Pellegrini & Long, 2002; Tattum, 1993). According to Olweus (1991), students' bullying refers to saying mean or annoying things to each other; or to beat, kick, threaten, or lock up each other. Bullying typically occurs repeatedly over time, and represents an imbalance of power between the bully (or a group of bullies) and the *victim* or scapegoat (Allport, 1948). *Victimisation* refers to the process of being bullied and refers to individuals experiencing aggressive, damaging, or destructive acts as a result of bullying. A student who is a victim of bullying often has difficulty defending him- or herself. Victim behaviour has been studied longitudinally and research indicates, for example, that victimisation in school is related to victimisation in the workplace later on (Smith et al., 2003).

Bullying should not be confused with teasing, where two or more persons challenge each other in more or less friendly ways (Mooij, 1992). Moreover, if two or more students quarrel or fight and are of roughly the same strength, bullying is not at stake either. A similarity between aggression and bullying is that both imply the breaking of the victim's will in a deliberate and conscious manner, although this does not need to mean that the perpetrator is always fully aware of the consequences of their actions. Bullying may take place for years and remain relatively unnoticed by others, particularly in cases of social exclusion. Aggression compared to bullying may be much outwardly damaging and therefore be recognised more easily.

A person or a group of people can be both bully and victim at roughly the same time. *Bully/victims* are individuals or groups who act as bullies and are bullied themselves (Wolke et al., 2001). This may, for example, happen in situations where social relations between individuals or groups are more or less hierarchic in nature, for example, in a street gang (Haagse Ondersteunings Functie, 1994). Research-based information about different concepts of bullying using Dutch students' self-descriptions can be found in Mooij (1992) where this author analysed the scores of 1,065 primary-school and 1,055 secondary-school students from Olweus' (1991) questionnaire and grouped the items on the basis of their statistical interrelationships. An overview of the empirical results with respect to six concepts is given in Table 8.1. The results revealed that a student being bullied or victimised is usually bullied both directly and indirectly, or physically and socially. Also, expressing a more negative attitude towards bullying is associated with higher scores for being bullied both directly and indirectly, higher scores for trying to stop bullying, and lower scores for bullying other students and bullying the teacher. Bullying other students and bullying the teacher also correlate highly.

Furthermore, Mooij (1992) checked whether self-description of bullying corresponded with description by the student's classmates (peer nomination). As expected, self-description of bullying other students and bullying the teacher was positively related to being described as a bully by classmates. Self-description of having a negative attitude towards bullying corresponded with being seen by others as sympathetic. Self-description of being bullied directly and indirectly co-occurred with being described by others as a scapegoat. These results confirmed that self-

Table 8.1 Bullying concepts, descriptions by items, and number of items included

Concept	Description of concepts by items	N items
1. Being bullied directly	Being bullied physically and continuously (last school-year, this school-year, during the last five days), everywhere (at school, on the way to and from school), and in different ways (being kicked, being told mean things, or called names)	6
2. Being bullied indirectly	Being socially isolated: disliking break-times, having hardly any good friends in class, often feeling lonely at school and during break-times, and more often thinking that you are less liked than the other students in class	5
3. Bullying	Bullying continuously (last school-year, this school-year, during the last five days) and everywhere (at school, on the way to and from school), and saying that you like bullying	5
4. Negative attitude towards bullying	Not liking that other children are bullied, helping a bullied child of your own age, and not liking children who bully other children	3
5. Bullying the teacher	Noticing children who tried to bully the teacher, more cooperation with other students in bullying the teacher, and having done this already more times during the last school-year	3
6. Stopping bullying	Observing that the teacher, other children, or other people on the way to and from school are trying to put an end to bullying	3

description of bullying and being bullied corresponded with classmates' reports of the student's behaviour.

Mooij (1992) also showed that, first, a student perceived as bullying and quarrelling with other students is also perceived as disrupting lessons, not being liked by the nominating student, and not being shy. Secondly, liking the other student, friendship and cooperativeness with respect to the other student tend to go together. Third, being bullied often, not being liked, and being non-assertive are characteristic behaviours of the victim or scapegoat. It is interesting to note that both bullies and victims are not liked or not considered as sympathetic by others. Without encouragement, a student will not usually assist or help students who become a victim or a scapegoat, because cooperation occurs only with 'sympathetic' students.

How Common is Bullying and Victimisation by Bullying?

Table 8.2 presents the prevalence of bullying and victimisation by means of bullying in a representative sample of 1,065 primary-school students aged 9–12 in the

Table 8.2 Percentages of children being bullied and bullying in primary schools

Frequency	Netherlands*		Belgium/Flanders**		Netherlands***	
	Being bullied	*Bullying*	*Being bullied*	*Bullying*	*Being bullied*	*Bullying*
Not this school-year	39	30	–	–	55	63
Only once or twice	38	50	–	–	28	32
Now and then/ regularly	15 (23)	14 (20)	23	16	6 (16)	3 (6)
Once a week	4 (8)	3 (6)	–	–	3 (10)	1 (3)
Several times a week	4	3	–	–	7	2

Source: *Mooij (1992); **Klasse (1994); ***Fekkes (2005).

Netherlands in the school year 1990–91 (Mooij, 1992), based on Olweus' (1991) bullying questionnaire. The findings show that being bullied 'several times a week' was reported by 4% of the students. If the criterion was bullied 'once a week', then the prevalence doubled to 8% (see the cumulative percentage between brackets), and figures further increased to 23% when the criterion was 'now and then'. The comparable percentage for bullying in Dutch primary schools was 20%. The Dutch results can be compared to results obtained in Flanders (the Dutch-speaking part of Belgium) which used the same questionnaire (Klasse, 1994). The percentages on being bullied 'now and then' or 'more' frequently in the Dutch and Flemish studies are identical (23%), while the percentages of bullying are similar (20% and 16%, respectively).

In a non-representative Dutch study, Fekkes (2005) studied 2,766 students aged 9–11 in a longitudinal quasi-experimental design. He used two items of Olweus' questionnaire on bullying and being bullied, but changed the answer categories, so the results cannot be directly compared. The last two columns in Table 8.2 show adaptation of his answer alternatives to those in the other studies.

Correlates and Multilevel Causes

Development of Truancy, Poor Academic Performance and Delinquency

Development of a child's social and affective adjustment is not only influenced by both genetic or biological and individually specific environmental or family characteristics (see Chapters 5 and 6, this volume), but also by peer characteristics (see Chapter 7, this volume) and other types of environmental variables (Goleman, 1995; Van Lieshout et al., 2001). There does not appear to be Dutch research on the genetic or biological determinants of bullying (see further Loeber & Farrington, 2001). Bullying or related aggressive behaviours may already be shown at a very young age, at home or in preschool (Olweus, 1980). Preschool teachers can notice various types of maladjusted or disturbing behaviours in students (Hermanns, 1979, 1980). However, adequate measures to stop or prevent such behaviours are not always taken. Longitudinal qualitative research by Mooij (1999a, 1999b) revealed how 4-year-old children, from their first day in preschool, needed an educational environment that supports their capabilities and potentials. He presented various examples of children who reacted individually to an unsuitable educational situation by either externalising problem behaviours (such as stubborn or aggressive behaviours towards other students and the teacher) or internalising problem behaviours (such as psychosomatic problems and preschool avoidance behaviour).

International research reveals that bullying may be accompanied by violence and truancy, poor academic performance, running away from home, dropping out of school, or developing a criminal career (Beirn, Kinsey & McGinn, 1972; Ferwerda, 1992; Jackson, 1968; Korte, 1992; Mooij, 1980; Reich & Young, 1975; US Department of Health, Education and Welfare, 1973; Van der Meer, 1988). Concerning Dutch primary-school students, however, no reliable or valid information with respect to the frequency of truancy, running away from home, dropping-out, or delinquency appears to exist,. One reason for this is that, in the Netherlands, information about students' disruptive behaviours is distributed among various domains such as schools, youth health and youth care organisations, and independent professionals (Moors, Pardoel & Bruinsma, 2005; Zeijl, Keuzenkamp & Beker, 2003). Moreover, no general judicial guidelines or measures exist for delinquent children (Gilsing & Keuzenkamp, 2004). The so-called 'twelve-minus' project has been designed to provide adequate treatment and support (Zeijl et al., 2003), but the project is not yet implemented countrywide.

Social Characteristics of Group Processes

Several social aspects of bullying and other types of aggressive processes may influence the development of desirable student behaviours. Examples are the rules and characteristics of social processes between persons or groups (Lewin, Lippitt & White, 1939; Marsh, Rosser & Harré, 1978; Mulder, 1977). Van Lieshout and colleagues (2004) investigated relationship networks of students in primary education (N=2,518) and secondary education (N=3,325). The authors distinguished between four relationship networks to indicate a student's social competence: only friendship; friendship and antipathy; only antipathy, and without friendship and antipathy. Moreover, the authors expected that a student's relationship network would be differentially related to his or her prosocial, disruptive, or socially reluctant behaviour. The results showed that the number of antipathies, gender, and time of measurement best accounted for individual differences in disruptive behaviours. Compared to girls, boys bullied other children more, were less prosocial, more disruptive and socially more clumsy. Moreover, older students in secondary schools were socially more active, bullied more and showed more prosocial, disruptive and socially clumsy behaviours than younger students in primary education. Students with the relationship network 'only friendship' scored lowest on being a victim of bullying; students with the relationship network 'only antipathy' scored highest on being a victim; and students with the relationship network 'friendship and antipathy' scored highest on bullying.

Classrooms, Teacher Management and School Characteristics

Characteristics at Different Levels

Classrooms constitute complex social group processes. Many interactional processes between students and between students and teachers occur simultaneously and take up a great deal of a teacher's attention and their attempts to control students' social interactions (Kounin, 1970; Mooij, 1982). Various social and didactical characteristics of academic lessons occur in classrooms. Examples are the degree to which the lessons are task- or content-oriented, directed at organisational or learning supporting activities, directed at social or group relationships between students or between students and teachers, order and discipline directed, or concentrated on external activities such as an excursion or visit to a museum. Furthermore, evaluation or assessment characteristics may stimulate or block either collaboration or competition between students. This may lead to success for some students and cause lack of success, demotivation, and compensating disruptive and bullying behaviour for others (Arbeitsgruppe Schulforschung, 1980; Kaplan, Gheen & Midgley, 2002).

A student's bullying can be influenced by educational characteristics at different levels and may, for example, partly reflect the teacher's shortcomings or reluctance to manage the social behaviour of all students in a classroom. In Japan, Yoneyama and Naito (2003) found that specific school circumstances and cultural conditions promoted a 'group dynamic' function of bullying between students and between students and teachers. The authors proposed that the following conditions contributed to bullying: stress as a result of achievement pressure and/or the perceived meaninglessness of studying, power-dominated relationships between teachers and students, and the social consequences of the use of corporal punishment by teachers. Thus, bullying processes can be influenced by characteristics or factors at different educational levels (Cronbach, 1983; Goldstein, 1995; Mooij, 1987).

Student and Classroom Level

To explore the relevance of the distinction between different levels in bullying research, Mooij (1992) calculated students' relative bullying scores by expressing these as deviations from the classroom mean of bullying. Principal-factor analysis of the relative scores on bullying of students in primary and secondary education led to the following factors. A first factor was labelled: 'a student who is being bullied relatively more', and the behaviours that loaded on this factor were: being bullied directly and indirectly with being bullied relatively more, being bullied elsewhere than at school, being identified by classmates as a scapegoat, and being less sympathetic. The second factor was labelled: 'a student who is bullying'. The behaviours that loaded on this factor indicated self-descriptive items about bullying relatively more, having positive opinions about bullying, being identified by classmates as a bully, bullying the teacher, and male gender. The third factor was named: 'student bullying as a class phenomenon'. This factor combined self-descriptions about seeing several children being bullied in the classroom, seeing several children bullying others in the classroom, bullying relatively more, being bullied directly relatively more, bullying the teacher, and attempts to stop bullying. This factor thus represents bullying as a collective social and teacher-related process, independent from individual-level variables (factors 1 and 2).

Classroom Level

At the classroom level, factor analysis can clarify interrelationships between teachers' didactical, organisational and social management behaviour, and mean and heterogeneity scores of students' bullying. Mooij (1992) used a principal-component factor analysis to provide more information about bullying as a collective or group phenomenon. A first factor united various characteristics of a primary class including higher mean scores on being bullied directly and indirectly. A second factor was labelled a 'bullying class with relatively more boys' and grouped characteristics of a bullying class (both primary and secondary education). The third factor revealed a 'class with a weak teacher's management and a high degree of bullying'. The fourth factor grouped characteristics with respect to a 'class with students from well-to-do families with easier teacher management'. In factor five, a 'class with a socially well-functioning teacher', the grouping of characteristics referred to higher percentages of time per week that the teacher spent on group management/social relations within class and on disciplinary aspects, a lower mean score of students on seeing that there was an effort to try to stop bullying, and less intensive surveillance during breaks.

Several groups of variables then seem relevant to long-range institutionalised class processes related to bullying and victimisation. The successive factors suggest that in the Netherlands, bullying is more characteristic of students aged 9–12 in primary education than for students aged 12–17 in secondary education (see factor 1) and to a specific class (see factors 2–5). Bullying of the teacher is related to a lack of effective management of bullying; in larger classes of students from higher socioeconomic backgrounds bullying occurs relatively more often, despite the higher percentages of time spent on social group relationships; finally, spending more time on social group and disciplinary processes in class is related to lower occurrences of trying to stop bullying, so this may prevent bullying. In particular, the third and fifth factors suggest teacher-dependent relationships between teachers' social, didactical and organisational behaviour, and bullying phenomena and social management and disciplinary variables in class.

School Level

School characteristics are variables located at the school level, which for example describe all students, the teachers, the management, or the social-pedagogical climate of a school. An often-stated opinion is that bullying and other forms of disruptive behaviours occur relatively more in schools with higher numbers of students (school size). To check this point, Mooij (1992) correlated school size with the bullying and victimisation school mean variables. In primary schools, mean bullying variables did not correlate with school size. In secondary schools, however, significant correlations were found. The higher the number of students in school, the fewer students experienced that they were bullied directly ($r=-.52$), the fewer students engaged in bullying (r=-.66), and the less heterogeneity in bullying existed in school (r=-.57). In addition, fewer teachers were bullied by the students (r=-.53). Three follow-up surveys examined bullying and violence in secondary education (Mooij, 1994, 2001, 2005; Mooij, Sijbers & Sperber, 2006). Again, the larger the numbers of students in secondary school, the lower the incidence of bullying and violence. These findings can be explained by the relationship between secondary school size and students' family background, teachers' social and didactical processes in class, and the level of education or 'educational type' of the school. Stated differently, students characterised by lower socioeconomic and educational family backgrounds usually attend smaller secondary schools characterised by lower educational levels, whereas students from higher socioeconomic and educational family backgrounds more often attend schools larger in size that provide higher educational levels.

Another factor relevant to bullying behaviour is the religious orientation of the school (Mooij, 1992). Students in secondary public and Roman Catholic schools were more accepting of bullying than students from secondary Protestant schools. In other words, students from Protestant schools behaved in more prosocial ways. Such differences may be caused by complicated interactional processes between family factors, teachers' pedagogical and managerial behaviour styles, and the pedagogical climate of schools (Baerveldt, 1990).

Risk and Protective Determinants: Interactional Multilevel Explanations

We can conclude that bullying processes can be characterised by person, home or family, peer group, educational and other environmental characteristics which interact in complex, multilevel ways. These interactional, multilevel processes can clarify the function or meaning of 'individual' and environmental determinants of disruptive or prosocial behaviours. Specific individual or environmental characteristics can act as risk factors for disruptive behaviours, whereas other individual or environmental variables may act as promotive factors (Tremblay & LeMarquand, 2001). It is important to unravel these different determinants to preclude wrong conclusions or irrelevant measures. Mooij's (1994) survey of student violence in secondary education can serve as an example. The results showed that students belonging to an ethnic minority group scored significantly higher on the perpetration of material violence, the perpetration of physical violence, and the possession of a weapon. However, in a factor analysis which included all individual factors, family background factors, and violence characteristics, ethnic minority group joined only family background variables and not violence characteristics. Multivariate analyses, in contrast to the bivariate analyses, thus demonstrated that belonging to an ethnic minority group was not related to violence, but was mainly related to family background variables.

The findings support the notion that many types of risk and promotive determinants at the individual, family, small group or class, and school level influence bullying and victimisation in schools. In particular, interactional processes with respect to variables at different levels are necessary to explain the social processes. This also becomes evident in the effects of intervention research designed to reduce disturbing, bullying, or otherwise disruptive behaviours of students. Van Lier (2002) concentrated on students aged 7–9 in primary education. The intervention goal was to promote prosocial behaviours by using 'Taakspel', a whole-class intervention programme using a team approach which focused on explication and reinforcement of positive behaviours and facilitation of the interaction between disrupting and non-disrupting children. Mann (2003) carried out research in group seven of primary education with students aged 10–12. This author used IATK (I Am The Key), a programme to promote self-respect and trust, coping skills and social support by participating in drama, role playing, arts and storytelling at school. Fekkes (2005) focused on fifteen intervention and thirty-five control primary schools. Intervention schools included the core intervention programme as originally described by Olweus: set clear rules against bullying; regular measurements of bullying; a curriculum of lessons on bullying and social skills; good supervision during intermission, and informed and involved parents. Students being bullied, bullying, and depressive symptoms decreased in experimental compared to control schools, whereas satisfaction with contact with other students increased. No significant changes occurred with respect to psychosomatic symptoms, delinquency, general satisfaction with school life, and satisfaction with contact with the teacher. However, a year later, positive intervention effects had disappeared. In conclusion, although a multilevel framework of risk and promotive variables applies to bullying, to have enduring impact, short-term effect interventions should be transformed into long-term, systemic approaches to the prevention of bullying and related disruptive behaviours.

Systemic Multilevel Prevention

Early Identification and Support at Home

The prevention of the development of bullying in children requires that from the beginning of each child's life the family situation should offer an accepting, child-oriented, positive and warm atmosphere combined with short, clear behavioural rules. Positively stated rules should be supported by clear procedures about how children and parents can create and maintain a mutually positive atmosphere. Social rewards stimulate the expected prosocial behaviours, while punishments should be applied to repeated violation of rules.

Instruments such as the Child Behaviour Check List (CBCL: see Achenbach, 1993) can be used to identify children's high-risk behaviour. It is important, however, to check whether the parents' childrearing practices fulfil the necessary pedagogical requirements as well (Bogenschneider, 2002; Goleman, 1995). The earlier the signs of persistent disruptive child behaviour, the more serious and more stable such behaviours may become (Loeber & Farrington, 2001). In this respect, Van den Boom (1995) and Stams, Juffer and Van IJzendoorn (2001) developed effective training programmes for mothers to improve, where necessary, their children's attachment process.

A more thorough assessment of children's problem behaviours can be based on an interdisciplinary approach to evaluate physical, physiological, psychological, or emotional characteristics that may interfere with the child's social development. What is needed, then, is a systematic set of concepts and reliable and valid instrumentation to diagnose and measure effects of specific treatments (Pijnacker Hordijk & Verwoerd, 2005). Here a 'pedagogical-didactical kernel structure' (PDKS) can assist to identify and support various competence domains including age-based normative diagnostics but also age-independent or criterion-based diagnostics, interventions and evaluations (Mooij, 2007). We will briefly discuss these issues.

Home-School Collaboration and Differentiated Learning

At the beginning of preschool, it is important to screen for the relevant characteristics of each child as perceived by different caretakers to synchronise perceptions and to check the need for specific pedagogical or didactical measures (for further discussions on screening, see Chapter 10, this volume). PDKS can function as a reference framework here. For example, a screening questionnaire developed by Mooij (2000) contains seven behavioural rating categories of different competence domains, including social behaviours. This instrument can be used by the parents at intake and by the preschool teacher after the child's first months in preschool when the child is about 4 years old. Communication about the outcomes of this screening procedure helps both parents and teachers get a clearer view of the child. Moreover, the procedure helps to improve agreement levels between parents and teachers about the child's behaviours. This facilitates further communication about the child and supports future development and learning processes, both in preschool and at home (Bennathan & Boxall, 1996; Mangione & Speth, 1998; Mooij, 2002; Walker et al., 1998).

The results of screening can also be used to assign specific playing or diagnostic and learning activities to particular children as a basis for further pedagogical and didactical support. This is most important for children scoring much lower than their peers on one or more competencies (Vermaas & Van der Pluijm, 2004), and for high-ability children who score much higher than their peers on one or more competencies (Mooij, 1999b). If indicated, a family diagnostic and intervention procedure can be developed and implemented with all family members in order to help both child and family rearrange home or family conditions (see, for example, Goderie, 2005).

Design of and Support by Integrating Information and Communication Technology

To allow the early identification and prevention strategy, Mooij (2007) constructed a systemic model reflecting multilevel educational and Information and Communication Technology (ICT) characteristics with a view to improving the cognitive and social learning processes of each child in school. This author related three types of contextual conditions (differentiation of learning materials and procedures, design and use of integrating ICT support, and improvement of development and learning progress) to four aspects of learning (Diagnostic, Instructional, Managerial and Systemic – or DIMS). The combination of contextual conditions and learning aspects produced fifteen theoretical guidelines, which were hypothesised to promote multilevel optimisation of learning processes and outcomes.

The guidelines include basic issues such as the identification of competence sub-domains in the PDKS and the consequent identification and stimulation of the learning progress of individual learners and groups of learners in varying contexts.

The ICT can provide Internet-based support of learning in multilevel ways, across various types of situations. ICT also assists in individual and group assignment, prosocial and collaborative improvement, teachers' coaching, and organisational and management transformation (Blumenfeld et al., 2000). To implement the guidelines, a software prototype was developed: 'Diagnostic and Instructional Management Systems' (DIMS).

The concept of 'learning arrangements' was then used to describe varying combinations of diagnostic, instructional and managerial characteristics which intend to support or meet the needs of specific learners in their development or learning progress (Mooij, 2004, 2007). Such arrangements differ in the degree to which they motivate and fit learners, so they correspondingly differ in their capacity to realise intended individual or group learning processes and effects. Development and implementation in practice were carried out in collaboration with teachers of some preschools and primary schools. For example, an instrument to diagnose a child's social problem behaviour in both preschool and primary education is the school behaviour scale of Bleichrodt, Resing and Zaal (1994). DIMS were used to connect school behaviour concepts to learning arrangements characterised by specific materials and procedures (Mooij & Smeets, 2006).

As a result of these activities, preschool teachers learned to assign specific playing or diagnostic and learning activities to their students, as a basis to further pedagogical and didactical support. Actual or potential risk characteristics received more preventive pedagogical attention by youth health specialists (for example, speech specialist, psychiatrist) in the school, and if necessary, from outside the school. Teachers learned that the differences between students were generally much larger than was accounted for in the existing play and learning materials, activities and diagnostic tools.

Next Steps

Many relevant materials and procedures are available to further develop such a preventive educational system (Faber & Steensma, 1995). A systemic combination of risk-reduction and promotive-enhancement programmes is necessary to adequately support children, teachers and parents (Van Haeringen, 1977; Kirschner, 1997). For example, Förrer, Kenter and Veenman (2000) focused on 'co-operative learning in primary education' and Hepler (1998) concentrated on social integration of children with various types of disabilities. DIMS can adopt an integrative role by ensuring that educational materials and instruments, coaching procedures, and the organisational conditions needed to stimulate and adequately monitor each student in and outside school, are sufficiently in place (Collier, 1994; Finn-Stevenson & Stern, 1997; Jones et al., 1998; Raver & Zigler, 1997; Skinner et al., 1998). In the Netherlands, this is particularly relevant to fine-tuning collaboration between youth health and education agencies according to an 'integral youth policy' (Gilsing et al., 2000; Scholte, 1998).

Conclusions

Bullying is often associated with truancy, poor academic performance, running away from home, dropping out of school, or developing a criminal career. Dutch research on a representative sample showed that about one in five students in primary education is either being bullied or bullying now and then, once a week, or several times a week. Being bullied several times a week happens to 4% of the students, and bullying several times a week is done by 3%. Students show different reactions to bullying. Some students may develop psychosomatic problems and school avoidance behaviour, while other students develop externalising problem behaviours such as stubbornness or conflict with other students or the teacher. Biological factors and other personal and environmental factors associated with bullying appear important (Loeber & Farrington, 2001), but have not been studied in the Netherlands. This chapter presented a multilevel approach to the causes of bullying that included individual and group disruptive behaviours in classrooms and schools.

We advocate the development of instruments to improve the assessment of individual and social functioning in preschool and primary school. Specifically, we propose a 'pedagogical-didactical kernel structure' (PDKS) to identify and support diagnostics, interventions and evaluations. Secondly, we advocate the use of an instrument to screen children's characteristics at the beginning of preschool to facilitate the synchronisation of teachers' and parents' perceptions and to establish whether there is a need for pedagogical or didactical intervention. A software prototype called DIMS can assist the systemic improvement of children's cognitive and social learning from preschool onwards. This Internet-based software supports learning in multilevel ways, across various types of practice situations. The preventive aspect of educational practice implies the involvement of parents, teachers, school management, school counsellors and youth or social welfare professionals from outside school.

Recommendations

We recommend that it is important to start as early as preschool with screening or identification of problem behaviours and support treatment interventions where indicated. We further advocate that parents of disruptive children need support and that ICT can be used to integrate support at home and at school. In schools, we stress the use of positive formulation and control of social conduct rules for students in classrooms, together with differential learning processes to adequately stimulate each student at his/her own level. We recommend the use of collaborative didactic procedures to improve prosocial behaviours between small groups of students, and adapt the student:teacher ratio to what is needed to adequately stimulate the students present in class. Finally, we see the integration of social behaviour professionals into teaching and learning processes as a promising option.

Chapter 9

A Cumulative Developmental Model of Risk and Promotive Factors

Rolf Loeber, Wim Slot and Magda Stouthamer-Loeber

Modern criminological theories aim to explain crime from childhood to adulthood, but they do so with different emphases on pathways to crime and ranges of explanatory factors (for example, Farrington, 2005; Thornberry & Krohn, 2003; Wikström, 2005). In addition, most theories focus on offending by adolescents and adults and rarely address offending during childhood (Loeber & Farrington, 2001). Theoretical explanations of serious delinquency and violence at any age are sometimes met with consistent empirical findings, and sometimes with equivocal results. On the one hand, meta-analyses indicate a high degree of replication of bivariate associations between explanatory and risk factors and later serious delinquency (for example, Howell, 2003; Lipsey & Derzon, 1998). On the other hand, results from multivariate analyses based on multiple predictors vary greatly from study to study (see Farrington, 2005; Thornberry, 1997; Thornberry & Krohn, 2003). This is partly caused by studies selecting relatively few of the known explanatory/risk factors of serious delinquency and under-emphasising other factors. Although theories of disruptive behaviour and delinquency often have several factors in common (for example, juveniles' relationships with parents and peers), they differ in their relative emphasis on domains, settings and details of explanatory factors, and the ways these factors are interrelated (see above sources and chapters in Farrington, 2005, and in Lahey, Moffitt & Caspi, 2003). The purpose of this chapter is to focus on shared elements between criminological theories as they are relevant to juvenile offenders, including very young offenders, for the purpose of explaining why some become offenders and others do not. The chapter examines escalation models representing increasing severity of offending with development and then reviews developmental aspects of risk and promotive factors, which together determine the likelihood of future offending (see also Chapters 5–8, this volume). The chapter closes with implications for assessments and interventions.

Criminological theories almost always share three elements with the goals of explaining (a) delinquency over the life-course, particularly in terms of prevalence, frequency and severity of delinquent acts; (b) individual differences in delinquency and developmental changes in these differences, and (c) non-offending or low-level offending. The key for researchers, practitioners and policymakers is to understand how the combination of (a), (b) and (c) explains why some juveniles and not others become serious property offenders or violent offenders, and to understand this both on the population level (for example, all youth in a particular city) and on the individual level (that is, a particular juvenile minor offender at risk of becoming a serious offender). Along these lines, there is a need for better life-course models that incorporate the development and accumulation of risk *and* promotive factors. Risk factors are defined here as events or conditions that are associated with an increased probability of serious forms of delinquency, distinguishing them from promotive factors, which are associated with a lowered risk of delinquency. Following the example of Sameroff and colleagues (1998), we distinguish between promotive and protective factors, with the former referring to main effects regarding positive outcomes (comparable to the main effects of risk factors, but then inverse), while protective factors, following the position put forward by Rutter (1985), are positive factors studied in situations in which individuals are exposed to risk factors or adversity (thus, an interactive term).

Theoretical approaches buttressed by empirical, longitudinal data and multivariate statistical models developed over the past four decades have demonstrated that disruptive child behaviour is explained by multiple factors (see Chapters 5–8, this volume; Loeber, Slot & Sergeant, 2001); that there are linkages between independent factors (in terms of mediation and moderation), and that it is useful to control for possible confounds. However, a number of limitations can be discerned. First, the results of the multivariate models have been enormously diverse. The second disadvantage is that most models have not delineated developmental pathways to serious forms of disruptive behaviours (such as violence) by the specification of developmental antecedents (such as earlier, less serious problems) to such serious outcomes. We presume that such a specification is necessary to identify both homotypic and heterotypic continuity of disruptive behaviours and delinquency with development. Homotypic continuity refers to the continuity of the same manifestations over time, whereas heterotypic continuity refers to different manifestations of disruptive behaviours that are developmentally linked in a successive manner over time. Against this backdrop of continuity and discontinuity of disruptive behaviours, we need to better understand selection processes, comparable to a successive sieving process, in which increasingly smaller groups of youths become at risk of the more serious behaviours (Loeber et al., 2008). The third limitation of current multivariate models is that they usually fail to address changes in the saliency of risk factors and their risk domains with development. Fourth, current models do not specify differences between individuals in their exposure to an *accumulation* of specific risk (or promotive) factors with development. A fifth disadvantage has to do with the fact that the majority of studies focus only on risk factors as a way of explaining disruptive behaviours and either neglect to consider promotive factors or the combined effect of risk and promotive factors on disruptive outcomes. A sixth limitation is that most research does not include factors occurring during early childhood. A final limitation is that studies that incorporate childhood data often lack theoretical considerations about the continuity or discontinuity between behaviours in childhood and delinquency in adolescence and early adulthood.

Two major strengths of current criminological theories are the explanation of current offending levels in populations and the risk of future offending. However, we argue that criminological theories can be enhanced in at least two other ways, first by incorporating past development, and second by incorporating possible future development based on knowledge of the development of children in other longitudinal studies. In the first category are differences in individuals' *past history of offending* (and history of problem behaviours that are precursors to delinquency); differences in the *individuals' exposure to earlier risk factors* (for example, prenatal exposure to toxins or child abuse during the preschool period), and *promotive factors* (for example, a good relationship with an adult). The second understudied area concerns two aspects of individuals' futures: first, the possible course of subsequent delinquent development (or pathways) as examined by longitudinal studies of young people who have been followed up into adulthood; and second, expected exposure to risk and promotive factors based on the observation of such factors in older populations of youths. Examples of 'new' risk factors that may enter individuals' lives are gang membership, victimisation and alcohol intoxication. In summary, we propose that developmental models should take advantage of knowledge of pathways and exposure to risk and promotive factors based on past studies, which can then provide a framework in which to place the development of specific individuals. In this sense, population data can describe both the stages in pathways to serious delinquency (the latter being the outer, more severe boundary) and the gradual accumulation of risk and promotive factors that can maximally take place in populations (another instance of an outer boundary). Knowledge of these two types of outer boundaries will make it possible to describe the past history of an individual's disruptive behaviours and delinquency, his or her past exposure to risk and promotive factors, and possible future exposure to ongoing or new risk and promotive factors.

One of the key advantages of such a model is that, in contrast to current statistical models, it may provide valuable information about choices and targets of intervention. This is very much in line with contemporary principles of prevention and intervention (see Chapters 11 and 12, this volume), with their focus on behavioural development and an emphasis on reducing exposure to risk factors while at the same time increasing exposure to promotive factors (Pollard, Hawkins & Arthur, 1999; Slot, 1995).

This chapter argues that an enhanced developmental model incorporating these aspects ideally should represent the following constituent components: behavioural development and the accumulation of risk and promotive factors with development. To construct such a model, it is necessary to review five key topics:

1. pathways representing a child's escalation toward serious property offences and violence;
2. differences between children in their exposure to risk and promotive factors at birth (called start-up factors) and subsequently during childhood, adolescence and early adulthood;
3. developmental accumulation of risk and promotive factors over time;
4. the existence of a dose-response relationship between the number of risk/promotive factors and later serious delinquency and violence, and
5. additive and compensatory effects of promotive and risk factors.

Finally, we integrate these five aspects into a single cumulative, developmental model.

Escalation and the Formulation of Developmental Pathways

The onset of violence is usually preceded by a history of escalation in the severity of aggression, which often – but not always – starts in childhood (Loeber, 1988; Loeber, Wung et al., 1993; Moffitt, 1993). Research shows that for some offenders, early involvement in status offences and delinquency are stepping-stones in pathways to serious, violent and chronic offending. About a quarter to a third of those children who engage in non-delinquent disruptive behaviours are at risk of escalating to minor delinquent acts. About a third to a half of child delinquents in the Pittsburgh Youth Study became at risk of escalating to serious delinquency (Loeber & Farrington, 2001; Loeber et al., 2008).

Many criminologists propose that a child's development from less serious problem behaviours to serious delinquency fits a hierarchical, developmental model that can represent individuals' escalation from persistent minor disruptive behaviours to serious delinquent acts. Le Blanc (2002) reviewed the extensive literature on methods and findings pertaining to escalation processes in delinquency (such as transition matrices, dynamic classification strategies, cluster analyses, semi-parametric or mixed Poisson regression analyses, and developmental sequence strategies) and found substantial evidence for developmental sequences from minor to more serious forms of delinquency (for example, Elliott, 1994; Elliott, Huizinga & Menard, 1989; Le Blanc, Côté & Loeber, 1991; Loeber, 1988). A developmental pathway is defined as the behavioural development of a group of individuals that is different from the behavioural development of other group(s) of individuals (Loeber, Keenan & Zhang, 1997).

The findings of several studies (for example, Elliott, 1994) focus on a single escalation pathway. In contrast, Loeber, Burke et al. (1993) tested a triple pathway model (Figure 9.1), which provided a better fit to the data. The pathways are as follows:

a) an *authority conflict* pathway prior to the age of 12, that starts with stubborn behaviour, has defiance as a second stage, and authority avoidance (for example, truancy) as a third stage;
b) a *covert* pathway prior to age 15, which starts with minor covert acts, has property damage as a second stage, and moderate to serious delinquency as a third stage, and
c) an overt pathway, that starts with minor aggression, has physical fighting as a second stage, and more severe violence as a third stage.

Within the third stage, homicide constitutes a separate and most serious component. Recent longitudinal research on the Pittsburgh Youth Study (Loeber et al., 2005) indicates that 94% of later homicide offenders have displayed violence earlier in life. The pathways are hierarchical in that those who have advanced to the most serious behaviours in each of the pathways have usually displayed persistent problem behaviours characteristics at the earlier stages in each pathway. The pathways are also related to neighbourhoods. For example, a higher percentage of youth in the

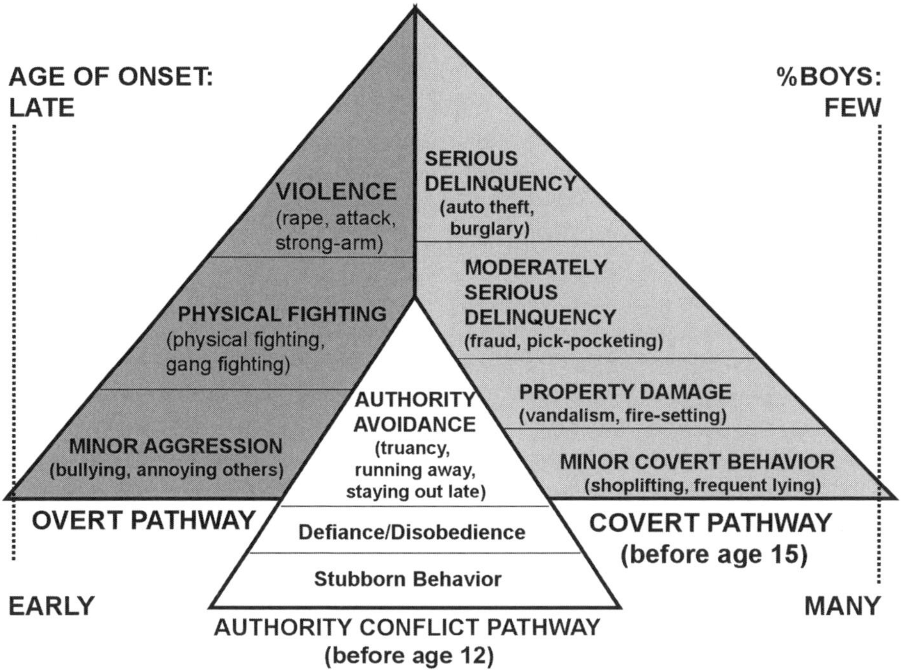

Figure 9.1 Developmental pathways to serious delinquency and violence

most disadvantaged neighbourhoods escalates from minor aggression to violence than youth living in more advantaged neighbourhoods (Loeber & Wikström, 1993).

Studies have replicated the three-pathway model on different populations. First, with the Pittsburgh Youth Study, the model has been replicated in two other samples of young males (Loeber, Wung et al., 1993; Loeber et al., 1998). Secondly, Tolan, Gorman-Smith and Loeber (2000) have also found empirical support for the triple-pathway model in a sample of African-American and Hispanic male adolescents in Chicago and in a nationally representative US sample of adolescents. Further, the Denver Youth Survey and the Rochester Youth Development Study have also largely replicated earlier findings (Loeber et al., 1999). Finally, recent analysis has shown that the pathway model also mostly fits the development of disruptive behaviours in girls (Gorman-Smith & Loeber, 2005).

The above studies primarily focused on males and show that with age, some of the children progress on two or three pathways, indicating an increasing variety of problem behaviours over time (Kelley et al., 1997; Loeber, Wung et al., 1993; Loeber, Keenan & Zhang, 1997). Also, Loeber, Wung and colleagues (1993) found evidence that development in multiple pathways is not interchangeable, in that boys who escalate in the overt pathway are more likely to escalate in the covert pathway as well, compared to a lower probability of boys in the covert pathway escalating in the overt pathway. Thus, aggressive boys are particularly at risk of committing covert acts, whereas boys engaging in covert acts are less likely to develop aggressive behaviours. Further, escalation in either the overt or covert pathway is often preceded by escalation in the authority conflict pathway (Loeber, Wung et al., 1993). In other words, conflict with authority figures is either a precursor or a concomitant of boys' escalation in overt or covert acts. Also, an early age of onset of problem behaviours or delinquency, compared to onset at a later age, is associated with boys' escalation to more serious behaviours in the pathways (Tolan et al., 2000). The pathway model accounts for the majority of the most seriously affected boys, that is, the self-reported high-rate offenders (Loeber, Keenan & Zhang, 1997; Loeber, Wung et al., 1993) and court-reported delinquents (Loeber, Keenan & Zhang, 1997). Evidence for the escalation of disruptive behaviours according to pathways also fits psychiatric findings of a hierarchical, escalation model in disruptive behaviours disorders (American Psychiatric Association, 1994). Research supports the notion that a proportion of boys who qualify for Oppositional Defiant Disorder are at risk of developing Conduct Disorder over time, whereas a proportion of boys with Conduct Disorder are at risk of developing Antisocial Personality Disorder[1] (Lahey et al., 2005; Loeber, Burke & Lahey, 2002). In summary, developmental pathways in disruptive behaviours and delinquent acts and developmental transitions between different disruptive diagnoses (that is, ODD and CD) share a conceptualisation of escalation in the severity of disruptive behaviours and delinquent acts in certain individuals over time.

It should be kept in mind that the formulation and tests of the above pathway model are limited in that they use retrospective information prior to age 7, which is not known to be consistently reliable. Keenan and Shaw (2003) formulated a dual-stage escalation model for the preschool period. One pathway, the *pathway to reactive antisocial behaviour*, starts with irritable behaviour during infancy. Children displaying persistent irritability are at risk of developing emotional difficulties as toddlers (low frustration tolerance, over-activity and being demanding) who, in turn, are at risk of developing disruptive, angry behaviours as preschoolers, including reactive aggression, crying, whining and defiance. A second pathway, the *pathway to proactive antisocial behaviour*, starts with children displaying under-arousal (that is, they are under-responsive to stimulation), who appear at risk of developing behaviour difficulties as toddlers (as demonstrated by persistent unresponsiveness to punishment and a high level of sensation seeking), who, in turn, are at risk of developing oppositional behaviours and conduct problems. The 'Keenan and Shaw' model may provide a link with the 'Loeber' pathway model in that the first two steps in the authority conflict pathway in the 'Loeber' pathway model (stubborn behaviour and defiance/disobedience; see Figure 9.1) may link to oppositional behaviours in the two 'Keenan and Shaw' pathways.

Both the Loeber and the Keenan and Shaw pathway models have in common the operation of selection processes, starting with a broad base of children with age-normative problem behaviours. From that group, a select proportion of children advance to the next stage, and from that group, an even smaller select proportion advance to the next, more serious stage of problem behaviours. This incremental

---

1 Even when controlling for the APD criterion of Conduct Disorder having been present prior to age 16 (American Psychiatric Association, 1994).

selection process, as children advance through deviancy pathways, can be conceptualised as a shift in the distribution of youth. Whereas at the initial level of age-normative problem behaviours the distribution is usually normal, as children advance through pathways the distribution becomes increasingly skewed as it increasingly represents the more deviant individuals.

The specification of developmental pathways can be contrasted with the identification of *developmental trajectories*, which are defined as the classification of individuals according to their behaviour *over time*. The assumption is that a population of individuals 'is composed of a mixture of groups with distinct developmental trajectories' (Nagin & Tremblay, 2001, p. 21). Typically, trajectory analyses have been based on repeated measurements of a single indicator of problem behaviours. Usually, the results of trajectory analyses have identified young males whose problem behaviours remain high over time; those whose problems behaviours remain low; those whose problem behaviours increase, and those whose problem behaviours decrease between childhood and early adulthood (Broidy et al., 2003; Bushway, Thornberry & Krohn (2003); Lacourse, Dupéré & Loeber, 2008; Lacourse et al., 2003; Maughan et al., 2000; Nagin & Tremblay, 2005; NICHD Early Child Care Research Network, 2004; Piquero, 2007; Shaw & Nagin, 2003).

In a longitudinal study of children aged 2–6, Côté and colleagues (2006) found a dual trajectory in the development of aggression. Physical aggression (that is, kicking, pushing, hitting) tended to decrease in early childhood. Most children followed either low or declining trajectories of this type of aggression, while almost 15% of the children followed a trajectory of high stable physical aggression. In contrast, indirect aggression (that is, group exclusion, rumour-spreading, breaking confidence) tended to increase, with approximately two-thirds of the children following the rising direct aggression and one-third the high rising indirect aggression trajectories.

Although the trajectory approach has provided new insights into the development of disruptive and delinquent behaviours, it has not usually illuminated heterotypic continuity of different categories of problem behaviours and, therefore, has not yet described escalation processes from less to more serious forms of delinquency in terms of timing of behaviour changes, emergence of high-rate serious offenders, and transition probabilities between less and more serious forms of delinquent acts. In addition, all attempts at trajectory analyses to date are postdictive rather than predictive in that the assignment of individuals to specific trajectories is only possible when all longitudinal data are used. Instead, it is our opinion that practitioners and researchers need developmental models for screening and intervention (see also Chapters 10–12, this volume) that can illustrate selection processes and the slow incremental nature within individuals of heterotypic transformations of different forms of disruptive and delinquent behaviours from childhood to adulthood.

Risk Factors

The majority of theories about the causes of disruptive and delinquent behaviours are generally based on risk factors alone, although different terms for such factors have been used (for example, Elliott et al., 1985; Farrington, 1996; Gottfredson &

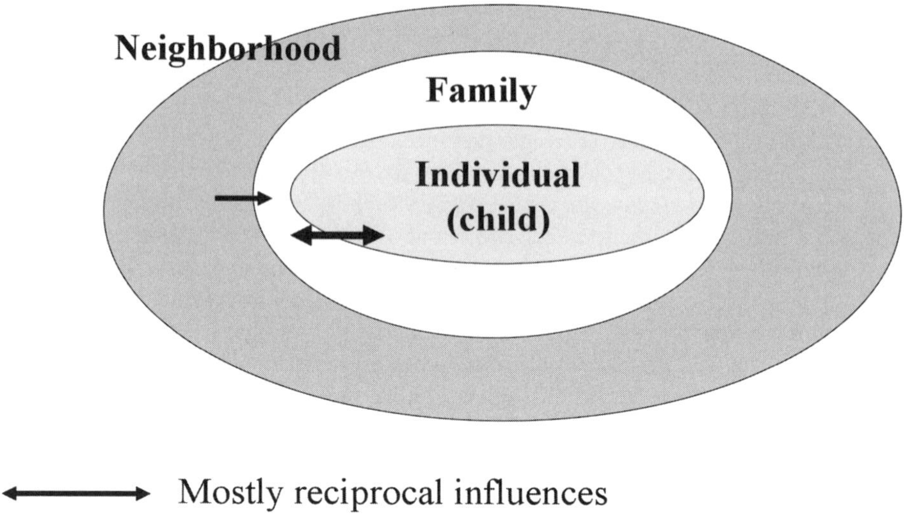

Figure 9.2 Nested domains of influences on children

Hirschi, 1990; Le Blanc & Fréchette, 1989; Loeber et al., 2008; Moffitt, 1993; Wilson & Herrnstein, 1985). Risk factors can be distinguished according to the different domains and contexts in which they operate. Overall, researchers and theoreticians agree (with some variation) to distinguish risk factors in the following domains: individual, family and peer group. In addition, some risk factors are associated with children's exposure to risk factors in specific contexts, including characteristics of the school attended and the neighbourhood in which the children reside or spend their time (Howell, 2003; Loeber et al., 1998; Stouthamer-Loeber et al., 2002). Data from prediction studies indicate that risk factors from each of the domains (individual, family, peers, schools and neighbourhoods) contribute to the explanation of why some individuals and not others progress from minor problem behaviours such as bullying, to physical fighting and to violence (for example, Farrington, 1997; Hawkins et al., 1998; Lipsey & Derzon, 1998, Loeber et al., 2008). Individuals' exposure to an accumulation of risk factors in multiple domains rather than in a single domain heightens the probability of later adverse outcomes (Rutter, Tizard & Whitemore, 1970). For example, Deater-Deckard and colleagues (1998) found that four domains (child characteristics, socio-cultural, parent and peer experiences) each contributed to the prediction of externalising problem behaviours.

Many researchers have been relatively silent about the developmental saliency and priority of different domains of risk factors (individual, family, peer, and so on), other than noting that children's exposure to family factors usually precedes their exposure to peer factors (for example, Loeber, 1985). Clinical theory, however, proposes that the relative saliency of risk domains may differ along different stages of development. Developmental saliency thus may serve as an explanation of why some individuals escalate from persistent minor disruptive behaviours to very serious forms of delinquency. No single domain is thought to fully explain this pattern of development. Instead, the data suggest that risk factors from all

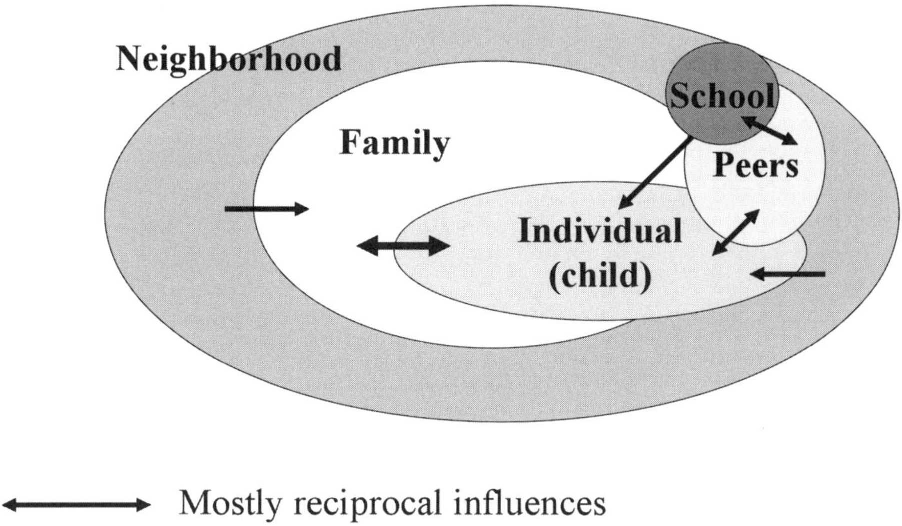

Figure 9.3 Changes in nested domains of influences on children from middle-childhood onward

three domains (individual, family and peers) and the two contexts (schools and neighbourhoods) contribute to the explanation of delinquency escalation processes. Figure 9.2 shows the typical thinking about the nesting of risk factors (based on Bronfenbrenner's (1979) model; for another variant, see Lerner & Castellino, 2002) in which, at a young age, the individual (child) is mostly affected by family factors (Winslow & Shaw, 2007), which in turn are affected by neighbourhood factors. In this conceptualisation, the child is only indirectly affected by neighbourhood factors through the family. In the course of their development, children become more mobile and also more active in selecting settings with their own risk and promotive factors (Wikström, 2005). This is represented in Figure 9.3, when children become exposed to risk and promotive factors of peers, school, and eventually, neighbourhood. Thus, with development, there is a reconfiguration of risk domains with new domains being introduced over time.

Developmentally Graded Risk Factors

Among the risk factors, some are thought to be present at birth or become manifest shortly afterwards, while other risk factors emerge later in individuals' lives. Before discussing each category of risk factors, our overall strategy is to view risk factors from a developmental angle in that children's exposure to different risk factors is gradual, that with development, children's exposure to different risk domains increases, and that many risk factors persist over time and, consequently, are 'stacked' over time. It would be clearly untenable to insist that all the risk and promotive factors mentioned in the preceding section are present in juveniles' lives from a very young age onward. Instead, it is much more likely that selection processes operate in

Table 9.1 Emergence of risk factors from birth to early adulthood

Domain	At birth	Early childhood	Middle to late childhood	Adolescence	Early adulthood
Individual	Low IQ	CONTINUITY OF EARLIER INDIVIDUAL FACTOR +	CONTINUITY OF EARLIER INDIVIDUAL FACTOR +	CONTINUITY OF EARLIER INDIVIDUAL FACTOR +	CONTINUITY OF EARLIER INDIVIDUAL FACTOR +
	Negative emotionality	NEW FACTORS Developmental delays	CONTINUITY OF EARLIER INDIVIDUAL FACTORS +	CONTINUITY OF EARLIER INDIVIDUAL FACTORS +	CONTINUITY OF EARLIER INDIVIDUAL FACTORS +
	Prenatal exposure to toxins	Language problems	NEW FACTORS Withdrawn behaviour	CONTINUITY OF EARLIER INDIVIDUAL FACTORS +	CONTINUITY OF EARLIER INDIVIDUAL FACTORS +
	Pregnancy/birth complications	Lack of guilt	Poor social skills	NEW FACTORS Heavy substance use	CONTINUITY OF EARLIER INDIVIDUAL FACTORS +
	Perinatal problems	Callous/unemotional behaviour	Cognitive attributional bias pertaining to aggression	Drug dealing	Unemployment
		Positive attitude to problem behaviours	Poor academic achievement	Weapon use	
		Impulsivity/daringness	Low school motivation	Delinquent victimisation	
		Attention problems	Positive attitude to delinquency		
		Poor executive functioning	Positive attitude to substance use		
		Counter control (child acts up more when disciplined)	Negative life events		

			Poor ability to plan for the future		
			Early puberty/ maturation (especially in girls)		
Family	Low SES	CONTINUITY OF EARLIER FAMILY FACTOR +	CONTINUITY OF EARLIER FAMILY FACTOR +	CONTINUITY OF EARLIER FAMILY FACTOR +	CONTINUITY OF EARLIER FAMILY FACTOR +
	Large family	NEW FACTORS Inconsistent discipline	CONTINUITY OF EARLIER FAMILY FACTORS +	CONTINUITY OF EARLIER FAMILY FACTORS +	CONTINUITY OF EARLIER FACTORS +
	Parental unemployment	Physical punishment	NEW FACTORS Poor parent-child relationship	CONTINUITY OF EARLIER FAMILY FACTORS +	CONTINUITY OF EARLIER FAMILY FACTORS +
	Welfare	Child abuse	Poor communication		
	Family delinquency	Neglect	Poor supervision		
	Parent psychopathology	Deviant siblings	Low aspirations for child		
	Parent substance abuse	No. of caretaker changes			
	Poor education of parent(s)	High parental stress			
	Teenage motherhood	Social isolation			
	Single parenthood	Poor relationship with partner			
		Parental positive attitude to child problem behaviour			

Table 9.1 continued **Emergence of risk factors from birth to early adulthood**

Peers		NEW FACTORS Peer rejection	CONTINUITY OF EARLIER PEER FACTOR +	CONTINUITY OF EARLIER PEER FACTOR +	CONTINUITY OF EARLIER PEER FACTOR +
		Victimisation (bullying)	NEW FACTORS Peer delinquency	CONTINUITY OF EARLIER PEER FACTORS +	CONTINUITY OF EARLIER PEER FACTORS +
			Peer substance use	NEW FACTORS Neighbourhood gangs	CONTINUITY OF EARLIER PEER FACTORS +
School			NEW FACTORS High school deviancy level	CONTINUITY OF EARLIER SCHOOL FACTOR +	
			Poorly organised school		
Neighbourhood			NEW FACTORS Disadvantaged neighbourhood	CONTINUITY OF EARLIER NEIGHBOURHOOD FACTOR +	CONTINUITY OF EARLIER NEIGHBOURHOOD FACTOR +
			High neighbourhood crime		

which certain categories of children and youths are incrementally exposed to certain risk and promotive factors as they grow into adults.

Table 9.1 summarises our knowledge of risk factors in each of the different domains as children grow into adults (largely based on Lipsey & Derzon, 1998; Hawkins et al., 1998; Howell, 2003; Loeber, 1990; Loeber et al., 2008; Van der Laan & Blom, 2006). To structure the review of the risk factors, we distinguish between different developmental periods, starting with risk factors present at birth, and those emerging during the following periods: preschool, elementary school, middle/secondary school and early adulthood. Emergence is defined as the probable earliest exposure of children to risk factors. Systematic knowledge in this respect is still wanting, and as a result we have made estimates (knowing that some of the onset of risk factors, such as poor executive functioning, partly depends on the state of measurement in that area). Note that emergence should not be taken too literally and may apply differently from one child to another. However, we maintain that an accumulation of risk factors may take place over many years, and that risk factors at birth (for example, low IQ, negative emotionality) may be followed by exposure to 'new' risk factors emerging during early childhood, such as language problems, which in turn may be followed by other novel risk factors emerging during middle to late childhood, such as poor social skills or poor academic achievement. During adolescence, novel risk factors may consist of heavy substance use or delinquent victimisation. These examples are risk factors in the individual domain, but Table 9.1 shows that a similar accumulation of new risk factors may occur in other domains as well, such as the family, peers, schools and neighbourhood (including work). It should be noted that – to some extent – risk factors emerging in one life period may persist across another life period and that even when they are time-limited (for example, child abuse), they may influence the probability of serious delinquency in a cumulative manner.

What developmental shifts in the saliency and accumulation of risk and promotive factors take place over time? Figure 9.4, based on Table 9.1, shows that the total number of risk factors associated with disruptive and delinquent behaviours to which children *can* be exposed is about equally divided at or close to birth (approximately fifteen), emerging in the preschool years (twelve), and emerging in the elementary school years (eighteen). Much lower numbers of risk factors probably first appear during the middle and secondary school years (five). Thus, the most salient risk window of children's exposure to risk factors is prior to adolescence. This must be true for early-onset cases of disruptive behaviours and delinquency. Even within the category of early-onset cases, the model is flexible in that we assume that none of the early-risk factors is necessary for the emergence of disruptive and delinquent behaviours. In that sense, there can be some substitution of risk factors that apply to some and not to other early-onset cases. This important point can be investigated by the examination of risk patterns for different categories of offenders.

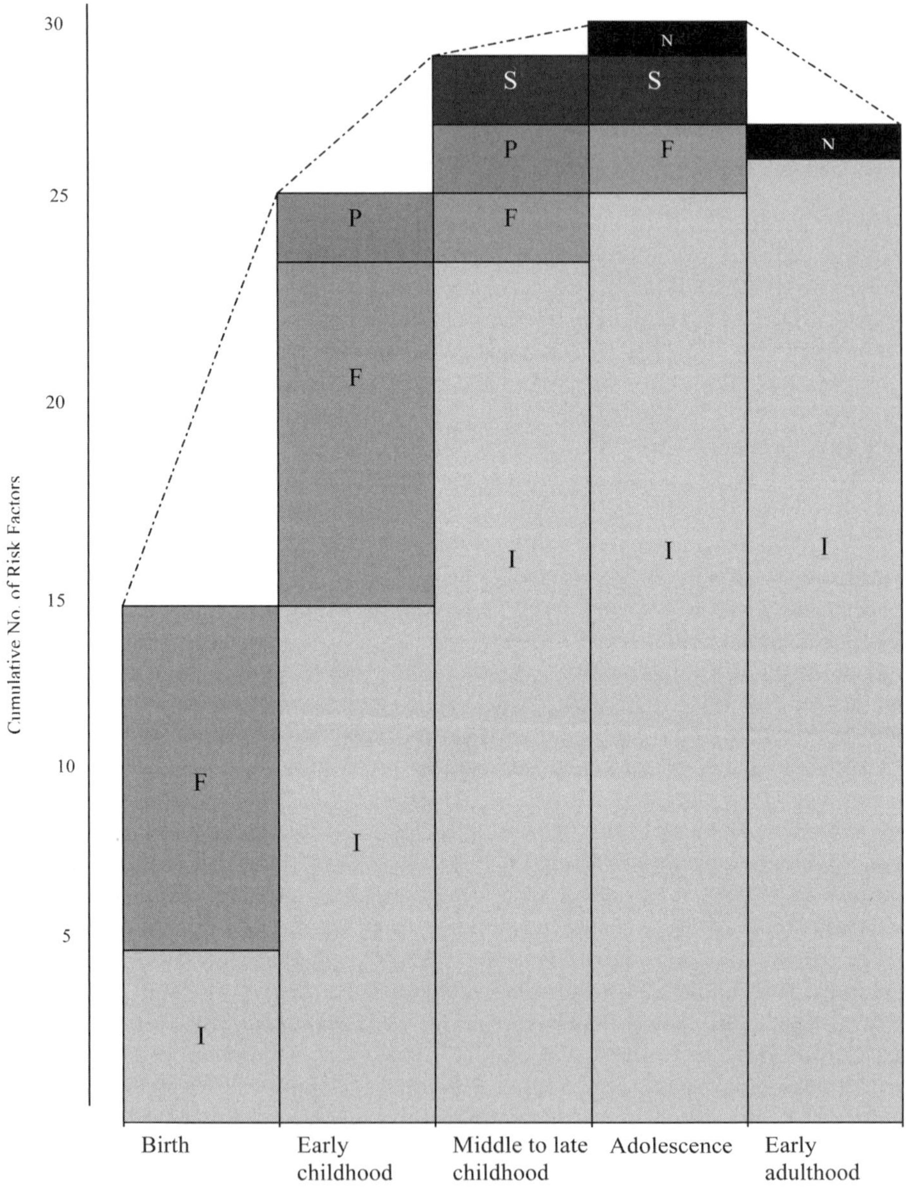

Figure 9.4 Developmental model of onset, accumulation, and continuity of risk factors

Note: I = Individual factors; F = Family factors; P = Peer factors; N = Neighborhood factors; S = School factors.

The emergence of later-onset cases of disruptive and delinquent behaviours can be explained in at least three ways:

a) the absence (or limited number) of risk factors early in life;
b) children's exposure to risk factors at a later age; and/or
c) the accumulation of risk factors with a later onset.

Thus, the explanations of both early-onset and later-onset of delinquent behaviours are similar in that children are likely to be exposed to an accumulation of risk factors rather than any one single risk.

The accumulation of risk factors represented in Figure 9.4 questions a commonly held assumption among practitioners, researchers and lay people, namely that endogenous individual risk factors manifest themselves mostly during early childhood, and that 'nurture' in the form of exogenous risk factors (in the family, peer groups, and so on) would manifest themselves more dominantly afterwards. In contrast to this notion, however, Figure 9.4 suggests that individual risk factors continue to increase in number after childhood and constitute a substantial proportion of all known risk factors after early childhood.

Dose-Response Relationship between Risk Factors and Delinquency

In the field of epidemiology, there are many examples of diseases and other negative outcomes that become more likely the higher the number of multiple risk factors that are present in an individual's life. Typically in epidemiological research, risk factors are dichotomised and the presence of each risk factor is counted as one. A summary score is then computed representing the number of known risk factors to which an individual is exposed (this is usually called the Burgess method of computing future risk). A key reason why we emphasise the Burgess method rather than a multivariate approach is that the former method is more suitable for the computation of false positive and false negative errors, which are essential pieces of information for the design and evaluation of screening devices to establish future risk of delinquency (and escalation to serious offending) for each individual (see Chapter 10, this volume). The computation of Receiver Operating Curves based on sensitivity and specificity is a further aid in determining the most optimal cut-off to use in such a screening score (for example, Loeber et al., 2008).

Studies agree that the higher the number of risk factors, the greater the likelihood that individuals will develop deviant behaviours such as serious delinquency. This association is usually called a dose-response relationship and has been demonstrated for the full range of indicators of disruptive behaviour: sociopathy (Robins, 1966), externalising problem behaviours (Deater-Deckard et al., 1998), conduct problems (Fergusson & Woodward, 2000; Sameroff et al., 1998; but see Gerard & Buehler, 2004), serious delinquency (Smith et al., 1995; Van der Laan & Blom, 2006) and violence and serious property crime (Farrington, 1997; Loeber et al., 2005; Loeber et al., 2008).

Figure 9.5 shows a prediction index in the Pittsburgh Youth Study constructed on the basis of the eleven strongest predictors of violence (Loeber et al., 2005):

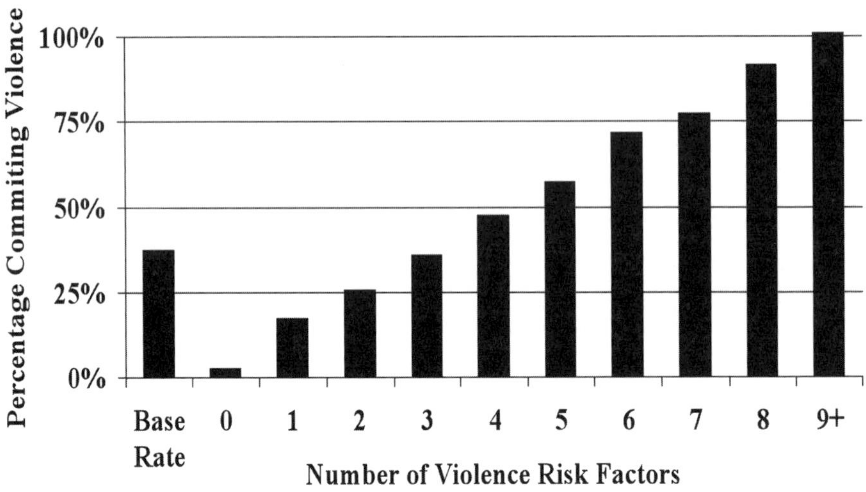

Figure 9.5 Proportion of boys committing violent offences for different levels of risk

Source: Based on Loeber et al., 2005.

truancy, low school motivation, onset of delinquency before age 10, cruelty to people, depressed mood, physical aggression, callous/unemotional behaviour, low family SES, family on welfare, high parental stress, and bad (that is, disadvantaged) neighbourhood (parent-reported). Figure 9.5 also shows that the dose-response relationship applies to the number of predictors and the probability of later violence (Odds Ratio (OR)=6.0 for four or more risk factors). Remarkably, the range of probabilities in the Pittsburgh data is from 3% at zero risk factors to 100% at eleven or more risk factors (that is, a much wider range than in Farrington's (1977) study).

Another important issue to be determined is whether homicide, as the most extreme form of violence, can be predicted among violent offenders, and whether, in this case as well, there is a dose-response association between the number of risk factors and later homicide. Figure 9.6 shows the prediction of homicide among the violent offenders (Loeber et al., 2005) based on the following risk factors: high risk score (of disruptive behaviour) at screening, positive attitude to substance use, Conduct Disorder by age 13, carrying a weapon, gang fighting, selling hard drugs, peer delinquency, repeating school years, and family on welfare. Figure 9.6 shows that the higher the number of risk factors the higher the probability of homicide. The probability of homicide is low for zero to three risk factors, but after that almost linearly increases to about 15% at six or more risk factors. The OR, based on four or more risk factors, amounted to 14.5. In summary, these results, and those of several other studies, indicate a robust association between the number of risk factors and the probability of later violence. Remarkably, the association holds even when slightly different risk factors are measured from study to study.

The dose-response relationship has also been demonstrated between risk factors and several other areas of functioning and maladjustment, including intelligence

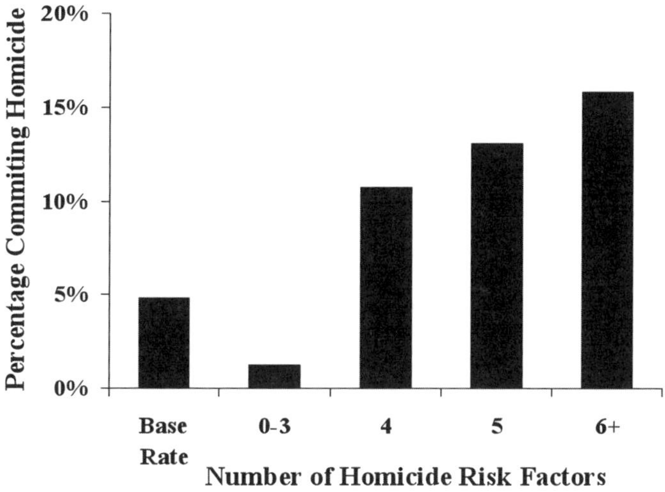

Figure 9.6 Proportion of violent boys convicted of homicide for different levels of risk

Source: Based on Loeber et al., 2005.

(Sameroff et al., 1993); some psychiatric disorders (Rutter, 1979); multiple problems (Fergusson et al., 1997); internalising problem behaviours (for example, Atzaba-Poria, Pike & Barrett, 2004); Attention-Deficit Hyperactivity Disorder (Biederman et al., 1995), and substance use (Bry, McKeon & Pandina, 1982; Smith et al., 1995). The dose-response relationship appears robust in that it applies to both genders (for example, Fergusson et al., 1997; Fergusson & Woodward, 2000; Sameroff et al., 1998; Van der Laan & Blom, 2006), different ethnic or racial groups (Atzaba-Poria, Pike & Barrett, 2004; Loeber & Farrington, 2004; Sameroff et al., 1998; Van der Laan & Blom, 2006), households with different income levels, children with single parents or two-parent families (Sameroff et al., 1998) and different neighbourhoods (Wikström & Loeber, 2000). Also, highly relevant for this chapter, the dose-response relationship also applies to child delinquents (Loeber et al., 2008). Thus, the dose-response relationship between risk factors and later negative outcomes is well replicated, robust across different populations, and also applies to disruptive and delinquent behaviours.

Against the backdrop of the replication of the dose-response relationship across different outcomes and populations, one should recognise that the strength of the association is not the same across studies and that the percentage of false positive and false negative errors varies greatly from study to study even if the same outcome is considered (for example, Farrington, 1997; Loeber et al., 2005). This has partly to do with different prevalence rates of outcomes (rarer outcomes are more difficult to predict) and different prevalence levels of the predictors (Deater-Deckard et al., 1998). The results are not dependent on the Burgess method but are also apparent when multiple regression analyses are conducted showing significant increments in variance accounted for (Atzaba-Poria, Pike & Barrett, 2004; Shaw & Emery, 1988).

It is important to know whether children whose exposure to risk factors decreases over time will have a lower probability of a negative outcome than those exposed to persistent risk factors. Sameroff and colleagues (1998) examined this in their follow-up of children and adolescents at ages 4, 13 and 18, and found that those children who were in a high-risk group at age 4 but had moved to a low-risk group by age 13, demonstrated an improvement in their IQ by 13 points (that is, more than one standard deviation). In contrast, those who were in a low-risk group at age 4, but moved to being in a high-risk group at age 13, saw a drop in their IQ by 15 points. It is our impression that positive or negative changes in exposure to risk factors over time similarly influence the probability of serious delinquency but, as far as we know, research in this area is currently lacking.

Figure 9.2, and to some extent Figure 9.5, suggests a linear association between the number of risk factors and the probability of later deviance. However, some studies have found a positively accelerating relationship (for example, Figure 9.6, and Rutter, 1979). The possible reasons behind divergent findings remain to be investigated. Several possible reasons present themselves, including non-equivalence of risk factors (where the presence of certain risk factors disproportionally increases the risk of a later negative outcome), or threshold effects (where there is a low impact in the presence of few risk factors, but a substantial impact in the presence of one or more additional risk factors).

Stability

It is implied in Table 9.1 that some risk factors may persist over time. Investigations of risk factors often ignore the fact that such factors, similar to the outcomes that they purportedly predict, may vary in their temporal stability over time. For instance, children's direct exposure to conflict and aggression between parents may decrease dramatically or stop completely once the parents separate or divorce, while heavy substance use by parents may be more persistent over time. On the other hand, exposure to some risk factors (such as familial crime) may be associated with a heightened risk of delinquency in the offspring that may have an impact that lasts from childhood at least until the adolescent period. Another category of risk factors that includes, for instance, exposure to the physiological effects of the mother's smoking during pregnancy, may occur during a sensitive period (in this case, that of brain development). Yet few studies have addressed the issue of stability of risk factors. An exception is Sameroff et al. (1998), who found that environmental risk factors correlate .77 over a five-year period (age 13–18), which is about the same level of stability as intelligence. Loeber et al. (2000) found that the year-to-year stability coefficient for the interactions between parents and their boys between age 6 and 18 averages .66 for bad parent-child relationship; .70 for poor parent-child communication, and lower for poor supervision (.56) and physical punishment (.46). Examination of absolute stability reveals that this is higher for bad relationships and poor communication, but decreases with age for poor supervision and physical punishment. It should be noted, however, that despite level changes in risk factors with development, many of the known risk factors continue to predict later negative outcomes, including delinquency, at different ages of children (for example, Loeber et al., 1998, 2008).

It is plausible that the presence of some risk factors sets in motion a cascade of other risk factors (Conger, Patterson & Ge, 1995). For example, the toxic teratogenic effect of maternal smoking may increase the probability of several other risk factors in the offspring, including poor executive functioning, poor academic achievement in school, low motivation to attend school, truancy and, subsequently, delinquency. As another example, the presence of several risk factors (for example, parents' exposure to enduring stress and parents' substance abuse) may increase the chance of disruptive and delinquent behaviours in the offspring at home, which in turn, may set the scene for heightened risk of problem behaviours outside of the home. Yet, it remains to be seen when and how risk factors operate as a cascade of successive, interrelated risk factors. It is clearer that the prevalence of different risk factors is higher in disadvantaged compared to advantaged neighbourhoods (Stouthamer-Loeber et al., 2002; Wikström & Loeber, 2000).

Promotive Factors

Most criminology and psychopathology studies with a public health slant have routinely neglected the study of promotive factors (but see Hawkins et al., 1992; Lösel & Bender, 2002; Werner, 2005). Promotive factors are associated with the likelihood of reduced disruptive and delinquent behaviours and/or increased positive outcomes, including positive adjustment and positive mental health. Some authors refer to variables as if they are either uniquely promotive or uniquely risk related (for example, Rae-Grant et al., 1989). Others emphasise that some promotive and risk factors are:

a) merely opposite ends of the same variable;
b) that the promotive and risk end of variables need not be just mirror images of each other but may differ in the magnitude of their relationship to an outcome, and
c) that there are unique promotive factors without a risk equivalent. (Stouthamer-Loeber et al., 1993, 2002, 2004).

Stouthamer-Loeber and colleagues (1993, 2002, 2004) advanced the investigation of promotive factors first as *main* effects, similar to the search for the main effects of risk factors, and then investigated the interaction effects between promotive and risk factors. Finally, protective factors have been conceptualized as processes that play a special role in the presence of risk (Rutter, 1990), reflecting interaction effects where a protective factor is greater when risk is high than when risk is low.

Developmentally Graded Promotive Factors

There is a growing body of research on promotive factors (see review by Lösel & Bender, 2003; Werner, 2005), but it is still miniscule in comparison to the number of publications on risk factors pertaining to disruptive and delinquent behaviours. Most

Table 9.2 Emergence of promotive factors from birth to early adulthood

Domain	At birth	Early childhood	Middle to late childhood	Adolescence	Early adulthood
Individual	Normal to high IQ	CONTINUITY OF EARLIER INDIVIDUAL FACTOR +	CONTINUITY OF EARLIER INDIVIDUAL FACTOR +	CONTINUITY OF EARLIER INDIVIDUAL FACTOR +	CONTINUITY OF EARLIER INDIVIDUAL FACTOR +
	Easy temperament	NEW FACTORS No developmental delays	CONTINUITY OF EARLIER INDIVIDUAL FACTORS +	CONTINUITY OF EARLIER INDIVIDUAL FACTORS +	CONTINUITY OF EARLIER INDIVIDUAL FACTORS +
	No prenatal exposure to toxins	No language problems	NEW FACTORS Not withdrawn behaviour	CONTINUITY OF EARLIER INDIVIDUAL FACTORS +	CONTINUITY OF EARLIER INDIVIDUAL FACTORS +
	No pregnancy/birth complications	Presence of guilt feelings	Good social skills	NEW FACTORS Believes likely to be caught if delinquent	CONTINUITY OF EARLIER INDIVIDUAL FACTORS +
	No perinatal problems	No callous/unemotional behaviour	No cognitive attributional bias pertaining to aggression	Many skills for getting a job	NEW FACTORS Being employed or in school
		Negative attitude to problem behaviours	Good academic achievement		Military service
		No impulsivity/daringness	High school motivation		Move away from disadvantaged neighbourhoods
		No attention problems	Negative attitude to delinquency		Positive relationship with partner
		Good executive functioning	Negative attitude to substance use		
		No counter control (child does not acts up more when disciplined)	Positive life events		
		Emergent skills/talent			

		Ability of plan for the future			
Family	Medium to high SES	CONTINUITY OF EARLIER FAMILY FACTOR +	CONTINUITY OF EARLIER FAMILY FACTOR +	CONTINUITY OF EARLIER FAMILY FACTOR +	CONTINUITY OF EARLIER FAMILY FACTOR +
	Small family	NEW FACTORS Consistent discipline	CONTINUITY OF EARLIER FAMILY FACTORS +	CONTINUITY OF EARLIER FAMILY FACTORS +	CONTINUITY OF EARLIER FAMILY FACTORS +
	No parental unemployment	Low physical punishment	NEW FACTORS Mentoring by adults	CONTINUITY OF EARLIER FAMILY FACTORS +	CONTINUITY OF EARLIER FAMILY FACTORS +
	No welfare	No child abuse			CONTINUITY OF EARLIER FAMILY FACTORS +
	No family delinquency	No neglect			
	No parent psychopathology	No deviant siblings			
	No parent substance abuse	Few or no caretaker changes			
	Moderate to good education of parent(s)	Low parental stress			
	No teenage motherhood	Social engagement			
	Two-parent family	Good relationship with partner			
		Parental negative attitude to child problem behaviour			
		Availability of supportive adults other than parents			

Table 9.2 continued

Peers		NEW FACTORS Good relationship with peers	CONTINUITY OF EARLIER PEER FACTOR +	CONTINUITY OF EARLIER PEER FACTOR +	CONTINUITY OF EARLIER PEER FACTOR +
		No victimisation (bullying)	NEW FACTORS Low peer delinquency	CONTINUITY OF EARLIER PEER FACTORS +	CONTINUITY OF EARLIER PEER FACTORS +
			Low peer substance use	NEW FACTORS Most friends attend school	CONTINUITY OF EARLIER PEER FACTORS +
				No gang membership	NEW FACTORS Marriage to prosocial partner
					Low number of sexual partners
School			NEW FACTORS Low school deviancy level	CONTINUITY OF EARLIER SCHOOL FACTOR +	
			Well organised school		
Neighbourhood			NEW FACTORS Advantaged neighbourhood	CONTINUITY OF EARLIER NEIGHBOURHOOD FACTOR +	CONTINUITY OF EARLIER NEIGHBOURHOOD FACTOR +
			Low neighbourhood crime		
			Move to a better neighbourhood		

studies have designated certain variables that operate as promotive (or protective) factors, and very few studies have empirically identified which variables operate mostly as promotive rather than risk factors (but see Loeber et al., 2008). In addition, we know very little about the developmental aspects of the accumulation of promotive factors through the life-course. The framework proposed by Hawkins and colleagues (Catalano & Hawkins, 1996; Hawkins et al., 1992) and ourselves (Stouthamer-Loeber et al., 2002) is unusual in criminology because it postulates changes within promotive factors to explain individual differences in the development of offending. We postulate that some promotive factors, like risk factors, may be present at birth, but that other factors emerge during the first decades of life. Table 9.2 shows promotive factors mentioned in the research literature (or factors that are probably promotive according to our view) as being relevant to disruptive and delinquent behaviours (based on Arthur et al., 2002; Bachman, O'Malley & Johnston, 1978; Farrington, 1994; Kandel et al., 1988; Loeber et al., 2008; Lösel & Bender, 2003; Pollard, Hawkins & Arthur, 1999; Rand, 1987; Sampson & Laub, 1990; Smith et al., 1995; Stouthamer-Loeber et al., 1993, 2002, 2004; West, 1982; Van der Laan & Blom, 2006). Where research appears wanting, we have inserted factors that we think are probable promotive factors. Most of the promotive factors are the inverse of risk factors, in that many, but not all, of the promotive factors represent the other pole of risk factors. However, we do not advocate that promotive factors are the complete inverse of risk factors (see Stouthamer-Loeber et al., 1993, 2005 for details). Loeber et al. (2008) found that several factors formerly thought of as risk factors mainly operated as promotive factors, including low ADHD, high persistence of discipline, low physical punishment, good supervision, involvement of boys in family activities, low parental stress, and living in a good neighbourhood. These results held across the two cohorts and across violence and theft. Loeber et al. (2008) also found that many factors had mixed promotive and risk effects, and these included psychopathic features, depressed mood, interaction with the interviewer, perceived likelihood of being caught, parental reinforcement, parental antisocial attitude, parental aspirations for the child, parental stress, peer delinquency, relationship with peers, academic achievement, attitude to school, family socioeconomic status, and housing quality. Most of these effects applied to the two cohorts (the exceptions were parental stress, peer delinquency and housing quality, which applied to the youngest cohort only) and applied across violence and theft (the exception was that psychopathic features were more a risk factor for violence than theft).

As with the development of risk factors, we assume that there is a developmentally graded emergence of promotive factors (see Table 9.2). Some of the promotive factors are thought to be present at birth (for example, moderate to high intelligence, absence of prenatal exposure to toxins), while other factors become manifest later. It is also thought that there is a high degree of temporal stability of promotive factors, although the data on this do not yet appear to have been reported. In the Pittsburgh Youth Study (Loeber et al., 2008), the strongest promotive factors predictive of a low probability of violence were high academic achievement, older mother at age of birth of first child, and good relations with peers. The strongest promotive factors predictive of a low likelihood of serious theft were low psychopathic features, high academic achievement, and high parental persistence of discipline.

It is likely that promotive factors, such as risk factors, are correlated, in that one promotive factor may set the scene for another promotive factor to emerge. For instance, association with prosocial peers may generate new prosocial behaviours, which, once adopted by an individual child, may further decrease the probability that that child will engage in delinquent acts. Hawkins and his colleagues (2003) are among the few who have specified prosocial pathways in the delinquency research that can be conceptualised as a string of promotive factors. They postulate that opportunities for prosocial behaviours set the scene for interpersonal involvement, which in turn produces rewards, improving bonding to others and promoting belief in a moral order. Research shows that the prevalence of different promotive factors is highest in the most advantaged neighbourhoods (Stouthamer-Loeber et al., 2002; Wikström, 2005).

Inverse Dose-response Relationship between Promotive Factors and Delinquency

Is there an inverse dose-response relationship between the number of promotive factors and later deviance? (That is, the higher the number of promotive factors, the lower the probability of deviance?) There are very few research studies addressing this question. Outside the area of delinquency, Sameroff et al. (1998) found that the higher the number of promotive factors, the lower the probability of problem behaviours, with the results mirroring the results of the risk factors: 'The more risk factors, the worse the outcomes; the more promotive factors, the better the outcomes' (p. 172). Smith et al. (1995) also found that the higher the number of 'protective' factors, the higher the probability of resilience to delinquency (that is, the higher the percentage of non-offenders or those not seriously delinquent). For example, in the presence of 0–5 promotive factors, only 18.9% of the young people were not seriously delinquent. The proportion of non-delinquent adolescents increased to 32.4% in the presence of 6–7 promotive factors, and to 75.5% for those exposed to eight or more promotive factors. In summary, those young people with many promotive factors 'were four times more likely to be resilient than youth with few protective factors' (p. 235). Similar results have been reported by Wikström and Loeber (2000) and by Van der Laan and Blom (2006), thus lending support to the notion that the accumulation of promotive factors in juveniles' lives counters the likelihood of later delinquent involvement.

Developmental Aspects of Promotive and Risk Effects

Very few studies have questioned whether the proportion of promotive and risk factors is more or less constant with development, or whether promotive factors are stronger in certain developmental periods and risk factors are stronger in others. Van der Laan and Blom (2006) and Loeber and colleagues (2008) have found that the proportion of significant associations between promotive factors and delinquency is highest before adolescence, and that during adolescence risk effects are more common than promotive effects. Thus, promotive factors relevant for the

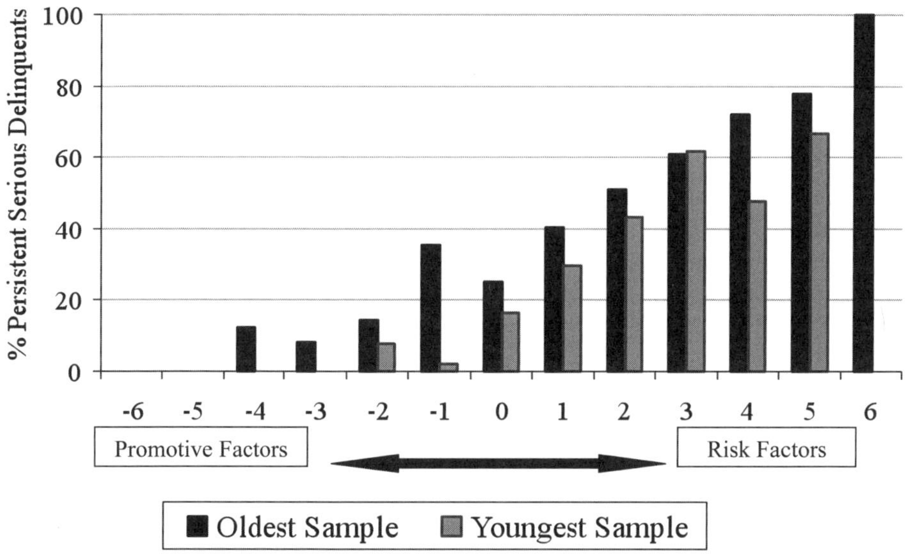

Figure 9.7 The higher the number of risk domains (and the lower the number of promotive domains) the higher the risk of later persistent serious delinquency

Source: Based on Stouthamer-Loeber et al., 2002.

prevention of serious delinquency had a greater effect at younger ages. This agrees with a community survey of risk and 'protective' factors reported in London which indicated that children's exposure to risk factors tended to increase with age, while their exposure to 'protective' (that is, promotive) factors tended to decrease with age (Communities That Care, 2005). Because of the relevance of these findings for early interventions, we will return to this in our conclusions.

Do Promotive Factors Offset the Impact of Risk Factors?

Do promotive factors buffer the risk for later persistent disruptive and delinquent behaviours? Research findings are sparse, but the data indicate that the additive mixture of risk and promotive factors predicts later deviance. For instance, Stouthamer-Loeber et al. (2002) showed that even at the level of the number of risk or promotive domains (child behaviour, child attitudes, school, peers, family, demographic characteristics), the sum of risk and promotive domains (where the number of promotive domains are deducted from the risk domains) linearly predicts persistent serious delinquency (Figure 9.7). The higher the number of risk domains to which a young person is exposed and the lower their exposure to promotive domains, the greater the likelihood of later persistent delinquency. Conversely, the higher the number of promotive domains and the lower the number of risk domains, the smaller the likelihood of later persistent serious delinquency. This was replicated for the youngest and oldest samples, for different degrees of neighbourhood advantage and

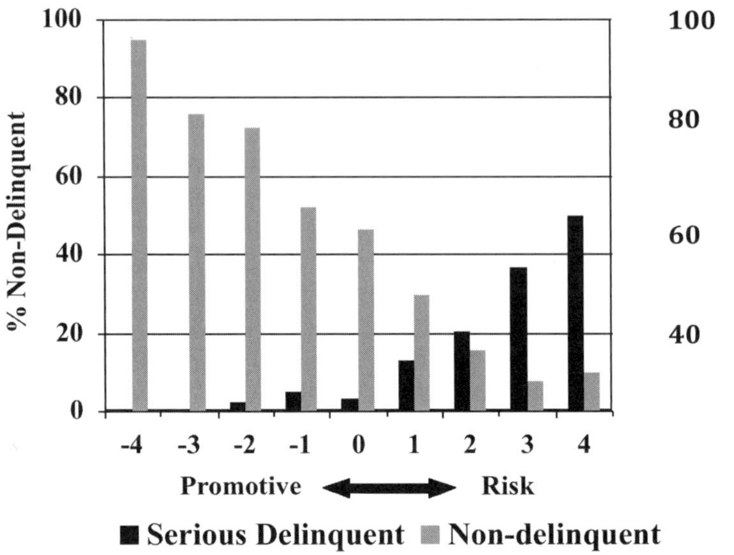

Figure 9.8 Promotive factors predominate for non-delinquents and risk factors predominate for serious delinquents

Source: Van der Laan & Blom (2006).

disadvantage, for specific risk and promotive factors, and for early- and late-onset forms of delinquency (Loeber et al., 2008; Stouthamer-Loeber et al., 2002; Wikström & Loeber, 2000).

Van der Laan and Blom (2006) in a cross-sectional Dutch study examined the proportion of domains of promotive and risk factors to which non-delinquent and seriously delinquent youth are exposed. Figure 9.8 shows that the balance between promotive and risk factors in the case of non-delinquents is in favour of promotive factors, while in the case of serious delinquents, risk factors tend to be dominant. In summary, there is replicated evidence that the balance between promotive and risk factors is associated with differences in juveniles' offending, and that the presence of promotive factors can buffer the impact of risk factors.

Not all researchers, however, have found that the relationship between risk and promotive factors is linear. For example, Pollard et al. (1999), studying such diverse outcomes as substance use, arrest and attack to hurt, found a non-linear effect, with the effect of risk factors greater as the level of risk increased. However, it is plausible that once neighbourhood context is taken into account, non-linear associations do occur. For example, Wikström and Loeber (2000) report that 'the overwhelming majority of boys with a high risk score were involved in serious offending regardless of the socioeconomic context of their neighbourhood' (p. 1130). However, neighbourhood matters greatly for those with a balanced score of risk and promotive factors.

Relevance of the Model for Assessments and Interventions

To summarise: first, we have reviewed developmental pathways from minor to serious delinquent behaviours (Figure 9.1). Secondly, we have discussed developmentally graded, cumulative onset of risk factors (Table 9.1; Figure 9.4) and developmentally graded, cumulative onset of promotive factors (Table 9.2). Third, we have seen that there are dose-response relationships between the number of risk factors and the probability of later delinquency and violence (Figure 9.5), and an inverse dose-response relationship between the number of promotive factors and the reduced probability of later delinquency and violence. Finally, we have seen that knowledge of the proportion of risk and promotive factors is more important than knowledge of either (Figure 9.7). The next question is: why is the cumulative, developmental model relevant for the assessment and the evaluation of preventive and remedial interventions?

Assessments

Advances have been made in the past decades in the area of more precise assessment of juveniles' problem behaviours in terms of the types of behaviour, their severity, and prognostic validity (see Chapter 10 and Appendix 1, this volume). In addition, screening instruments are now available to go beyond the range of problem behaviours of juveniles that also include the past history of risk factors to which juveniles have been exposed (for example, Koegl, Webster & Levens, 2001 (see also Appendix 1, this volume); Lodewijks et al., 2003). However, based on the information provided in this chapter, we argue that assessments can probably benefit from two other components. The first is an appraisal of current and past promotive factors to which juveniles are or have been exposed, because it is the mixture of risk and promotive effects that appears most crucial in determining the future risk of serious offending as well as the probability of full desistance or lower-level offending. And secondly, we also argue that the next generation of risk assessment devices could potentially also benefit from an appraisal of juveniles' expected future exposure to risk *and* promotive factors based on knowledge gained from longitudinal survey studies. Specifically, assessments of developmentally graded exposure to risk factors, based on longitudinal survey studies, could be employed to calculate the probability that juveniles will be exposed in the future to risk and promotive factors typically emerging for that age group.

One might argue that cross-sectional studies contain such information. There are several reasons why this is not the case. First, in contrast to cross-sectional studies, longitudinal studies have the power to specify selection processes determining which groups of youth are most likely to be exposed to future risk and promotive factors. Secondly, longitudinal studies can identify promotive factors predictive of nondelinquency, de-escalation from serious to minor offending, or desistance from offending. Since juveniles' engagement in delinquency varies from year to year, it is important to establish which promotive factors are associated with persistent non-offending or, alternatively, with a stable de-escalation in the severity of offending.

Longitudinal studies rather than cross-sectional studies are the best methods by which to identify promotive factors.

Preventive and Remedial Interventions

Chapters 11 and 12 and Appendix 1 (this volume) deal with prevention and intervention, and we will limit ourselves here to points that derive specifically from our cumulative, developmental model. We agree with Hawkins and colleagues (1992) and Howell (2003) that a developmental approach to offending needs a reconceptualisation of when interventions, preventive or treatment, can best take place (see Figure 1.1 in Chapter 1). Howell (2003) has been a primary proponent of the influential Comprehensive Strategy that addresses the full continuum of disruptive and delinquent development with two foci for implementing change: prevention and early intervention, and graduated sanctions. We believe that this orientation, which is based on knowledge of risk and promotive factors (which Howell calls protective factors), can also greatly benefit from the assessment of future risk through developmentally graded expectations of exposure to risk and promotive factors. We argue that this is especially important because even the most effective interventions still do not reduce the risk of recidivism by more than 40% (Lipsey & Wilson, 1998) and that the reoffending rate of high-risk populations of youth still remains extraordinary high (Loeber & Farrington, 1998). One of the highest risk populations is child delinquents who are at high risk of becoming tomorrow's serious and violent offenders. Whereas in normal development, promotive processes appear to dominate prior to adolescence, in the case of child delinquents, risk processes appear to dominate already early in life.

It should be understood that knowledge of risk and promotive factors as listed in Tables 9.1 and 9.2 does not mean that we have available the tools to change each of them, and of course some risk (and promotive) factors are not malleable (for example, single parenthood). However, we hope that our list of the risk and promotive factors and our model will stimulate the development of other forms of interventions that can augment the overall efficacy of interventions currently available. It is our impression that many treatment programmes can use knowledge gained by longitudinal survey studies to increase the range of promotive factors to enhance treatment efficacy. We foresee that interventions that mobilise or enhance promotive factors (together with the reduction of risk factors) eventually are likely to improve treatment efficacy and, possibly, the maintenance of treatment effects. We agree, however, with Pollard et al. (1999) that a sole focus on interventions enhancing promotive factors only, because of the compensatory function of risk and promotive factors, is likely to be inadequate. Another possible beneficial result of our model specification is the further individualisation of interventions tailored to a child's past, present and possible future exposure to risk and promotive factors.

Finally, we should stress that our cumulative model of disruptive and delinquent behaviours has certain limitations. Most of the work on risk and promotive processes has been accomplished outside of the Netherlands (but see Loeber & Slot, 2007; Loeber, Slot & Sergeant, 2001; Van der Laan & Blom, 2006). In addition, we mainly focused on the cumulative processes of risk and promotive factors rather than the specifics of mediation and moderation within and between risk and promotive factors. In addition, we do not focus on possible reciprocal processes between risk and promotive factors and negative or positive child behaviour, or the fact that as children's mobility in the community increases with age, they become more able to select settings and situations in which novel risk and promotive factors may present themselves. We are also aware that our model may have different components depending on the subject population of study (girls vs. boys, different ethnic groups), but we think it is generic enough to serve as an example to explain a range of maladjustments other than serious delinquency. The model depicts escalation in the severity of disruptive and delinquent behaviours better than de-escalation to lower severity levels, but de-escalation could perhaps be incorporated in the next iteration of the model. In addition, we have presented the model in a three-dimensional space (Loeber, Slot & Stouthamer-Loeber, 2006) so that the dynamic inter-relationships between its components can be better visualised. Also, there is a need to transfer the basic mathematical properties of our model into future model testing and particularly apply this to children who start offending at a very young age, which is the topic of this volume. It is clear that many tasks await, and we hope that this chapter will inspire others to improve on our current knowledge.

Acknowledgments

This chapter is partly based on Loeber, R., Slot, N.W., and Stouthamer-Loeber, M. (2006). A three-dimensional, cumulative developmental model of serious delinquency. In P.-O. H. Wikström & R. Sampson (eds), *The Explanation of Crime: Contexts and Mechanisms* (pp. 153–94). Cambridge: Cambridge University Press. The research was supported by grant 96-MU-FX-0012 from the Office of Juvenile Justice and Delinquency Prevention, grant No. 50778 from the National Institute of Mental Health, and grant No. 411018 from the National Institute on Drug Abuse. Points of view or opinions in this document are those of the authors and do not necessarily represent the official position or policies of the US Department of Justice, the National Institute of Mental Health, and the National Institute on Drug Abuse. We are indebted to Anna Neumann for assistance with this chapter.

Part IV
Prevention and Intervention

Chapter 10

Screening and Assessments

Lieke van Domburgh, Robert Vermeiren and Theo Doreleijers

Research has shown that prevention programmes can be effective in curtailing the escalation of disruptive or delinquent behaviours displayed by children at a young age (see Chapter 11, this volume). To be effective, interventions need to be well-timed, directed at the appropriate risk groups, and aimed at malleable, causal risk factors (Dryfoos, 1990; Durlak, 1995; Van der Ploeg & Scholte, 1997). To make sure that a prevention or intervention programme is applied at the appropriate risk group, screening and risk assessments are needed. To make sure that the subsequent prevention or intervention programme is aimed at the right criteria, needs assessments are required also.

First, screening refers to a (short) method to select at-risk children. Screening can take the form of 'explicit' identification of at-risk children within a larger population using a short actuarial screening instrument. In addition, screening can take place more 'implicitly' by professionals (for example, teachers, general practitioners, day-care professionals and police officers) who come into contact with children showing signs of delinquency, truancy, substance use, or violence. Although it may not be the job of some professionals, or within their expertise, to assess children (for example, the police), it is crucial that these signs are reported to and picked up by the appropriate agency (for example, a juvenile health care agency).

Secondly, risk assessment aims at predicting future risk of offending by individuals within an at-risk group. In addition to actuarial information, risk assessment focuses more on risk factors that require professional expertise to assess, such as impulsivity or potentially negative parenting practices. Moreover, a risk assessment generally requires a professional judgement of risk based on the gathered information.

Finally, needs assessment refers to the assessment of factors that need to be taken into consideration to prevent future offending by the individual. Although risk and needs assessments overlap somewhat, needs assessment focuses on dynamic risk factors, while risk assessment can use both static and dynamic risk factors. Dynamic predictors are malleable and therefore important for intervention, since risk can be reduced through treatment, for example, by improving social capacities. Static predictors on the other hand cannot change over time and are therefore immune to intervention (those such as sex or age of onset) but can be highly predictive of a negative development (for example, number of previous offences).

This chapter describes screening and assessment practices for at-risk children in the Netherlands. In order to evaluate existing practices, a framework of principles of effective screening and assessment will be presented. First, some general principles will be described (Le Blanc, 1998, 2000; Scholte and Doreleijers, 2001) that are considered essential in this perspective. Secondly, a description of relevant methods of screening and assessment will be given, from short screening lists to longitudinal multi-stage assessment procedures. Third, limitations of existing instruments and ethical issues will be discussed. Finally, Dutch practice will be described with emphasis on methods of active screening, but also on processes designed to ensure that signs observed by professionals in their daily practice reach the appropriate agency.

Theory of Effective Screening and Assessment

Principles of Effective Assessments

Le Blanc (1998, 2000) formulated principles to ensure effective and reliable assessment, which also apply to screening procedures to identify the appropriate at-risk children. The principles are guided by the following three main underlying issues (for details, see Le Blanc, 1998).

What Do We Want to Predict?

When assessing a child in order to identify at-risk children, one must decide on the exact outcome and a criterion representing the outcome. For instance, if we want to predict risk for violent offending, the criterion might be future arrest by the police or future self-reported offending. Particularly when screening within the general population, the problem is often the low prevalence, or base rate, of certain behaviours such as violent offending in the population. In the case of a low base rate of a criterion (for example, future arrest for sexual offence), the best prediction is that nobody will meet the criterion because the inherent 'margin for error' for prediction of the outcome hampers accurate prediction of such a rare outcome. Moreover, in children, relevant criteria – such as sexual recidivism – have very low base rates and cannot easily be replaced by a 'better' criterion. Therefore, it may not be feasible to predict specific types of externalising problem behaviours in general populations (for example, sexual offending at first screening in school), while this may be possible in at-risk populations (for example, sexual reoffending in children referred for sexual unwanted behaviour). On the other hand, more serious behaviours displayed by a small proportion of children often evolves from less serious behaviours displayed by a larger proportion of children. These less serious and more prevalent behaviours can serve as predictors of the more serious behaviours. Whatever prediction method is used, prediction errors are unavoidable and include false positives (falsely predicting the child will become delinquent) and false negatives (falsely predicting the child will not become delinquent). Acceptance of such error relates to the severity of outcome, impact of intervention, and specific characteristics of the individual case. For example, when a child is assessed to decide the child's out-home placement, consequences of the decision are far more dramatic than when a child is assessed for referral to social-skills training at a school.

What Predictors Should We Use?

Selection of specific predictors in screening instruments should be based on theory as well as empirical information (preferably related to the target population: for example, primary-school boys). Since the causes of disruptive and delinquent behaviours are multifaceted phenomena, a wide variety of factors are involved and should be covered in screening and assessment. These factors include family, peers, environment and individual characteristics (see Chapters 5–9, this volume). Some predictors can be highly predictive but are rare in a population and may therefore not be useful in a short actuarial screening instrument applied in a general population (Loeber & Dishion, 1983). However, low base-rate factors may have substantial predictive value in screening and in risk and needs assessments. For instance, although truancy at elementary school is rare in general populations, it can be a marker for deviant development and, therefore, can be a reason for a schoolteacher to refer the child for a risk assessment.

Decisions of what to include in needs assessments should also cover dynamic risk factors (Bailey, 2002). In addition, optimal intervention also requires the assessment of general needs and psychosocial functioning of the child. Extensive assessment will provide more information to optimally tailor the intervention to the child. Several studies have shown a high prevalence of mental health problems and academic underachievement among juveniles in the juvenile justice system (Grisso, Vincent & Seagrave, 2004; Vermeiren, Jespers & Moffitt, 2006; Maguin & Loeber, 1996). A general needs assessment is essential to optimise intervention and thereby reduce future risk of serious offending. Some authors have argued that the younger the child, the more interventions should consider optimising the child's overall functioning and well-being (Grisso & Zimring, 2004).

How to Gather Reliable Information?

In daily practice, it may be difficult to gather reliable information or to even gain insight into the reliability of the gathered information. All data sources have their advantages and disadvantages. For example, children tend to underreport their externalising problem behaviours, while parents tend to underreport their child's internalising problem behaviours (Sawyer, Baghurst and Mathias, 1992). Reliability may also largely depend on the nature and the possible impact of screening. A parent who is being assessed while voluntarily seeking help is likely to report differently from one who is being assessed for involuntary out-of-home placement of the child. Methods of data gathering (for example, questionnaires vs. interviews) have their own limitations. For each predictor, the most reliable method of data gathering available should be used. For example, psychiatric diagnoses should be made only by trained mental health professionals, whereas for the purpose of prevention or screening an assessment should be based on standardised interviews or a standardised screening instrument. To optimise a reliable assessment, all variables should be clearly defined and scoring guidelines should be used, which should also make explicit the required training level of the assessor. In practice, sources of information can be restricted; for example, it may not be possible for a mental health professional to gather official court or school data without the permission of the parents. The challenge then is to optimise reliability of the available information about children's behaviours.

Effective Assessment Strategies

Once the information has been gathered, several methods can be used to evaluate the information. First, actuarial screening instruments combine risk factors without requiring weighting of the information and are therefore suited for quick screening of children within large populations. Since actuarial screening instruments use static, unchangeable risk factors (for example, past delinquent behaviour), which are objective and countable, the instruments can be accompanied by strict scoring guidelines, thus avoiding interpretation of the findings by the professional. Although actuarial screening instruments can assess risk well, they are not useful for guiding individual intervention (Douglas & Kropp, 2002). Risk assessment instruments, such as the Early Assessment of Risk Lists (EARL20-Boys; EARL21-Girls) for children age 6–12 require the professional to give a clinical judgement of risk based on the score (Augimeri et al., 2001; Levene et al., 2001; see Appendix 1, this volume). Research in adult populations indicated higher predictive accuracy of these latter instruments than of the actuarial method (for example, de Vogel et al., 2004). The main advantage is that these instruments use both static and dynamic factors and are thus sensitive to changes in risk level (Ruiter, 2005). On the other hand, these instruments are time-consuming and require a high professional standard, making them less appropriate for large-scale population screening.

Regardless of the method used to evaluate the findings, different strategies can be used to select the appropriate risk group of children, ranging from using a single screening instrument at a single point in time to step-wise screening over a period of time. Stepped screening, or screening in multiple phases – also called multiple-gating methods (see Figure 10.1) – can be a cost-effective solution to the low base-rate problem of predictors and outcomes (Loeber, Dishion and Patterson, 1984). The strategy of multiple-gating is first to do a low-cost screen for general problem behaviours within a general population sample in order to identify a moderately high-risk group of youth. A subsequent slightly more expensive screen on the identified moderately high-risk sample helps to further narrow down the high-risk group to those most likely to become deviant later. In the example provided by Loeber and colleagues (1984), a school-based sample of children that could benefit from intensive treatment to avoid escalation to violent offending was first screened by the teacher on a five-item questionnaire measuring risk behaviour. Individuals scoring high on this screening questionnaire were then evaluated by the teacher through a more extensive questionnaire, which measured aggressive problem behaviours. At the third and last stage, children displaying aggressive problem behaviours were assessed by a psychologist, who then involved parents as informants as well, so that individuals could be selected who could benefit from the treatment. This method was cost-effective and 58% less expensive than a single-stage screening (Loeber et al., 1984).

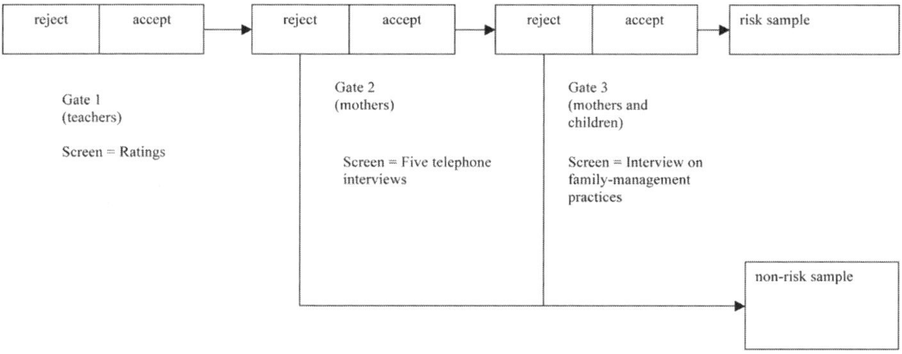

Figure 10.1 Diagram of the multiple phase design for a three-phase screening procedure

Source: Loeber et al. (1984).

Step-wise screening can also be used to address another problem in the assessment of children, namely the instability of their behaviour. For example, most children are oppositional at some point in their lives. For behaviour to be predictive of future disruptive and delinquent behaviours, it must be stable over time. When applying the multi-stage method with young children (age 6 and 7), research showed that multiple observations over time were necessary in the first assessment stage to achieve adequate predictive power (Charlebois & LeBlanc, 1994). Children had to score high on a screening instrument at the first stage for two years in a row to be considered at risk, in order to rule out children whose deviancy is temporary (for example, because of a recent life event). A multi-stage screening method can be implemented in an institute that children attend for a long period of time, such as a school. The method does not need to be restricted to one organisation. Collaborative use of information collected by multiple organisations may serve as multi-stage assessment as well (for example, between police and youth care agencies).

Which strategy is appropriate to select at-risk children depends on the setting. Longitudinal, multi-phase screening should take place either in agencies that already follow children throughout their development, such as schools, public health services and day-care centres, or in various agencies working together. Incidental risk signs gathered by different agencies (for example, general practitioner, teacher, or the police) should be reported to a central agency. In order to make screening and assessment feasible in daily practice, the use of time-consuming instruments that require expertise can best be done in agencies where screening and diagnostic assessment is part of their daily practice. Other professionals – such as police officers or schoolteachers – should only be requested to report signs of child problem behaviours and to use short instruments that require no specific expertise.

Limitations and Ethical Considerations

Screening instruments for children are only as good as they are sensitive to developmental processes. The prediction of future child deviant behaviour is complicated because children's development from minor to serious, violent and persistent offending entails intricate processes in which numerous factors have main effects on child deviancy and, sometimes, interaction effects over time as well (Loeber & Farrington, 2000; see also Chapters 5–9, this volume). For example, impulsivity and living in a disadvantaged neighbourhood independently predict deviant child behaviour (that is, each has a main effect). However, research has shown that impulsivity carries a much higher risk in poorer neighbourhoods (which is an interaction effect; Lynam et al., 2000). Thus, including interactions between predictors in screening instruments may have the potential of enhancing predictive accuracy.

There are limitations to the prediction of persistent disruptive behaviours and delinquency based on pre-adolescent behaviour. A child's personality is still developing during this period of life. Moreover, many risk factors at this age are indicators of later general problem behaviour, rather than antecedents of a specific condition such as delinquent acts. Also, many child problem behaviours often are temporary variations of normal behaviour. Since no assessment instrument for the pre-adolescent period is fully sensitive, using an assessment tool can never entirely replace professional and clinical judgement, as well as responsibility, when deciding on an individual's future risk As the developmental characteristics of various age groups are different (for example, emotional development, peer relationships, school attendance), we should warn against the adaptation of assessment instruments used for older age groups for use with children.

The main ethical aspect to consider when screening at-risk children is the possible negative impact of adults' labelling a child as deviant, which may negatively affect their interaction with the child's behaviour, and in a self-fulfilling prophecy generate deviant child behaviours (Rock, 2002). However, empirical evidence for this mechanism is very limited. Although several studies have shown formal criminal interventions can increase the risk of future offending (for example, Farrington, Osborn & West, 1978; Farrington, Loeber & Stallings, 2007), it remains unclear whether labelling is the mechanism causing this effect. We have been unable to find Dutch studies on the effect of incarceration or institutionalisation on later offending. Recent studies have shown adolescents who received justice interventions to be at higher risk to affiliate with deviant others, which in turn leads to higher reoffending rates as compared to adolescents with similar initial delinquency levels who did not receive an intervention (for example, Bernburg, Krohn & Rivera, 2006). Whatever the mechanism, the important thing to keep in mind is the possible negative effect of an intervention on the development of the child.

To avoid duplication of information and reduce burdens on families, administrators have stressed the increased need to exchange information among social service agencies. Exchange of information can, however, also have a negative impact. Controls for the reliability of the information are often not in place, and once information is lodged in a database it is often difficult to correct or remove.

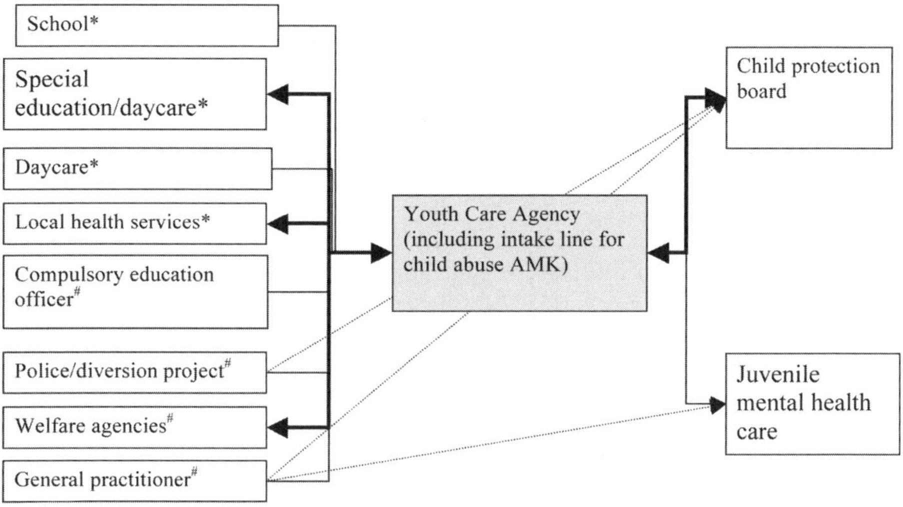

Figure 10.2 Dutch agencies involved with potential at-risk children

Note:*Organisations with regular contact with all children; # organisations with incidental contact with at risk children.

Finally, systematic screening of children creates an obligation to act on the results. In other words, once social services have identified some children as at risk, the agencies have to be able to offer treatment to the children and their families. Otherwise, the systematic screening of children is unethical because it may give the false hope to the child and their family that treatment is to follow. However, in daily practice, it is very difficult to guarantee follow-up on the screening outcomes due to lack of funds and shortage of facilities.

Screening and Assessment of Children with Disruptive Behaviours in the Netherlands

Where Screening and Assessments Take Place

As can be seen from Figure 10.2, many Dutch agencies are involved in the screening of (at-risk) children, and different professionals in these agencies have their own unique opportunities of identifying such children. Almost all children are reached by professionals from three services: the Local Public Health Services (GGD), day-care/child centres, and schools. Local authorities are legally obliged to offer children, from birth to age 19, both mental and physical healthcare. Ninety per cent of all Dutch newborns regularly attend the Local Public Health Services from shortly after birth until age 14: care for children from birth to age 4 is provided at local child centres (*Consultatiebureau* or *Ouder-Kind Centrum* in Dutch [Consultation Bureau for Children and Parents]). From age 4 onward, care is provided at school by the same service. Over 90% of children in the Netherlands start to attend kindergarten at age 4 and many Dutch children attend some sort of day care prior to that age. Therefore kindergarten and day-care centres offer nationwide opportunities for longitudinal screening. In addition, the long-term contact between kindergarten and day-care centres and parents offers many possibilities to try to motivate the parents and the child. If motivation fails the first time, it may succeed the second, third, or fourth time as the behaviour of the child becomes more apparent and the bond between the parents and the professionals has possibly become stronger.

When more specialised help is needed, children and parents can turn to the Youth Care Bureau (*Bureau Jeugdzorg*), which forms the main gateway to professional mental health care assistance in the Netherlands. The Youth Care Agency determines whether and in what form specialised help is needed. When specialised help is indicated, the Youth Care Agency refers the child to the most appropriate mental health agency. If no specialised care is needed, the Youth Care Agency can itself offer short interventions (Doreleijers, 2004). Aside from parents, professionals can also refer a child to the Youth Care Agency (examples are a police officer who catches a child who steals from a shop, or a general practitioner who notices a child who uses drugs). Only in cases of immediate danger to the child can a direct referral be made to the child protection board.

Instruments for Screening and Assessment of Dutch Children

Recently a Dutch government committee summarised the evidence of screening instruments for children's externalising problem behaviours (Hermanns, Öry & Schrijvers, 2005). The committee concluded that few screening devices have been developed or translated for the detection of disruptive and/or delinquent behaviours in children. Some broad instruments that include a section on externalising problem behaviours have been translated into Dutch and could be used for screening children, such as the Strengths and Difficulties Questionnaire (SDQ: Goodman, 1997; Van Widenfelt et al., 2003) and the Child Behaviour Check List (CBCL: Achenbach, 1991). Both instruments have parent, teacher and self-report versions and do not require professional expertise to administer. The CBCL, however, specifically provides information on externalising problem behaviours in at-risk sub-groups (Vreugdenhil et al., 2006). The only risk assessment instrument specially designed for children below age 12 is the Early Assessment Risk List. This instrument consists of twenty (twenty-one for girls) items that are related to the family (for example, socioeconomic status, coping, and so on), the child (for example, hyperactivity, academic deficits) and responsivity or motivation for treatment. Each item can be rated absent, partially present, or definitely present (EARL20b for boys: Augimeri et al., 2001; and EARL21g for girls: Levene et al., 2001; see also Appendix 1, this volume). The EARL is being translated and will be validated in the Dutch population. Administration of the instrument requires the training of professionals.

Recently several short self-report instruments for various forms of disruptive behaviours have been translated into Dutch and can be used with children, for example, the Youth Psychopathic Inventory Child Version (YPI-CV): Baardewijk et al., 2007), the Antisocial Process Screening Device for psychopathic characteristics (APSD: Frick & Hare, 2001, Das et al., 2003), and the Reactive and Proactive

Questionnaire for pro- and reactive-aggression (RPQ: Raine et al., 2006; Domburgh & Popma, 2003) for the purpose of scientific research. Their value has, however, not yet been established for individual risk assessment.

Recent Developments in Screening and Assessments

In the past, the use of validated and standardised methods for screening, assessment and referral was rare. In addition, the goals of the various agencies have made assessment very specific to particular agencies. This has resulted in a lack of cooperation between agencies, which in turn has led to duplication in assessments and gaps in essential data. In past years, many authors, agencies and Dutch governmental reports (such as *Operatie Jong* <www.operatiejong.nl>; Jeugd Terecht, 2006) have stressed the importance of early detection of at-risk children by means of screening and collation of the knowledge across agencies. This has resulted in screening, prevention and intervention initiatives by various agencies throughout the country. The initiatives have stressed the need to improve cooperation between agencies, reduce duplication, collate knowledge, and to assure actual care is provided after referral. One of the most important developments in this regard has been the installation of the Youth Care Agency as the central agency in the referral to Juvenile Mental Health Care. In addition, several agencies have made referral agreements. For example, the police and the Office for Juvenile Care have agreed on a referral method. Although promising, these referral agreements do not guarantee actual referral or follow-up within a short time span. A better guarantee is by means of structural meetings between involved agencies that have been instituted where children at risk are discussed between disciplines. An example of this is the chain units (*Ketenunits)* in Amsterdam, which brings together the Child Protection Board, the police, the Diversion Project Agency (*Bureau HALT*), and the Youth Care Agency. Another promising development is the linkage of information from the computerised registration systems of several agencies.

Although cooperation has improved, there is much room for further improvements. At the moment, several services have started screening in parallel. This results in duplication, which is not only costly and inefficient but also forms an unnecessary burden on the children and their parents. Furthermore, duplication of screening creates confusion in the parents and children who then do not know what can be expected from the various agencies. It becomes even more confusing if the results of screening and subsequent advice on intervention differ. Further, it is not uncommon that screening, decisions and the identification of at-risk children is still based on unstandardised screening assessments which have not been validated, and in addition, screening is seldom based on multi-phase and/or longitudinal screening techniques. Finally, increased screening by agencies creates a demand for treatment of the identified at-risk children in a field that already is struggling with long waiting lists and shortages of treatment facilities and funds. Therefore, it should be kept in mind that an improvement in screening will have to be accompanied by an improvement in intervention facilities. Despite these difficulties, the new initiatives can form an excellent base for validated assessments and referral methods. We will now turn to the most promising practices.

Promising Dutch Examples and Opportunities

Screening/Assessment in the School: the SPRINT Project for Longitudinal Multi-phase Screening

As mentioned, the school system is an excellent place to conduct multi-phase screening for mental health problems including problem behaviours. A promising longitudinal multi-phase method called SPRINT (Van Leeuwen & Bijl, 2003a, 2003b) is currently being evaluated in elementary schools in Amsterdam. SPRINT is based on multiple-gating method (Loeber et al., 1984) as described above, but applied repeatedly over time. SPRINT aims to detect children with persistent disruptive behaviours at a young age, and to offer them (and their parents) a 'preventive' intervention. The screening consists of three 'gates' or steps. First, the potential risk group is selected by a global screening list filled out by the teacher. Teachers assess every child in the classroom on five problem areas. Secondly, the potential risk group resulting from this first screen is screened three times in one year. Screening consists of teacher reports using an instrument measuring disruptive behaviours (WAS: Slot, Orobio de Castro & Duivenvoorden, 2000), supplemented with some items on family risk factors (*Signaleringslijst*: Orobio de Castro, 1999). Children who score above a threshold on two or more measurements are considered at risk. Third, parents of the at-risk children are asked to fill out the WAS and the CBCL. Following from this, the at-risk children and their parents are offered an intervention suited to their specific problems. Results are promising, showing that at-risk children can be identified (PI Research, 2002). Motivating non-Dutch parents in particular to accept intervention remains difficult. However, for those parents who refuse intervention, a support system has been developed. Parents are told intervention remains available, and schools contact parents on a regular basis to discuss the development of the child. In sum, SPRINT is one of the few screening methods using standardised instruments in a multiple-gate, multiple-time design, accompanied by empirical research to test whether the goals of screening are met. The design is thereby sensitive to the screening standards described in the first part of the chapter.

Longitudinal Screening in the Local Public Health System: Rotterdam Youth Monitor

In Rotterdam, all children are systematically screened on several possible problems, including disruptive behaviour, by the public health agency (GGD) from birth to age 18 using multi-phase screening (called the Youth Monitor) with standardised and validated instruments (*Rotterdamse Jeugdmonitor* <www.jeugdmonitorrotterdam.nl/web.cijfers.html>). Screening takes place at age 2, 5, 11, 13 and 15. The first wave (age 2) is incorporated in the regular visit at the local child centre. Parents are sent a short child mental health questionnaire (SKIPPI <www.skippi.nl>) prior to the appointment. All items that are scored negative are discussed with a nurse at the appointment. Afterwards, the nurse decides whether advice or referral is needed based on the parent information, the nurse's own observations, and the dossier at the child centre. The conclusions of the nurse are registered in a standard form. At age 5 and age 11, screening of the children is incorporated in school visits by the school public health agency. Both parents and teachers fill out the SKIPPI. At age 11, parents and teachers fill out the SDQ. Children are considered to score high if they score in the highest 20%. Again, the juvenile nurse decides whether advice or referral is needed. At age 13 and 15, screening is based on self-report. Currently, specific risk protocols (for example, on disruptive behaviour) are being developed allowing specialised assessment in multiple phases. Besides individual screening, results are collated at the school and neighbourhood level. School-specific reports are produced and discussed with school personnel. If needed, school-specific interventions, such as social skills training, are offered.

Although very promising, the Youth Monitor still needs to be developed further. First, screening of children takes place at several different ages. However, information from the different assessments at the various time points is not automatically combined in an overall developmentally-oriented screening method. For that reason, the Youth Monitor fails to use one of its main potential strengths, that is, screening from birth to adolescence. Secondly, although the decisions made by the nurse are recorded in a standard form, there is no standardised way to interpret the results. Third, the interventions offered to the school have to be funded by the school itself, which means that there is no guarantee that children most in need will receive an intervention. Finally, in the near future, the Youth Monitor will need to be evaluated on whether indeed the highest-risk children have been identified using the most optimal predictors, reporters and outcome criteria.

Screening and Assessment after Police Encounters: Screening Instruments and Local Referral Initiatives

Children's encounters with the police at a young age constitute important warning signs for the development of disruptive and delinquent behaviours. Such encounters can stimulate professionals and parents to seek or accept help for individual children. Although children below age 12 are not criminally liable and therefore cannot be prosecuted, police encounters are registered in local police systems. Consequently, police officers have to decide what action to take with a child (for example, referral to a voluntary diversion project or reporting to the Youth Care Agency). However, screening children is not considered to be in the expertise of the police. This apparent contradiction has resulted in a variety of practices and checklists throughout the country. Over the past years, the police introduced nationwide a form which is filled out when a juvenile is registered as a suspect in an offence (*Landelijk Overdrachts Formulier – versie 2: LOF*). It lists risk factors described in the international literature and should be used for all juveniles, including children. It is unclear why certain risk factors are included on the form while others are not. The form is used as a signalling instrument for contacts with other agencies, and collates information gathered by the police, but does not encourage the formulation of standard advice on the information collected. Furthermore, standardised protocols have not been developed on how to gather the information needed to complete the form. Consequently, many forms, especially those relating to children, are filled out incompletely. Scientific evaluation of risk factors used in this form and formulation of standardised protocols would greatly enhance the efficacy of the instrument.

Aside from the LOF, some of the locally designed cooperation and referral practices with public services and the Youth Care Agency deserve to be mentioned (*JPP*, *JPT*, *Vangnet Jeugd* and *Pak je Kans*). These initiatives mostly follow the same principle by which the police refer – based on a first screening – children and their families to a mental health worker who collaborates with the police. Within a given period of time (for example, forty-eight hours) after the referral, the mental health worker visits the family and offers them a short intervention if needed. The mental health worker can in turn refer the child or the family to other mental health agencies if further diagnostic assessment or treatment is needed. These cooperative methods do not yet use a standard instrument for screening, but would form an excellent base for multi-phase screening.

One of the oldest and best-studied interventions is a family-oriented prevention programme called the Youth Prevention Programme (*Jeugd Preventie Programma: JPP* <www.collegio.nl/poducgroep/dienstfiles>). A trained police officer judges all locally registered information covering risk behaviour of children. If such signs are present, the officer visits the child and parents. If the child shows persistent high-risk behaviour, and if the family shows difficulties in three or more life domains (school, work, finances, police/justice, housing, relationships and social environment, health and leisure time), the police officer will refer to the family to the JPP. In a given year, about 17% of the children who enter the JPP range in age from birth to age 10, and 38% are 10–14-years-old (internal information by *collegio* <www.collegio.nl>). If the family is referred to the JPP, they are offered a twelve-week intervention, followed by further referral or by less frequent family coaching by a JPP worker. The programme was evaluated in 1995, but evaluation research has not yet been conducted to examine the effect of the screening. Police and JPP workers are trained to perform the screening and assessment, but no hard criteria are specified to determine if a problem is present in one of the life domains. The programme will be included in the national database on effective youth interventions by the NIZW International Centre (*Nederlands Instituut voor Zorg en Welzijn*). The JPP also aims to receive a certificate on its quality and effectiveness. To achieve this, a plan will be presented on how to measure the effectiveness of the programme on an annual basis. Although these initiatives are very promising, they have been implemented on a local basis only and often lack standardised screening methods.

Child Protection Board

Since 1999, the Child Protection Board uses a standardised (preliminary) assessment procedure in juvenile law cases called BARO (*Basis Raads Onderzoek*; Doreleijers et al., 1999; Doreleijers & Spaander 2002). The BARO is based on the POSIT (Dembo, 1994) and has been validated for the Dutch adolescent population in a sample of arrestees. The BARO comprises a questionnaire and an interview protocol. The procedure results in a standardised report and an indication as to whether further diagnostic assessment is required. A separate survey carried out by an independent research team found that using the BARO had added value to the methods previously used (Herwaarden, 2004). Compared to the previous methods used for files, the use of the BARO has improved the quality of files and subsequent advice based on them. In addition, interviews revealed that all stakeholders such as juvenile judges, child protection board workers and parents were much more satisfied with the BARO method than with other methods. Currently, the Board is considering the validation of the instrument for use in civil cases, including civil cases for children below the age of criminal responsibility. In Finland, the BARO is already implemented in civil cases. In Switzerland, the German version of the BARO has been validated (Gutschner & Doreleijers, 2004, 2006) and is now used in a nationwide survey of institutionalised youths. However, it remains to be seen whether the BARO is as effective for children as it is for juveniles, or whether an adapted child-version needs to be designed.

Computerised Information Exchange: The National Referral Index for At-risk Youth (Verwijsindex risicojongeren) and the Electronic Child File (Electronisch Kinddossier)

As mentioned above, most at-risk children do not yet have an extensive dossier at an agency. For that reason, the collation of information from different agencies would enable earlier detection of children in need of help. One way of combining information is the use of shared registration software. Software implemented nationwide will also ensure that information will not get lost when children move, which is important since many at-risk children and their parents are highly mobile. When using shared software, the privacy of clients must be guaranteed. One solution may be to limit the authorisation of professionals to certain domains. Two promising examples of this method are the Referral Index for At-risk Youth for local juvenile agencies and the Electronic Child File for juvenile mental health care agencies.

The Electronic Child File is the initiative of the Ministry of Health, Welfare and Sport. It will replace the existing paper files of local juvenile healthcare agencies (*GGD* and *Thuiszorg* in the Netherlands). The main goal is to standardise and combine registration to improve efficacy and follow-up of children. It will be available nationwide, assuring that no information on children will get lost when they and their families move home. The registration will contain information on the mental and physical health of the child, family circumstances and school functioning. The file will be used by the local juvenile health professionals such as medical doctors, nurses and juvenile health care staff. The Electronic Child File will in practice be available nationwide for all children from birth to age 19 from 2008–09. However, it is still to be decided who will get access to the information and how this is to be done. In the future, software may be designed to automatically screen for at-risk children using the central registered data.

The National Referral Index for At-risk Youth is a proposal of the inter-departmental initiative *Operatie Jong* (<www.operatiejong.nl>). It is designed to be a software application in which all agencies (for example, school, police, general practitioners, housing services, mental health care and local health care) will be involved. The application will report only that a contact has taken place but will not record the content of the contact. If two or more agencies have reported potential signs of risk, the different agencies will be able to contact each other to coordinate any follow-up. Currently, pilots for the development of the index are being carried out in different cities in the Netherlands. It has yet to be decided whether the index will be implemented nationwide and who will be the central coordinator of the index. If agencies register all possible risk signs and standard follow-ups can be guaranteed, the index will be an important step forward in the screening of at-risk children. With time, it is hoped that it will show how effective both indices will be in screening at-risk children.

Conclusions

The practices and local standardised screening methods described above show that Dutch agencies are becoming aware of the need to screen and assess children in a more standardised way. In addition, it has become more widely accepted that screening should not be regarded as a one-off event, but should be viewed as a longitudinal process in which cooperation between agencies is essential. However promising, more information is needed on the validity of the screening and assessment instruments and on the advice given based on the results. In particular, up until now designers of information systems have paid little attention to the fact that there are differences in predictive validity of risk factors within specific populations. It cannot be automatically assumed that a known risk factor within the general adolescent population will have the same predictive value within a population of children with a police encounter. This requires scientific validation of the methods within each setting. Aside from the development of new methods and instruments, useful screening and assessment tools have been translated into Dutch and their validity is currently being evaluated. It is expected that these instruments will soon become available to practitioners in the Netherlands. In addition, screening and prediction instruments are likely to be enhanced when knowledge of the interaction between risk factors is incorporated into new instruments and screening strategies. If these standardised screening methods are adopted nationwide and if the subsequent increased demand for interventions can be met, more at-risk children will be served at a young age.

Chapter 11

Prevention

Harrie Jonkman, Tom van Yperen and Bert Prinsen

Violence and persistent disruptive and delinquent behaviours in children and adolescents are serious social problems. They have consequences for individuals as well as for society, now and in the future. In addition to psychosocial damage to victims, there may also be substantial financial consequences (Keating & Herzman, 1999; Loeber & Farrington, 2001; Van Lier & Crijnen, 2003). Violence and delinquency are often linked to early disruptive behaviours. They are also related to other problem behaviours in later developmental phases, such as substance abuse, dropping out of school, teen pregnancy and adult mental health problems (Dryfoos, 1998; Kipke et al., 1999; Loeber, Slot & Sergeant, 2001; Rutter, Giller & Hagell, 1998; Rutter & Taylor, 2004). In this respect, intuitively, efforts to prevent early delinquency cannot be wrong.

In the Netherlands, the appeal of preventive efforts has led to a flourishing practice of projects and programmes. In recent years, however, a number of critical questions have been put forward. Are these preventive efforts really effective? Are they feasible? Can they be implemented at the right place, the right moment and as early as possible? Can people and institutions really use them? Thus far, many of these questions remain to be answered. Nevertheless, in the Netherlands as elsewhere, in the last five years a new practice has risen of critically evaluating existing prevention programmes and searching for and implementing effective, 'evidence-based' interventions. This practice has shown that in the Netherlands there is a long way to go towards identifying and implementing early, usable and effective prevention programmes.

In the 1990s, youth delinquency – and in particular violence – had become a social problem of the first order (Van der Laan, 2005). This phenomenon gained much attention in the media, and it became a serious political topic at national and local levels. The result was that on the one hand, the Netherlands followed the course of the US and the UK by introducing a 'culture of control' (Garland, 2001): there was an increasing emphasis on repression of delinquency on different levels. More violent and delinquent youngsters were locked up or placed in special treatment facilities. On the other hand, pleas for prevention policy and programmes were growing strongly. However, the theoretical foundations for this preventive path were still limited. Moreover, the empirical research on the validity of these foundations and the effectiveness of the programmes was still very scarce. Prevention policy was mostly based on intuition rather than a more scientific approach (Junger-Tas, 2001).

At the same time, our knowledge of the development of these problem behaviours had increased enormously. Research revealed the risk factors in early development, and shed light on the biological, familial and social influences in the developmental pathways of these youngsters (Elliott & Tolan, 1999; Junger-Tas, 2001; Loeber et al., 1993; Loeber & Farrington, 1998; Rutter et al., 1998; Rutter & Taylor, 2004; Tremblay & Craig, 1995). It became clear that these developmental pathways can best be influenced at an early stage, when behavioural patterns are still fluid and have not yet become stable. In addition, studies showed that some preventive interventions were working better than others and yielded increasing insight into 'what works' in the prevention of delinquency (Dryfoos, 1990, 1998; Durlak, 1997; Elliott & Tolan, 1999; Elliott, 1997; Sherman et al., 1996). These studies, however, came mainly from abroad and the findings were only marginally adopted in the ever-growing number of Dutch prevention projects.

As we will discuss later, studies show that in the 1980s and 1990s a wide range of prevention programmes had been developed of which only a very few had an explicit, up-to-date theoretical rationale (Hermanns & Vergeer, 2002; Verdurmen et al., 2003). Moreover, almost none of these programmes have been adequately evaluated for effectiveness. This is a dramatic finding in view of the growing problem of youth delinquency in Dutch society. It calls for a drastic renovation of both the prevention and evaluation practice in this country. The first step in this process is to examine the theoretical concepts that should be at the foundation of this practice. The second is to learn as much as possible from the few programmes that have a sound rationale and a proven success record.

A Theoretical Framework for Prevention

The Developmental Perspective

The prevention of delinquency at an early stage is made possible by current knowledge of the behavioural development of disruptive and delinquent behaviours from childhood onward. The knowledge of the factors that cause, maintain, or aggravate child problem behaviours comes from epidemiological and longitudinal research (Catalano & Hawkins, 1996; US Public Health Service, 2001; Jonkman, Junger-Tas & Van Dijk, 2005). The results of this research have substantially improved our knowledge. It has become clear that a successful prevention strategy can be anchored in the early phases of the developmental pathways that lead to youth delinquency (see also Chapters 5–9, this volume). One of the key elements of this kind of developmental prevention is that the programme is aimed at suppressing or eliminating risk factors that increase the probability of children becoming tomorrow's delinquents. The intervention, then, can be considered as a promotive factor that serves as a counterbalance to compensate for stable risk factors. For example, children from low-income families with both parents working are offered cheap facilities for after-school activities that are supervised by adults. The programme can also change dynamic risk factors into promotive factors. For example, a programme may encourage teachers and parents, who use negative disciplinary strategies (such as giving warnings, uttering threats and administering punishment) to use more positive strategies (such as ignoring negative behaviours and praising children for their positive behaviours).

Our theoretical framework of prevention programmes follows the example set by Van Yperen and Boendermaker (Chapter 12, this volume): The first issue concerns *which* mediators are influenced by a particular intervention. In line with a developmental approach, these mediators extend to the different developmental stages of the child. Accordingly, a preventive programme is likely to be effective if: (a) the programme addresses true risk factors that are causally related to later delinquency, and (b) the programme enhances promotive factors that buffer the presence of risk factors.

The second issue concerns *how* these mediators are addressed in interventions. This calls for knowledge of how and when the mechanisms and associated factors can be changed.

We will now discuss these two aspects of prevention.

Which Risk Factors and Mechanisms?

It is common to consider these factors and mechanisms in relation to four actors in the development of children: the child itself, the family, significant others and the broader environment (community, state). Constitutional and physiological factors and the genetic make-up of *the child* can act as risk factors and mechanisms which influence children's development of externalising problem behaviours (see Chapter 5, this volume). For example, the use of drugs, cigarettes and alcohol by the mother during pregnancy, and problems during birth may affect the child's brain development, which in turn is associated with higher risks of later child problem behaviours (Jessor, 1998; Moffitt, 1997; Loeber & Farrington, 2001; Van Lier, 2002). Furthermore, we know that children born with a difficult temperament often show a lack of self-control in different social settings and react with anger and impulsivity. This in turn leads to a higher risk of later disruptive and delinquent behaviours (Moffitt, 1997). In addition, young children who show early behavioural, cognitive and school problems have a higher likelihood of showing later disruptive and delinquent behaviours.

As to *the family*, lack of communication, poor bonding, lack of love and trust, but also frequent tensions and quarrels are known to have a negative impact on children's development (Damon, 1997; Furstenberg et al., 1999; see also Chapter 6, this volume). Also relevant are parents' internal management qualities (how they run family life) and their external management qualities (how they control and follow what their children do outside the home; see Furstenberg et al., 1999). The latter become increasingly important when youngsters begin to expand their activities outside the home.

The quality of the *school* environment is another important factor (Greenberg et al., 2003). Failure to recognise and deal early on with children who show behavioural and school problems may have far-reaching consequences. These children have a higher likelihood of later delinquent behaviours. They may also be a risk for other children in the school, as they may act as a negative role-model for peers, contribute to a negative social climate in the school, and persuade children to join in their disruptive activities (see Chapter 7, this volume). In other words, a lack of positive classroom management competencies in the teacher and the absence of effective programmes to prevent or diminish beginning behavioural or school problems pose a high risk for both children with and without these problems.

The influence of peers is also important in the development of disruptive and delinquent behaviours. Peers who are engaged in delinquent acts can influence the behaviours of youngsters in a negative way. Membership in a gang can also do this (Loeber & Farrington, 1998).

As to the *broader social context* of the community, lack of social control, an economically disadvantaged neighbourhood with a high prevalence of delinquency, the presence of drug abuse and other delinquent behaviours, are all important threats to the development of the children living in these environments (Wilson, 1987). That these risks are linked to specific neighbourhoods does not mean that this is a local problem only. Comparative studies show that the prevalence rates of violence and delinquency differ much from one country to another. This may be the result of historical, political and cultural factors (McCord, 1997; Garland, 2001; WHO, 2002).

Since the risk factors in the development of persistent disruptive behaviours can be found in the prenatal period, in the child, in the familial environment, in the school, and in the community, the question of how to intervene seems simple: one should have a broad set of programmes in each of these domains in order to optimise the conditions under which children grow up. One could also argue that these interventions should be targeted at as many people and situations as possible. However, things are not always as easy as they may appear. A plethora of preventive interventions may be redundant or far too intrusive, and the results may be disappointing in view of the enormous costs involved. Instead, programmes should be well targeted and, if possible, highly selective so that resources are used with optimal effect. In other words, preventive activities have to be performed at the right place, at the right moment and with the right tools.

Current knowledge about developmental pathways and risk and promotive factors allows us to pinpoint four life-stages in the developmental trajectories of children and adolescents that can serve as anchor points for preventive interventions:

- The *pre- and perinatal period (-9 months–+2 months).* Prevention interventions in this period should offer support to parents during pregnancy, stimulating them to refrain from the use of alcohol, cigarettes and drugs, and help them to prepare to become effective parents.
- *The preschool period (birth–age 4).* Prevention interventions in this period should support parents with information and training programmes on healthy lifestyles, positive parenting, adequate family communication and providing a supportive social network (Damon, 1990).
- *The elementary school period (age 5–11).* Prevention interventions in this period should continue to support the parents and teach them to control the external environment of the child, support them in training children with difficult temperaments to function well, and educate and train teachers in

adequate classroom management (Damon, 1997; Kellam et al., 1994).

- *Puberty and the adolescent period (age 12–18).* Prevention activities for this group should continue to support the parents, youngsters and teachers, involve the community in practising social control and offering youngsters substantial chances to participate in social, cultural, and economic activities (Sampson, Raudenbusch & Earl, 1997). Societies with few social differences between groups and in which groups are not discriminated against and isolated show less juvenile problem behaviours (Keating & Herzman, 1999; McCord, 1997). Such societies seem to provide a protective environment against disruptive and delinquent behaviours.

How: The Working Ingredients of Prevention

The next question is: how are the mechanisms and factors addressed? Four types of working ingredients can be distinguished here:

- *Activities that address the children directly.* A well-known example of a preventive factor is the scheduling of violent television movies late in the evening in order to limit the exposure of young children to models of disruptive behaviours. Another example is the use of school programmes to teach children and adolescents how to cope with provocative situations in a prosocial manner.
- *Supporting parents and families* can be a very effective way of preventing disruptive and delinquent behaviours in children and youngsters. Interventions with parents and families to prevent these problems are based on theoretical and empirical evidence (Kumpfer & Alvarado, 2003). Early family interventions are, for example, home visitation (programmatic support of parents by nurses or volunteers) and early educational enrichment (programmatic family stimulation to improve children's later educational chances). Other kinds of interventions include family therapy (preventive programmes for at-risk parents) and family skills training (behavioural skills training for parents, their children and the family together).
- *Activities directed at significant others in the child's environment* with particular focus on peers and teachers in school. Peers can influence each other strongly in a positive sense (see Chapter 7, this volume). An example is tutoring programmes in which at-risk youngsters are tutored by other youngsters who are socially and emotionally positive. Teacher programmes are often orientated at academic skills, but also on social-skills and classroom management (Greenberg et al., 2003; Ferrer-Wreder et al., 2004).
- *Activities addressing the school, neighbourhood and the state.* The influence of social context as a factor in supporting the health and development of children and adolescents is gaining increasing interest, for example in environmental change programmes that target broader population groups and reach schools and other community settings (Wandersman & Florin, 2003; Ferrer-Wreder et al., 2004).

Mrazek & Haggerty (1994) and Offord et al. (1999) suggested another way of making a distinction between different ways in which prevention programmes address risk factors and mechanisms:

- *Universal interventions* are those interventions targeted at whole populations, without any selection of groups characterised by specific risk factors. They consist, for example, of simple information campaigns, or a standard training of professionals who work in institutions that support children and parents, teachers and youth workers.
- *Targeted and clinical interventions* focus on groups characterised by specific risk factors, for example, young mothers in low-income families without an adequate social network. These programmes usually work with narrow-targeted activities such as informing or training the children and/or parents.

Summary: The Developmental and Dimensional Model

In summary, the developmental perspective on disruptive and delinquent child behaviours and the different dimensions that characterise prevention efforts constitute a framework that can be used to analyse the available programmes (Table 11.1). The key question is how to fill this matrix with a selection of activities that are effective? To answer, we need a detailed understanding of the course of development, the factors that lead to different directions and turning points in pathways, and ways that these factors can be influenced (Tolan & Gorman-Smith, 1998; Elliott & Tolan, 1999). The current state of knowledge relating to these factors permits us to fill in this matrix with many different options. There is a growing body of evidence of 'what works', which has contributed to a better understanding of the prevention of disruptive and delinquent behaviours in children under age 12.

Preventive Interventions

What Works: International Reviews

There are several reviews and meta-analyses that have shed light on the effectiveness of prevention programmes. These studies have helped to identify 'evidence-based' interventions. Although there is no explicit consensus on the number and type of studies and the sample size required for 'evidence-based' status, a number of them with (quasi) experimental design have shown positive results from prevention programmes and interventions. A further analysis of the 'evidence-based' interventions helps us to understand what risk factors can be addressed effectively at a particular moment at a particular target group. This has led to the formulation of the famous 'What works' principle in crime prevention (Andrews et al., 1990). However, in the Netherlands, the literature on the effectiveness of programmes aimed at the prevention of the first offence is scarce. Elsewhere, however, we have seen a shift towards a more scientific approach to prevention and improved knowledge about effective and promising interventions for children and youngsters.

Two pioneering reviews are worth mentioning here. Sherman and colleagues in *Preventing Crime: What Works, What Doesn't, What's Promising* (1996) reviewed the quality of hundreds of programmes for the prevention of violence and delinquency. They looked for factors underlying criminality and the effectiveness of different preventive programmes. The study, based on a growing body of knowledge, is a critical assessment of the effectiveness of a wide range of crime prevention strategies operated at the local level, with and without the support of federal funds. The authors distinguished between four different types of programmes:

- *Programmes that work*: those programmes that are known to prevent delinquency or reduce risk factors in the social context for which they are set up. The results are transferable to comparable settings and at different intervals.
- *Programmes that don't work*: these are programmes that have been shown to be ineffective.
- *Promising programmes*: there is not enough data yet to make conclusive generalisations about the efficacy of the programmes.
- *Other programmes* of which we know a little and which cannot be placed in any of the above categories.

Sherman and colleagues' (1996) review can be seen as a guide to what works in preventing crime. The authors argue that until nations invest more to evaluate preventive interventions, we will continue to use programmes without known efficacy. There needs to be a better balance between funding and evaluating programmes and developing scientifically recognised standards and methodologies. At present, according to the authors, most funding is devoted to policing and prisons. In addition, family, school and community environments can be more effective in the prevention of delinquency and violence through knowledge gained from funding substantive, effective research.

The second major review – the Blueprints for Violence Prevention – has been undertaken by the Centre for the Study and Prevention of Violence, which evaluated hundreds of prevention programmes for violence and delinquency (Elliot, 1997; <www.colorado.edu/cspv/blueprints>). The authors selected eleven *blueprint* programmes based on clear and high standards of effectiveness. The three criteria for these model programmes are:

- *Evidence of deterrent effect with a strong research design*: The evaluation studies used an experimental or quasi-experimental design with matched groups. This category of interventions has both a good research design and a large sample size.
- *Sustained effects*: effects post-treatment are still present after one year.
- *Multiple site replications*: programmes have been implemented in more than one setting and with diverse populations.

Although much is known about the criteria for model programmes, far less is known about implementation problems. For that reason, current research efforts focus on what makes a programme a success and how to identify factors that enhance

Table 11.1 Features of prevention programmes

What *(Mediators)*		***How***	
Actors	*Developmental stage*	*Actors*	*Broadness target group*
Child • Constitutional and physiological risk factors • Difficult temperament • Early behavioural, cognitive and scholastic problems	Pre/perinatal (-9–12 months) • Parents refrain from drugs, alcohol, smoking • Parents prepare for their roles	Activities directed at the child, for example • Limiting exposure to risk factors • Educating children	Universal, targeted at whole populations, for example • Information campaigns • Standard training of professionals
Family • Internal family management (lack of communication, bonding, love and trust, regular tensions and quarrels) • External family management (lack of control over the activities of the child outside the home)	Preschool (ages 0–4) • Healthy family lifestyle • Positive parenting • Adequate family communication • Supportive social network	Activities directed at the family, for example • Parent or family support • Family skills training	Selective, targeted at high risk groups, for example • Informing young mothers with low income • Training professionals who deal frequently with these mothers

Significant others • Inadequacy of dealing with behavioural and scholastic problems. • Lack of positive classroom management • Peer delinquency • Gang membership	Elementary School (ages 5–11) • Parental control over external environment • Child's control over his/her own functioning • Adequate classroom management	Activities directed at significant others (peers, teachers), for example •Peer-to-peer programmes •Classroom management programmes	Indicative, targeted at groups on individuals with identified risk factors or with beginning problems, for example • Informing young mothers with low income and drug use • Training professionals to support these mothers in adequate care of the child
Community, school, state • Lack of social control • Economically disadvantaged neighbourhood • Historical, political and cultural factors	Puberty/adolescence (ages 12–18) • Parental and social control • Child's chance to participate in social, cultural and economic activities	Activities directed at the community, school, state, for example • School change programmes • Community intervention programmes	

implementation of effective programmes (such as site selection, training, technical assistance, fidelity and sustainability (Elliott & Mihalic, 2004)).

Prevention in the Netherlands

There is a broad spectrum of programmes, projects and methods in the Netherlands to prevent problem behaviours in young children. However, this field is characterised by a lack of transparency. Recent studies have offered insight into the programmes that are used in child public health, mental health and youth care (Brezinka, 2002; Buskop-Kobussen & Cox, 2003; Verdurmen et al., 2003; Prinsen & Ligtermoet, 2006). In reviewing this field, Verdurmen and colleagues (2003) concluded that evaluation research is scarce, the methodology of effectiveness assessment is generally poor, intervention costs and treatment integrity are often ignored, and the outcomes are mixed. In addition, Ince and colleagues (2004) reviewed the Dutch programmes aimed at preventing crime and supporting families, school and communities. They labelled a programme as promising if there was a clear definition and description of:

- the target group (youngsters between birth and age 18) who are not yet showing signs of problem behaviour, and/or their social context);
- the target (reduction of risk factors, strengthening of promotive factors);
- the method (a clear description that makes replication in other settings possible), and
- the intervention theory (an explanation of why this method is effective for this target in this target group).

An additional criterion for effective programmes is:

- positive results from effectiveness research (with both internal validity and external validity).

Ince and colleagues (2004) concluded that there are five effective programmes in the Netherlands (*Opstap*, *Overstap*, *Taakspel*, *Levensvaardigheden* and *Gezonde School*). In addition, there are twenty-six promising programmes (those lacking the fifth criterion). Most of the preventive programmes in the Netherlands, however, are neither effective nor promising. Hermanns, Öry and Schrijvers (2005) also undertook a review of Dutch prevention programmes and concluded that only six interventions were effective or probably effective in the early prevention of delinquency. The latter category includes programmes that are implemented in the Netherlands because research from abroad has shown that these interventions are highly effective, although this is not yet validated by Dutch research (the exception is *Taakspel*). There are six programmes, arranged by developmental period below.

Pregnancy to Age 2: Home Visitation

VoorZorg is based on the Nurse Family Partnership Program (Olds, 1998; Olds et al., 2004a, 2004b). The key features of the original programme were to improve the outcome of pregnancy and to improve the quality of care by mothers for their children. In addition, the programme advanced the mothers' achievement of life goals, such as the completion of education, finding employment, and so on.

Age 2–3: Preschool

Kaleidoscoop based on the *High/Scope Perry Preschool* (Schweinhart, 2003, 2007; Schweinhart et al., 2005). The original programme focused on 3–4-year-olds and consisted of a daily preschool programme aimed at children's intellectual enrichment, increased thinking and reasoning for later school achievement. On average, this programme took place over a period of two years.

Age 2–9: Parent Management Training

A Dutch version of *The Incredible Years Program* (Webster-Stratton & Mihalic, 2001; Webster-Stratton, Reid & Hammond, 2001), typically, this parent-training programme focuses on for children age 2–7. The training is done in groups of ten to fourteen parents using videotapes to increase parents' childrearing skills. This programme is currently being implemented in a random clinical trial at Utrecht University (Matthys, 2005).

The *Triple P*, a programme on positive parenting (Sanders et al., 2002a) has been evaluated for children age 2–9. The programme is described below.

Age 7–11: School-based Programme

Taakspel, based on the Good Behaviour Game (Barrish et al., 1969; Dolan et al., 1993), has been replicated in the Netherlands (Van Lier, 2002; Van Lier, Vuijk & Crijnen, 2005) and is reviewed in Chapter 7.

The above effective interventions pioneered abroad have not yet been implemented on a nationwide basis or evaluated in the Netherlands. However, this situation is bound to change in the near future. Also, Hermanns and colleagues (2005) identified promising Dutch interventions meeting quality standards but lacking evaluations such as the *Healthy School Program* and the *Opvoeden Zo* parenting training course (Kooijman & Wolzak, 2004; Prinsen & Ligtermoet, 2006). The state of the other programmes, however, is qualified as 'a thousand flowers flourishing …'.

In summary, there is evidence on what works in crime prevention. This body of evidence is growing rapidly, and a small set of programmes has gained the status of 'evidence-based' interventions. A problem is, however, that our knowledge of 'what works' is dominated by the programmes that have been evaluated for their effectiveness. In other words, we are still ignorant of those characteristics of promising programmes that may work but that have not yet been evaluated. In the short term, the situation in the prevention field in the Netherlands calls for a pragmatic approach to prevent violent and delinquent behaviours. We have to learn as much as possible from the 'evidence-based' programmes, and at the same time increase efforts to evaluate the promising programmes. In the Netherlands, this process is beginning to take shape. Therefore, we need to take a closer look at the effective and promising programmes.

Effective and Promising Prevention Programmes for Children Age 0–12 in the Netherlands

Our review of prevention programmes in the Netherlands is based mainly on the two Dutch studies mentioned earlier: Ince et al. (2004) and Hermanns et al. (2005). Most of the programmes described in these studies focus on one or more of three risk factors: the persistence of early problem behaviours, academic failure, and family management problems. In addition, there is a group of programmes that focus on other risk factors. Table 11.2 offers an overview of the twenty-nine known prevention programmes in the Netherlands. Nine of them proved to be effective abroad and/or in the Netherlands. These nine programmes have been implemented in the Netherlands or are in a developing phase in this country: *Opstap*, *Overstap*, *Taakspel*, *Triple P*, *Voorzorg*, *Incredible Years*, *Kaleidoscoop*, and *Pad and Match*. They are currently used (or will be used in the near future) on a broad scale in Dutch cities and organisations. Only three of these programmes have been thoroughly tested for effectiveness in the Netherlands using (quasi) experimental designs. The other twenty programmes shown in Table 11.1 are promising because they have a sound rationale, although empirical evidence for their effectiveness is still lacking. We will now describe in more detail the programmes that have been shown to be effective in the Netherlands or abroad.

Prevention of School Problems: Opstap

Opstap is a preventive programme for children age 4–6. It has been developed to improve the educational chances for children in disadvantaged neighbourhoods. The central risk factor here is academic failure. As mentioned, young children who show early cognitive and scholastic problems have a greater chance of developing problem behaviours later on in their lives. *Opstap* aims to stimulate the cognitive and language development of children, their active learning-attitude and the pedagogical interaction in the family. This preventive family programme is for children in group 1 (or nearly group 1) of the primary school. The parents of these children tend to have median or a low level of education. *Opstap* is a structured curriculum of play and learning activities. Parents with their children engage in these activities centred around six development areas at least five times a week. In addition, parents are guided by a contact person individually and in groups. *Opstap* is mostly implemented regionally by welfare agencies. Researchers from the University of Utrecht evaluated *Opstap* (Van Tuijl, 2001, 2002, 2006). Children from Moroccan and Turkish families who participated in the programme were compared with children who did not participate in the programme. The children were assessed at the start (group 1), after completion of the programme (group 3), and two years later (group 5). In addition, the families were observed at home, and data was collected on school achievement, passing grades, demographic facts of the family, and aspects of programme implementation. The research showed some significant differences between the experimental and control group on school achievement, passing grades and parental attitudes. Although there were some differences within the experimental group, there were general positive programme effects in the long term.

Prevention of Persistent Behavioural Problems: Taakspel

Taakspel is aimed at the prevention of children's disruptive behaviours, the promotion of task-oriented behaviours, and a positive educational climate in the classroom. The aim is to decrease early disruptive behaviours (attention-deficit hyperactivity problems, oppositional defiant problems and conduct problems) and enhance positive behaviours at an early stage (grades 4–8 in primary school at age 8–12). The underlying factor of risk here is early and persistent disruptive behaviours. *Taakspel*, based on the American 'Good Behaviour Game', is group-orientated and consists of regular lessons in which children learn through play how to better follow rules in the classroom. After a period of orientation, the teacher divides the class into several teams. Team players stimulate each other to follow the rules and thereby become eligible for a reward. *Taakspel* can focus on a few or on many rules, it can be played for different lengths of time, and the rewards can be given immediately or sometime later. As a result of the intervention, teachers learn to pay better attention to positive child behaviours. In addition, the children receive attention when they show positive behaviours. *Taakspel* has been developed for children of Class 4 and 5 of the primary schools (age 8–10) and serves as a universal prevention programme for the whole class.

Taakspel has been evaluated in a quasi-experimental design with improvement shown in children's task orientation and rule violation. The behaviours of the children in the experimental group improved, while the behaviours of children in the control group became worse. The programme has also been evaluated through follow-up studies, showing that children with moderate levels of problem behaviours responded best to the intervention. Children with serious problem behaviours responded partly to the intervention. This is in keeping with the goal of the programme: intervention in early problem behaviours. None of the evaluation studies showed zero or negative results. American and Dutch evaluations also have shown positive results in large-scale epidemiological studies (Van Lier, 2002; Van Lier, Vuijk & Crijnen, 2005; Barrish et al., 1969).

Prevention of Family Problems: Triple P

Triple P stands for Positive Parenting Program, which is based on an Australian intervention aimed at supporting parenting skills for parents of children and adolescents from birth to age 16 (Sanders et al., 2002b). It is the only multi-level system of parenting and family support specifically developed as a population-level strategy and a public health approach to promote children's well-being (Sanders et al., 2005). *Triple P* aims to prevent severe behavioural, emotional and developmental problems in children

Table 11.2 An overview of prevention programmes in the Netherlands

Programme	***Risk factors addressed***	***Age (timing)***	***Activities (ingredients)***	***Where effectiveness has been demonstrated***
School problems				
Opstap	Academic failure	0–6	Selective activities in school	NL
Overstap	Academic failure	6–8	Selective activities in school	NL
Kaleidoscoop	Academic failure	2–6	Preschools/schools/ universal/selective	Abroad
Instapje	Academic failure	0–2	Families/selective	-
Boekenpret	Academic failure	0–6	Schools/selective	-
Bij de Hand	Academic failure	1–4	Families/selective	-
Opstapje	Academic failure	2–4	Families/selective	-
Piramide	Academic failure	2–6	Schools/selective	-
Startblokken en Basisontwikkeling	Academic failure	2–8	Schools/selective	-
Fantasia	Academic failure	4–12	Schools/universal	-
Rugzak	Academic failure	4–6	Families/selective	-
Stap door!	Academic failure	7–8	Schools/selective	-
Persistence of problem behaviours				
Taakspel	Early and persistent disruptive behaviour	8–10	Schools/universal	NL
Match (Big brothers, big sisters)	Early and persistent disruptive behaviour; Early initiation of problem behaviour; rebelliousness	4–14	Schools/friends/ selective	Abroad

Pad	Early and persistent disruptive behaviour; friends with problem behaviour; positive attitude towards problem behaviour	6–12	Schools/universal	Abroad
Leefstijl	Early and persistent disruptive behaviour; friends with problem behaviour; positive attitude towards problem behaviour; early initiation of problem behaviour	4–18	Schools/universal	-
Marietje Kessels	Positive attitude towards problem behaviour; friends with problem behaviour	10–12	Schools/universal	-
Schooladoptieproject/ Doe effe normal	Positive attitude towards problem behaviour; friends with problem behaviour; early initiation of problem behaviour	10–12	Schools/universal	-
Psycho-educatieve gezinsinterventie KOPP	History of problem behaviour; constitutional factors	4–14	Families/selective	-
Kopp-preventieprojecten	History of problem behaviour; constitutional factors	8–16	Peers/selective	-
Family problems				
Triple P	Family management problems	0–16	Families and communities; universal/ selective and indicated	Abroad
Moeders informeren Moeders	Family management problems; constitutional factors	0–2	Families/selective	-
Home-Start	Family management problems; family conflicts	0–6	Families/selective	-
Opvoeden: Zo	Family management problems; family conflicts	3–12	Families/universal	-

Table 11.2 continued

Mixed				
Drukke kinderen	Family management problems; family conflicts; early and persistent disruptive behaviour; constitutional factors	4–12	Families/selective	-
Voorzorg	Family management problems; history of family problem behaviour; family conflicts	-0–2, 5	Families/selective	Abroad
Incredible years	Family management problems; parenting style; history of problem behaviour; early and persistent disruptive behaviour; lack of commitment towards schools	3–9	Families/schools/ indicated	Abroad
Thuis op straat	Mobility; lack of bonding and disorganisation in the community	2–19	Community/universal	-
Waarden en normen in jeugdwerk	Norms that invoke problem behaviour; lack of bonding and disorganisation of the community	0–18	Community/universal	-

Note: Effectiveness: NL=One or more (quasi) experimental studies in the Netherlands showed positive outcomes; Abroad=One or more (quasi) experimental studies outside the Netherlands showed positive outcomes; -=No (quasi) experimental studies.

by enhancing the knowledge, skills and confidence of parents. It incorporates five levels of intervention on a tiered continuum of increasing strength (from the universal Level 1 to the enhanced Level 5). Interventions target everyday social contexts that influence parents, including the mass media, primary health care services, preschool, childcare and school systems, religious organisations, and the political system. Parents learn to use ongoing interaction in the family to support their children emotionally and to stimulate their social competencies and problem-solving skills. This approach reinforces the positive forces in the family and empowers the parenting skills of the parents as well as counteracting risk factors. *Triple P* applies principles and strategies derived from social learning theory to increase parents' self-efficacy in raising their children. It targets five core-parenting principles: creating a safe engaging environment for children; creating a positive learning environment; assertive discipline; reasonable expectations, and looking after oneself as a parent. Parents learn how to encourage children to develop a variety of social and emotional skills to succeed at school and in relationships. Children learn how to communicate and get on with others, manage their feelings, become independent and solve problems for themselves. All together, the different kinds of family and parenting supports constitute an integrated system of interventions that fully responds to the needs of parents for information and parenting support. In that sense, *Triple P* is cost effective. Some parents are satisfied by getting information, while others need more intensive support in order to become empowered. One of the characteristics of *Triple P* is its flexibility. The programme varies by the age of the children and it can be offered in different ways: individually or to a group, digitally or by printed material, and also by a self-help programme. The different levels are: a mass media information campaign, information and advice about behaviour and development of children, support for serious problem behaviours, and family interventions when serious problem behaviours occur. The Trimbos Institute, the Dutch national institute on mental health, in cooperation with the universities of Nijmegen and Leiden, has undertaken a controlled group design study during the experimental phase of the programme's implementation in 2005 and 2006. Results supported the outcomes of research in Australia where *Triple P* has been researched by twelve RCTs (Randomised Control Trials). The conclusion is that *Triple P* can be seen as an effective programme (Hermanns et al., 2005; De Graaf et al., 2007). Significant effects were found especially at the intervention Levels 2, 3 and 4 (Bor et al., in press). The effects are positive and were maintained over six months after the conclusion of the programme. Thus, evaluations using different designs at various intervals and different cultures showed that *Triple P* is effective in the prevention of problem behaviours in children and encouraging the participation of parents in educating their children (Hermanns et al., 2005; Sanders et al., 2002; Sultana et al., 2000).

Conclusions

We described the principles of effective prevention of persistent disruptive and delinquent behaviours from a developmental perspective. We examined the first steps of improvements in prevention and evaluation practices that have taken place in the Netherlands. The prevention of disruptive and delinquent behaviours is not new and research on this topic has had a long history. We see changes in prevention practices as an answer to the growing problem of youth delinquency in Dutch society. New and interesting programmes have been initiated, at first abroad but more recently in the Netherlands, based on the principle of 'what works'. These initiatives focused on programme results and programme efficiency.

We presented a developmental model for prevention which can be used to examine the extent to which prevention is practised and to set the agenda for future prevention efforts. Important questions for prevention include; the underlying risk factors (where), the timing (when), and the targeting (how). Seen from this developmental perspective, we presented nine effective and probably-effective Dutch programmes: *Opstap*, *Overstap*, *Taakspel*, *Triple P*, *Voorzorg*, *Incredible Years*, *Kaleidoscoop* and *Pad and Match.* In addition, there are many promising programmes that have good underlying theory and a clear methodology.

In our review of the Dutch prevention field, we noted that there are effective or probably effective programmes for children. They have been researched elsewhere, and sometimes in the Netherlands. For other programmes, Dutch experimental research is planned in the near future. At present, several Dutch programmes are promising, but evaluation research needs to be set up in the near future. We can also see that most of the effective and promising programmes are geared towards families and schools. There are few programmes for peers and communities. Thus, family management problems and academic failure are covered whereas many other risk factors are not.

There are more promising and effective preventive programmes in the Netherlands than is often assumed. We are hopeful that in the near future we can further expand the number of preventive programmes and strengthen the positive social development of children. For this investment to continue, it is important that we can indicate which programmes are effective and which ones are not and that this knowledge is accessible to people who work with children on a daily basis as well as to organisations that are funding this important work. It is also important that we not only know what works but also what the conditions are under which effective programmes work well. Questions about implementation and dissemination of effective programmes on a broader scale are sometimes neglected and do not receive the scientific interest they need. The prevention of disruptive and delinquent behaviours is important and needs national and local investment. Our children and our society deserve this support, now and in the future.

Chapter 12

Interventions

Tom van Yperen and Leonieke Boendermaker

Chapter 11 of this volume reviewed issues pertaining to the prevention of disruptive and delinquent behaviours in children. This chapter focuses on treatment interventions for children with disruptive or delinquent behaviours. Research has offered insights into the general principles of effective interventions in juvenile delinquency. Unfortunately, empirical evidence of intervention efficacy in children is very scarce. This chapter addresses the ingredients of promising programmes for children who are disruptive or delinquent. A sound theory is an essential basis for any programme. For that reason, we will discuss a theoretical framework of interventions treating children with disruptive and delinquent behaviours. This is followed by a brief review of the different types of possible programmes. We will then present a selection of the programmes available in the Netherlands in the context of the core elements of promising programmes. To conclude, we will formulate recommendations for future programmes.

A Theoretical Framework for Interventions

The problem shared by children who offend is their disruptive behaviours and the risk for later delinquency. The ultimate goal of interventions is to reduce disruptive behaviours to a more normal level and reduce the risk of a criminal career. Each intervention is usually based on an implicit or explicit theory on how this goal is to be attained. This theory is not necessarily comprehensive, abstract and scientifically well-formulated. It can be a simple statement on why a particular intervention is expected to be the right way to attain the goal that has been set. Several authors have stressed the importance of good theory behind interventions (for example, Kazdin, 2001; Rossi, Lipsey & Freeman, 2004; Swanborn, 1999; Weersing & Weisz, 2002). Theories should address at least two issues: the mechanisms and factors that are in play, and the working ingredients of the intervention. In this section we will discuss these two issues, illustrated with the case of Frank (Box 12.1).

Which Mechanisms and Factors?

Each of the problem behaviours mentioned in Box 12.1 has a number of factors or mechanisms that cause, maintain, or aggravate the child's problem behaviours, or prevent it from getting worse. In this respect, it is important to discriminate between

Box 12.1 A case history of Frank

Frank is a 10-year-old boy living with his mother in a neighbourhood characterised by poverty and criminality. Frank always had 'a difficult temper'. He is now clearly entering puberty. His parents got divorced after a long period of severe conflicts. His mother complains that Frank is aggressive and defiant. The teacher reports that Frank is bullying other kids. The school psychologist thinks that Frank's behaviour is not only a matter of temper and his early puberty, but that he is also very angry and sad about the divorce. Furthermore, Frank often interprets the intentions of others as hostile. The psychologist thinks that anger-coping training may help him to control his aggression and that Frank's mother should talk with him about what the divorce means for Frank, so that he can express his feelings about it.

two types of factors (see also Holmbeck, 1997; Petrosino, 2000; Offord & Kraemer, 2000; Van Yperen, 2001; Van de Wiel, 2002), represented in Figure 12.1.

- *Mechanisms and factors that can change as a result of a particular intervention*: These include causal mechanisms of risk and promotive factors, often referred to as the dynamic factors or mediators. Examples in Box 12.1 are Frank's anger-coping strategies, social cognition, and his feelings about the divorce. Thus, interventions should focus on dynamic factors and mediators in order to achieve the desired outcome of change in child behaviours. Holmbeck (1997) has put this in the following terms: the intervention (the independent variable) 'causes' the mediator to change, and this 'causes' changes in the outcome of the intervention (the dependent variable: the degree to which the goal of the intervention is attained).
- *Mechanisms and factors that* cannot *be influenced by a particular intervention*: These factors may interact with the dynamic factors, and may therefore have an important facilitating or inhibiting influence on the outcome. These factors are usually stable and outside the scope of the intervention. Research literature often refers to these factors as moderators. Examples in Box 12.1 are male gender, having divorced parents, Frank entering puberty, and the fact that he is living in a bad neighbourhood. All of these factors may limit the effectiveness of the intervention.

Effective interventions for young offenders tend to focus on mediating dynamic risk factors, such as the juvenile's social competencies or their family's functioning. The moderators may be obstacles for success. However, it is important to stress that moderators are not fixed entities. They can change into mediators by taking a broader perspective. For example, most youth care workers cannot change neighbourhoods. However, Frank's environment could change for the better with a social policy promoting the creation of jobs, improving housing conditions and reducing the availability of drugs and weapons.

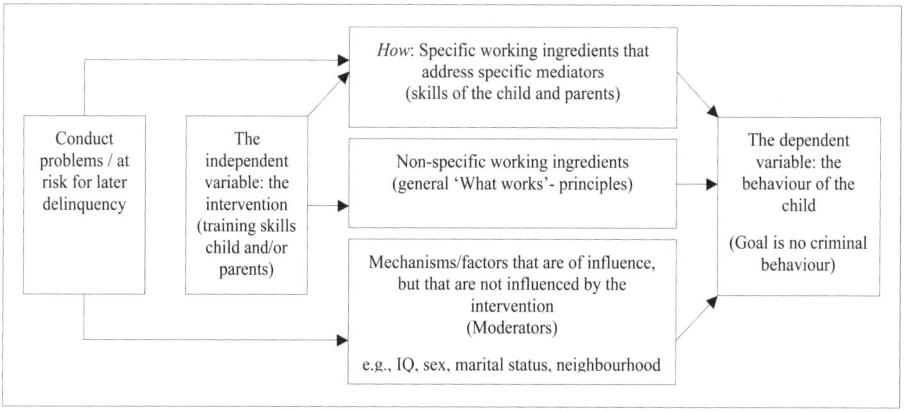

Figure 12.1 Mechanisms and factors that can change as a result of a particular treatment, and mechanisms and factors that cannot be influenced by a particular treatment

An important principle to enhance the success of interventions is to increase the number of dynamic factors used for intervention and to control the moderators as much as possible, or turn a moderator into a mediator, as in the example above. If the latter is not possible, then one should not set the goals too high, as the moderators may have a strong impact on the outcome. This principle applies in individual cases (like Frank's) as summarised in Box 12.1 as well as in target groups (that is, all boys like Frank).

How Do Treatments Work?

In the section above, our focus was on *which* factors are to be influenced by the treatments. The next question is *how* the intervention will influence these factors. This is the other part of programme theory. Two types of factors (Figure 12.1) are relevant here: general or non-specific ingredients, and specific ingredients.

General or non-specific intervention ingredients are elements of an intervention which contribute to the outcome irrespective of the type of intervention, the type of problem, or the target group. Reviews and meta-analyses show the importance of the following factors (see, for example, Drieschner, Lammers & Van der Staak, 2004; Farrington & Welsh, 2003; Schippers & De Jonge, 2002; Shirk & Karver, 2003; Weisz, Donenberg et al., 1995; Van Yperen, Booy & Van der Veldt, 2003):

- There should be a good fit between the severity and complexity of the child's problem behaviours and the type of treatment. With respect to preventing delinquency, this means that the intensity of the treatment should correspond to the risk of offending (the higher the risk, the more intense the treatment). The treatment should focus on the characteristics, risk factors, and needs that are directly related to delinquency, and the treatment should consist of different modalities, using different methods that effectively address different risk factors (Andrews, 1995).

- The therapist should be well trained. A related factor is that the working conditions of the therapist should be favourable (normal caseload, good supervision, safe circumstances), but studies do not agree about optimal working conditions (see, for example, Weisz, Weiss et al., 1995).
- The treatment is delivered in accordance with the protocol (the principle of 'programme integrity').
- There should be a good fit between the treatment and the motivational stage of the client. If necessary, the treatment should be adapted to the specific characteristics of the client, the therapist and the general context of the treatment programme (the principle of responsivity; Andrews, 1995).
- The treatment should be well-structured (clear goals, good planning, and a process that is structured in phases).
- There should be a good relationship between the client and the therapist.

Specific treatment ingredients are responsible for the effectiveness of treatments that focus on the particular dynamic factors relevant for young children's disruptive behaviours or delinquency. What do we know about 'what works' for children with disruptive and delinquent behaviours? There are more evaluation studies on the effectiveness of treatments for adolescent than for child problem behaviours (see also Chapter 13, this volume). In the well-known meta-analysis by Lipsey (1995), for instance, only 1.8% of all participants in the treatment studies were between age 6 and 11. We know from these studies that the use of problem-solving skills training, or cognitive-behavioural training and family interventions, are essential in working with young children with severe externalising and internalising problem behaviours (Bennet & Gibbons, 2000; Brosnan & Carr, 2000; Lipsey & Wilson, 1998). The efficacy of skills training in young children is enhanced if the treatment involving the child is combined with parental-skills training (Kazdin, 1997; Perkins-Dock, 2001). This is also true for young children treated in a residential setting: better outcomes are achieved when parents are trained and involved in the treatment of their child (Sunseri, 2004).

Interventions with children under age 11 often focus on parental-skills training (Farrington & Welsh, 2003). For example, Taylor and Biglan (1998) reviewed effective behavioural family treatment studies. The authors concluded that essential treatment components were the training of parents in positive parenting strategies and effective discipline, together with training in the effective use of mild, brief, non-physical punishments such as 'time out' or loss of privileges. Better outcomes were achieved if these components were combined with the training of parents focused on the reduction of stressors, such as self-control training for parents, assistance with marital difficulties, and social training in problem-solving skills. Serketich and Dumas (1996) conducted a systematic review of twenty-six studies on the outcomes of behavioural parent training. They found an average effect size of .86 for overall child outcome (as rated by parents, observers, or teachers), which shows that training of parents has a large effect on the problem behaviours of children, and an effect size of .44 for parental adjustment.

Studies agree that parental-skills training programmes improve outcomes, especially when combined with interpersonal skills and problems-solving skills training of children as well (Behan & Carr, 2000; Brestan & Eyberg, 1998; Webster-Stratton, Reid & Hammond, 2001). Thus, two mechanisms are essential in treatments with disruptive children: skills and competencies training in children and in their parents.

Interventions in the Netherlands

We will now review Dutch treatment programmes designed to (a) reduce disruptive and delinquent child behaviours, and (b) prevent child delinquents from becoming serious offenders (Brezinka, 2002). Thus, these treatment interventions differ from the prevention programmes described by Jonkman, Van Yperen and Prinsen in Chapter 11 (this volume).

The treatment programmes can be assigned to four broad categories:

1. interventions focused on factors associated with a first offence;
2. interventions focused on the competencies of children;
3. interventions focused on the competencies of children and adult/parents and/ or teachers, and
4. interventions focused on family functioning.

In the following section, we will discuss examples of the different types of treatments, with an emphasis on interventions that have some empirical evidence of treatment efficacy and interventions which are currently being researched (see Table 12.1).

Interventions in Response to a First Offence

A first offence can be considered a marker of an incipient criminal career. The goal of treatment for first-time offenders is to prevent recidivism by addressing a variety of risk and promotive factors. Metselaar, Tönis and Van Lakerveld (2000) presented short descriptions of nine programmes in several large cities in the Netherlands for juvenile offenders known to the police. We will review three programmes for which evaluations are available: the *Twelve Minus Project*, the *Youth Prevention Programme* and the *STOP-reaction*.

The Twelve Minus Project

The *Twelve Minus* project of Haaglanden, an urban region in the mid-west of the Netherlands is a prototypical example of a project that received limited process evaluation (Van den Hoogen-Saleh, 2000). The risk factors addressed varied between children and mostly comprised ineffective parenting, poor supervision, financial debts, parental problems, poor neighbourhoods, and child problem behaviours in school and in the neighbourhood. If a child was brought to the attention of the police, police officers completed a simple screening task that focused on the mediators and moderators of delinquency. If the officer considered the child 'at risk', a social worker would then analyse the child's and the family's situation and discuss with them what should be done to prevent recidivism. Usually, the social workers succeeded in motivating the families to get help from regular youth care agencies. A study by Van den Hoogen-Saleh, (2000) showed that most of the young offenders received an intervention, for example, a *STOP-reaction* (explained below), or youth care. Unfortunately, the contents and efficacy of these treatments is unclear.

The Youth Prevention Programme

The Youth Prevention Programme is situated in the south-east of Brabant (a mostly rural area in the middle of the Netherlands with some larger cities), for which a convenient documentation of the treatment is available. Social workers can draw on nine specific ingredients of the treatment, such as learning to deal with practical issues, activating the social network, increasing parental skills, or resolving family conflicts (Lieverse, Heineke & Hoffman, 2002). In most cases, social workers offer short-term support. The theories that underlie these treatments are typically hybrid in nature. As a basis, there is the simple idea that risk factors may aggravate the present problem behaviours of the child. Motivating the children and their parents to participate in treatments can reduce these risk factors.

The *Youth Prevention Programme* has received a preliminary evaluation to document its effectiveness. Project social workers rated 109 clients on four areas at the start and finish of the intervention: social surroundings, school, leisure time activities and police contacts. The results showed that social workers rated most of their clients as functioning better at the end of the intervention. One year after the intervention, about 16% of the referred children had one or more new police contacts (Van't Hoff et al., 1995).

STOP-reaction

STOP-reaction is another, nationwide intervention in response to delinquency by children. Although children under age 12 are not criminally responsible in the Netherlands, this intervention falls under the responsibility of the Public Prosecutor. The goal of *STOP-reaction* is to promote avoidance of offending. The *STOP-reaction* is applied on a voluntary basis in response to minor offences, such as shoplifting or vandalism with little damage. If the police encounter serious problems with the children or the families, they refer the case to a regular youth care agency. The *STOP-reaction* focuses only on 'predelinquent' child behaviours. A police officer talks to the parents and child and if the parents agree, the child is ordered to work with a social worker on tasks such as rules, punishment and saying 'no' to friends with disruptive plans. The way the tasks are carried out depends on the parents and the child. Some children work on their tasks in groups with a social worker of the *STOP-reaction* programme. Other children work individually on their tasks with the social worker, or do their tasks at home. One of the tasks is to attend to victim(s) of crime and to make restitution and/or apologise to victims.

The theoretical underpinnings of the *Stop-reaction* programme are the introduction of promotive factors by means of children's explicit learning that their behaviour has caused damage or grief, and that this behaviour is not tolerated by society. This learning experience is promoted by intervention elements such as the brief involvement of an authority figure, confrontation with the damage or the victim, and giving the child a chance to set things right. These activities can be seen as a helping hand to parents in correcting their children's behaviours. In 2005, around two thousand children received a *STOP-reaction* intervention.[1]

Tsjebanova, Harland and Versteegh (2006) collected data in the region of Haaglanden on the number of successful *STOP-reaction* interventions involving 348 children. In 2003, 75% of the cases were considered 'successful', 69% in 2004, and 58% in 2005. Unfortunately, the authors did not provide details of the content of the *STOP-reaction* and the criteria that made a reaction 'successful'.[2] An evaluation of the effectiveness of *STOP-reaction* was started by the Research and Documentation Centre of the Dutch Ministry at the end of 2006.

Interventions Focusing on Children's Competencies

A wide variety of programmes focus on social-competence training of children. Evaluation research on this kind of programme is scarce, however, and only two programmes have been thoroughly evaluated.

Self-Control is a programme that focuses on the training of new skills in children with problem behaviours (Van Manen, 2001). The author developed a cognitive-behavioural training called *Self-Control* which is for children between age 9 and 12 who display aggressive and oppositional-defiant behaviours. The goals of the programme are to reduce behavioural problems and impulsive behaviours, and improve social-cognitive skills and self-control. The programme is based on the theory of social information processing by Dodge (1986) and trains children how to interpret social information to improve self-control and reduce impulsivity. The programme consists of eleven well-described sessions of about 70–90 minutes, with a small group of between four and six behaviourally disordered children. In the sessions, the children learn to observe their own behaviour, ask themselves what they feel and think, and as a consequence, what they do. They are also trained in interpreting social situations, as well as given skills in problem solving (that is, how to react in a non-aggressive manner). The intervention is focused mainly on changing problem behaviours in children. Parents and schoolteachers attend a special information session and are kept informed by weekly telephone contacts. Parents are asked to sign a 'contract' in which they promise not to reward aggressive behaviours, but do not receive further training in how to do this. The theory behind the treatment is that improvements in social-information processing, and self-control and problem-solving skills, will reduce aggressive and oppositional-defiant behaviours. Alongside

1 <www.halt.nl>, accessed 9 October 2006.

2 Klooster and colleagues (2002) investigated which children and parents dropped out of the interventions, but this study is not discussed here.

these specific working ingredients, the fact that the training follows a well-described protocol for each session is an important non-specific working factor.

There are two studies available on the *Self-control* programme by Van Manen (2001). Both can be classified as quasi-experimental studies in daily practice, one with and one without a follow-up. The first study by Van Manen, Prins and Emmelkamp (2004) assigned ninety-two boys between age 9 and 13 to one of the following three conditions: the *Self-Control* programme (forty-two boys); social-skills training (forty boys), and a waiting-list control group (fifteen boys). Most boys were of Dutch origin (79.5%) and were formally diagnosed with either a disruptive behaviour disorder, such as ODD, or a non-specific behaviour disorder. Therapists were supervised in applying the programme as intended, and well-known and valid instruments (like the Child Behaviour Checklist (CBCL), or the Matson Evaluation of Social Skills with Youngsters (MESSY)) were used on three occasions: at the start of the programme, at the end, and at a follow-up one year later. The results showed that the *Self-control* programme and the social-skills training produced positive outcomes in comparison to the control group, both directly after the treatment and one year later. The boys who had followed the *Self-control* programme showed significantly better outcomes in comparison to the social-skills training group. The mean effect sizes of the *Self-control* programme are .50 directly after treatment and 0.76 one year later. The comparable effect sizes were 0.41 and 0.56 for the social-skills training. Thus, the results showed that this cognitive behavioural programme works with Dutch disruptive children.

The second study was conducted in a school setting (Muris et al., 2005). In this study, forty-two children (boys and girls, between age 9 and 12), who were reported as having problem behaviours in school, were randomly assigned to either the *Self-control* training or a waiting-list condition. About 80% were of Dutch origin. Data were collected with valid instruments (like the CBCL, the Strengths and Difficulties Questionnaire (SDQ), and other measures) on three occasions: at the start of the programme, at the end, and three months later. Here the mean effect size was 0.62. In summary, the *Self-control* programme showed moderate reductions of disruptive child behaviours.

Interventions Focusing on the Competencies of Children, Parents and Teachers

There are three programmes in the Netherlands which focus on a combination of the skills and competencies of children and their parents, *The Utrecht Coping Power Programme*, *Stop 4-7* and *SPRINT*.

The Utrecht Coping Power Programme (UCPP)

Van de Wiel (2002) evaluated *UCPP*, which aims to decrease oppositional-defiant and/or disruptive behaviours and to improve social behaviours by developing the parental skills of adults and problem-solving skills in their children. The programme is meant especially for children with a disruptive behaviour disorder between age 8 and 12, and their parents, but can also be applied to children at risk of developing a disruptive behaviour disorder. The programme has several working ingredients. First, treatment staff formulates a protocol for each session, which means high treatment integrity. Activities in each session can be chosen to fit the problems and learning style of the children. Specific working ingredients are the parental-skills training and the training of the children themselves. Parental-skills training consists of eighteen sessions with a group of five to eight parents. Several topics are reviewed in the sessions: the observation of behaviour, the use of rewards and other means of positive reinforcement, how to react to disruptive behaviour, how to create a positive atmosphere within the family, and how the parents can look after themselves. The children have their own eighteen sessions and are trained in more or less the same way as in the *Self-control* training programme described above. They learn to recognise their feelings and to 'stop and think' before they act.

The intervention theory of this treatment programme focuses on the interaction between parents and children: if the parents learn to reward prosocial behaviours and to use mild punishments (as in the use of a 'time-out'), they will influence their children's behaviours in a positive way. The training of the children has the same rationale as the *Self-control* programme described above, that is, improving social-information processing, and developing self-control and problem-solving skills, which are thought to reduce aggressive and oppositional-defiant behaviours.

Van der Wiel (2002) evaluated the first version of the *UCPP*. She used a random control trial in which 116 families were randomly assigned to one of three conditions: *UCPP* (N=38), 'care as usual' (N=39), or a non-treatment control group (N=39). Treatment drop-outs (four children in the experimental condition and five children in the control condition) were included in the analysis. Data were collected at the start and the end of the training and after a follow-up period of six months. Interviews, direct observations and valid measurements such as the CBCL and the DISC (Diagnostic Interview Schedule for Children, a structured psychiatric interview) were used. The evaluation showed a significant decline in disruptive behaviours in the experimental as well as the control groups. Also, a significant increase in prosocial behaviours was found. The mean effect sizes ranged from 0.24 to 0.69 in the *UCPP* group, and 0.23 and 0.54 in the 'care as usual' group. In the experimental as well as in the 'care as usual' groups, the disruptive behaviours decreased. However, prosocial behaviours increased in the *UCPP* group. In a further analysis of the results, Van de Wiel et al. (in press) found that cases in the 'care as usual' condition (who received family therapy) showed significantly less improvement compared to the *UCPP* condition (effect Size=1.07). There was no significant difference between *UCPP* and cases that received normal behaviour therapy. Six months after the intervention, the difference between the *UCPP* and 'care as usual' groups had disappeared. Since *UCPP* is much cheaper than the 'care as usual', *UCPP* is to be preferred. In a long-term follow-up, Zonnevylle-Bender and colleagues (in press) found that five years after the intervention, children who were treated with *UCPP* smoked fewer cigarettes and used less marijuana (17%) compared to the 'care as usual' group (42%). The level of substance use in the *UCPP* group was the same as in a matched group of 'normal' children. The *UCPP*, 'care as usual' and 'normal' group showed no difference in delinquency.

In summary, *UCPP* was cheaper compared to 'care as usual'. Moreover, in the short term, *UCPP* seemed more effective than cases treated with family therapy, and just as effective as in cases treated with behaviour therapy. Long-term differential effects of *UCPP* compared to 'care as usual' are only found in terms of substance use.

STOP 4-7

This programme has a somewhat broader orientation than the *UCPP* and has recently been developed in Belgium, the name being a Dutch abbreviation of 'together back on track' (*Samen Sterker Terug op Pad*). The programme promotes a reduction in disruptive behaviours in young children age 4–7 (De Mey et al., 2005) and focuses on the training of children, their parents, and teachers. Parents and children each follow their own ten-session training with more or less the same content as in the *Self-control* programme or *UCPP*. The extra component of teacher training consists of four sessions and explains the development of disruptive behaviour and teaches how to influence child problem behaviours by using rewards and positive feedback, how to handle difficult situations and how to communicate with the parents of conduct-disordered children. A special notebook is also used to stimulate communication between child, parents and teacher. Thus, *Stop 4-7* has the extra ingredient of working with the teachers. This is derived from the idea that, other than parents, teachers often have more influence than anyone else on children's problem behaviours. The rationale of the *Stop 4-7* is that disruptive behaviours develop as a result of many risk factors in the child, the family and the school. Intervention efforts, therefore, should involve all three systems. The *Stop 4-7* programme is currently being evaluated for effectiveness and no research outcomes are yet available.

SPRINT

The last programme discussed here is *SPRINT*, which is the Dutch abbreviation for 'screening of and preventive intervention with disruptive behaviour' (*Signalering van en Preventieve Interventie bij Antisociaal Gedrag*) (Van Leeuwen & Bijl, 2003a, 2003b). *SPRINT* is applied in twenty-five primary schools in Amsterdam. Teachers and the so-called 'internal advisers' fill out a screening list for all children age 7–10. The screening is done three times, at six-month intervals, and divides the children into those who are possibly at risk and those who are not.[3] The parents of the 'at risk' group are invited to attend individual consultations where parenting skills, communication within the family, social support and communication with the school are discussed. The children attend a short cognitive-behavioural training activity (individually or in a small group) which focuses on problem-solving and positive-thinking skills. The rationale of *SPRINT* is more or less the same as in the programmes described earlier in this section. The starting point of *SPRINT*, however, is different

3 Children who come out of the first screening as in need of direct help do not have to wait until the whole screening procedure is over: in these cases, services are immediately provided.

because it lies in the schools and uses a well-described screening procedure. The exact content of the parent-child training has not yet been documented. Nevertheless, the specific working ingredients appear the same as in *Self-control* and the *UCPP*. This programme is also currently being evaluated for effectiveness.

Family Interventions

Several reviews of treatments for families with disruptive or delinquent children are available (Berger, 2006; Orobio de Castro et al., 2002; Veerman et al., 2004; Welsh & Farrington, 2006). Veerman and colleagues (2004) concluded that in the Netherlands there are ninety-two programmes for intensive treatments in families with disruptive children. These treatments are applied by youth care agencies over the whole country. Their main focus is on risk factors related to parenting skills, family management, personal problems of the parents and social support. Veerman and colleagues (2004) examined seventeen of the ninety-two available programmes. The central idea of these seventeen treatments is based on what is known about the development of disruptive and delinquent behaviours. An early onset of problem behaviours is seen as an important risk factor for the further development of disruptive and delinquent behaviours. The aim of the programmes is to prevent such an unhealthy development and prevent the problems from becoming worse. The treatment consists of training parents and children, and creating support for families with financial problems and for parents with their own problems such as alcoholism or depression. The programmes are highly characterised by general working ingredients. Most programmes use social workers trained in goal-setting, and behavioural and motivational techniques. As to the specific ingredients, the family treatments are focused on the use of elements of behavioural therapy, family therapy, social-skills training for children, parenting-skills training, enhancing family communication, and improving parental support.[4] The treatments are individualised depending on the goals set for each family.

Only two of the seventeen treatments focused on preventing children from becoming delinquents. Together with a third and similar programme, these two were the subject of a study by Orobio de Castro (2002). Of particular note in these treatments is the use of screening instruments to identify children in a certain neighbourhood at risk of delinquency. Families of high-risk children can choose either to participate voluntarily in an intensive family treatment or be referred to a child protection agency to receive a court-ordered supervision order. The study shows that almost all families could be motivated to take part in the family treatment. Each family was assigned a social worker who was available to them for about ten hours a week during a one- to two-year-period. Veerman et al. (2004) also analysed the effectiveness of the seventeen treatment programmes. Information was available on two outcomes: externalising problem behaviours of 1,259 children and parental stress measured at the start and conclusion of the treatment. There were no 'non-treated' control groups

---

4 The seventeen methods include, for instance, *Families First* (a well-developed method for crisis intervention in families to prevent the child from being placed in care), an intensive orthopedagogical family treatment programme, a psychiatric family treatment programme, or video home-training.

Table 12.1 An overview of intervention programmes in the Netherlands

Programme	*What: Dynamic factors addressed*	*How: ingredients*	*Age*	*Subjects in the study*	*Type of study*	*Results*	*Mean Effect Size*
	Factors related to first offence						
Twelve-Minus Programme (Van den Hoogen-Saleh, 2001)	Different factors in child and/or family, related to first offence	Various, depending on individual risk factors identified	<12	387 participants in the Twelve-Minus Programme	Descriptive	Description of the number of children in the programme and participating organisations	-
Youth Prevention Programme (Van 't Hoff et al., 1995)	Different factors in child and/or family, related to first offence	Various, depending on individual risk factors identified	≤12	About 180 clients of the youth prevention programme	Descriptive	Social workers rated their clients as doing better after treatment and 16% committed (a) new offence(s) in the first year after the intervention	-
STOP-reaction (Tsjebanova et al., 2006) Current research by RDC/Ministry of Justice	(Lack of) awareness of an offence causing grief and/or not being tolerated	Brief involvement of authority figure; writing a letter to the victim; giving the child the chance to set things right	≤12	348 children in the region Haaglanden referred to STOP in the period 2003–05	Descriptive	Percentage of cases marked as 'Successful': 2003 75%; 2004 69%; 2005 58%. The low percentage in 2005 might be due to lack of data on the last year.	-
	Competencies of children						

Self-control: Study 1 (Van Maanen et al., 2004)	Cognitive processing of social information	Intervention protocol; training children in eleven sessions of a small group of 4–6 behaviourally disturbed children; informing parents and teachers weekly	9–12	92 boys in an experimental group (42), a social-skills training group (40) and a waiting-list control group (15).	Experimental study, six months follow-up	The self-control participants display less problem behaviour at the end of the intervention and at a six-month follow-up than comparable participants in social- skills training or on waiting list.	Self-control group: 0.50 directly after treatment and 0.76 one year later. Social-skills group: 0.41 and 0.56
Study 2 (Muris et al., 2005)				42 boys and girls known by the school to have problem behaviours, 31 in the experimental group, 11 in waiting-list control group.	Experimental study, three months follow-up	Participants in the self-control training had significant reduction in problem behaviour and significant growth in cognitive skills directly after treatment and three months later.	Overall mean E.S. is 0.62
	Competencies of children, parents and teachers						
UCPP (Van de Wiel, 2002; Van de Wiel et al., in print; Zonnevylle-Bender et al., in print)	Problem-solving skills; children and parenting skills parents	General: structuring the intervention by using a protocol. Specific: training children in eighteen sessions in a small group of behaviourally disturbed children, group training of their parents in eighteen sessions	8–12	116 problem behaviour children in UCPP, care as usual (CAU) and no-treatment control group	Experimental study, six months follow-up	UCPP has somewhat better outcomes than care as usual at the end of treatment. Six months later, there is no difference between the two groups. Long-term effects only on substance use. However, UCPP is more cost-effective.	ES in UCPP: 0.24–0.69. CAU: 0.23–0.54. ES UCPP vs. CAU Family therapy: 0.61–1.07; UCPP vs. CAU Behaviour therapy: 0.19–0.24.

Table 12.1 continued

TOP 4–7 (Current research by De Mey)	Problem-solving skills children; parenting skills; parents, teacher behaviour towards children and parents	General: structuring the intervention by using a protocol. Specific: group training children in ten sessions, their parents in ten sessions, and their teachers in four sessions	8–12	-	-	-	-
SPRINT (Current research by Van Leeuwen)	Problem-solving and positive-thinking skills; children, parenting skills; communication in the family; communication with school; social support	Individual or small group training for children; individual consultations for parents	7–10	-	-	-	-
Family interventions (Veerman et al., 2004)	Parenting skills, family management, personal problems parents, social support	General: goal setting; motivational techniques. Specific: behavioural therapy; family therapy; social-skills training for children; training of parenting and communication skills	All ages	Between 7 and 266 families in each of the seventeen interventions pre- and post-test information on roughly 1,250 children	pre-test/post-test design without control group	Family interventions have moderate effect on problem behaviours of the children and on parental stress (significant reduction).	Mean overall effect size externalising problem behaviour: 0.52; parental stress: 0.55
(Orobio de Castro et al., 2002)				62 families in two interventions	pre-test/post-test design without control group	Family interventions have moderate effect on problem behaviours of the children (significant reduction).	Mean effect size problem behaviour: 0.56

available, which makes this a non-experimental study. The mean effect sizes for both outcomes were similar: 0.52 for externalising problem behaviours and 0.55 for parental stress, indicating that there was a significant reduction in both behavioural problems and parental stress during the family treatment. However, a substantial proportion of the children still showed severe behavioural problems at the end of the treatment.

As mentioned, Orobio de Castro and colleagues (2002) evaluated three family intervention programmes and found a decrease in the behavioural problems of the children and in family problems at the end of two of the interventions. Since the study did not have a 'non-treated' control group, it can also be classified as a non-experimental study. The mean effect size on behavioural problems in this study was 0.56. The third project failed to organise for proper inclusion rates. Therefore, the number of families on which pre- and post-test information was measured was too small to be analysed.

Future Developments

In this chapter, we discussed treatments in four areas:

- interventions in response to a first offence;
- interventions focused on the competencies of children;
- interventions focused on the competencies of children as well as parents, and
- family interventions.

We will now discuss recent developments in three of the four areas.

Interventions in Response to a First Offence

A promising development is the planned research on the *STOP-reaction* programme. This research will focus on the implementation as well as the effects of the intervention on children's problem behaviours (Verwers & Van der Laan, 2006).

Interventions Focused on the Competencies of Children and Parents

We described a single treatment with a focus on competency training of children and two treatments with a training component for parents. Only recently has parenting-skills training been implemented in the Netherlands for families with problem children. Four training programmes on parenting skills have been started with (quasi-experimental or experimental) evaluations. The first treatment is the *Parent Management Training* (*PMTO*) (Patterson, 2005), directed at parents of conduct-disordered children up to age 12. In ten to twelve individual sessions, parents are trained in positive parenting skills, such as rewarding positive behaviours and setting clear limits. Next, several pilot programmes based on the Australian *Triple P* programme (*Positive Parenting Programme*) (Sanders, Dadds & Turner, 2003) are being carried out. In the *Triple P* programme, interventions range from Level 1 (general information on parenting in the media) to Level 5 (intensive and individual training of parental skills in families with severe problems). In addition, over the last few years, a special training programme has been developed for parents of delinquent children and adolescents (up to age 17): *Parents of Recalcitrant Youth* (Van Veluw, 2006). Like *Triple P*, the programme makes available interventions with different levels of intensity and focusses on skills for positive parenting. In contrast to *PMTO* and *Triple P*, this programme includes group sessions in which parents practise new skills and exchange experiences and ideas. A fourth and final programme is the *Incredible Years* (Webster-Stratton, Reid & Hammond, 2001). This programme for parents of young children (age 3–8) is currently being implemented in a random clinical trial at Utrecht University (Matthys, 2005). Aside from the *Parents of Recalcitrant Youth* package, all three treatments are evidence-based in that research done abroad has demonstrated an increase in positive parental skills and a decrease in child problem behaviours.

Family Interventions

Recently, a fourth family treatment known as *IOG-Erger voorkomen* (The prevention of worse outcomes) has been developed (Berger, 2006). This programme has many similarities with the family treatments described by Veerman and colleagues (2004). The main difference is the special aim at crime prevention. The treatment is directed at young people between age 8 and 18 and will be implemented in the coming years.

Residential Care

Our review did not include residential treatments. Van der Ploeg and Scholte (2000) presented an overview of residential programmes in the Netherlands to reduce disruptive and delinquent behaviours for children and young people with serious externalising and internalising problem behaviours. They found only two residential programmes for children. In one residential setting, children with developmental disorders received social-skills training through the use of videos. The second setting used social-skills training for a group of children with pervasive developmental disorders. Unfortunately, no further information on the children and the interventions is given in the report.

Recently, an organisation in Rotterdam started two small residential groups, each with five disruptive or delinquent children age 9–12 (Horizon Jeugdzorg, 2006). These groups are special because they offer accommodations with low-profile security in contrast to non-justice residential care for children with severe behavioural disorders where, due to a recent change in Dutch law on youth care, special security measures that were formerly restricted to juvenile justice institutions only are now being applied. In these residential programmes, children live in a building with a locked front door, an isolation cell and an alarm on the doors of the children's rooms. They cannot get out of their rooms unnoticed. Evaluation research on the implementation and treatment efficacy is being conducted.

Conclusions

There are many programmes available in the Netherlands, but only a few are based on an articulated treatment theory and very few have been properly evaluated. The interventions applied in a police context have more or less the same goals as the family interventions described by Veerman and Orobio de Castro (Orobio de Castro et al., 2002; Veerman et al., 2004). The family interventions, however, compared to the police interventions, are based on a more articulated treatment theory, and explicit attention is paid to general working ingredients like proper goal-setting or motivational techniques. Both types of intervention try to reduce the influence of moderators in the child's family.

The treatments which focus on training competency for children, parents and/or teachers can be arranged on a continuum of an increasing number of mediators (that is, risk factors) and increasing complexity of the treatment theory. In the *self-control* training, Van Manen and colleagues (2004) recommend a combination of self-control training with parental-skills training to improve the important moderating influence of parents on child behaviours. The other interventions (*UCPP*, *STOP-4-7*) combine these components or even extend the intervention to the training of teachers (*SPRINT*).

Unfortunately, the number of programmes with detailed information on treatment effectiveness is limited. Furthermore, we do not have much information on the application of the treatments described in this chapter. We conclude that we have detailed information on two of the programmes presented (*Self-control* and *UCCP*), and we have less detailed information on the widely applied family interventions (as investigated by Veerman et al., 2004). Self-control training, the *UCPP* and family interventions have a positive effect on child problem behaviours, parental skills and parental stress. If not combined with training of the child, family programmes show moderate effects, but a substantial proportion of the children still have behavioural problems at the end of the programme.

In summary, the number of treatments meant for children with disruptive and delinquent behaviours is growing. The government and youth care providers are recognising the importance of treatment at an early stage of development of persistent and delinquent behaviours as well as working with several systems (child, parents and family). In the coming years, there will be strong pressures on providing evidence that the treatments work. However, resources for studying the effectiveness of programmes remain scarce.

We call for a new approach in the development of treatments. We expect that only a few treatments will be fully investigated and developed. These treatments should set the benchmark for the quality of other programmes, which should at least incorporate the general – and a number of specific – intervention factors that have been proven to contribute to the effectiveness of the benchmark treatments. Furthermore, standard monitoring of the extent to which interventions are implemented (treatment integrity) and the outcome of the treatments should result in empirical data showing whether the programmes meet the standards. Last but not least, we need more advanced effectiveness research with (quasi) experimental studies in which children are assigned to experimental and control groups or repeated N=1 studies.

Chapter 13

Cost-Benefit and Cost-Effectiveness of Prevention and Treatment

Djøra I. Soeteman and Jan J.V. Busschbach

In the Netherlands hardly any research exists on the cost-benefit and cost-effectiveness of crime prevention and treatment programmes for child delinquents (the terms 'cost-benefit' and 'cost-effectiveness' are defined below). This is remarkable as the odds are that crime prevention or treatment programmes will show a favourable cost-benefit ratio compared to alternatives such as detention or 'doing nothing'. The assumption of a favourable cost-effectiveness ratio is based on a straightforward line of reasoning: we know that any long-term residential treatment is very expensive and we know that detention is not an effective way to reduce crime. This reasoning implies that the odds are that any non-residential treatment with even modest effectiveness in reducing recidivism will show a favourable cost-benefit ratio as compared to detention. This lack of evidence is even more remarkable, as research from abroad shows that crime prevention and treatment programmes for children can be cost-effective (for example, Aos et al., 2004; Greenwood et al., 1996).

Despite these two arguments, efforts to report convincing empirical evidence on the cost-benefit or cost-effectiveness of these programmes fall short. This can be considered a problem because the introduction of new prevention and treatment programmes for young offenders is of high interest to policymakers who usually are forced to make policy decisions in the absence of any knowledge of the cost-effectiveness of existing programmes. Until now, this lack of evidence has legitimatised a policy of building additional, often expensive, facilities to incarcerate young offenders and providing grants to projects of which the cost-effectiveness is at least questionable. Thus, whereas professionals in forensic care have a strong interest in establishing the cost-effectiveness of their programmes and finding alternative treatments for incarceration, criminological research is still dominated by themes such as aetiology and epidemiology. This focus of research can well be legitimatised by 'a scientific point of view'; it fails, however, in providing policymakers with 'evidence-based' arguments for alternative policies beyond restrictive measures such as incarceration.

In this chapter, we will focus on how cost-benefit and cost-effectiveness analyses can be used to optimally inform the general public and, more importantly, policymakers in policy decisions regarding treatment interventions. In this respect, the choice of the outcome measures and the perspective of the cost-analysis are crucial. In many studies, the choice of outcome measures is based on a therapeutic framework, which can be understood if one is interested in the working mechanisms of the treatment. However, in order to be meaningful to the policymaker, a more generic outcome measure has to be chosen. Indeed, policymakers are not so much interested in an answer to the question 'how does the treatment work?', but rather their primary interest is 'does the treatment work better than what already has been implemented and reimbursed?' To answer this question, we need generic outcome measures, which allow for meaningful comparisons between different treatment options. We will argue that the most commonly used generic outcome is the monetary value of the benefits, but we will also show that there is a limit to what can be valued meaningfully in terms of money. For instance, the monetary value of an avoided murder is unlikely to be helpful for policymaking, as there is a lack of consensus about quantifying its value. Furthermore, we will argue for a policymaker perspective in cost analyses. A cost-benefit analysis is of limited value for policymaking if the parameters which define the policy dilemma are not included. We will illustrate our argument with examples from health economics and a short overview of the main findings existing in international cost-effectiveness literature on crime prevention and treatment. By providing meaningful generic outcome measures and emphasising the policymaker perspective, we hope this chapter will help researchers in producing studies that can guide policymakers to the next level in crime policy.

Different Forms of Economic Evaluation

Cost-Benefit Analyses

The terms 'cost-benefit' and 'cost-effectiveness' are often used confusedly. Strictly speaking, they are different forms of economic evaluation. Cost-effectiveness analysis can be seen as a special case of cost-benefit analysis. In cost-benefit analysis, costs and benefits are both measured in monetary units. For instance, we can calculate the costs of a crime prevention or treatment programme and at the same time estimate the effects in terms of money saved. When the effect is measured in terms of the number of crimes avoided, we have to attribute a monetary value to a crime avoided in order to calculate the benefits in monetary terms. This approach can lead to a simple decision rule: if a programme's net benefits exceed its net costs, then it should be adopted. In other words, we can estimate if we lose money, or if we gain it. Aos and colleagues (2004) adopted this approach in their rank ordering of benefits and costs of crime prevention and treatment programmes for young people from a persuasive taxpayer perspective. By using the cost-benefit approach, the authors argued that effective prevention and treatment programmes are not costs to the taxpayer but rather an investment, as the cost-benefit ratio is positive. When cost-benefit analyses are based on valid data sources and reasonable assumptions, one really has no choice rather than adopting the recommendations based on cost-benefit studies, otherwise money is spend irrationally.

Notwithstanding the powerful arguments cost-benefit analyses may provide, they do not dominate health economics because they have an important methodological limitation. The problem is that cost-benefit analyses require the monetary valuation of all benefits. This can cause serious problems for relevant outcomes in health care or other fields of interest such as criminal justice. For instance, it is very difficult to find a meaningful monetary value for 'a life year gained' or 'an increase in the quality of life'. Despite years of research, there is still no consensus about the true monetary value of 'a life year'. The problem is not so much that we cannot ascribe a monetary value to a life year; rather the problem is that different research estimates provide very different values ranging from around €20,000 to several million. A similar problem emerges when implementing cost-benefit analyses in crime prevention and treatment programmes. It is reasonable to assume that a valid estimate of the material damage done can be proposed, but a monetary estimate of immaterial suffering is much more difficult. In the end, those estimates will always involve some form of value judgement for which the validity has not yet been established.

Cost-Effectiveness Analyses

If there is no consensus about the monetary value of important entities in the cost-benefit analysis, a solution is to keep these entities as recognisable items in the evaluation and thus without a monetary conversion. In this case, the analysis is referred to as a cost-effectiveness analysis. For instance, we could decide not to attribute a monetary value to the avoidance of a crime. Concordantly, our economic evaluation ends with monetary savings and costs of all other items, and the number of crimes avoided. We could then calculate the cost per avoided crime. In other words, how much should we invest in order to avoid one crime? Typical examples of outcomes in these studies in health care are: cost per life year gained and cost per quality-adjusted life year (cost per QALY). The difficulties in the valuation of these immaterial elements are the major reason that cost-effectiveness analyses have emerged as a favoured technique for economic evaluation in health care. Or as Neumann describes it: 'it allows analysts to quantify health benefits in health rather than in monetary terms' (Neumann, 2005, p. 15). For this reason, cost-effectiveness ratios, such as cost per life year gained, cost per avoided cardiac event and cost per QALY, dominate the health economic literature. Whereas in health economics, cost-effectiveness analyses are the preferred and most commonly applied technique, in the field of criminal justice, cost-effectiveness analyses are considered incomplete cost-benefit analyses, and accordingly are attributed less validity.

A Policymaker Perspective

The most commonly used perspective in economic evaluations is the 'policymaker perspective'. This is not surprising if one considers the main purpose of economic evaluations, which is to provide the policymaker with cost-effectiveness data on two alternatives from which a reimbursement decision can be made. Therefore, a cost-benefit or cost-effectiveness analysis is of limited value in policymaking if the parameters concerning the policy dilemma are not included. In other words, the choice of perspective is important because it determines the costs and consequences that will be included in the analyses.

By using a policymaker perspective, costs are most often calculated from a societal viewpoint. This means that not only the costs of the treatment or programme under consideration are included in the analysis, but also the costs and savings that occur elsewhere in society. The underlying idea is that health care programmes, or in this case prevention and treatment programmes, are not only a cost to society but may also generate or save money because of the treatment effects. These 'savings' in other areas of care can then be subtracted from the costs of the treatment programmes under evaluation.

Cost-Effectiveness Analyses in Health Care

In health care, cost-effectiveness analyses are a well-established decision-making tool in reimbursement policy. Manufacturers of new pharmaceuticals that try to launch their products into the market in, for instance, the UK, Australia, Canada and the Netherlands, and who want to qualify for reimbursement by the various national social health insurances, have to submit their data with an extensive cost-effectiveness analysis. Typically, such an evaluation should not only present evidence that the new treatment is effective as compared to doing nothing or taking a placebo, but it also has to show that the new treatment is a cost-effective alternative to the treatments already reimbursed.

One of the reasons health economics is mostly applied in the pharmaceutical industry, is because it can be considered an additional line of defence by the social national health insurances against the commercial interests of the pharmaceutical industry. Accordingly, health economic evaluations are often called 'the fourth hurdle', on top of the three standard requirements for reimbursement: efficacy, safety and effectiveness. Despite this negative connotation, the science of health economics has developed rapidly over the past decades from an *ad hoc* methodology in the early 1980s to standardised methods and consensus about the presentation of the results at the turn of the century. In the leading countries on health economics, this consensus has resulted in official guidelines for this type of research. The research available on the economic analysis of crime prevention and treatment programmes for youth is often considered in the light of these official guidelines. One might wonder if applying these sophisticated guidelines is not too strict, considering the early stage of this type of research in crime prevention and treatment programmes. Indeed, this is a legitimate question and therefore we will discuss it further below. First, however, we will provide an overview of the existing literature on economic evaluations of crime prevention and treatment programmes for youth.

Benefits and Costs of Crime Prevention and Treatment

There are several cost-benefit analyses of crime prevention and treatment programmes in which the immaterial benefits were assigned some monetary value, or just left out of the analysis. Leaving these effects out is the same as valuing the effects with a monetary value of zero. Obviously, a point of criticism on these analyses could be that not all of the effects and costs are included, or wrongly valued at zero. On the other hand, if the costs omitted in the analysis are of little value to the policymaker in a particular area of interest, this might not be considered a problem. Indeed, to what extent these intangible aspects should be included in the analyses is a matter for debate. Below we will describe two milestone studies that have provided monetary estimates of immaterial gains and losses in crime prevention and treatment.

Benefits and Costs of Prevention and Early Treatment Programmes for Youth (Aos et al., 2001, 2004)

In 2004, the Washington State Institute for Public Policy (Aos et al., 2004) published an extensive report on the comparative costs and benefits of prevention and treatment programmes for youth to reduce crime. In order to write this report, the authors systematically reviewed over 3,500 programme evaluations conducted mostly in North America over the last three decades. Their initial study (2001) was limited to evaluations that measured the costs and benefits of only crime-related outcomes; however, the 2004 report is an expansion of the earlier work and also examined the non-crime-related benefits such as education outcomes, substance abuse outcomes, teen pregnancy outcomes, and child abuse and neglect outcomes. Only the studies that had a randomised research approach were included in the review, following the trend of 'evidence-based medicine'. Findings from evaluations in highly controlled research settings (not 'real-world' programmes) were excluded. The costs and benefits of the programmes were calculated from three perspectives. First, from the taxpayer's perspective, by spending a taxpayer dollar now on a programme, how many dollars will be saved in the years ahead? Secondly, the crime victim's perspective was considered: if a programme can reduce rates of future delinquency, there will be fewer crime victims; and third, the programme participants' perspective. The standard economic measure – that is, the benefit-to-cost ratio – was calculated for all programmes. In calculating the total costs and benefits, the same assumptions were made and the same model was applied to all programmes. Because of this internal consistency, programmes can be compared to each other on a relative basis.

Aos and colleagues (2004) concluded that investments in effective programmes for juvenile offenders have the highest net benefit (benefits minus costs). Such programmes yield net benefits from $1,900 (Diversion Programmes with Services[1]) to $31,200 (Dialectical Behaviour Therapy[2]) per youth. Some forms of home-visiting programmes that target high-risk and/or low-income mothers and children were also effective, returning from $6,000 (Home Visiting Programmes for At-Risk Mothers

1 Diversion Programmes with Services are programmes typically designed for low-risk, first-time juvenile offenders who would otherwise have their cases handled formally in the juvenile court. These programmes typically have citizen accountability boards with counselling services provided by social service agencies (Aos et al., 2004).

2 Dialectical Behaviour Therapy is a comprehensive cognitive-behavioural treatment for individuals with complex and difficult-to-treat mental disorders. The focus of the programme is on the enhancement of the youth's behavioural skills to handle difficult situations; motivating to change dysfunctional behaviours and ensuring the new skills are used in daily life (Aos et al., 2004).

and Children[3]) to $17,200 (Nurse Family Partnership for Low-Income Women[4]) per youth. Moreover, early childhood education for low-income 3–4-year-olds and some youth development programmes provided very attractive returns on investment. In addition, while their net benefits were relatively low, many substance-use prevention programmes for youth were still cost-effective, because the programmes were relatively inexpensive. Only a few programmes were effective at reducing teenage pregnancy.

The Monetary Value of Saving a High-Risk Youth

Cohen's (1998) paper on this topic provides estimates of the potential benefits from saving a high-risk youth, by calculating the lifetime costs associated with the typical career criminal, drug abuser and secondary-school dropout. Cohen's publication is exemplary for a study that makes an effort to estimate monetary values for 'intangible' costs, such as the costs of the pain, suffering and lost quality of life of crime victims. For instance, in the case of fatalities, he derived the value of an additional year of life from consumer behaviour in buying life-saving products and from worker willingness to accept riskier jobs in exchange for a premium wage. Results of this study showed that the typical career criminal causes $1.3–1.5 million in external costs; a heavy drug user $370,000–970,000,; and a high-school dropout $243,000–388,000. That these intangible costs can make a substantial difference in the total costs of a programme was illustrated in Cohen's (1988) re-analysis of Austin's (1986) cost-benefit calculations of an early release from prison programme. When Cohen added pain and suffering components to Austin's estimates of the direct losses incurred by crime victims, the total costs of the programme increased sixfold, showing the impact of these intangible costs on the total costs.

Cost-Effectiveness Studies on Young Offenders

Besides the two studies described above, there is little published evidence on the cost-benefit and cost-effectiveness of crime prevention and treatment programmes for young offenders. We found only three reviews that included (but were not limited to) treatment and prevention programmes for young offenders. Two of these focused primarily on the costs and benefits of correctional interventions (Welsh & Farrington, 2000; McDougall et al., 2003). The third review covered a broader scope of criminal justice interventions, for example, crime-prevention programmes involving young offenders, and treatment programmes and sentencing (Swaray, Bowles & Pradiptyo, 2005). Welsh and Farrington (2000) concluded in their review that little is known

3 Home Visiting Programmes for At-risk Mothers and Children focus on mothers considered being at risk of parenting problems. The content of the programme consists of instruction in child development and health, referrals for service, or social and emotional support (Aos et al., 2004).

4 Nurse Family Partnership for Low-Income Women provides intensive visitation by nurses during a woman's pregnancy and the first two years after birth. The goal is to promote the child's development and provide support and instructive parenting skills to the parents (Aos et al., 2004).

about the economic efficiency of correctional intervention strategies. Only seven published studies were identified that have presented information on monetary costs and benefits. McDougall et al. (2003) argued that even the seven studies found by Welsh and Farrington lacked important information to shed light on the economics of crime interventions. For instance, all seven studies had omitted the indirect/intangible costs to victims and three studies of the seven postulated their conclusions in the absence of a control group. They found nine studies that satisfied their criteria; they included studies that specified costs and benefits of sentencing options, and all had to be rated at Level 3 or above on the Cost Benefit Validity Scale (Cohen, Swaray & McDougall, 2002). Their recommendation for future research, besides more rigorous research designs such as randomised controlled trials, was to focus on developing a standardised methodology for calculating the relative costs and benefits of criminal justice programmes to allow comparisons between different sentencing options.

The most recent review of Swaray and colleagues (2005) found only ten published studies, out of a total of 154 studies reviewed, that were judged to encapsulate rigorous applications of economic analysis to criminal justice interventions. Besides emphasising the paucity of economic analysis of interventions in the criminal justice field, the authors also stressed that there is a need for more refined application of appraisal and evaluation techniques in this particular field of interest.

Research specifically studying prevention or treatment programmes for juveniles is even more diluted. Welsh (2001) reviewed the available evidence on the economic costs and benefits of early developmental prevention of delinquency in children under age 13 and could only identify five studies. His earlier work on correctional intervention programmes (Welsh & Farrington, 2000) did not turn up any studies of programmes that had intervened with delinquents under age 18. There are, however, a few studies in this sub-group that are worth mentioning. Robertson, Grimes and Rogers (2001) performed a cost-benefit evaluation of two community-based intervention programmes for juvenile offenders. In their quasi-experimental study, they evaluated the effects of community-based intensive supervision and monitoring (ISM) and cognitive-behavioural (CB) intervention techniques on justice system expenditures for court referrals and court-ordered detention. The sample consisted of 293 offenders between ages of 11 and 17 who were on probation or parole. The outcomes were analysed in comparison to the outcomes of a control group consisting of participants on standard probation or parole. They found the cognitive-behavioural intervention technique to be cost-beneficial: for every dollar spent at the margin for the CB programme, almost $2 were saved in terms of lower justice system expenditures on additional court referrals and days of detention for juvenile offenders in the programme. However, a limitation of this study is that only the direct, short-run costs and benefits incurred by the local justice system were estimated and thus the study probably provides a conservative estimate of potential costs and benefits.

A report by the RAND Corporation (Greenwood et al., 1996) describes a study that compared the costs and benefits of four different approaches to intervening early in the lives of children at some risk of eventual trouble with the law with a high-profile incarceration alternative (California's 'Three Strikes' law). This study is of particular interest as it is one of the few studies focusing on prevention techniques rather than treatment techniques. Moreover, it compares the alternative treatments to treatment-as-usual, which is a condition for research to be useful in policy decisions. Results showed that three of the approaches compared favourably in cost-effectiveness with incarceration. These programmes were school-based interventions, for example, incentives to graduate; treatments for families with children who are 'acting out'; and treatments for troublesome youths at an early stage in their delinquency career. The programme graduation incentives for high-risk youths appeared the most promising with costs of $4,000 per crime avoided. Furthermore, the effects of such a programme will be felt within a short period of time because the targeted young people are approaching their most crime-prone years. Parent training intervention could be relatively cost-effective over the long run at a cost of $6,500 per serious felony prevented. Delinquent supervision programmes cost nearly $14,000 per serious crime prevented. Although these costs per avoided crime are higher than the programmes mentioned before, the impact is almost immediate because the intervention comes just prior to the peak in the age-crime curve. The fourth programme – early home visit and day-care intervention – was not as cost-effective as the three other programmes and incarceration. One reason is the delay of almost fifteen years between the intervention and the time the effects were most likely to occur (that is, the crime-prone years). The cost per crime prevented was $29,400. A limitation of this study is that only the direct programme costs were estimated. Indirect and intangible benefits, such as averted incarceration or prevented victim trauma, were not included in the analyses. This is probably the reason that the cost-effectiveness ratios are not dominated by negative costs, that is to say savings, as was demonstrated in the cost-benefit analyses of Aos et al. (2001, 2004) and Cohen (1998) discussed above.

The main findings of the RAND report suggest that prevention programmes targeting problem youths, either children who act out or delinquent youths, are more cost-effective than prevention programmes that target general populations of youths. This is in line with a rule often found in cost-effectiveness analysis: cure is more cost-effective than prevention. In addition, another factor influencing the programme costs and benefits is the time lag between the intervention and the appearance of effects: the effects of earlier interventions have more opportunity for decay before children reach a crime-prone age. Furthermore, the researchers conclude that prevention is more cost-effective in the long run than incarceration.

That a prevention programme can yield money to society becomes apparent in the High/Scope Perry Preschool Study (Schweinhart et al., 2005). This study randomly assigned 123 African-American children, born in poverty and at high risk of failing in school, to a high-quality preschool programme or no-programme control groups. The study shows that the preschool programme, over the children's lifetimes, improved their educational performance, contributed to their economic development, helped prevent them from committing crimes, and provided a high return on taxpayer investment. A cost-benefit analysis showed that the average cost of the programme was $15,166 per participant. For this cost, the programme yielded public benefits of $195,621 per participant, a cost-benefit ratio of 12.9:1. The sources of benefits per participant were, in order of magnitude, costs saved by the potential victims of

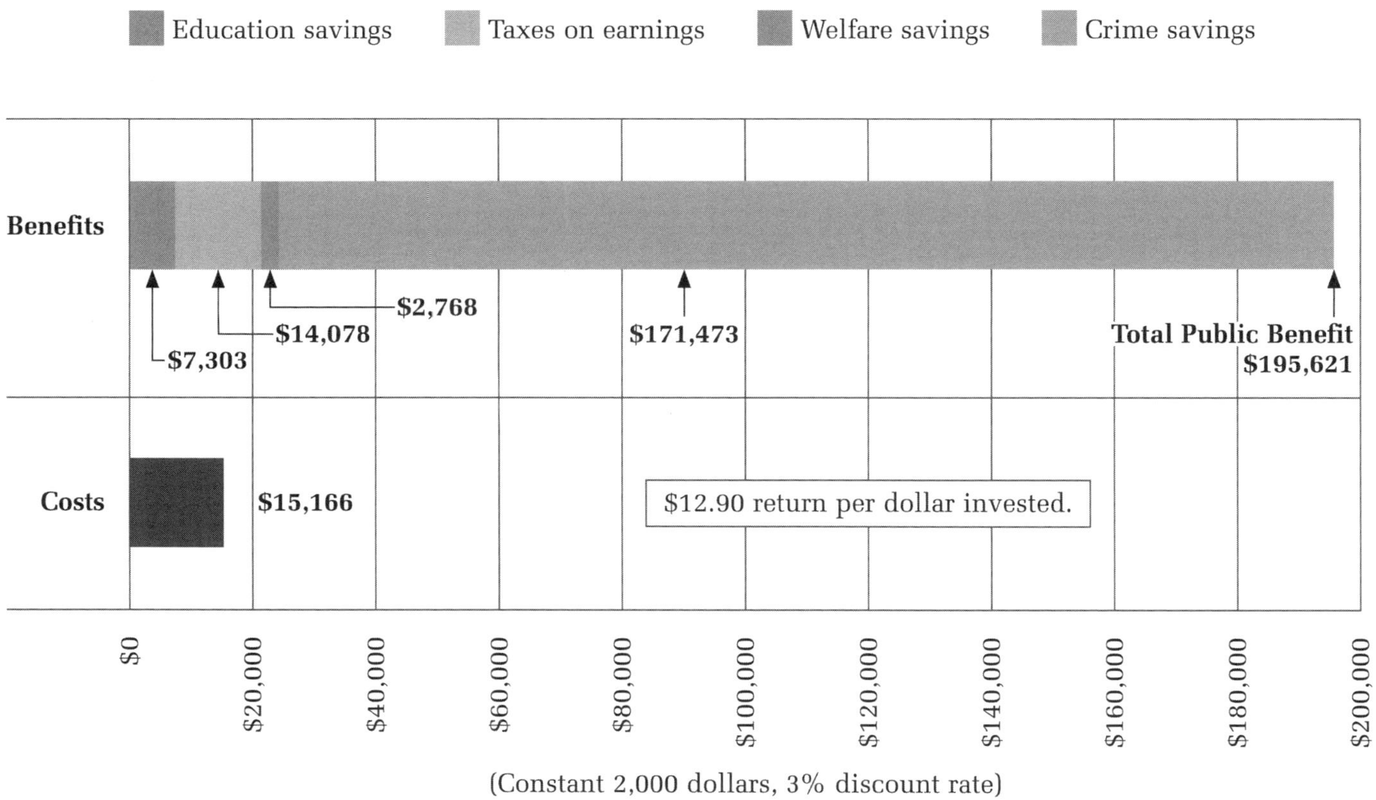

Figure 13.1 The public costs and benefits per participant of the High/Scope Perry Preschool Programme

Source: Schweinhart et al., 2005

crimes never committed and accordingly the reduced justice system costs, increased taxes paid by preschool programme participants because they had higher earnings, costs saved due to reduced need for special education, and reduced welfare costs. These public benefits are displayed together with the programme costs in Figure 13.1. The authors concluded that this high-quality preschool programme for.young children living in poverty was an extremely good economic investment, comparing favourably with alternative uses of public resources and even with private-sector investments.

Although the quality of the research is not always according to the high standards of systematic reviews, the international literature on economic evaluations of prevention and treatment programmes for juvenile offenders is growing. Moreover, the existing evidence suggests that crime prevention and treatment programmes for this particular population can be cost-effective.

Cost-Effectiveness Studies in the Netherlands

To the best of our knowledge, there are no published economic evaluations of crime prevention or treatment programmes for young offenders based on Dutch data. This seems remarkable as the Netherlands is one of the leading countries in economic evaluations of health care. Concordantly, knowledge of the methodology of performing such evaluations is amply available. It is therefore puzzling why there are no such evaluations performed in the field of childcare, since persistent disruptive and delinquent behaviours in youth can be considered a serious problem. In the Netherlands, 1.6–5.1% of young people can be considered seriously violent or delinquent (Loeber, Slot & Sergeant, 2001). Juvenile delinquents – in particular those who are extremely violent and aggressive – are known to be expensive to society. In a recent investigation of the Research and Documentation Centre of the Dutch Ministry of Justice (abbreviated to WODC in Dutch), it was found that criminality cost society €9.1 billion per year. This provides a good reason to search for the most cost-effective treatments. Nevertheless, cost-effectiveness research in childcare is not as common as it is in health care. For instance, none of the prevention and treatment programmes which have emerged in recent years has been evaluated properly in terms of cost-effectiveness.

To apply cost-effectiveness research to crime prevention and treatment programmes in youth, we have to adopt some scientific basics. First of all, good evidence on the effectiveness of a programme is necessary before performing a cost-effectiveness analysis can even be thought of. Another condition is that only treatment protocol programmes that have well-operationalised principles can be used for the evaluation of their cost-effectiveness. It is useless estimating the (cost-) effectiveness of a particular programme of which the treatment principles have changed over time or are performed differently somewhere else. In childcare, a lot of the existing prevention and treatment programmes are not applied according to well-specified treatment protocol and standards.

A stimulating development is that the Dutch Ministry of Justice is striving to fund in the future only those programmes that have proven cost-effectiveness. In anticipation of this, it has asked ECORYS, an economics research and consulting agency, to develop a prototype of a generally applicable cost-benefit analysis computation model for the economic assessment of judicial interventions. The general model, described in an extensive report (Versantvoort et al., 2005), compares the costs and benefits of the intervention programme under consideration with a zero alternative, that is, the current policy of imposing a sentence. The user can specify a number of aspects to be included in the model, for example, the duration of the zero and project alternative, the horizon of effect determination, the offence categories considered, the number of participants in an intervention, the effects per intervention and offence type to be included, the costs of the intervention, the costs per type of offence, and the recidivism frequency per type of offence in the zero and project alternative. These aspects together eventually determine the net benefits of the intervention. Although the model itself looks very promising, the developers remark that there is insufficient data available in the Netherlands to completely specify the new-developed model.

Conclusions

Economic evaluations in the field of childcare are in their infancy, and only a small number of cost-benefit and cost-effectiveness studies are available. Additionally, the methodological quality of the research has been questioned in systematic reviews. However, despite the fact that the quality of much of the research falls short of the highest quality standards that apply in other fields such as medicine, realising the necessity of this kind of research for the continued existence of prevention and treatment programmes in childcare is a good development. Moreover, some evidence for the effectiveness and cost-effectiveness of a prevention or treatment programme is always more evidence-based than having no evidence at all. Therefore, we have to be careful not to reject the existing research which on initial consideration may not be considered optimal.

A good example of this is Multisystemic Therapy (MST), an intensive home-based treatment programme for chronic violent, delinquent, or substance-abusing juvenile offenders age 12–18 (Henggeler et al., 1998). The treatment services of MST are typically delivered in the young person's home, school and community settings. In the field of childcare, MST was set as an example of an evidence-based programme concerning its cost-effectiveness. This role as a model was seriously put to the test when Littell, Popa, and Forsythe (2005) recently argued that there were serious flaws in the publications about the effectiveness of MST. Littell and colleagues concluded: 'MST is not consistently more or less effective than other services in preventing restrictive out-of-home living arrangements (e.g., incarceration, psychiatric hospitalization), reducing arrests or convictions, or improving youth and family functioning. There is no evidence that MST has harmful effects' (p. 11). When reading this review, it may be difficult to believe that MST is even near qualifying as an evidence-based effective treatment programme. However, it is important to realise that the flaws reported in the recent Cochrane review of MST refer to a standard of research without precedent in the field of childcare. In a

Cochrane review, evidence about the effectiveness of an intervention is judged by the highest standards, as found in the field of medicine, for example, randomisation methods such as sealed envelopes or even/uneven registration numbers are not seen as a 'proper randomisation'. Another example is that the close involvement of the developers of MST with the effect studies was seen as a devaluation of the evidence. Further, Littell considered the lack of standardisation of the follow-up (no full intention-to-treat and no fixed follow-up measurement periods) a major concern. Does this criticism mean that MST can no longer be considered an evidence-based and/or cost-effective treatment programme? If we use the scientific state-of-the-art of the field of childcare as a reference, MST is among the best-documented and evidence-based programmes available. However, compared to medical evaluation studies, the research done on MST has not yet been performed according to high-quality standards.

High-quality research is therefore needed to avoid future economic analyses on crime prevention and treatment programmes for young offenders being rejected due to a lack of adherence to the highest research standards, resulting in their cost-effectiveness being discredited. Moreover, this research should be conducted from a policymaker's perspective. With this perspective in mind, the research will have the best chance to assist the decision makers in directing scarce public resources toward economically successful programmes and away from unsuccessful programmes, thereby producing net overall gains to society.

Part V
Legal and European Contexts

Chapter 14

Juvenile Justice: International Rights and Standards

Jaap E. Doek

From an international human rights perspective, the administration of justice is first and foremost a matter of fair trial based on the right of everyone charged with a criminal offence to be presumed innocent until proved guilty according to law. This emphasis on fair trial – that is, a fair and public hearing by a competent, independent and impartial tribunal established by law (and not, for example, by a presidential or monarchical decree) – results in the elaboration of various procedural rights and standards in, for example, the International Covenant on Civil and Political Rights (ICCPR) such as:

- the right to be informed promptly about the charges;
- the right to be tried without undue delay, to defend oneself in person or through legal assistance of one's own choosing;
- the right to examine witnesses, and
- the right not to be compelled to testify against oneself or to confess guilt (see Art. 10 and 11 ICCPR for more details).

The other predominant aspect of international human rights and standards regarding the administration of justice concerns the treatment and punishment of persons accused of having committed an offence. In this regard, the most widely accepted standard is the right of everyone *not* to be subjected to torture or to cruel, inhuman, or degrading treatment or punishment (Art. 7 ICCPR and the Convention against Torture and Other Cruel, Inhuman or Degrading Treatment or Punishment). Secondly, when it comes to the sentencing of the offender, the international human rights focus is on the limitation of the death penalty (Art. 6 ICCPR) and the deprivation of liberty (Art. 9 and 10 ICCPR). Most of these international standards are also included in the UN Convention on the Rights of the Child (hereafter: the CRC; Art. 40 and 37 CRC). In that regard, the CRC is a confirmation of the applicability of existing international rights and standards for the administration of juvenile justice. However, there are some significant differences. First, the UN Convention on the Rights of the Child is the only human rights treaty that contains a description of the overall aims of the administration of justice concerning juvenile offenders (Art. 40, par. 1 CRC). Secondly, the CRC explicitly recommends (whenever appropriate and desirable) dealing with children who infringe the penal law without resorting to judicial proceedings (Art. 40 par. 3 under b CRC). Third, the CRC requires that a variety of non-custodial measures are made available as alternatives to institutional care, or deprivation of liberty (Art. 40, par. 4 CRC).[1] In line with this provision, Article 37 under b, CRC states that deprivation of liberty shall be used only as a measure of last resort and for the shortest appropriate period of time, a provision unknown in other human rights treaties.

Finally, the implementation of the rights and standards for juvenile justice as enshrined in the CRC are supported by and elaborated in three sets of Guidelines, Standards and Rules:

- UN Guidelines for the Prevention of Juvenile Delinquency: The Riyadh Guidelines,[2]
- UN Standard Minimum Rules for the Administration of Juvenile Justice: the Beijing Rules, and[3]
- UN Rules for the Protection of Juveniles Deprived of their Liberty: the Havana Rules.[4]

The Riyadh Guidelines and the Beijing Rules are unique international documents. There are no similar documents for the prevention of adult delinquency or for the administration of justice for adult offenders.

With regard to the deprivation of liberty, various other international rules and principles have been adopted by the General Assembly of the UN.[5] The Havana Rules can be considered as a child-specific elaboration of at least part of these general rules and principles. There are other international and regional (European and inter-American) conventions and rules that can be of relevance for the treatment of juvenile offenders.

This chapter focuses on the international rights and standards of direct relevance for the administration of juvenile justice. It will be impossible to fully present and discuss all the international rights and standards relevant for juvenile justice, even

1 On 14 December 1990, the General Assembly of the UN adopted (Resolution 45/110) United Nations Standard Minimum Rules for Non-custodial Measures (the so-called 'Tokyo Rules'). These rules are important because States committed themselves to the implementation of these rules. But, these rules are not legally binding and it is striking that they are not based on a specific provision in one of the human rights treaties. The consequence of this is that the implementation of the rules is not included in the monitoring activities of (one of the) human rights treaty bodies.

2 Adopted by the General Assembly of the UN by Resolution 45/112 of 14 December 1990. The short name of these Guidelines is linked to the name of the city where the drafting was completed, in this case Riyadh. The same applies to the other documents.

3 Adopted by the General Assembly of the UN by Resolution 40/33 of November 29, 1985. The drafting was completed in Beijing.

4 Adopted by the General Assembly of the UN by Resolution 45/113 of 14 December 1990. The drafting was completed in Havana.

5 See for example, Standard Minimum Rules for the Treatment of Prisoners approved by the Economic and Social Council (ECOSOC) of the UN by its Resolutions 663c (XXIV) of 31 July 1957 and 2076 (LXII) of 13 May 1977; Body of Principles for the Protection of All Persons under Any Form of Detention or Imprisonment adopted by the General Assembly of the UN by Resolution 43/173 of 9 December 1988.

if I were limiting myself to those contained in the CRC and the three documents mentioned above. For these reasons, I will limit myself to highlighting the major rights and standards, while identifying difficulties in implementing these rights and standards. This will be based on the experiences of the CRC Committee in reviewing the performances of States Parties to the CRC, experiences which are also reflected in General Comment No. 10 on Children's Rights in Juvenile Justice.[6] Where appropriate, I make reference to Dutch rules, regulations and practice to illustrate what the possibilities and problems can be in a country that is a State Party to the CRC.[7]

Some General Observations

Up to this point I have been using the terms 'rights' and 'standards'. They are not interchangeable and in order to avoid misunderstanding the following explanations might be helpful. The 'rights' of juvenile offenders can be found in international human rights treaties and in particular in the CRC. Among other things, 'rights' are specific provisions that entitle the child to certain protections or services. States Parties to the treaty have committed themselves to undertake the necessary measures to ensure that these rights are fully respected and implemented. In case of violation of one of these rights, the State is under the obligation to provide the child (and/or their parents/guardians) with adequate ways and means to remedy the violation. 'Standards' can be defined, in this context, as internationally agreed-upon principles and/or rules for promoting/enhancing a minimum level of quality of the various activities in the administration of juvenile justice.

Documents containing recommendations for the States to undertake specific actions are often called 'guidelines'. An example is the Guidelines for Prevention of Juvenile Delinquency. The guidelines, however, can also contain (explicitly or implicitly) certain standards and the recommendations usually aim at the development of a minimum level of quality of actions by States.[8]

The UN Committee on the Rights of the Child (the CRC Committee) is the elected international body of experts mandated to examine the progress made by States Parties to the CRC in achieving the realisation of the obligations undertaken under the CRC (Art. 43 CRC). States Parties must report to the CRC Committee for the first time on their achievements and the difficulties they are facing in their

---

6 This General Comment contains various recommendations for States Parties and was adopted at the forty-fourth Session of the CRC Committee; UN Doc. CRC/C/GC/10, 9 February 2007 (unedited version).

7 To avoid misunderstanding, the Kingdom of the Netherlands, which includes the Dutch Antilles and Aruba, is a State Party to the CRC. But my references to developments in the Netherlands will be limited to the European part (usually called the Netherlands) of the Kingdom of the Netherlands.

8 See, for example, the Guidelines and Measures for the Prohibition and Prevention of Torture, Cruelty, Inhuman or Degrading Treatment or Punishment in Africa (The Robben Island Guidelines, adopted by the African Commission on Human and Peoples' Rights at its thirty-second ordinary session, 17–23 October 2002.

efforts to implement the CRC within two years after their ratification of the treaty and thereafter every five years. The examination by the CRC Committee is based on this report and additional information it receives from national and international non-government organisations (NGOs) and from UN agencies, in particular UNICEF. This examination takes place in a public discussion between a delegation of the State Party and the CRC Committee. After this discussion, which takes place in Geneva, the CRC Committee issues a set of Concluding Observations containing specific and concrete recommendations for further actions to be taken by the State Party.

Finally, some remarks on the terminology: the CRC uses in Article 40 the phrase: a child 'alleged as, accused of or recognised as having infringed the penal law'. In order to avoid rather cumbersome repetition of this phrase, I will use the terms 'juvenile offender' or 'child delinquent', which cover all persons who are accused or who have been found guilty of having committed an offence and who were younger than age 18 at the time of the (alleged) commission of the offence (see also Rule 2.2 of the Beijing Rules). In addition, and in line with the Riyadh Guidelines, the term 'juvenile delinquency' is used and covers all activities that constitute an (alleged) infringement of the penal law by a person under age 18.

The CRC Committee is of the opinion that States Parties to the CRC should make prevention an integral part of their juvenile justice policy. I shall therefore start with some observations regarding prevention and follow with a presentation and discussion of the basic rights and principles of juvenile justice. Thereafter I will deal with the other key rights and standards of juvenile justice: the (minimum) ages for application, diversion, fair trial and dispositions. I will conclude with some remarks about the implementation of the rights and standards of juvenile justice.

Prevention

The CRC does not contain a specific provision requiring States Parties to develop and implement a policy aimed at the prevention of juvenile delinquency. But the need for such a policy can be based on one of the most important goals of the implementation of the CRC: the promotion of the full and harmonious development of the child's personality, talents and mental and physical abilities (Art. 6 and 29 CRC). In the light of these and other provisions of the CRC, it is obviously not in the best interest of the child (Art. 3 CRC) to grow up under circumstances that may cause increased and serious risks of becoming involved in delinquency. The CRC Committee is, therefore, of the opinion that States Parties should undertake targeted and systematic measures to prevent juvenile delinquency, and in particular to prevent a child becoming a serious and/or chronic offender.

States Parties developing and implementing prevention policies or programmes should fully take into account the Riyadh Guidelines for the prevention of juvenile delinquency. This document contains *inter alia* the fundamental principles that should be observed when implementing prevention policies. For example, 'Young persons should have an active role and partnership within society and should not be considered as mere objects of socialisation or control'; and, prevention policies 'should avoid criminalizing and penalizing a child for behaviour that does not cause serious damage to the development of the child or harm others'.

The Guidelines recommend that emphasis should be placed on preventive policies facilitating the successful socialisation and integration of all children and young persons, in particular through the family, the community, peer groups, schools, vocational training and the world of work, as well as through voluntary organisations. The Guidelines provide detailed recommendations for:

- The role of the family and the need to assist the family in providing care and protection, with special attention for particularly vulnerable children, such as children belonging to indigenous, migrant or refugee families;
- The role of education *inter alia* in extending special care and attention to children and young persons who are at social risk. Teachers and other professionals within the educational system should be equipped and trained to prevent alcohol, drug and other substance abuse.
- The role of the community in providing or strengthening a wide range of community-based support measures for young persons, including community development centres, recreational facilities, and services for children who are at social risk.

Other specific recommendations concern the role of the media, the need to develop a comprehensive social policy, to enact legislation, to undertake or encourage research and to establish mechanisms for an effective collaboration between all the professionals and organisations involved, including proper coordination of their activities.

In conclusion, States Parties to the CRC must develop and implement comprehensive prevention policies, and the Riyadh Guidelines provide them with detailed information about the key elements of such policies.

The Basic Rights and Principles

The CRC Committee has identified four provisions in the CRC which it considers as General Principles. These provisions should be an integral part of the implementation of the other provisions relevant for juvenile justice, in particular Articles 37 and 40. I will briefly comment on these four General Principles.

Non-Discrimination (Art. 2 CRC)

States Parties shall respect and ensure the rights set forth in the CRC of each child within its jurisdiction without discrimination of any kind, irrespective of, for example, the child's race, colour, sex, language, religion, national, ethnic or social origin, disability, birth, or other status. Within the context of juvenile justice, this means that States must abolish all discriminatory rules and regulations and prevent *de facto* discrimination, particularly of vulnerable groups such as street children and children belonging to indigenous peoples and other minorities. In this respect, particular attention should be given to the *de facto* discrimination of former juvenile offenders in their efforts to get access to education or to the labour market. Extra support and assistance may be necessary to overcome this *de facto* discrimination in order to allow these juveniles to reintegrate and to assume a constructive role in society in line with the overarching goals of juvenile justice (Art. 40, par. 1 CRC). As an example, I refer to the plan of the Dutch government to establish a well-organised care programme for juveniles who have completed their sanction, especially when they are released from a detention or treatment centre. The government emphasises the practical nature of this so-called after-care (*nazorg* in Dutch), for example, support for finding adequate housing, for the continuation of education, for finding a job, or if necessary, for applying for social security benefits.[9]

The right to non-discrimination is a core provision not only of the CRC but also of the other human rights treaties. It means *inter alia* that activities of adults that are not considered to be an offence should not be criminalised if a child is the actor. To quote paragraph 56 of the Riyadh Guidelines, 'legislation should be enacted to ensure that any conduct not considered an offence or not penalized if committed by an adult, is not considered an offence and not penalized if committed by a young person.' In line with this rule, the CRC Committee recommends that States Parties abolish the provisions on so-called status offences. Children's problematic behaviours, such as vagrancy and running away, must not be criminalised, but should be dealt with via child protective measures and effective support for parents and other caregivers.

The Best Interests of the Child (Art. 3, CRC)

'The Best Interests of the Child' (Art. 3, CRC) shall be a primary consideration in all actions concerning children. Children and adolescents differ from adults in their psychological development and their emotional, educational and other needs. These and other differences are the justification for a separate system of juvenile justice and require different treatment of juvenile offenders. This means, for example, that repressive objectives of criminal justice must give way to rehabilitation and restorative justice objectives when dealing with juvenile offenders.[10]

---

9 See the Dutch policy paper *Vasthoudend en effectief. Versterking van de aanpak van jeugdcriminaliteit* (Tenacious and effective. Strengthening the policy on juvenile delinquency), 2002.

10 In this regard, I would like to refer to the US Supreme Court decision in *Roper* v. *Simmons* (543 US 2005) of 1 March 2005 that rejection of the death penalty for juvenile offenders under 18 is required by the Eighth Amendment. The court identifies three general differences between juveniles under 18 and adults:

- Juvenile susceptibility to immature and irresponsible behaviour means their irresponsible conduct is not as morally reprehensible as that of an adult.
- Their own vulnerability and comparative lack of control over their immediate surroundings mean juveniles have a greater claim than adults to be forgiven for failing to escape negative influences in their whole environment.
- The reality that juveniles still struggle to define their identity means it is less supportable to conclude that even heinous crimes committed by a juvenile are evidence of an irretrievably depraved character.

The Right to Life, Survival and Development (Art. 6 CRC)

This right should guide and inspire States Parties in their development of effective programmes and policies for the prevention of juvenile delinquency because it goes without saying that delinquency has a very negative impact on the child's development. It should also result in a policy of reacting to juvenile delinquency in a manner that supports the child's development.

The death penalty and life imprisonment without parole are explicitly prohibited (Art. 37 CRC). But deprivation of liberty for many years can have very negative consequences for the child's right to harmonious development and seriously hamper their reintegration into society. It is therefore important to ensure that deprivation of liberty is only imposed for the shortest appropriate period of time so that the child's right to development is respected as much as possible.

The Right to Be Heard (Art. 12 CRC)

The key provision for juvenile justice in the CRC, Article 40, does not contain a specific provision elaborating on the right to be heard, but Article 12 CRC underlines the importance of the implementation of this right throughout every stage of the administration of juvenile justice. Article 12, par. 2 CRC requires that a child be provided with the opportunity to be heard in any judicial and administrative proceedings affecting the child, either directly or through a representative or an appropriative body in a manner consistent with the procedural rules of national law.

It is obvious that for a child who is alleged, accused, or recognised as having infringed the penal law, the right to be heard is a fundamental element of the right to a fair trial. It is equally obvious that the child should have the right be heard directly and not only through a representative or an appropriate body. This right of the child should be fully observed in all stages of the process starting with the pre-trial stage, when the child must be heard by the police, the prosecutor and the investigating judge. But it also applies to the adjudication and judicial disposition stage, and to the stage of execution of the imposed measures or sanctions.

The right to be heard is not limited to the alleged infringement of the penal law. Children should be given the opportunity to express their views freely and those views should be given due weight in accordance with the age and maturity of the child throughout the juvenile justice process (Art. 12, par. 1 CRC). It means that the child should be informed not only about the charges, but also about the juvenile justice process as such and about the possible measures and/or sanctions. Children should also be given the opportunity to express their views concerning the (alternative) measures/sanctions that may be imposed, and the specific wishes or preferences they may have in this regard should be given due weight. Assuming that the child is criminally responsible implies that they should, to the degree possible, participate in the decisions regarding the most appropriate response to their infringement of the penal law. It may go without saying that the prosecutor and the judge involved are responsible for and make the decisions. But to treat the child as a passive object does not contribute to an effective response to their delinquency. This also applies to the implementation of the measure/sanction imposed. According to the CRC Committee

(General Comment No. 10, par. 23c), research shows that actively engaging the child in this implementation will in most cases contribute to a positive result. However, most of the research on the right of the child to be involved or to participate deals with activities or decisions other than in the field of juvenile justice (see, for example, Sylwander, 2001; Van Beers et al., 2006; Lansdown, 2005).

Minimum Age of Criminal Responsibility

Article 40, par. 3 CRC expects States Parties to set a minimum age for criminal responsibility (MACR) without indicating what an acceptable minimum age is. The Beijing Rules (par. 4) recommend setting a MACR at not too low a level. The MACR has been, and still is, subject to sometimes heated discussion. Some States Parties favour a very high MACR, even up to age 18, which would make most of the provisions of Article 40 CRC redundant. To avoid misunderstanding, the MACR is not about the capacity of a child to infringe the penal law (as suggested by Article 40, par. 3 CRC), but about the age at which a child who commits an offence can be held criminally responsible. That is the age at which the child can be charged under the penal law and be sentenced if found guilty.

The CRC Committee has recommended States Parties with a low MACR to increase it to an internationally-acceptable level. From these recommendations it can be concluded that a MACR under age 12 is *not* internationally acceptable. At the same time, the Committee expects States Parties to raise the MACR to a higher level than 12 years and *not* to lower an existing higher MACR – for example, 14 or 16 years to age 12 (General Comment No. 10 paragraph 16).

A high MACR contributes to a juvenile justice system which, whenever appropriate and desirable, deals with juvenile offenders without resorting to judicial proceedings (Art. 40, par. 2 (b) CRC). But the CRC requires that the human rights and legal safeguards be fully respected in the treatment of juveniles below the MACR who have committed an offence. The general principles discussed in paragraph 4 should be fully respected and implemented. Treatment of the offending children must be appropriate to their well-being and proportionate both to their circumstances and the offence.

In the Netherlands, as in some other States Parties to the CRC, proposals have been made to lower the MACR. The Dutch government did not support the proposals and rightly so, because a MACR of 12 years is considered by the CRC Committee as the absolute minimum (See General Comment No. 10, par. 16). But children below the MACR do commit offences, and the challenge for every government is to develop an adequate and balanced response to these acts with a view to preventing recidivism and the development of a criminal career.[11] Child protection interventions are the traditional response in many countries.

As mentioned, the *Stop-reaction* serves children younger than age 12 who commit an offence (see Chapter 12, this volume). This programme offers support to

---

11 For the importance of early intervention in cases of crimes committed by young children, see Loeber & Farrington, 2001.

parents in their efforts to correct their child's problem behaviours. A special bureau has been established for organising and implementing alternative measures for children under age 12. The parents' cooperation is necessary, but should be given on a voluntary basis and there is no sanction if they do not cooperate. Evaluation of this project shows that the overall results are positive; but more outreach work is needed to gain the parents' cooperation, in particular of those parents belonging to ethnic minorities.[12]

It is especially important that the General Principles of the CRC are fully respected and that the response is proportionate to the circumstances of the child and the offence. This approach can reduce the sometimes popular pressure to lower the MACR.

The rights and standards of juvenile justice should apply to all persons below age 18, starting at the MACR. The CRC Committee has regularly encouraged States Parties to abolish provisions that allow the imposition of adult sanctions on juveniles who were below age 18 at the time of the commission of the offence. Such a provision exists in the Dutch criminal code (Art. 77b, (Sr.) Book 1, section VIIIA, Special Provisions for Young Persons, Art. 77a–hh). It allows the juvenile court judge to impose an adult sanction on 16- or 17-year-old adolescents (at the time of the offence) on one of the three grounds mentioned in Art. 77b (Sr). A recent study shows that the use of this exception is declining: from 205 in 2001 to 143 in 2004 (or 2.4% of the total sentenced cases to 1.2%). In more than 50% of these cases, the imposed sanction was below the maximum possible under the rules of juvenile justice.[13] The CRC Committee recommended to the Dutch government in 2004 to abolish this exception (UN Doc. CRC/C/15/227, 30 January 2004, par. 58 and 59). A special problem in this regard is that it also allows for the imposition of life imprisonment. The Dutch government noted that this possibility is purely theoretical since it is never used in practice. The CRC Committee has explicitly recommended that at least this possibility be abolished. In the light of the Dutch government's caveat, just mentioned, it should be very easy to implement this recommendation, but it has yet not been done.

Diversion[14]

One of the distinct features of juvenile justice is the rule that States Parties, whenever appropriate and desirable, should deal with juvenile offenders without resorting to judicial proceedings (Art. 40, par. 3(b) CRC). It is left to the States Parties to make this rule a reality, by developing, for example, alternatives to a formal criminal procedure, such as community service, family conferencing, and other forms of restorative justice. These alternatives can also be used in the course of judicial proceedings as an alternative

12 See, for example, *Stopreactie. Bereik, ervaringen en effecten tijdens het experimentele jaar* (Ministerie van Justitie, The Hague, 2000) and *Stopreactie. Redenen van niet bereik* (Amsterdam, 1 October 2002).

13 See J. Weijers (2007), Art. 77b Sr: weinig gebruikt, maar slecht gemotiveerd, *Tijdschrift voor Familie- en Jeugdrecht*, *1*, 14–20.

14 See also Beijing Rules, Section 11 on Diversion (with commentary).

to a traditional punishment, for example, deprivation of liberty. In the Netherlands, for example, about 40% of all cases of juvenile delinquency registered with the police (2005: ±60,000) are diverted by the police. In addition, avoiding judicial proceedings may also result in non-intervention, particularly in cases where the juvenile is a first offender and/or has committed a non-serious offence and the family (parents), school, or community have reacted to the offence in a constructive manner.

However, the preference for diversion comes with a caveat: human rights and legal safeguards should be fully respected. In this regard it is important that States Parties establish clear criteria and rules for the practice of diversion in order to ensure that the right to non-discrimination is fully respected. Measures of diversion should only be used if there is convincing evidence that the juvenile committed the offence of which he or she is accused. Furthermore, the juvenile should give a well-informed consent to the proposed measure. 'Well-informed' means that the juvenile should receive adequate and specific information on the content and duration of the measure and the consequences of a failure to cooperate and complete the measure. Undue pressure on the juvenile either to confess to the alleged offence and/or to give consent to the proposed measure of diversion must be prevented.

The completion of the diversion by the juvenile court should result in a definite closure of the case without any public criminal record. It goes beyond the scope of this chapter to elaborate more on diversion. But reports from States Parties and a considerable body of literature show not only that there is a wide variety of diversion measures, but also that in many instances results of diversion have been positive (Greenwood et al., 1996; Bazemore & Walgrave, 1998; Ferwerda, Jakobs and Beke, 2006). Finally, a well-structured and organised international exchange of information sharing regarding good and bad practices is necessary to establish and/or strengthen diversion activities in States Parties to the CRC.

Guarantees for a Fair Trial

If diversion is not considered to be an appropriate response, the public prosecutor in most countries will initiate judicial proceedings. Article 40, par. 2 CRC contains various provisions meant to ensure that the right of juveniles to a fair trial is fully respected. Many of these provisions can already be found in Article 14 and 15 ICCPR and par. 2 of Article 40 CRC is to a large degree a confirmation of the fact that these rights and standards are also applicable to juvenile offenders. This applies, for example, to the presumption of innocence; the right to prompt information about the charges and to free assistance of an interpreter; the right to examine or have examined the witnesses; the right not to be compelled to testify or confess guilt, and the principle of non-retroactive justice.[15] For practical reasons, I will limit myself to highlighting some of the juvenile-specific aspects of the guarantees for a fair trial for juveniles.

15 This principle also known as *nullum crimen sine lege* means that no one can be held guilty (or accused) of any criminal offence on account of an act or omission which did not constitute a criminal offence at the time it was committed (see Art. 15 ICCPR and Art. 40, par. 2(a) CRC). Art. 15 contains provisions that cannot be found in Art. 40 CRC: the right not to be subjected to a heavier penalty than applicable at the time of the crime and to benefit from

The Right to Assistance (Art. 40,2(b)(iii)CRC)

A juvenile has a right to legal or other appropriate assistance in the preparation and the presentation of his/her defence. This provision means that the States Parties must take measures to provide juveniles with such assistance without charge. 'Other appropriate assistance' means that this assistance is not necessarily provided by a lawyer. This may depend on the case, but the 'assistant' (for example, a social worker), must have adequate knowledge of the rules, regulations and practice of the juvenile justice system. With reference to Article 12 CRC and Article 14, Article 3(b) ICCPR, States Parties should also allow a child/juvenile to express their views and have their preference/choice taken into account. The Netherlands made a reservation with regard to this provision: this right is not applicable for cases dealt with by a cantonal judge (*kantonrechter* in Dutch) because these cases concern only petty offences. There are no detailed figures available, but it is likely that only very few juvenile offenders appear before such judges and most cases will be settled out of court. The CRC Committee has recommended withdrawing this reservation (UN Doc. CRC/C/15/227, 30 January 2004, par. 10 and 11).

Decisions without Delay (Art. 40, par. 2(b) (iii) CRC)

It should be noted that this provision does not, like similar provisions in other treaties (Art. 14 ICCPR, Art. 6 ECHR) use the qualification 'undue'. This confirms the widely accepted principle that for juvenile offenders the time between the commission of the crime and the final response to it must be as short as possible. The right to have the matter determined without delay should be balanced with the right to a fair and carefully conducted trial in which the human rights of the child and legal safeguards are fully respected. However, a determination without delay can be facilitated if States Parties would introduce specific time limits, for example, the completion of the police investigation, the decision to bring charges (or not), and the final adjudication and disposition by the court.

The Right to Appeal (Art. 40, par. 2(b) (v) CRC)

The child delinquent has the right to have his conviction and sentence by the court reviewed by a higher, competent, independent and impartial authority or judicial body. The same right can be found in Article 14, par. 5 ICCPR. The expression in this provision 'according to law' does not mean that the very existence of this right of review is left to the discretion of the national law. It only means that the determination of the modalities for carrying out this review, and by which higher tribunal, is a matter for domestic law. The Netherlands has made a reservation to this provision: it is not applicable in cases decided by a cantonal judge (see also above under the Right to Assistance). It is noteworthy that a similar reservation was not made under Article 14, par. 5 ICCPR. This constitutes an interesting legal conflict

---

the fact that lighter penalties were introduced by law after the commission of the crime. These rules apply to juvenile offenders in State Parties to the ICCPR (see Art. 41 CRC).

since the ICCPR is also applicable to juvenile offenders. So far the rule that limits the right of appeal for juvenile offenders has not been challenged in court, but I would submit that this limitation is a violation of Article 14, par. 5 ICCPR. Nevertheless, the CRC Committee has recommended that the Netherlands withdraws this reservation (UN Doc. CRC/C/15/227, 30 January 2004, par. 10 and 11).

The Right to Privacy (Art. 16 and 40, par. 2(b) (vii) CRC)

The provision that the right to privacy must be fully respected at all stages of the proceedings is specific to juvenile offenders. A similar provision for adults does not exist. The reason for this provision is to avoid stigmatisation of the juvenile offender via negative publicity. Many States Parties have the rule that court hearings for juvenile offenders should take place behind closed doors.[16] Some States Parties allow for an exception to this rule. This exception should be limited to well-defined cases and subject to the decision of the court, with the possibility for the juvenile to have this decision reviewed by a higher court (see Art. 40, 2(b) (v) CRC).

If the hearing is public, the media should be under legal obligation not to make public the name of the juvenile or other information that may facilitate identification. Violations of this obligation should be punished by disciplinary measures, such as exclusion from juvenile justice hearings and penal law sanctions. Article 495b of the Dutch Criminal Procedures Code allows the judge to decide that the case, by way of exception, shall be tried in a public hearing. But there are no specific rules that require the media to report in such a way that the juvenile's privacy is protected. Respect for the privacy of the juvenile offender also means that a public authority should not issue statements for the press/media in cases against juvenile offenders, unless there is a compelling public interest to make such statements. But even then the identity of the juvenile offender must not be revealed.

Finally, the right to respect for privacy also means that criminal records of juvenile offenders shall be kept confidential and closed to third parties except for those directly involved in the investigation, adjudication and disposition of the case. With a view to avoid stigmatisation and/or pre-judgements, criminal records of juvenile offenders shall not be used in adult proceedings in subsequent cases involving the same offender (Beijing Rules 21.1 and 21.2). States Parties should introduce rules for removal from the criminal records of the name of the juvenile who committed a crime, either automatically – such as when they reach age 18 – or at the request of the juvenile, if necessary under certain conditions, such as the individual not having committed a crime within three years of the last conviction.

Disposition

After the initiation of the juvenile justice proceeding, the juvenile offender will be formally charged and tried before a juvenile court or a specialised judge or similar

16 See in this regard also Art. 6 ECHR that allows for an exception to the rule that criminal cases should be dealt with in a public hearing where the interests of juveniles so require.

authority (in some countries a council or administrative board). The establishment of this specialised court/judge and other specialised institutions (for example, juvenile police units within the police and specialised prosecutors) is required under Article 40, par. 3 CRC.[17] If the juvenile offender is found guilty, the trial results in the imposition of a measure/sanction. In the following section, I will make some observations on the applicable rights/standards.

First, I want to emphasise that initiating a judicial proceeding does not necessarily result in a court sentence. It is in the spirit of the CRC (in particular Art. 40, par. 3(b)) to continuously seek for alternatives to the traditional imposition of a sanction by the court. In this regard, States Parties should introduce well-regulated possibilities (to avoid discriminatory use of discretion) for prosecutors to divert cases via alternative measures such as a community service order or other forms of restorative justice. For this practice and the applicable standards, see also the paragraph on diversion. An appropriate use of this possibility can mean that the prosecutor's office takes only a small percentage of the juvenile delinquency cases it is dealing with to the juvenile court/judge. For example, in the Netherlands the prosecutor 'diverts' about two-thirds of the cases he is considering. It means that only 20% (or less) of the cases registered with the police are dealt with in a procedure before the juvenile court/judge.[18]

Secondly, a variety of dispositions such as care, guidance, supervision, probation, foster care, vocational training programmes and other alternatives for institutional care, shall be available (Art. 40, par. 4 CRC and Rule 18 of the Beijing Rules). This is meant to ensure that juvenile offenders are dealt with in a manner appropriate to their well-being and proportionate both to their circumstances and the offence (see also Rule 5 of the Beijing Rules). But it is also meant to promote the implementation of the rule that deprivation of liberty should be a measure of last resort. Article 40, par. 4 CRC implies that a strictly punitive approach to juvenile offenders is not in accordance with the CRC.

Below are some more specific remarks on the rules and standards that should be applied regarding disposition measures.

- The death penalty shall not be imposed for offences committed by persons below age 18 (Art. 37 CRC). It is important to note that this rule (in line with Art. 6, par. 5 ICCPR) does not use terminology related to the age of majority

---

17 This is the CRC Committee's understanding of the text: 'States Parties shall seek to promote the establishment of institutions specifically applicable to children (juvenile offenders).' It should be noted that the Beijing Rules do recommend specialisation within the police (Rule 12.1) but do not recommend the establishment of specialised juvenile courts (when appropriate, that is, fitting in the legal system of the country).

18 In the Netherlands, one can distinguish between 'primary' and 'secondary' diversion: 'Primary' diversion takes place at the police level; a formal judicial procedure has not been initiated; 'secondary' diversion takes place at the prosecutor's level. Each of these forms of diversion deals with about 40% of cases so that ultimately 20% of all juvenile delinquency cases (registered with the police) are tried in court.

or any other qualitative criteria.[19] In other words, for example, if a person is 20 years old at the time of the court decision, they cannot be sentenced to death for a crime committed before they turned 18.

- Life imprisonment without the possibility of release (life without parole) shall not be imposed for offences committed by a person below age 18 (see the remarks made in relation to the death penalty).[20] Life without parole is certainly not compatible with the objective of juvenile justice enshrined in Article 40, par. 1 CRC. Personally, I think this is also true for life imprisonment with parole. In many countries the possibility of release is not considered before the prisoner has served a minimum sentence, for example, twenty years or more. Often there is discretionary power to (not) grant a release. In short, a convicted juvenile may spend most of his life in prison, which certainly does not contribute to achieving the goals of juvenile justice. For that reason, the CRC Committee strongly recommends that States Parties to the CRC abolish all forms of life imprisonment for juveniles (General Comment No. 10 on Children's Rights in Juvenile Justice, par. 27).
- Deprivation of liberty must be a measure of last resort and for the shortest appropriate period of time (Art. 37 (b) CRC). This applies both to pre-trial detention and the detention/imprisonment imposed in a sentence of the court. Unfortunately, the CRC does not contain specific standards for pre-trial detention, although in many countries children frequently are held in pre-trial detention for many months without any possibility to challenge the legality of this deprivation of liberty. But the Beijing Rules contain some specific provisions (Rule 13): the need to replace detention pending trial by alternative measures is emphasised (Rule 13.2, with some examples). Juveniles in detention pending trial are entitled to all rights and guarantees of the Standard Minimum Rules of the Treatment of Prisoners. This means *inter alia* that these juveniles should be kept separate from convicted peers (Rule 8 (b) Standard Minimum Rules). They should also be kept separate from adult untried prisoners.[21] This rule also applies to juveniles who are deprived of their liberty due to a conviction (see Art. 37 (c) CRC). 'Separated' means in a separate institution (building) or in a separate part of an institution, or prison that is also holding adults (see Beijing Rule 13.4). But this rule does not mean that a juvenile serving a detention sentence in an institution for juveniles

---

19 For instance, in Iran a judge can declare that a person of 16 years has reached puberty and should be considered an adult, including the possibility of imposing the death penalty for a crime committed. For reasons to prohibit the death penalty for persons below 18 years when they committed a crime see *Roper* vs. *Simmons* (543 US 2005).

20 It should be noted that other human rights treaties, in particular the ICPPR, do not prohibit life imprisonment. Persons age 18 or over who commit a crime can be sentenced to life imprisonment with or without parole.

21 It should be noted that there are different terms used in UN documents. In the Beijing Rules, the term is 'detention pending trial'. In the Standard Minimum Rules for Treatment of Prisoners, the term is 'untried prisoners'. This is likely the result of a different approach: on one hand, emphasis on the detention (Beijing Rules); on the other hand, focus on the individual (Standard Minimum Rules).

> who turns 18 should be moved to an institution for adults. It would result in a discontinuity in treatment, which is not in their best interest. But if the juvenile has still to serve many years in detention, under certain conditions clearly defined in the law, a transfer to a facility for adults could be made possible. In many States Parties to the CRC, children in need of care and protection are placed in the same institutions as juvenile offenders. The CRC Committee has systematically recommended to these States, including the Netherlands, that they terminate this practice. The Dutch Minister of Justice announced (letter, 1 July 2004) in line with the recommendation of the CRC Committee (UN Doc. CRC/C/15/227, 30 January 2004, par. 59), that non-offending children, who are for reasons of care and protection in need of a placement in a secured facility, will not be placed in the same facility as juveniles in conflict with the penal law. Measures will be taken to introduce this new policy of placement and should be completed by 2010.[22]

Juveniles in detention pending trial shall benefit from a special regime. Rules for this regime can be found in Beijing Rule 13, but in more detail in the Standard Minimum Rules (see par. 84–93). For instance, untried (juvenile) prisoners shall sleep singly in separate rooms, with the reservation of different local customs with respect to climate; an untried (juvenile) prisoner shall be allowed to wear their own clothing and if prison clothes are worn they shall be different from those supplied to convicted prisoners. These and other rules, for example, rules regarding access to information, medical and dental care, and visits, are meant to respect the presumption of innocence: as long as a juvenile is not tried and convicted they have the right to be treated differently.

Every child deprived of their liberty (awaiting trial or convicted) has the right to *prompt* legal or other appropriate assistance. In addition, children have the right to challenge the legality of the deprivation before a court and to a *prompt* decision in any such action (Art. 37 (d) CRC). In my opinion, the term 'prompt' comes very close to 'immediate' and underscores that children, even more than adults because of their different perception of time, need quick decisions in order to make periods of uncertainty as short as possible.

In addition to the rules and standards mentioned previously, there are many more rules and standards established for the protection of persons deprived of their liberty and more specifically for juveniles. It is fair to say that of all the different elements of juvenile justice, the most attention is given to the deprivation of liberty.

Rule 27 of the Beijing Rules requires that efforts shall be made to implement the relevant principles of the Standard Minimum Rules for the Treatment of Prisoners to the greatest possible extent so as to meet the varying needs of juveniles. In practice, it means that the general rules/principles are applicable as far as they are

---

22 This decision was based on a study by the Verweij-Jonkers Institute (rapport *Samenplaatsen van jongeren in justitiële jeugdinrichtingen*, Utrecht: Verwey-Jonkers Institute, May 2004) and a report of a working group established by the Minister of Justice (*Optimalisering van zorgaanbod voor jeugdigen met ernstige gedragsproblemen*, Ministerie van Justitie, The Hague, June 2004).

not included in the specific UN Rules for the Protection of Juveniles Deprived of their Liberty (Havana Rules). This document contains detailed rules and standards for, *inter alia*, the management of juvenile facilities; the physical environment and accommodations; education/vocational training and work; medical care; the use of physical restraint and force; disciplinary procedures; inspection, and complaints.

It goes well beyond the scope of this chapter to even summarise all of these rules. But a careful reading of them shows that life in a prison or detention facility for juveniles should be well-protected and human rights should be well-respected and implemented. Unfortunately, that is not the case in many institutions for juveniles. The Netherlands has enacted a special law for juveniles in institutions (*Beginselenwet justitiele jeugdinrichtingen*) that can be considered as an example of how the rights of juvenile offenders in institutions can be protected, including an elaborate system for filing complaints in cases of violations of the rules (see, for example, Liefaard, 2005).

Implementation and Conclusions

Finally, with reference to my remarks in the introduction to this chapter, I will discuss the implementation of all these rights, rules and standards based on my experiences as a member of the CRC Committee, *the* international body for monitoring the implementation of, among others, the rights, rules and standards applicable in the field of juvenile justice.

One of the rather shocking facts is that there are still judges dealing with juvenile offenders who are not aware of the existence of the CRC or who think that the CRC does not have any relevance for their practice. The same applies for public prosecutors, policemen and policewomen, probation officers and professionals working in institutions for juvenile offenders. It is also reflected in the recommendations of the CRC Committee that most States Parties to the CRC must take (many) measures to ensure that information on human rights in general – and children's rights in particular – is an integral part of the education of professionals working in the field as part of regular curricula in education. The good news is that many States Parties have taken or are taking legislative measures to bring their domestic law in compliance with the CRC and other international standards and to establish an adequate juvenile justice system.

At the same time, there is a move – in some countries at least – towards a more punitive approach, reflected in proposals to lower the MACR and/or to become tougher on juvenile delinquency, particularly in relation to the alleged increase of serious crimes and in response to youth gangs. There is not enough information that lends empirical statements to justify this move to more punitive juvenile justice as so far the information is rather anecdotal.[23] However strong the movement towards a more punitive approach may be, there is also a growing demand – at least on paper

23 For instance, there is the suggestion that public pressure to reduce the MACR is high. But, so far, only Japan lowered the MACR from 16 to 14 years. A proposal in Panama to lower the MACR was not successful due to actions of NGOs supported by professionals in juvenile justice, including a member of the Supreme Court. There are more examples of increasing the MACR than there are of lowering it.

– for alternative measures, diversion, and restorative justice. This development may contribute to a reduction in the use of deprivation of liberty for juveniles. At the same time, however, the conditions in juvenile detention centres in many States Parties are a far cry from the standards internationally accepted in the Standard Minimum Rules for the Treatment of Prisoners (1957/1977) and the UN Rules for the Protection of Juveniles Deprived of their Liberty (1990). Quite often juveniles are detained together with adults and the separation of untried and convicted juveniles is hardly practised. That raises the question: what can be done to make all these rights and standards a reality? Without going into detail, I would like to make the following observations:

- First and foremost, governments of States Parties must establish a comprehensive national policy and programme of action for the prevention of and intervention in juvenile delinquency based on the CRC and related international standards. This policy and the related plan of action should set time-specific targets and priorities for a step-by-step well-coordinated implementation plan together with adequate allocation of necessary financial and other resources. An example of such a comprehensive policy can be found in the Netherlands, although the country struggles with the familiar problem of coordinating its implementation.[24]
- Secondly, systematic and ongoing training of all actors in the field of juvenile justice is imperative.
- Third, non-governmental organisations (NGOs) should undertake well-planned and coordinated action to put pressure on governments/parliaments to improve the practice of juvenile justice and where appropriate provide direct services in this regard. For instance, establish in juvenile detention centres an independent information/consultation service and publish its hours/days of opening. Other activities can be awareness-raising campaigns in cooperation with the media; mobilising and supporting specific groups of professionals such as lawyers (and where necessary urging them to provide legal assistance without charge), and social workers (probation services; group leaders in juvenile detention centres); and initiating alternative measures, such as restorative justice.
- Fourth, the academic world should be involved in and promote systematic evaluation of the different aspects of the juvenile justice system such as pre-trial detention, the right to fair trial, the use and effects of alternative measures, and the deprivation of liberty. The results of evaluations and other research should be used to impact policies and practices, and academics and NGOs should join hands to produce that impact.

---

24 See the Nota (policy document) *Vasthoudend en effectief. Versterking van de aanpak van jeugdcriminaliteit*, presented to the Dutch Parliament on 28 March 2002 and the related *Actie programma* (Programme of Action) *2003–2006 Jeugd Terecht* with various time-bound targets. An ambitious and comprehensive policy, although it is not clear how the actions of various ministries (Justice, Health/Welfare, and Interior) are coordinated, also with regard to actions at the local level in order to be as effective and efficient as possible. Reports on the results of this programme will be produced in the course of 2007.

In conclusion, there are many rights and standards relevant to the treatment and protection of juvenile offenders which can create a juvenile justice system that is not only humane but also effective, both for the individual juvenile and for the society as a whole. For the next decade, the slogan should be: not more standards but (much) more implementation.

Chapter 15

Early Interventions with At-Risk Children in Europe

Rob Allen

There are wide disparities in the minimum age of criminal responsibility for juveniles in different countries in Europe (see also Chapter 14, this volume). Among the forty-six countries in the Council of Europe, there are three main clusters of relevant ages. Some countries hold children criminally liable from age ten or below. These include the three UK jurisdictions and Switzerland. A second group, including France, Germany and Italy as well as the Netherlands, stipulates the minimum age at 12, 13, or 14. A third group restricts the role of the criminal justice system to young people above age 15 or even 18 (the Scandinavian countries, Spain and Belgium) (Allen, 1996).

The concept of criminal responsibility is not entirely straightforward, however. Some jurisdictions have different ages for different types of offences. Ireland, which has recently raised the age from 7 to 12, allows children as young as 10 to be charged with serious crimes such as murder or rape. Other countries such as France allow children to be prosecuted from age 10 with the possibility only of educational sanctions (including closed residential care), while in Scotland, although the age is 8, all but the most serious offenders under age 17 are dealt with by a welfare tribunal called the Children's Hearing.

In most countries, children below the age of criminal responsibility who commit 'delinquent' acts obviously cannot be prosecuted, but this does not prevent authorities from taking other actions. The type and nature of intervention is generally a matter for the child welfare or education agencies, although in some countries, the courts play an important role.

In Italy, the Ministry of Justice can only become involved in criminal cases involving young people over age 14. However, when a child is under age 14 and if the court considers him or her to be a danger to society, they can be placed in a judicial reformatory. This illustrates the typical difference between penal measures on the one hand and civil, administrative, or protective measures on the other. It is estimated that there are approximately 10,000 juveniles under age 14 who commit crimes, but the only applicable measures are civil ones, which are non-custodial and do not restrict freedom. Action taken against under 14-year-olds is a matter for the local social services. In Finland, juveniles under 15 years olds can be held responsible for damage they cause, in which case either the parents pay or the debt is met when the young person reaches adulthood. Again, referral is to the child welfare authorities, although children can also be directed by police to a reconciliation meeting. Finland has also introduced fast-track responses to petty property offenders under age 15 in projects developed by the police, businesses and security companies. Success has been claimed for the impact of a pilot project in Oulu, even though some practical difficulties arose because it is the social services department rather than the other agencies which are under a statutory duty to respond to young people under age 15 who commit crimes (Buckland & Stevens, 2001). Better cooperation was achieved in the Erwischt 'Caught you' project in Magdeburg, Germany. This enabled a speedy referral from police to social workers based in the police station. Following discussion with the child, a meeting with the victim is held and compensation negotiated in almost a third of shoplifting cases (Buckland & Stevens, 2001).

German courts dealing with family cases have been empowered to issue socio-educational orders for children who have committed unlawful acts. If a case is dismissed on grounds of lack of culpability, the guidelines relating to Section 1 of the *Jugendgerichtgesetz* (Youth Court Act; JGG) stipulate that the public prosecutor must examine whether anyone is to be informed, and if so who (generally, schools or the family courts), and must determine whether action should be taken against those with supervisory obligations.

The goal of this chapter is to describe several initiatives in Europe for different agencies, including welfare officials, school personnel and the police, to intervene with child delinquents in order to prevent their becoming serious, violent and chronic offenders (for a Canadian example, see Appendix 1, this volume). The focus will be especially on programmes aimed at families, schools and the community.

The Response of Child Welfare Authorities

Evidence on how delinquent children are dealt with by child welfare systems is hard to obtain because statistics about their use do not often distinguish between the various reasons for referral. Finland is typical of Scandinavian countries where youth crime is not seen as a separate phenomenon that requires the construction of a programme specifically to combat it. Young people's problems are basically social problems, of which criminal activities are an indicator (Kuuire, 2003). There is a debate about the desirability of designating intervention measures in terms of their crime prevention potential. A German commentator has suggested that one problem with the term 'crime prevention measures' to describe tried and tested provisions for leisure activity is that the new label makes potential criminals of all children who take part in service activities out of a desire for adventure (understandable at their age) or because they lack other opportunities (Schäfer, 2004, p. 52).

Legislative provisions do sometimes specify what is possible in the way of intervention through welfare agencies. Typical is the new criminal law for minors in Switzerland, which entered into force on 1 January 2007. Section Four of this law deals with offences committed before age 10 (the minimum age of criminal responsibility in Switzerland). Measures foreseen in Section Four are: contact with the parents and, if necessary, transmission of the case to the child welfare authorities in order to decide measures of educational protection (Queloz, 2007).

In Denmark, in order to investigate delinquent cases the police can detain children at the police station (though not in a cell), but the police must summon a representative from the local authority and notify the parents. Social authorities then decide what to do with the child and have a wide range of options, the choice of which in principle depends on the needs of the child rather than on the seriousness of the offence, which is not in itself a deciding factor (Kyvsgaard, 2004, p. 366). Options include participating in a supervised activity, such as sports, youth work, or education; and practical or financial support to the home, including family therapy, or the appointment of a personal adviser. Similarly, in Sweden, police turn child cases over to social authorities. The measures they can take include assigning a contact person or family member, providing need-based personal support, or assigning the child to a non-institutional care programme. In 2001, 3,662 children aged 10–14 received help in this manner. Only 226 in this age group needed placement in institutions in 2000.

In Germany, child and youth services' areas of responsibility and their scope for intervention are defined by the *Kinder und Jugendhilfe* (KJHG – Child and Youth Help), which in Section One gives as its goal defending the right of children to promote their personal development and supporting their claim to be brought up as personally and socially responsible human beings. This gives the services a clear socio-educational mandate for crime prevention among children and young people. Prevention of delinquency is chiefly a socio-educational task, which they pursue without firm support from legal institutions. Thus 'social training courses', introduced as means of increasing the social skills of young offenders to prevent delinquency, have formed the basis of various provisions devised by the child and youth services. The aim of the courses is to tackle developmental difficulties and problem behaviours among children below the age of criminal responsibility. (Schäfer 2004, p. 50).

Child and youth services working with children are subject to parental agreement in most of the jurisdictions discussed above. However, there is some evidence that in difficult cases the services frequently find it hard to gain the cooperation and consent of parents (Schäfer 2004).

In almost all countries, the child welfare system allows children to be placed in an institution, foster family or other approved place of residence. In many countries, this is largely done with the parents' consent, but when the child is at risk of harm (including in some cases through their continued offending), they can be placed without parental consent. In Denmark, this happens in 10% of residential placements. In these cases, a local politician, judge and child expert must approve placement decisions. In Norway, interventions generally involve community-based casework services (in eight out of ten cases). Of those who are taken into care, four-fifths are placed with foster parents (Nova, 2007).

Secure accommodation is also available in most child welfare systems, but it is generally said to be used 'as a last resort'. In Denmark it is only available for up to two months in the case of those under 15 years old, and longer only in the case of those over the age of criminal responsibility. These secure care establishments are not prisons. They are closed establishments, which generally have higher staffing ratios than prisons and staff trained in psychology or education. This enables more individualised programmes of care and treatment and more flexible arrangements for education, family visits and temporary release.

Types of Programmes for Disruptive Children

In many countries, the thresholds for intervention with children under the age of criminal responsibility by social services are too high to give priority to preventive work. Partly in response to criticism of the adequacy of social welfare responses (Allen, 1993), there has been a growth in some countries in the number and variety of specific programmes. But in other countries, such as France and Spain, there is reliance on a general social welfare approach.

There are several ways to categorise programmes, but given their multi-faceted nature categorising them as 'preschool' or 'parenting' or 'family' can be fairly arbitrary. The typology below considers programmes that focus on a) families, b) schools, and c) the community. The examples draw heavily on an excellent review of good practices in preventing juvenile crime across the EU (Stevens et al., 2006). The examples emphasise work that takes place with individual cases, although much recent activity takes a more universal or primary prevention approach. A discussion of work undertaken in German schools, for example, justified targeting entire school classes on the assumption that delinquency is very common among this age group (Schäfer, 2004).

Family Programmes

In Sweden, work with children under the age of criminal responsibility has included Functional Family Therapy (FFT) and multidimensional treatment foster care (Utting et al., 2007). The Strengthening Families Programme has also been introduced, which is a family skills training programme to increase resilience and reduce risk factors for problem behaviours in 6–11-year-olds. An example of FFT is a project carried out in Bergsjon, a deprived district in Gothenburg. The family services unit responsible for investigations carries out the work for children and young people from birth to age 21, under the governance of the Swedish Welfare Act (SOL) and Special Provisions for the Care of Young People Act (LVU). A special project called 'Turning Point' was started in 2004 aimed at children reported for a crime for the first time because ordinary social services did not have the capacity to work with the children. Initially financed by the Swedish National Council for Crime Prevention, the project was due to become part of ordinary social services in 2006. The project makes contact at the police station when a child is arrested. The approach of the therapeutic involvement, which is entirely voluntary, is to empower the parents to help their children through a series of discussions. Of the seventy-eight children involved in the first two years of the project, twenty-five were under age 13. Offences committed predominantly were shop theft and assault but included six cases of robbery. Eight children of the caseload had been known to reoffend (Larsson, undated).

Interventions involving parents are increasingly common across Europe, with projects including EFFEKT in Germany, KOMET in Sweden and the Webster Stratton approach used in the UK. In France, there are parent centres providing assistance to families, and Germany has experimented with short-term residential support for families with follow-up – the Integrative Family support model developed by Caritas, using a 'coaching model' (Zimmer, 2000).

The UK has recently embarked on an ambitious strategy for supporting parents which builds on the extensive Sure Start programme which is due to create three thousand children's centres by 2008. Specific parenting initiatives include:

- Early Learning Partnerships demonstration projects supporting parents of 1–3-year-olds at risk of learning delays;
- Transition Information Session Demonstration projects which make parents more aware of how they can support their children during the transition from preschool to primary, and from primary to secondary school;
- Parenting Early Intervention Pathfinders in fifteen local authorities are increasing support for the parents of 8–13-year-olds;
- Parent Support Advisers in over six hundred primary and secondary schools in the most deprived areas;
- Ten health focused parenting support demonstration projects testing intensive home visiting from pre-birth to age 2;
- Fifty Respect Family Intervention Projects offering a range of rehabilitation measures to families engaged in antisocial behaviour, and
- A doubling of the number of parenting support interventions (to 11,000 per year) for the families of children known to the Youth Offending teams which administer youth justice locally. [Department for Education and Skills, 2006]

It is estimated that there are currently over ninety types of parenting programmes being implemented in the UK. King's College London, the Family and Parenting Institute, and Parenting United Kingdom, have recently been awarded £30 million by the Department for Education to create a new centre of excellence called the National Academy for Parenting Practitioners. The centre, which will carry out parenting research and provide quality support for parents, was opened in November 2007.

In England and Wales, parenting orders can be imposed by courts following the conviction of a child for a delinquent act, and the conviction of a parent for failure to ensure school attendance or following expulsion of their child from school.

Several countries have seen the development of multi-systemic therapy (MST) over the last five years (described in Chapter 12, this volume). In Norway, a replication of the MST model developed in the US is funded by the ministry of children and the municipalities and coordinated by the University of Oslo (Ogden & Halliday-Boykins, 2004).

School Programmes

The second focus of programmes for disruptive children is educational, where programmes fall into three categories: first, the reliance on schools to respond to emerging problems; second, enhanced programmes for use by teachers; and, third, the deployment of police officers in educational settings. While the focus of many initiatives is on secondary schools, some of the interventions apply to children under age 12.

Some countries have continued to see the prevention of delinquency as part of a generic educational function. In Finland, where school is compulsory from age seven, it is the school health services and the student welfare team who are responsible for the pupils' well-being, with referral to special services or child protection when different forms of disturbance become apparent. Internal school welfare and support systems are the most significant forms of preventative social work for children of this age.

Among the specific programmes for teachers and other educators to use in the prevention of delinquency, perhaps the best known is Olweus' Bullying Prevention Program, widely used in Norway, Germany and elsewhere (Olweus, 1993; Olweus et al., 1999). This violence prevention and intervention programme is directed against so-called bullies who torment, mob, or exhibit aggressive behaviour or violence towards peers, put them under pressure, or steal from them (see also Chapter 7, this volume). The programme targets three levels: the whole school, classrooms and individual pupils. School-wide measures include closer supervision during break periods, classroom initiatives which comprise the development of rules through classroom meetings, and options at the individual level which include discussions with particular pupils involved in incidents, the notification of the parents of the perpetrators, and the holding of a meeting with the parties, which can involve entire classrooms. The adoption of a clear set of procedures, a victim focus, and an approach which makes incidents public, has helped victims become confident that a 'cry for help' will prompt consistent and resolute action by the school. Evaluation of the programmes in various settings have found reductions of direct forms of bullying, tangible and measurable improvements in the social climate at the school, and organisational changes such as new rules for break periods and redesign of the area used during break periods (Olweus, 1995).

Baldry and Farrington (2007) recently reviewed anti-bullying programmes in schools in many different countries and found that out of sixteen evaluations, eight showed desirable results, two mixed results, and four produced small or negligible results. However, enthusiasm was tempered by the fact that only four out of ten controlled studies produced desirable results, indicating a great need for future evaluation studies of anti-bullying programmes.

Other programmes developed for use in schools include mediation to reduce violence. In Germany, the programme is targeted at pupils aged 9–12 with an aim of discovering what is at the root of interpersonal conflicts, learning to change negative reactions and improve social relationships, helping young people recognise and name their emotions, and familiarising students with conflicts without dramatising them. Students are put in groups of four by teachers and specially trained mediators to take part in four-hour workshops once a week. During this time, they role-play and participate in other exercises that allow them to gain a deeper understanding of the emotions which are experienced during conflict.

Restorative justice (RJ) in schools has also been developed with some success in England where an evaluation of programmes in twenty secondary and six primary schools found that restorative conferences reached agreements in nine out of ten cases and that participants were very satisfied with the results. Impact on further victimisation, exclusions and pupil attitudes were mixed, but after the introduction of RJ, pupils at one primary school reported a 10% reduction in spreading rumours, an 8% reduction in racist name calling, and a 17% increase in pupils thinking that the school was doing a good job in stopping bullying (YJB, 2004).

Schools in many countries have developed life-skill training with an emphasis on avoiding delinquency and resolving conflicts peacefully. Skill-based training programmes include the American 'Lions Quest' <www.lions-quest.org>, which is known in Germany as 'Erwachsen Werden' or 'Becoming Autonomous'. The Skills for Growing programme is aimed at students in primary schools (years 1–6) to prevent involvement in drugs and violent crime. The specific aims are to enhance social and life competencies as well as autonomy, to support the development of socially and emotionally sensible behaviour and to enhance conflict-resolution abilities. Teachers receive special training and incorporate this programme into the curriculum (forty-two lessons for years 1–4 and twenty-one for years 5 and 6). In the beginning, the subject matter is general, but as the students get older they begin to learn about specific topics such as bullying and stress reduction. Parts of the programme are done through role-play and theatre as well as meditation and relaxation workshops. In addition, work with parents is done to support the programme. In a quasi-experimental evaluation, the conflict-solving competencies, empathetic behaviour and communication skills of students in the experimental group were higher than those in the control group (Wibord & Hamewinkel, 2005), but no information appears to be available on whether the programme had an impact on disruptive or delinquent child behaviours.

The Skills for Growing Programme is similar to the Social Emotional Learning, another American model aimed at reducing delinquency, drug use and school exclusion (Stevens et al., 2006). The programme, which is being made available in Sweden, involves structured exercises for pupils to teach them self-awareness, empathy, the handling of emotions, and social skills. Teachers and other school personnel also receive training, as do parents, who are provided with information so that they are able to help and encourage their child to learn. Pupils also take part in role-play, modelling and positive reinforcement with opportunities to test new skills in different situations. A similar programme has been introduced in Norway. For example, the '*Lev vel*' (live well) teaching package was sent to all 3,335 schools in Norway by the Crime Prevention Council.

In some countries, schools are looking beyond the socio-educational approach to prevent crime. In Germany, the police have now become more active in schools, where they have always been involved in traffic education schemes but have recently started to play a broader role (Stevens et al., 2006).

In the UK, the Safer Schools Partnership (SSP) was introduced in 2002 as a way to reduce bullying, truancy and exclusion from school, as these are linked with higher rates of delinquency. Police officers are placed in schools and the aim is to build closer working relationships between the police and schools. The partnerships are organised in different ways, depending on how they are funded and on the strategy adopted by the school. Some involve an operational police officer and a supporting team located full-time in a secondary school. In other schools, a police officer is part of a multi-agency partnership attached to a cluster of schools (at three secondary, plus at four of the primary schools that feed into it). There are also local variants, with the police presence in school playing a less central role. This category of programmes, which constitutes the majority of SSP, includes police officers who specialise in youth work being based in a central city location and supporting a variety of schools and youth organisations. The time allocated to a single school is thus limited, sometimes to as little as half a day each week.

Evaluation of SSP by the Youth Justice Board (2004) has shown increased trust in the police by pupils and their parents resulting from becoming more used to having a police officer in the school. The initiative also produced more activities and pastoral work for pupils, a quicker response to problem behaviours, more engagement with the local community, better attitudes and ethos in the school, with greater emphasis on mutual respect and inclusion. The presence of SSP staff was supporting, challenging and engaging pupils (Bhabra et al., 2004). The only major problem was in setting up a team of non-teaching staff to work with teaching staff in a bid to improve school safety. This task was time-consuming, and some school staff members were uncomfortable with having a police officer around full-time and were unsure about the officer's role in the school. Data about pre-offending rates in schools was only available in the three schools participating in the programme funded by the Youth Justice Board and the Association of Chief of Police Officers. A comparison of before and after measures suggests that approximately 139 offences may have been prevented annually in schools which introduced SSPs. Pupils in intervention schools also tended to feel safer and there was some evidence to suggest that students in participating schools were less likely to be victims of crime. It is difficult to know how far these effects are due to the specific impact of the programme, however. Although truancy levels decreased significantly in the fifteen intervention schools in comparison to non-participating schools, expulsions fell in all of the schools, so it is not possible to isolate the effect of SSPs.

Community Programmes

The third constellation of programmes focuses on the community. Examples include various restorative justice (RJ) approaches. Norway's child welfare law allows RJ, overseen by a national network of mediation boards, for those under the age of criminal responsibility. In Germany, the youth services have begun to employ reparation of damage done, seeing it as a successful way of helping children to appreciate the cause-and-effect aspects of their delinquent acts.

Other examples of community-based programmes include efforts to target communities or neighbourhoods which are particularly at risk. England and Wales have recently introduced Youth Inclusion and Support Panels (YISPs), which aim to prevent disruptive and delinquent behaviours by those 8–13-year-olds in the most deprived neighbourhoods who are considered to be at high risk of offending. YISPs are multi-agency planning groups that offer early intervention based on assessed risk and need. Parenting support in the form of contracts and programmes is offered as part of a range of tailored interventions.

To date, 122 YISPs have been established. Of this total, thirteen pilot areas have received additional support from the Youth Justice Board to develop procedures and innovative practice, alongside a management information system. When fully evaluated and quality-assured, this programme will provide a framework of best practice for other YISPs. The core principles of YISPs include voluntary engagement: any child or young person referred only participates voluntarily, after their full, informed consent and that of their parent or caregiver have been obtained. Participants have the right to withdraw from the YISP at any point without prejudice (that is, they can re-engage at a later, perhaps at a more appropriate time in their life).

The YISP focuses on children and young people aged 8–13 who are identified by two or more partner agencies and/or parents or carers as those youth who are most at risk of disruptive or delinquent behaviours. The YISP requires a multi-agency response to involve children, young people and their families in the planning of interventions and participation in all aspects of programme delivery. Although organised as part of the youth justice system, the YISP recognises the paramount importance of the needs of the child or young person. It is committed to safeguarding the health and well-being of those engaged in YISP activities at all times and to steering them away from the dangers of crime. A focus of every YISP intervention is improved access to mainstream and statutory services (YJB website).

The 'Neighbourhood Tutors' Project in Portugal, which takes a rather different approach, seeks to work with children and adolescents from immigrant and ethnic minority families (6–18-year-olds). Effectively, this is a mentoring programme focused on young people involved in disruptive and delinquent behaviours. The aim of the work is fairly conventional: to support social inclusion, decrease truancy and early school leaving, promote cognitive, social and personal competencies and support more efficient parental guidance through family and community involvement in school dynamics. The method, however, is innovative in that it chooses a group of young people at risk and trains them to be 'neighbourhood tutors' who will work with selected young people and link school, family and community. The tutors are then integrated into schools along with a psychologist and social worker. Through the use of pedagogical activities, organised sports, leisure time and psychological intervention, the programme aims to tackle social exclusion.

In similar vein, a Berlin scheme originally aimed at Bosnian Roma children developed provisions that successfully involved children who are normally extremely difficult to reach. *Fallschirm* (Parachute) was established in 1998 as a community-based alternative to the residential childcare institutions where young offenders normally would have been placed away from their families. Until the end of 2000, it was a model financed by the German state lottery. Since the beginning of 2001, it has a regular contract with the Berlin youth service system, and since then it has worked with families and children of a variety of different origins including Turkish, Lebanese and former Yugoslavian as well as German children, most of them boys. Currently, the project targets young repeat offenders who are under age 14 and are suspected of having committed more than six offences against the law during the preceding six months (with a probable minimum sentence of three months for at least one offence, if older than 14), or suspected of more than ten offences during the preceding twelve months (again with a minimum sentence of three months, if older than 14). It is estimated that in Berlin there are between twenty and forty such children. The offences are mostly theft and robbery, but also arson, grievous bodily harm, slander and damage of property. More than 60% of these young people refuse to go to school regularly. The children often live in isolated families where parents do not exercise control, where involvement in education is sporadic and positive role models are few. The children are mostly left to themselves and their delinquent peer-group becomes more influential as a surrogate for a non-existent family life. *Fallschirm* is a non-residential project, which works intensively with these young offenders by offering support and alternatives to delinquent behaviours. The project tries to maintain contact, even if the young people are hostile, by seeking to build on the strengths and competencies of the children, keeping in regular contact with the family in order to help them to learn to deal with crises and to set boundaries for acceptable behaviours. The project workers work closely with the social services, the school and the parents in order to challenge the ways children can justify their delinquency and encourage them to take responsibility for their actions. The project also tries to get young people back into school and take part in legal leisure time activities such as youth/sport clubs. The programme includes individual or group leisure activities combined with social-skills training and regular sessions with parents to improve their educational skills. Sixty per cent of the children needed to be accompanied to school every morning for several weeks, as well as to the police when necessary. The project is available to the young people twenty-four hours a day through a hotline. Self-evaluation shows that the project's targets – reducing delinquency and truancy, changing leisure activities and reinforcing parental responsibility – are met in about half of the cases.

Similar projects were established in the Turin region of Italy in the 1990s. For example, in the town of Giaveno, a voluntary organisation that aimed to encourage vulnerable young adolescents to stay in school and set up a neighbourhood centre where young people could come every day. Similar centres were set up by social cooperatives in Moncalieri and the Mirafiori Sud area of Turin. Activities were organised every day for 9–15-year-olds who were referred by the local social and health services due to educational, family, or psychological difficulties. Younger children were targeted by a project called 'Ludoteca', or gameplace. The project aimed to support nursery schools and families to integrate 3–14-year-olds at risk of social exclusion, attracting an average of seventy children every day (Buckland and Stevens, 2001). This approach has something in common with the Danish 'Family Folk High school', a community-based social and life-skill training programme aimed at 10–15-year-olds from minority backgrounds.

Conclusions

This brief essay cannot do justice to the very large range of programmes being undertaken with at-risk children in several European countries. The review identified several programme themes. First, a few countries in Northern Europe have started to implement a programme-based approach, often inspired by American models, sometimes home-grown. While these programmes have a good deal of empirical and theoretical backing, there is a question of how far it will be possible to mainstream such programmes. Other countries seem steadfastly committed to an approach based on social casework and meeting needs as they arise. However, the political and media climate in many countries is increasingly concerned about crime. Consequently, a social casework approach may be hard to sustain, particularly where the intervention thresholds are high and resources for proactive and preventive work are limited.

Secondly, it is clearly important that projects and programmes do not become a substitute for entitlement to mainstream education, health and social services. Whatever the efficacy of school-based interventions, their positive impact can be undone by structural factors, such as truancy and expulsion rates, cuts in pastoral care and support services and increasing classroom sizes.

Third, the danger of inadvertently reinforcing rather than combating social exclusion is probably greatest with respect to ethnic minorities. Some of the most interesting projects have been attempting to meet the needs of hard-to-reach children, often from ethnic or immigrant minorities. Prisons all over the world show strong over-representations of such minorities and developing effective prevention and treatment approaches must be a priority.

Fourth, there is the question of the relationships between the social agencies and the police and criminal justice agencies. Some commentators feel uncomfortable about the presence of police officers in schools, but evidence from the UK suggests that most teachers and pupils like the sense of security it brings. There does seem to be a need for clear rules of engagement when agencies with very different aims and objectives are working together. This is true in relation to some of the police-led attempts to stimulate speedy action in relation to child offenders under the age of criminal responsibility. As far as the minimum age of criminal responsibility is concerned, jurisdictions need to make sure that they respond to the Council of Europe's recommendation that 'culpability should better reflect the age and maturity of the offender, and be more in step with the offender's stage of development, with criminal measures being progressively applied as individual responsibility increases' (Council of Europe, 2003: par. 9; see also Chapter 14, this volume).

Fifth, there are important issues arising relating to the practice of prevention work. Some people are uneasy about schemes which mix children who have committed unlawful acts with children who have not (or have not been caught). Mixed groups can try to harness the skills and influence of non-delinquent peers in helping young offenders discover alternative ways of behaving, but run the risk of contamination effects (see Chapter 7, this volume). Clearly, group interventions need to ensure that positive, prosocial norms prevail as far as possible. There are also some concerns that preventive work with children operates mainly on a verbal basis, focusing on conversations with individuals or groups. Detached youth work, arts, music and sport can all be vehicles through which positive relationships can be fostered.

Finally, there are issues relating to the emphasis on cases rather than places, and the argument for more vigorous efforts to increase social capital in the most deprived areas. This requires an approach which concentrates not so much on risks, deficits and so-called 'criminogenic' needs, but focuses instead on identifying and building strengths in individuals, families and communities.

Part VI
Conclusions

Chapter 16

Conclusions and Recommendations

Rolf Loeber, Peter H. van der Laan, Wim Slot and Machteld Hoeve

This volume concerns tomorrow's criminals. Recent research has substantially expanded our knowledge of the manifestations as well as the correlates and causes of disruptive and delinquent behaviours in children and adolescents. This knowledge has important implications for treatment and prevention and can be crucial for optimising the economic and social consequences of decisions by local and national policy and decision makers. However, as this volume has highlighted, application of a large variety of consistent research findings for prevention and intervention (that is, treatment) in countries grappling with the issue of young delinquents is still scarce and incidental. This holds true for the Netherlands and many European countries as well.

This chapter summarises the conclusions presented in the previous chapters, supplemented by more general conclusions, and discusses key research and policy recommendations addressing the behaviours and needs of disruptive and delinquent children. We organise our conclusions according to the questions raised in Chapter 1 (but in a slightly different order).

Why Focus on Disruptive Children and Child Delinquents?

Increasingly, Dutch citizens express concerns about safety in their everyday lives (Boutellier, 2005). Since there is a direct connection between safety and delinquent acts committed by offenders, society must be concerned about the origins or possible causes of delinquency and how to prevent delinquency in future generations of children. One of the main reasons for this volume is to show the developmental link between disruptive children, child delinquents and adolescent and adult chronic, serious and violent offenders (Figure 1.1). This sequence is repeated for *each new generation* of youth.

As mentioned in Chapter 1, one of the key, replicated findings in criminology is that a relatively small number of chronic offenders in adolescence and adulthood account for more than half of all crimes including serious property crime and violence (see Figure 1.1). Most of these chronic offenders start their delinquent careers in childhood. Of all children below age 12, a small proportion show persistent disruptive behaviours (usually known as 'disruptive children'). Some disruptive children will start committing delinquent acts (known as 'child delinquents'). Child delinquents have a two to three times higher likelihood of becoming violent, serious and chronic offenders, and have longer delinquency careers. Viewed retrospectively, the majority of eventual chronic serious offenders in adolescence and adulthood are former child delinquents. Therefore, a proportion of disruptive children and child delinquents constitute a high-risk group for later serious, violent and chronic delinquency, and because of their eventual substantial infliction of harm on others, they form a disproportionate threat to the safety and property of citizens.

How Common are Child Delinquents and Disruptive Children?

As shown in Chapter 2, there are about 131,000 child delinquents in the Netherlands, which is about the population of a small town. Also, we know from these studies that 1–5% of children reported having stolen at home or at school, and reported having committed burglary or assault. About 6% reported having committed vandalism and supposedly minor fire-setting. Such delinquent behaviours tend to be more common in the most disadvantaged neighbourhoods. Some of the children qualify for a diagnosis of a psychiatric disorder. A recent study of low SES areas in Amsterdam and Utrecht showed that about one in ten (11%) of 3rd–5th-graders qualified for an impairing externalising disorder (ODD or CD) or ADHD (Zwirs et al., 2007). Thus, the number of youth with disruptive behaviours, ADHD, or delinquency in the Netherlands is considerable, and is probably more prevalent in the large cities.

Only a proportion of all child delinquents are known to the police. Estimations are that on a yearly basis between 4,000 and 5,000 young children come into trouble with the law (that is, they are registered in a police database). Around 15% of these child delinquents are recidivists in that they are registered on more than one occasion. Thus, recidivism is not uncommon for this age category. It should be kept in mind, however, that children under age 12 cannot be prosecuted and, therefore, are not necessarily fully included in criminal police and court statistics.

Disruptive behaviours are common in young children and are part of normal development (Chapter 3), but repeated and atypical disruptive behaviours are markers for disruptive processes that can forewarn that a child is on the road to a life of crime (see below). As an example of 'normative' child problems, three-quarters of parents in a general Dutch sample of pre-12-year-olds reported high rates of oppositional behaviours, including temper tantrums and disobedience, sulking and teasing. In contrast, covert child problem behaviours (such as stealing, lying and vandalism) and aggression were reported by about one in five parents.

Externalising problem behaviours, including aggression, tend to decrease in prevalence when children grow older. However, the decrease is less for aggression than for non-aggressive behaviours, meaning that aggressive behaviours tend to be more stable over time. Against this backdrop of decreasing problem behaviours, delinquency and violence tend to increase in prevalence after childhood.

A proportion of children with disruptive behaviours fail to outgrow normative disruptive behaviours and, instead, develop persistent patterns of problem behaviours that show increasing variety and increasing severity over time. These are the children who eventually are more likely to become child delinquents.

Depending on who is reporting (parent, teacher, child, or professional) and the type of sample, the prevalence rate of disruptive children varies from around 5%

(parents) up to 28% or more (professionals). Children from the general population have the fewest problems, followed by children with an intellectual disability and clinically referred children. It is estimated that 5–7% of Dutch children have serious problems and are in need of professional help.

In general, the prevalence data of disruptive and delinquent children should be viewed with caution. Official registration of children with persistent disruptive behaviours is usually lacking or incomplete, and cut-off scores to identify children who score in the clinical range are often arbitrary and not necessarily based on external criteria, such as impairment. National or regional secular trends are difficult to discern due to the absence of longitudinal monitoring and research. Tick (2007) by comparing parent and teacher ratings in Dutch samples, concluded that there were no secular changes in externalising problem behaviours,[1] but noted 'a small increase [over the past years] in the proportion of children with serious parent- or teacher-reported rule-breaking behavior scores' (p. 98). Thus, notwithstanding the small numbers, there is ample reason to take changing indications of persistent disruptive and externalising problem behaviours of young children seriously.

How Important are Ethnic and Cultural Factors?

Juveniles from minorities are over-represented in the justice system and in institutions for delinquents. Data from the juvenile justice system on 12–18-year-old youths show that 58% of the youngsters held in detention or pre-trial custody are from non-Dutch cultures, which is a substantial over-representation. Given the considerable continuity between child problems and problems and offending during adolescence, one might expect that minorities are already over-represented among disruptive and delinquent youth at a young age. Studies reviewed in Chapter 3 show that Turkish children in the Netherlands seem to have more problem behaviours than children from other ethnic groups. Studies show inconsistent prevalence rates of problem behaviours of Moroccan children. While parents report similar levels of problems compared to Dutch parents, teachers identified more problems in Moroccan than in Dutch children. With respect to delinquent acts at a young age, reliable information is lacking since police and other crime statistics cover only suspects and/or arrestees aged 12 and older.

The causes of cultural and racial differences are difficult to interpret. The fact that children from a certain cultural or ethnic background present more externalising problem behaviours does not necessarily imply that cultural background or racial discrimination itself is the only primary cause. Other factors such as low SES or living in poor neighbourhoods are more frequent in populations from non-Dutch cultural backgrounds and may contribute to a higher proportion of externalising problem behaviours in children. We agree with Van der Laan and Blom (2006) who, on the basis of Dutch research, concluded that interventions for minorities should focus on the presence of risk factors and the lack of promotive factors and not on the ethnic origin. At the same time, however, interventions should be culturally sensitive.

---

1 Including no secular change in the emotional and behavioural problems of preschoolers.

How Important are Gender Differences?

Chapters 2–4 and 7 show that delinquency and disruptive behaviours, including aggression, are more common in boys and are consistent across different cultures. Self-report studies on delinquency demonstrate that the gender ratio varies depending on the type of disruptive and delinquent acts. Girls do not differ from boys in shoplifting and hitting parents, but show considerably lower involvement in theft, aggression outside the home and graffiti. Not surprisingly, the ratio of being questioned by the police during the previous year is 5% for boys and ten times less (0.4%) for girls.

More boys than girls have externalising problem behaviours. Girls, compared to boys, tend to have more internalising problem behaviours during adolescence. However, clinically referred girls (day-care and outpatient) have relatively more severe externalising and attention problems than boys. This is in accordance with previous studies from abroad that found some evidence for the 'gender paradox', which states that although boys show higher rates of problem behaviours, clinically referred girls show more severe problems than boys. Data from a Dutch study showed that among clinically referred children, relatively more girls than boys had deviant scores on two or three behavioural syndromes (that is, delinquency, aggression and attention problems).

In terms of exposure to risk and promotive factors, Van der Laan and Blom (2006) in a Dutch study found that more girls compared to boys are exposed to domains of promotive factors. In contrast, boys more so than girls on average are exposed to a mixture of risk and promotive factors in which risk factors dominate.

Are there Developmental Pathways to Serious Delinquency?

The development of serious and chronic offending is not a random process, but in most young people evolves over time in an orderly fashion along developmental pathways. Basically, young individuals can be on *one or more* of three developmental pathways (see Figure 9.1). A first pathway, called the Overt Pathway, consists of the development of overt, confrontational disruptive acts in three steps or stages. The first step in this pathway is minor aggression (such as bullying and annoying others), followed by physical fighting (including gang fighting) as the next step, and serious violence (includes rape, attack with a weapon, to seriously harming another person, and strong-arm or robbery) as the third step. The majority of individuals, who display behaviours characteristic of step three, usually have progressed through the preceding steps.

The second pathway is the Covert Pathway, prior to age 15, which starts with minor covert acts as a first step, has property damage as a second step, and moderate to serious delinquency as a third step. The third pathway is the Authority Conflict Pathway prior to the age of 12, which starts with stubborn behaviour as a first step, has defiance as a second step, and authority avoidance (for example, truancy, running away from home and staying out late at night) as a third step.

Knowledge about pathways has implications for preventive interventions that focus on curtailing or stopping individuals' progression from persistent minor forms of disruptive behaviours to the most serious delinquent behaviours. The pathway model cited above is valid for age 7 upward until adolescence, but for the period from birth to age 7 is based on less than ideal retrospective information. Distinct pathways of disruptive behaviours based on prospective data collected during the preschool period have been less well-researched.

What are the Negative Consequences for Juvenile Delinquents?

Aside from child delinquents' infliction of harm on others there are many negative consequences of early-onset delinquency that can affect the quality of life of the offenders themselves (see Chapters 3–5, 8 and 9; Loeber & Farrington, 2001). These negative consequences have been listed by and include:

Years of engaging in delinquency robs youths of many opportunities to learn prosocial behaviours.

- Persistent disruptive behaviours and delinquency often are associated with poor social skills, leading to major and repeated disturbances in social relationships, initially with relatives and peers, and later with partners, employers, and co-workers.
- Persistent disruptive behaviours tend to elicit enduring negative reactions in others, which can further aggravate disruptive behaviours.
- Disruptive behaviours in classrooms in combination with low interest and motivation in educational matters, eventually increases the risk of chronic truancy and early school dropout with a detrimental effect on later employment opportunities and lifetime income. In addition, there are several problems associated with child delinquents who become recidivist offenders:
- Child recidivists are more likely to become fathers at a young age and often are unable or unwilling to fulfil the father role or to assume financial responsibilities for the partner and child. For this and other reasons, the children of very young offenders are at risk of disruptive behaviours.
- Young aggressive delinquents have an especially high risk of internalising problem behaviours, such as depression.
- Early-onset offenders often start using potentially addictive substances at a young age and are at risk of becoming substance abusers.
- A high risk of criminal victimisation in the community.
- A high risk of employment problems and chronic unemployment.
- Referral to social and/or special educational services for long-term help and/or training. A study on the annual costs of services necessary to address the needs of youth with Conduct Disorder (many of whom are aggressive) shows that such costs increase from year to year as these children grow older. (Foster et al., 2005)

In summary, there are many negative consequences to children starting delinquent activities at an early age. Research shows that in the long run, compared to delinquents, non-delinquents tend to be healthier, better educated, more often employed, earning more money and paying more taxes (Schweinhart, 2003, 2007).

What are Correlates and Causes of Disruptive and Delinquent Child Behaviour?

Children's exposure to known risk factors for serious delinquency increases as they grow up. Early in life, the most important risk factors are individual factors (for example, birth complications, exposure to lead, difficult temperament, hyperactivity, impulsivity and sensation-seeking) and family factors (for example, parental delinquent behaviour, parental substance abuse, parents' poor childrearing practices, mother's smoking during pregnancy, teenage motherhood). Later risk factors are peer influences, school influences, and community factors. Although genetic causes for child delinquency cannot be excluded (see below), there is abundant evidence that factors in the child's social environment influence long-term outcomes.

Individual Factors

It is rare that disruptive and delinquent behaviours in childhood emerge without one or more individual predispositions being in place, often at a very young age. Among these predispositions are a child's emotional, cognitive, physical and social characteristics, which may set the stage for the development of disruptive behaviours and thus function as risk factors (reviewed in Chapter 3).

Research has focused on several biological factors that may influence individual predispositions to disruptive and delinquent behaviours. Among these are genes, but there is very limited information on this so far, and certainly no single, relevant gene has been identified. Heritability appears stronger for aggression and violence than for property crime, and genetic influences are found to be more important for early-onset disruptive behaviour/delinquency cases than for those who become delinquent in adolescence. Genetic susceptibility and adverse influences of environmental factors add up to an increased risk of developing disruptive behaviours (this is also confirmed in a recent meta-analysis by Taylor & Kim-Cohen, 2007). Studies show that the *interaction* between genetic and environmental factors results in a risk that is far higher than the sum of the individual risk factors. Adoption studies, for example, show that an adverse adoptive home environment interacts with the antisocial personality of the biological parents in predicting increased aggression in the offspring. In summary, disruptive and delinquent behaviours may increase when genetically vulnerable children are confronted with adverse familial and peer contextual influences.

Decreased autonomic arousal in children is believed to be a stable, genetically determined marker of the development of persistent disruptive and delinquent behaviours. Similarly, decreases in neuro-endocrine responses are related to disruptive and delinquent behaviours. However, the role of sex hormones and of pubertal hormonal changes is unclear. Neuro-cognitive deficits are most germane for early-onset and persistent disruptive and delinquent behaviours, as is low IQ, low verbal IQ and discrepancies between verbal and performance IQ. Executive functioning – in particular, inhibitory control – predicts onset and persistence of disruptive behaviours from early preschool onwards. Deficits in executive functioning are related to lesions in the orbito-frontal cortex. Their associations with disruptive behaviours are most consistent among children with ADHD symptoms. Furthermore, disruptive children are more inclined to focus on reward signals while ignoring signals for punishment, often resulting in poor self-regulation.

Family Factors

The importance of family processes and parent and child personality characteristics is reviewed in Chapter 6. Research from the Netherlands and from elsewhere shows that externalising problem behaviours are the result of interactions between individual characteristics of the child and their social environment. As such, the child is an active participant in the parenting process. The effects of parenting also partly depend on the combination of parent personality characteristics and those of the child. Parents' negative childrearing practices, such as lack of supervision, overprotection, weak family relationships, rejection and inconsistency in discipline, have stronger associations with delinquency compared to more structural family factors such as single-parenthood and large families. Moreover, many parenting factors are modifiable and, therefore, of great importance for the prevention and treatment of disruptive and delinquent child behaviours (discussed below).

Peer Factors

Research on the influence of peers has focused on three different but equally important processes (Chapter 8): (a) bullying, (b) rejection by peers, and (c) peer affiliation. Bullying by peers may elicit disruptive behaviours in non-aggressive child victims, and may accentuate the already existing externalising problem behaviours of other children. Turning to rejection, approximately 5–10% of children experience chronic rejection by their peers. Peer rejection has been related to many negative consequences for the child, including early-onset conduct problems and delinquency and also internalising problem behaviours. Peer rejection can cause cognitive biases in the victims, such as hostile attributions about neutral peer behaviours. The link between peer rejection and later disruptive behaviours may depend on a child's age. Younger children are more susceptible to the adverse effects of peer rejection than older children. The third process concerns affiliation with deviant peers. Children who are at risk of developing externalising problem behaviours tend to affiliate with disruptive peers, who subsequently foster the development of the child's disruptive and delinquent behaviours.

School and Neighbourhood Factors

Some risk factors are associated with children's exposure to risk factors in specific contexts, including the characteristics of the school attended and the neighbourhood in which the children reside or spend their time. Data from prediction studies indicate that risk factors from different domains and different contexts contribute to the explanation of why some individuals and not others progress from persistent minor disruptive behaviours to child delinquency, and eventually, to chronic, serious delinquency and violence (see Pathways, above).

What are Promotive Factors that Protect Against Disruptive and Delinquent Behaviour?

Promotive factors are defined as factors that predict a low probability of later disruptive and delinquency in the general population or predict desistance from offending in populations of known disruptive or delinquent children. Thus, promotive factors are associated with increased positive outcomes, including positive adjustment and positive mental health. Most criminology and psychopathology studies have routinely neglected the study of promotive factors.

Chapter 9 reviewed the developmental changes in children's exposure to promotive factors as they grow older. Some promotive factors emerge at birth, others in early, middle, or late childhood, and again others in adolescence or early adulthood. Typical promotive factors in the individual domain at birth are normal to high IQ, or absence of pregnancy or birth complications. Absence of callous behaviour or impulsivity become visible when entering early childhood, whereas good academic achievement and skills for getting a job show up in middle or late childhood and adolescence respectively, stable employment appears even later in early adulthood. The same can be said for promotive factors in the domain of the family. Medium to high SES or absence of delinquency in the family may already be present at birth, whereas positive parenting and supervision tend to show up at later stages. Promotive factors in the domains of peers, school and neighbourhood predominantly appear by the time children start socialising with other children, begin attending school, or go outside and play with their peers.

Promotive Factors Buffering the Impact of Risk Factors

Promotive factors can offset or buffer the impact of risk factors, that is, it is the *mixture* of risk and promotive factors that appears most crucial for determining the future risk of serious offending (as well as the probability of desistance). Thus, for serious delinquents, the balance between risk and promotive factors weighs in favour of risk factors, whereas for non-delinquents the opposite occurs: the balance between risk and promotive factors favours the promotive factors. More is to be learned about how promotive factors buffer the impact of risk factors and predict favourable and unfavourable child outcomes in the Netherlands.

What is the Role of Victimisation?

Chapters 4 and 7 reviewed three types of victimisation: child maltreatment, children's witnessing violent among adults, and bullying. As to the first two, there are no national data on how many children experience victimisation in the form of psychological abuse or neglect, sexual abuse, by witnessing interparental violence, or by being exposed to repeated bullying.[2] Physical abuse of young children increases the risk of violent offending. Child maltreatment in the Netherlands represents an understudied area. However, a recent study shows that sexually abused children as well as children who witnessed interparental violence show high levels of problem behaviours. Forty-seven per cent of the children who witnessed interparental violence scored in the clinical range on externalising problem behaviours, while 71% scored in the clinical range of internalising problem behaviours. Sexually abused children exhibited significantly more externalising problem behaviours (63% scored in the clinical range) than children who witnessed and/or were victims of interparental violence and 66% of the sexually abused children were in the clinical range of internalising problem behaviours.

Another key form of victimisation is bullying (Chapter 8). Bullying can occur in many settings, but has been most studied in schools. One out of five pupils in Dutch primary schools bullies other children occasionally or more frequently. About 3% of the children bully several times a week. Prevalence rates of victimisation of bullying (being bullied) are similar. Bullying tends to elicit aggressive and internalising problem behaviours in both non-aggressive children and children with persistent disruptive behaviours. In summary, improvements in the safety and well-being of young child delinquents in home, school and neighbourhood are important priorities.

Summary: What are Some Important Principles of Child Development?

Several principles of development have emerged from the scientific literature, which are relevant to disruptive and delinquent children:

- *Early-onset principle*: an early onset of delinquency or persistent disruptive behaviours, compared to later onset, is predictive of later chronic, serious and violent offending.
- *Age-crime curve*: is a universal phenomenon showing that the prevalence of offenders is low in late childhood, increases in early adolescence, peaks in middle to late adolescence and decreases subsequently.
- *Dose-response principle*: there is a dose-response relationship between risk factors and outcomes, meaning that the higher the number of risk factors that a child is exposed to, the more likely it is that that child will become seriously delinquent. There also is an inverse dose-response relationship between promotive factors and outcomes, meaning that the higher the number of promotive factors that a child is exposed to, the lower the likelihood that that child will become seriously delinquent.
- *Buffering principle*: the higher the number of promotive compared to risk factors juveniles are exposed to, the more likely it is that the promotive factors will buffer or negate the impact of risk factors. Thus, non-delinquency

2 However, the information is collected from secondary-school students in the Netherlands.

is more likely when promotive factors outstrip risk factors. The same applies to desistance from delinquency: desistance becomes more likely the higher the number of promotive compared to risk factors.

- *Developmental prominence principle*: there is emerging evidence that promotive factors tend to predominate in childhood, whereas the number of risk factors that children are exposed to tends to increase between childhood and adolescence.

These five principles are of importance in assessing children, and particularly their risk of future serious delinquency, but the principles are also highly relevant for the formulation and evaluation of interventions.

How Early Can Child Delinquents be Identified and What are Early Warning Signs?

Is it possible to predict future serious delinquency and violence on the basis of disruptive behaviours in the first decade of life? Although some studies show that early problem behaviours in the preschool years are correlated with later delinquency (for example, Caspi et al., 1996; Tremblay, Pihl et al, 1994), the fact is that there are currently no studies showing which children in the preschool period are likely to become tomorrow's chronic, serious and violent offenders. Wakschlag and colleagues (2007) in reviewing this area concluded that developmentally informed diagnostic criteria are badly needed for deviant preschool behaviours.

Although it may appear laudable to conduct research on criteria that would facilitate such early identification, there are several important complications attached to this strategy (Loeber & Farrington, 2001). First, studies that start in the primary-school age period show that there is substantial behavioural change with some children stopping their disruptive behaviours and others starting to display these behaviours. Further, the solidification of disruptive behaviour and early forms of delinquency often takes place over a number of years and is a function of juveniles' exposure to risk factors during that period. Secondly, childhood is a period in which most young people learn about what is good and bad, what is permissible and not permissible, and how to solve interpersonal conflicts without resorting to violence. Childhood is also characterised by age-normative problem behaviours which most children overcome as they grow up. Usually, in this period of trial-and-error learning, many children engage in problem behaviours of a relatively minor nature for a short time and therefore are not of major concern.

However, the following *persistent* disruptive behaviours are important warning signs of future problems (Loeber & Farrington, 2001):

- disruptive behaviour that is either more frequent or more severe than in children of the same age;
- disruptive behaviours such as temper tantrums and aggression which persists beyond the first two to three years of life;
- physical fighting;
- cruelty to people or animals;

- covert acts such as frequent lying and theft, and fire-setting;
- not getting along with others;
- low academic motivation during elementary school, and
- substance use (without parental permission).

What are Effective Screening Methods?

The growing interest in a developmental and multiple risk and promotive factor approach in understanding juvenile delinquency has led to increasing efforts to predict problem behaviours in young people (Chapter 10; see, for example, Walker et al., 1988, 1990, 1994; Feil, Severson & Walker, 1995, 1998). Understanding the potential impact of risk and promotive factors on the emergence of persistent disruptive behaviours and delinquency, and the acknowledgement that such factors often are present and operate at a relatively young age, have enormous potential for designing effective prevention and intervention strategies. As a result, the development and use of assessment and screening instruments is receiving more attention from both policymakers and researchers. Undoubtedly, national and local authorities and agencies working with young children are currently investing in the development of new, or the translation and implementation of standardised, instruments from abroad. Screening and assessment is regarded as an ongoing activity in which various agencies and care organisations should collaborate. Still, much effort must be put into strengthening the validity of screening and assessment (for example, to make screenings gender sensitive; see Appendix 1), and also the validity of advice and actions taken on the basis of screening and assessment. Furthermore, more is to be learned about the predictive validity of screening for specific populations of children and families.

Also, it is unlikely that a single screening method would provide the greatest utility in identifying those at highest risk; instead, it is much more likely that screening methods applied in sequence would have a greater utility (as is currently being applied at the SPRINT programme in Amsterdam (Van Leeuwen & Bijl, 2003a, 2003b). In addition, the advantage of screening based on continuous development instead of on a single moment in time supplies multiple opportunities to try to motivate the parents and the child to bring about behavioural change. Yet researchers are not in agreement about at what age(s) such sequential screening should be optimally administered (Le Blanc, 1998; Howell, 2001).

Many Dutch agencies are involved with at-risk children, and these professionals have their own unique opportunities to identify such children. Professionals from three services – the local public health agency, day-care/child centres, and school – reach almost all children. Local authorities are legally obliged to offer children from birth to age 19 both mental and physical juvenile health care. Ninety per cent of all Dutch newborns are in regular consultation with the Local Health Services (GGD) from shortly after birth until age 14: care for newborns to 4-year-olds is provided at local child centres (*Consultatiebureau of Ouder-Kind Centrum* – Consultation Bureau for Children and Parents); from age 4 onward, care is provided at school by the same service. Eighty per cent of Dutch children attend some sort of day care and over 90% of children attend school, starting with kindergarten at age 4. Therefore, these agencies offer nationwide opportunities for longitudinal screening.

In the Netherlands, the use of *validated* and *standardised* methods for screening, assessment and referral used to be rare. In recent years, however, the importance of early detection of at-risk children by means of screening, and integrating the databases of different agencies, has been stressed by many authors, social service agencies and in Dutch government reports. It is recognised that better, empirically based, reliable screening instruments are needed to discriminate between child delinquents who are at high risk of becoming serious and violent juvenile offenders and those who are not.

What are Relevant Judicial and Legal Interventions?

The minimum age of criminal responsibility for young people in the Netherlands starts at age 12 (see the legal basis discussed in Chapter 14). However, some children below age 12 commit acts that are considered delinquent for older children. A proportion of cases of child delinquency come to the attention of the police. The police may refer parents of young children to voluntary care and support agencies, but it is not known how often this is done. In more serious cases, the police are required to formally notify the Council of Child Care and Protection (*Raad voor de Kinderbescherming*). In the administration of the Council, these cases are not registered as 'penal cases' but as 'complaint or protection cases'. In 2005, the Council of Child Care and Protection conducted enquiries in more than 7,300 protection cases that were brought to its attention in which young children were involved. In very few of these enquiries, delinquent behaviour of the child is mentioned as the core problem. In 4% of the cases, the reason for the referral was disruptive behaviours. Police in the Netherlands can also refer children to *Stop*, a short, pedagogical programme in which the children are instructed on several aspects of delinquent behaviour, including its harm to victims. Systematic evaluation of the *Stop* programme is needed to establish whether the programme prevents children's escalation to chronic, serious and violent forms of delinquency.

The fact that there are children below age 12 who are actually committing delinquent acts does not have to imply that legal age limits should be lowered. Arguments against decreasing the age of criminal responsibility are the absence of evidence that the justice system works for young children, as well as possible violation of the protection of children, and their inadequate understanding of legal procedures.

Recently, Allen (2006) advocated increasing the minimum age of criminal responsibility in the UK from age 10 to 14. He recommended that the change be accompanied by the phasing-out of prison custody for 15- and 16-year-olds, and moving the responsibility for youth justice from the Home Office to the Department of Education and Skills. We do not advocate raising the minimum age of criminal responsibility in the Netherlands. However, we consider this an important issue for periodic review and recommend the appointment of a panel of experts to report to the government on this matter.

Finally, proposals have been put forward to make parents legally more responsible for the lawbreaking of their children, and especially to provide sanctions for parents who do not prevent their children's access to guns (Junger-Tas & Slot, 2001; Seelye, 1999). Whether this is politically feasible remains to be seen. More important is the difficulty of demonstrating that such a measure would inhibit young offenders from recidivism.

What are Effective Preventive Interventions for Disruptive Child Behaviours and Child Delinquency?

If the criminal justice system has limited responsibility for child delinquents, which institutions are responsible for this group of troublesome youth? How effective are preventive interventions by other gatekeepers for child delinquents than the police, such as day-care attendants, workers at health agencies, and teachers? Nowadays, much information about the type and efficacy of preventive programmes for children is available on the Internet. Table 16.1 summarises key information sources of programmes in the Netherlands and North America.

In the Netherlands there is a broad spectrum of programmes, projects and methods for the prevention of problem behaviours in young children (see reviews in Chapters 8, 9, 11–13). But this field is characterised by a lack of transparency; the research is scarce; the methodology of effectiveness assessment is generally poor; the cost-benefit aspects of the intervention and treatment integrity are often ignored, and the outcomes are mixed. However, several foreign and a few Dutch intervention programmes can be classified as effective in the early prevention of persistent disruptive behaviours and delinquency. These programmes focus on the following risk factors: academic failure, early persistent coercive behaviour, poor parenting, positive attitudes towards problem behaviour, and problematic influence by deviant peers and environmental risks.

The positive findings are reinforced by a recent meta-analysis of school-based prevention programmes (Hahn et al., 2007) showing that classroom-based prevention programmes on average led to a 15% reduction in aggression and violence. There was a trend for effect-sizes to be larger for programmes in preschool and elementary school compared to middle school (32.4%, 18.0% and 7.3% respectively) which supports the notion that early intervention had higher yields. A second recent meta-analysis (Wilson & Lipsey, 2007) focused on both school prevention and school-based treatment programmes for aggressive or disruptive youth and demonstrated not only significant reductions in aggression, anger/hostility/rebelliousness, and problem behaviour, but also improvements in social skills, school participation, school performance and several other outcomes.

Intervention prevention programmes rarely help all children with disruptive or delinquent behaviours. However, even a 10% reduction in aggression or violence is beneficial for victims, reduces costs to society, but also can pay off in the cost-benefit ratio of programmes (Foster, Jones & Conduct Problems Prevention Research Group, 2005; Welsh, Farrington & Sherman, 2000).

Table 16.1 Directory of selected Dutch and North American programmes related to evidence-based interventions for children (and their websites)

Dutch programmes and websites	
Operatie Jong [Operation Young]	www.operatiejong.nl
Rotterdamse Jeugdmonitor [Rotterdam Youth Monitor]	www.jeugdmonitorrotterdam.nl/web.cijfers.html
Jeugd Preventie Programma [Youth Prevention Programme]	www.collegio.nl/poducgroep/dienstfiles
Centrum of Criminaliteitspreventie en Veiligheid [Centre for Crime Prevention and Safety]	www.hetccv.nl
Netherlands Jeugd Instituut	www.jeugdinterventies.nl
North American programmes and websites	
Blueprints for Violence Prevention	www.colorado.edu/cspv/blueprints
Model Program Guide, US Office of Juvenile Justice and Delinquency Prevention	www.dsgonline.com/mpg2.5/mpg_index.htm
Bulletins on Child Delinquency, US Office of Juvenile Justice and Delinquency	www.ojjdp.ncjrs.org
Promoting Relationships and Eliminating Violence (Canada)	www.prevnet.ca
Guide to Community Preventive Services, US Center of Disease Control	www.thecommunityguide.org

Chapters 11 and 12 make it clear that there are different forms of effective preventive interventions for disruptive and delinquent child behaviours, each of which address different age populations of young people. This is clarified in the top portion of Figure 16.1, which summarises in a generic manner the most effective prevention programmes ('evidence-based' programmes) reducing aggression, delinquency and/or violence. The earliest intervention is the home visitation programme by Olds (Olds, 1998; Olds et al., 2004a, 2004b), discussed in Chapter 11 which focuses on the mother when she is pregnant up to age 2 of the child. The next opportunity for intervention is the preschool period, and the High/Scope Perry Preschool Program (Schweinhart, 2003, 2007; Schweinhart et al., 2005), discussed in Chapter 11, is among the best for that developmental phase (age 3–4).

Next, two types of evidence-based programmes in elementary schools focus on increasing children's social competence. An example is the Good Behaviour Game (*Taakspel* in the Dutch; Dolan et al., 1989), reviewed in Chapters 7 and 11, can be applied by teachers in classrooms at age 7–11. Another example is Olweus's anti-bullying programme (Olweus, 1993; Olweus et al., 1999), which can be instituted in classrooms between age 7 and 12.

In summary, along the developmental time-line when some children develop persistent disruptive behaviours and a minority start displaying delinquent acts as well, there are available several proven preventive interventions (note, however, that most of the evaluations have taken place abroad). Most programmes have been evaluated for boys, while preventive interventions for girls are lagging behind (Hipwell & Loeber, 2006).

Policymakers' choice of preventive interventions should not so much focus on the question of whether a single type of intervention suffices but, instead, be developmentally informed, in that not all at-risk circumstances are present early in life and may develop from childhood through adolescence. Therefore, a sequence of preventive interventions, each with their age-relevant agent of change (for example, first parents, then teachers) should be the standard inventory for local and national prevention programmes.

What are Effective Treatments for Disruptive Child Behaviours and Child Delinquency?

Even with the best of prevention programmes, one can expect that some children will need treatment for their disruptive and delinquent behaviours. Many forms of treatment for children are available in the Netherlands (see Chapters 4, 7, 8 and 12), but only a few have a thorough theoretical and empirical underpinning and few have been properly evaluated. Problem-solving skills training, or cognitive-behavioural training and family interventions turn out to be essential components of treatment for disruptive and delinquent children. Interventions linked to the police as well as family interventions try to reduce the influence of risk factors in the child's family or broader social system. As a rule, the family interventions are based on a well-articulated treatment theory, and pay explicit attention to general working ingredients like proper goal-setting or motivational techniques. Evaluations of these family interventions involving twenty programmes yielded moderately strong effect sizes for externalising problem behaviours and for parental stress, indicating that there is a significant reduction in both problem behaviours and parental stress during family interventions.

Which treatment programs should be applied at what ages of disruptive and delinquent youth? The bottom portion of Figure 16.1 presents a selection of the major proven ('evidence-based' treatments) for different ages of children. Several parent management programmes to teach parents improved childrearing practices and improved control over their lives are now available for parents of children from age 2–3 up. Examples of programmes, discussed in Chapter 12, are *The Incredible Years* programme developed by Webster-Stratton (Webster-Stratton & Mihalic, 2001; Webster-Stratton, Reid & Hammond, 2001) and The *Triple P*, a programme on positive parenting (Sanders et al., 2002a) for children between age 2 and 9. Further, children's self-control training in the form of the SNAP programme is highlighted in Appendix 1. Because of the focus of this volume on children below age 12, we did not elaborate on other effective treatment programmes for older age groups (see, for example, Farrington & Welsh, 2007). In summary, a choice of effective treatment programmes is available for children with disruptive and delinquent behaviours. However, at the moment, the evaluation of programmes for girls is very inadequate (Hipwell & Loeber, 2006).

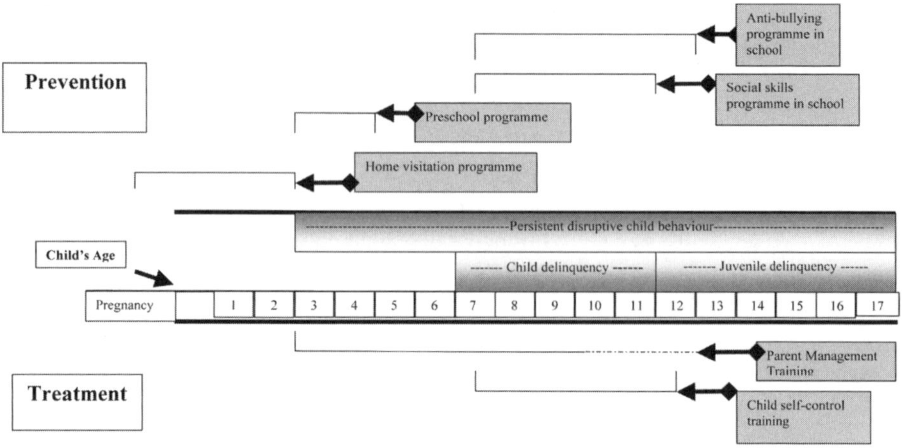

Figure 16.1 Effective programmes for prevention and treatment of disruptive child behaviour and delinquency by age of the child

Interventions require more than effectiveness only. For example, the manual for the SNAP programme (described in Appendix 1) has much to say about optimising implementation procedures that are a prerequisite for effective programmes. The central features of the SNAP programme are: 1) the creation of a referral mechanism to facilitate clients' direct access to relevant services; 2) clinical risk assessment (that is, screening) procedures, and 3) gender-specific evidence-based interventions tailored to the needs of this population of children and their families.

Are Interventions for Child Delinquents Taking Place Sufficiently Early?

Overall, society appears more prepared to carry the huge costs of dealing with serious and violent juvenile offenders in adolescence and adulthood rather than to take cost-effective preventive measures in childhood. Currently, most juvenile justice resources are spent on adolescent juvenile offenders rather than on child delinquents, and are not spent in proportion to the probable risk of long-term serious outcomes. The same typically applies to schools, where most of the resources of special education and behaviour management are funnelled into middle and secondary schools, rather than primary schools or preschools. Similarly, programmes for child delinquents undertaken by welfare agencies often are directed at children whose disruptive and delinquent behaviours is already persistent.

We strongly argue for professionals in schools and those working with families to shift their perception of an 'early intervention' time-frame from childhood to adolescence. A reorientation of agencies toward 'early' prevention is urgently needed to redirect resources to deal with children at a younger age. This needs to be accomplished along with interventions for serious forms of delinquency by juveniles of any age.

For Which Problems (Other than Delinquency) Do Disruptive and Delinquent Children Require Services?

As shown in Chapters 3–5, 8 and 9, a proportion of disruptive and delinquent children have co-occurring problems and, therefore, can be considered multiproblem juveniles. Examples of problems other than persistent disruptive behaviour or delinquency are:

- ADHD,
- early substance use,
- internalising problems, especially depressed mood,
- peer rejection, and
- educational problems, including academic under-achievement, repeating grades, and truancy.

Knowledge of the co-occurring problems is important because they can compound the negative consequences of disruptive and delinquent behaviours over time, and because each of these problems requires unique interventions.

Are there Treatments that Can Do Wrong?

Some interventions do go wrong (Chapters 5 and 7). When children with problem behaviours are brought together in group treatment sessions, 'deviancy training' may occur by which children inadvertently learn disruptive behaviour from their peers. Social reinforcement of rule-breaking conversations and behaviours cause increased rates of delinquency and tobacco, marijuana and alcohol use. Deviancy training has been demonstrated in several studies. Low-disruptive adolescents who were assigned to mixed groups (comprising adolescents who were high and adolescent who were low on conduct problems) showed unfavourable higher levels of externalising problem behaviours after the intervention. Other intervention studies substantiate that deviancy training is not only related to poor development, but also can undermine the outcome of treatment. In other words, it is not the affiliation with deviant friends *per se*, but the consequent learning of, and reinforcement for, deviant behaviours that shapes a child's own disruptive behaviour.

Do Services Need to be Integrated?

A US survey of practitioners indicated that they were almost unanimous (99%) in agreeing that more integration between agencies (juvenile justice, child welfare, mental health, schools, and so on) was needed to deal with very young offenders (Loeber & Farrington, 2001). In the Netherlands, Ferwerda and colleagues (1996) complained of uncoordinated, independent actions by agencies without interagency planning. Several of the pioneering programmes currently being evaluated involve consistent coordination between different agencies concerned with child delinquents (see Appendix 1).

Currently in the Netherlands, at least five governmental departments (Health, Justice, Education, Internal Affairs and Social Affairs), twelve provinces, and 483 municipalities deal with the prevention of violence (Junger et al., 2007b). Coordination, streamlining of separate funding sources, reduction of overlapping responsibilities, and the elimination of duplicative programmes should become a high and routine priority. On a local or municipal level, no single agency (such as the juvenile justice system, schools, mental health agencies, or child welfare agencies) is best equipped to reduce child delinquency in the community. Instead, partnerships between different local agencies are likely to be more productive and efficient in dealing with child delinquents. This task is supported by the *Centrum of Criminaliteitspreventie en Veiligheid* (Centre for Crime Prevention and Safety <www.hetccv.nl>) in Utrecht, which assists agencies in obtaining access to documents relevant to prevention programmes.[3]

What are the Monetary Costs of Crime and What is the Cost-Benefit Ratio of Interventions?

The monetary costs, not to mention the human costs, of a life of crime are very high. In addition, government costs for dealing with crime are exceedingly high. Molenaar (2007) estimated that in the Netherlands the care of victims of crime (by offenders of any age) cost the government €33 million in 2006, expenditures for crime prevention (defined very broadly) amounted to €2.198 million and €1.887 million was spent on tracking down offenders. These figures do not include the costs of private security firms for businesses, insurance premiums and anti-crime measures undertaken by private citizens. A recent investigation of the Research and Documentation Centre of the Dutch Ministry of Justice found that criminality costs society €9.1 billion per year, which is €570 per capita.

Cohen (1998) calculated that in the US the costs of a *single high-risk youth* engaging in four years of offending as a juvenile and ten years as an adult ranged from $1.7 to $2.3 million (in 1997 dollars). Given that many of these high-rate offenders start their delinquent and disruptive careers early in life, we can safely assume that the cost to society of child delinquents is considerable. Welsh and colleagues (in press) were the first to examine the costs of self-reported offending between age 7 and 17. Most of the costs of offending comes from violence as opposed to property offences. Welsh and colleagues (in press) showed that the costs of early-onset offenders were much higher than those of later-onset offenders, while chronic offenders (those accounting for half of all self-reported offences), compared to other offenders, caused five to eight times higher average victim costs. The above costs do not include the costs of agencies working with at-risk or delinquent youth, or the costs of incarceration and other special services. This makes it clear that the

3 Other, good examples are the US Office of Juvenile Justice and Delinquency Prevention Delinquency Prevention's Model Program Guide <www.dsgonline.com/mpg2.5/mpg_index.htm>, the Promoting Relationships and Eliminating Violence <www.prevnet.ca> in Canada, and the US Center of Disease Control's Guide to Community Preventive Services <www.thecommunityguide.org>.

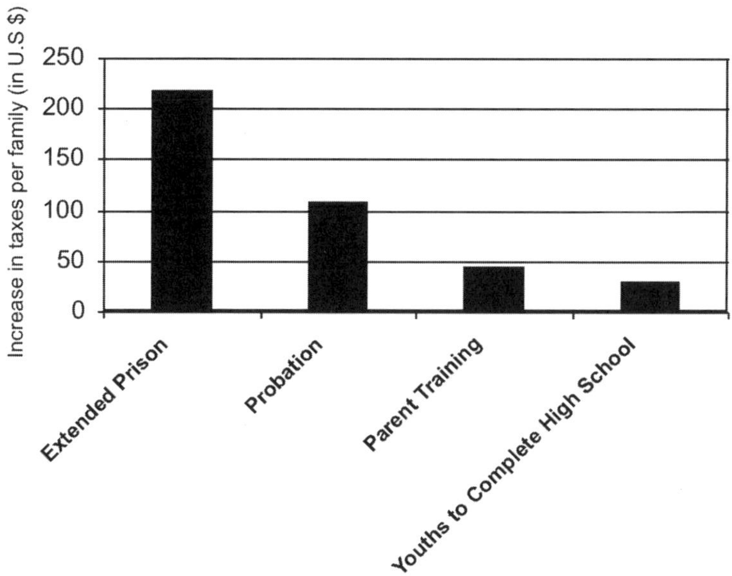

Figure 16.2 Per family tax increase to bring about a 10 per cent decrease in community crime is highest when extended prison is used as prevailing practice, and is much lower when probation, parent training, or young people completing secondary school are used as prevailing practice

Source: Waller 2006.

above costs to society are an underestimate of the real costs of child delinquents. Victim and system costs of child and juvenile delinquents need to be studied in the Netherlands and in other European countries.

Costs to society also depend on the efficacy of prevention and treatment programmes. In a landmark study in the US, Aos and colleagues (2001, 2004) calculated that effective programmes for juvenile offenders may have net benefits (benefits minus costs) ranging from $1,900 to $31,200 per youth, whereas non-effective programmes had negative 'benefits' ranging from -$408 to -$12,478 per youth. In the Netherlands, such a cost-benefit approach to the problem of young offenders and children with serious problems has yet to emerge.

Yet another way of looking at crime reduction is to pose the question of what taxpayers might expect if they were asked to pay higher taxes to bring about a reduction in community crime. Waller (2006), using information from the Rand Corporation in California (see Figure 16.2), estimated that a reduction of 10% in community crime could be effected by extended prison sentences, but this strategy of incarceration would cost an average family $220 in extra taxes. In comparison, a 10% reduction in crime could also be effected by probation (at half the cost of increased taxation), or by means of parent training ($45 increase in taxes), or youths completing secondary school ($30 increase in taxes). These figures are likely to be different for the Netherlands or other European countries, but the principle behind them is probably the same: the financial burdens on taxpayers is highest when incarceration is the prevailing practice and lowest when preventive strategies prevail such as parent training and young people completing secondary school. Further, this example illustrates that a modest increase in taxes when used for the prevention of crime is a much better use of tax money than when applied to incarceration.

Why do International Rights and Standards Apply to Children?

Children have special needs which often are distinct from the needs of adults. Several of these special needs are recognised in the UN Convention on the Rights of the Child (CRC), which is the only human rights treaty that contains a description of the overall aims of the administration of justice concerning juvenile offenders. The CRC explicitly recommends (whenever appropriate and desirable) dealing with children who infringe the penal law without resorting to judicial proceedings. In addition, the CRC requires that a variety of non-custodial measures be made available as alternatives to incarceration and institutional care. The CRC states that deprivation of liberty shall be used only as a measure of last resort and for the shortest appropriate period of time. A key concept in the CRC is 'the best interest of the child'. That means that the responsibility of the State Parties to the treaty does not end when alternative non-judicial proceedings and non-custodial alternatives have been developed. The CRC clearly states that these alternatives should serve the best interests of the child. These interests have been articulated in one of the most important goals of the implementation of the CRC: the promotion of the full and harmonious development of the child's personality, talents and mental and physical abilities. In the light of these and other provisions of the CRC, it is obviously not in the best interest of the child to grow up under circumstances that may cause increased and serious risks of becoming involved in delinquency. The CRC Committee is, therefore, of the opinion that States Parties should undertake targeted and systematic measures to prevent juvenile delinquency, and in particular, to prevent that a child becomes a serious and/or chronic offender.

Common Myths Revisited

In Chapter 1, we listed seven common myths about disruptive children and child delinquents. We will now readdress these seven myths and for each add our retort:

- Myth 1: *There is a new and more serious 'breed' of children who become delinquent at a young age.* Retort: There is *no* evidence of a new and more serious 'breed' of children who become delinquent at a young age.
- Myth 2: *Today's child delinquents are destined to become tomorrow's 'hard core' or chronic offenders.* Retort: Today's child delinquents are *not necessarily* destined to become tomorrow's 'hard core' or chronic offenders.
- Myth 3: *Many early problem behaviours are relatively harmless and, therefore, can be safely ignored.* Retort: Although indeed many early problem behaviours of children do not cause great harm, for a proportion of children

persistent or age-atypical disruptive or delinquent behaviours can constitute a stepping-stone to more serious problem behaviour. For that reason, these children should be monitored over time to facilitate the decision by teachers and other adults to seek intervention at an early rather than late stage of deviant development.

- Myth 4: *We can accurately tell which preschoolers will become child delinquents and, subsequently, serious and violent juvenile offenders.* Retort: With current knowledge, we cannot accurately predict which preschoolers will become child delinquents and, subsequently, serious and violent juvenile offenders.
- Myth 5: *Most disruptive and delinquent children will 'grow out' of their problem behaviour.* Retort: Although a proportion of disruptive and delinquent children will grow out of their problem behaviour, this is less so for aggressive children. At this stage of development, screening methods are far from good in forecasting which children will outgrow disruptive behaviours and which children will not. Under these circumstances, it is best to actively prevent children's escalation to more serious behaviours.
- Myth 6: *The implementation of harsh sanctions in the juvenile justice system (incarceration in a detention centre or correctional facility) is effective in reducing child delinquency.* Retort: Harsh sanctions in the juvenile justice system (incarceration in a detention centre or correctional facility) are not known to be effective in reducing child delinquency. They certainly are among the most costly interventions for society and for all taxpayers. Moreover, harsh sanctions run counter to the UN Convention on the Rights of the Child.
- Myth 7: *Going soft on crime by advocating prevention is a waste of resources.* Retort: This is a fallacy. Economic data show that a reduction in community crime can be effected through prevention at a cost for taxpayers that is substantially lower compared to incarceration. Cost-benefit analyses show that several preventive and treatment interventions have a high return on the funds invested. Increasingly, leading researchers advocate prevention as a key method of addressing serious and violent forms of delinquency in society (for example, Farrington & Welsh, 2007; Ferwerda et al., 2006; Greenwood, 2006; Hermanns, Öry & Schrijvers, 2005; Ince et al., 2004; Junger et al., 2007a, 2007b; Junger-Tas, 2001; Van der Laan, 2004; Waller, 2006).

What are High Priority Recommendations for Research?

Research findings to buttress evidence-based decision making by practitioners and policymakers concerning children with disruptive and delinquent behaviour are badly needed. Specifically, knowledge is needed on:

- What are other warning signs signalling a deviant development towards offending at a young age and, eventually, serious and violent forms of delinquency?

- What are developmental pathways towards these outcomes, particularly during the preschool years?
- What are common combinations of risk factors associated with these outcomes?
- What are promotive factors associated with the absence of disruptive child behaviour and the presence of nondelinquency, and what are promotive factors with desistance in disruptive behaviour and child delinquency?
- Which aspects of peer processes increase the probability of later disruptive child behaviour and delinquency?
- What are the best risk-needs assessments and screening methods to be used by the police, juvenile court officers, teachers, mental health officials and child welfare professionals?
- How can the range of effective interventions for child delinquents be expanded?
- What are the most cost-effective interventions?

What Kinds of Annual National or Regional Surveys are Needed?

The proportion of the population in the Netherlands who are children has somewhat increased over the past couple of years (from 1,935,000 10-year-olds in 1995 to 1,973,000 in 2007; Statistisch Jaarboek, 2007). We argue that the rate of child delinquency will increase proportionate to future increases in the size of the population of children. Larger numbers of child delinquents in the population means that communities will experience higher levels of crime spread over several decades as child delinquents achieve their maximum level of delinquency during late adolescence and early adulthood (recall the age-crime curved discussed in Chapter 1). In addition, a larger numbers of child delinquents will mean that service agencies (for example, *Bureau Jeugdzorg* (Youth Care Bureau), *Jeugd GGZ* (Juvenile Mental Health and Addiction Care) and *Jeugdpolitie* (Juvenile Police) in the Netherlands) will see increasing workloads in the future. Increasing the size or number of service agencies in response to larger numbers of child delinquents is costly, but such costs can probably be offset or rendered unnecessary by improved preventive interventions (see Chapter 12).

Even if the population in the Netherlands (or any other country) were to remain constant, crime in the community, including juvenile delinquency, may show secular increases or decreases. There is no dispute that annual crime data for a country are essential for policymakers and planners of services. However, police and other crime statistics mostly cover suspects and/or arrestees aged 12 and older (see, for example, Tonry & Bijleveld, 2007b). For that reason, it is difficult to obtain reliable and valid data regarding prevalence and secular trends of delinquent behaviour of young children in the Netherlands. As a result, we do *not* know in which locations (that is, cities and regions) child delinquents are most prevalent nor do we know how many child delinquents are noted by agencies outside of the justice system in the community but not recorded. Thus, there is a basic lack of knowledge about tomorrow's potential delinquents, which impedes the channelling of resources to early, preventive interventions.

For these reasons, we highly recommend that WODC and/or another Dutch government agency undertake *annual* self-reported delinquency surveys of 8–11-year-olds (in addition to their survey of older youths). Such surveys ideally should also record juveniles' exposure to known risk and promotive factors to better track children's and adolescents' well-being (see, for example, Communities That Care, 2005; Society for Prevention Research, 2004). In addition, it is crucial to have accurate countrywide uniform recording of physical injuries attended to in hospitals and trauma centres to track changes in violent victimisation of young people (as well as to prevent revictimisation of high-risk individuals). The information gathered on an annual basis will be essential to inform policymakers and local decision makers where and when to allocate resources to identify tomorrow's delinquents and prevent serious and violent offending in years to come. However, we argue that policymakers should not make taking action dependent on an observed increase in child delinquency. Instead, they need to focus on creating programmes designed to break the linkage between child delinquency and later chronic, serious and violent forms of delinquency.

Conclusions and their Relevance to Policy

Several countries have new juvenile justice legislation (for example, Canada and the UK) or have such legislation in the making (US). Currently, the effectiveness of legislation to reduce recidivism of child delinquents is far from clear. Legislation in many countries, including the Netherlands, has become more punitive in the application of justice to juveniles (Junger et al., 2007b), as evident from stiffer legal sanctions for child delinquents within the juvenile court system, and increasing numbers of juveniles in institutions and prisons. However, it is unclear to what extent this is appropriate and/or effective for child delinquents. The media, legislators and policymakers all have the responsibility to avoid creating legislation under the influence of crises (Junger et al., 2007b), or rare forms of delinquency involving children as offenders that do not reflect the majority of offences committed by young people. Sherman (2003) argued for a more informed citizenry to surmount legislators' short-term views of crime solutions. Such initiatives are more likely to succeed when supported and maintained by an informed media.

Increasingly evidence-based interventions that have proven efficacy are becoming the norm and are on the agendas of several government departments in the Netherlands (Junger et al., 2007b) and can lead to the weeding-out of ineffective programmes. Although pharmacological studies are required by the government to have information about cost-effectiveness and cost-benefit, this is not a routine requirement for psychosocial interventions, such as the prevention of child delinquency, or treatment interventions for known disruptive or delinquent children. Cost-benefit analyses are needed to increase knowledge about the cost-benefit ratios of different interventions and to weed out interventions that have been implemented for many years but are not cost-effective. We advocate that routine evaluation studies need to be put in place to document and maintain high standards of treatment efficacy and cost-benefits ratios.

In summary, persistent disruptive behaviours and child delinquency are necessary conditions for later serious and violent offending. For that reason, we argue that our efforts to reduce serious forms of juvenile delinquency should not consist of a single-track focus on either known adolescent delinquents or known chronic offenders. We maintain that a dual focus on children with persistent disruptive behaviours *and* child delinquents has several major advantages:

- Both groups at a young age are less likely to be exposed to additional risk factors that are characteristic for such youths at a later age.
- Both groups are less likely to have incurred the many negative social and personal consequences of disruptive and delinquent behaviours persisting over many years.
- Parents of children in both groups probably will be more motivated to participate in preventive as well as treatment interventions in contrast to parents of older children over whom parents have been losing control because of persistent disruptive and delinquent behaviours outside the family home.
- There are effective interventions to reduce both persistent disruptive behaviours and delinquency offences at an early age, which prevent serious, violent and chronic offending in the long run.
- The monetary savings to society of such interventions will be very large, and the reduction of harm to victims can be expected to be enormous.

Appendix 1

A Canadian Programme for Child Delinquents

Christopher J. Koegl, Leena K. Augimeri, Paola Ferrante, Margaret Walsh and Nicola Slater

Child delinquents have received special attention in Canada over the past several decades. Through the *Young Offenders Act* in 1985 in Canada (which was replaced by the *Youth Criminal Justice Act* in 2003) the minimum age of criminal responsibility was established at 12, which means that delinquent children under that age cannot be criminally prosecuted. Provincial and territorial child protection statutes stipulate that delinquent children who are not adequately supervised can be deemed 'in need of protection' and, as such, apprehended. Once under the purview of the child welfare system, families can access a range of remedial services, although there is wide variation across Canada in terms of the extent to which child protection statutes specifically address disruptive and delinquent behaviours committed by young children. There are even greater differences across provinces and territories in terms of the range of services available to children once they enter the child welfare system.

In the years following the implementation of the *Young Offenders Act*, child welfare systems across Canada did not systematically respond to this group of high-risk youths, but maintained their focus on child protection matters and not child delinquency *per se*. In addition, children's mental health services in Canada were not geared towards meeting the specific needs of this population (Augimeri, Koegl & Goldberg, 2001). Also lacking were reliable referral mechanisms to direct at-risk children to appropriate services and risk assessment procedures tailored to the types of issues faced by these children and their families.

In an effort to address these gaps, the Child Development Institute in Toronto began to develop a comprehensive, gender-sensitive approach to respond to children under age 12 in conflict with the law (Figure A.1). The Institute (which is an amalgamation of the former Earlscourt Child and Family Centre and the Crèche Child and Family Centre) is a multi-service, not-for-profit, community-based organisation with a history of over ninety years of working with high-risk, disruptive and delinquent children and their families.

The central features of our approach are as follows:

- referral mechanisms that facilitate direct access to relevant services;
- clinical risk assessment procedures geared toward children in conflict with the law, and
- gender-specific, evidence-based interventions tailored to the needs of this

population of children and their families.

In the sections that follow, we describe these components in reference to supporting research.

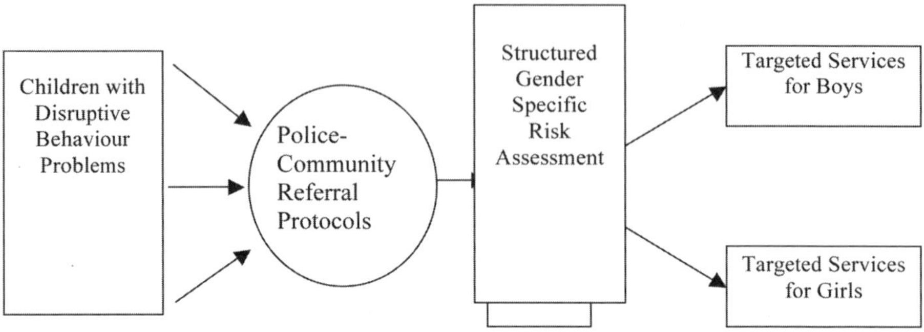

Figure A.1 A comprehensive approach to responding to children in conflict with the law

Referral Mechanisms: Police-Community Referral Protocols for Children under Age 12 in Conflict with the Law

In 1997, the Child Development Institute spearheaded a task force in Toronto to explore the feasibility of developing a community-wide referral mechanism for children under age 12 in conflict with the law. It began with the simple idea that access should be direct (that is, via a single entry point) and timely (that is, contact with potential service providers should be made immediately). Because police officers are usually the first responders when children get into serious trouble, it was decided that they should be integrally linked to any plan that directs at-risk children and their families to specialised mental health services.

With no legal authority under the Canadian *Criminal Code* to initiate formal proceedings based on a child's misbehaviour, early research on the police response to these children revealed that the police typically return children to their parents, or in more serious cases, refer families to child protection authorities or community-based agencies providing general programmes (Augimeri, Goldberg & Koegl, 1999). The absence of formal police policies and procedures across Canada with respect to handling this population of young people (Augimeri et al., 1999) was considered undesirable as it means that some children and their families will not have equitable access to evidence-based programmes. In addition, not having a single-entry access point also makes it difficult to gauge the extent of the problem as there is no primary organisation monitoring the number or severity of referrals. This point is particularly relevant in the context of developing community-level crime prevention strategies. It is often important to understand at the outset the number of young children who are at risk of becoming adolescent or adult criminal offenders. By having a centralised entry point, the volume of referrals can be monitored over time.

To overcome these limitations, the Child Development Institute worked with the Toronto Police Service and other organisations to develop a city-wide protocol. The first of its kind in Canada, this community mobilisation project brought together the Toronto Police and Fire Services, child protection authorities, school boards, children's mental health and other child service agencies to establish a single-entry access point through a Central Intake Line housed at the Child Development Institute. Signed on 1 February 1999, this Protocol mandates that the fifteen participating organisations make referrals to the Child Development Institute within forty-eight hours, which – if the family agrees to participate – triggers a more in-depth clinical assessment within five working days.

From the beginning, however, it became clear that the Protocol is a 'living agreement' in that in order to assess its effectiveness and maintain a steady flow of referrals, there must be constant communication and coordination among Protocol stakeholders. In the nine years that the Protocol has been in place, we have been able to identify a number of key ingredients and challenges associated with such an endeavour. Specifically, we have learned that there needs to be:

1. *A protocol champion*, or a person within a lead organisation who coordinates and corresponds with partnering agencies to: a) assess and monitor the volume of referrals, b) determine whether children are being admitted into services, c) inform referral sources about the status of referrals (for example, whether families followed through with treatment), d) determine whether partnering organisations are actively participating in the referral process, and e) ensure that staff are adequately trained to provide services. The protocol champion should also be in a position to mobilize local stakeholders and resources, and secure external funding when needed to support its continued development.
2. *A protocol marketing strategy*, which ensures that front-line personnel within participating organisations (that is, those most likely to encounter at-risk children) are aware of the protocol and know how to make a referral through the Central Intake Line. For example, in Toronto, a Protocol poster was widely distributed to elementary schools, community centres, police and fire stations, child welfare offices and children's mental health centres to advertise the Protocol. We learned, however, that many of these posters were either never displayed or were removed over time. This led us to extend our marketing efforts beyond the poster itself to key personnel within the community who occupied positions of influence, and who could ensure that their staff would become aware of the Central Intake Line.
3. *A protocol for ongoing dialogue between the referral source and service provider.* Our normal practice with the Toronto Police Service is to inform referring officers about the status of their referrals. In the absence of providing this information, we have found that there is a tendency for officers – especially in cases where the family does not pursue treatment – to become cynical about the efficacy of the Protocol, which has historically led to a reduction in referrals.

Two phases of evaluation indicate that the Toronto Protocol has helped to seal a significant crack in the system by bringing organisations together to serve this specific population of young people. From these positive evaluations, and the fact that protocol costs are relatively low, the protocol model has been subsequently replicated in eight other communities across Canada, which includes a province-wide protocol in Manitoba. With these referral mechanisms in place, it is now possible for any child in these communities to access specialised services in a timely fashion based on an assessment of his or her unique risk factors and needs. In the following section, we describe two gender-specific tools that were designed specifically to assist with the assessments. Researchers and practitioners at the Child Development Institute were the first to develop comprehensive psychosocial risk assessment tools specifically focused on young children in trouble with the law.

Gender-Specific Childhood Risk Assessment Tools

Early work by Loeber (1982, 1990, 1991) and CDI researchers (Day 1998; Day & Hunt, 1996) helped to shape our thinking as we began to develop a structured risk assessment scheme for young children. Our first attempt at an assessment list consisted of fifty-three items (Augimeri & Levene, 1994, 1997), which was later condensed into twenty factors, each of which was scored on a three-point scale (0–not present, 1–possibly present, 2–definitely present). This format was adapted from other structured clinical guides such as the Hare Psychopathy Checklist-Revised (Hare, 1991) and the HCR-20 (Webster et al., 1997).

Fairly early in the development process, it became apparent that separate tools for boys and girls were needed, as it was important to consider that childhood risk factors may not be the same or may operate differently for boys and girls across developmental stages (Moffitt et al., 2001). Accordingly, we first began working on a draft version of the tool, dedicated specifically to the assessment of potential for disruptive and delinquent behaviours in boys (Augimeri et al., 1998). Version 2 of the EARL-20B (*Early Assessment Risk List for Boys*) was published in 2001 (Augimeri et al., 2001) after an extensive literature review and consultation with leading experts in the field. Soon after the release of Version 2, we published a parallel Consultation, Version 1 of the *Early Assessment Risk List for Girls* (EARL-21G; Levene et al., 2001). Most of the EARL-21G item headings parallel the EARL-20B headings, although the content of items and coding guidelines differ in as much as the research literature revealed gender differences in the manifestation and influence of individual risk factors. Two distinct items, *Caregiver-Daughter Interaction* and *Sexual Development*, were added, and one item – *Authority Contact* – was subsumed under *Antisocial Behaviour* to yield a 21-item tool for girls. Table A.1 lists the items included in the *Early Assessment Risk List for Boys* (EARL-20B, Version 2) and the *Early Assessment Risk List for Girls* (EARL-21G, Version 1).

Table A.1 Items in the early assessment risk list for boys and girls

Family (F) Items	Child (C) Items	Responsivity (R) Items
Household Circumstances	Developmental Problems	Family Responsivity
Caregiver Continuity	Onset of Behavioural Difficulties	Child Responsivity
Supports	Abuse/Neglect/Trauma	
Stressors	Hyperactivity/Impulsivity/ Attention Deficits (HIA)	
Parenting Style	Likeability	
Antisocial Values and Conduct	Peer Socialisation	
Caregiver-Daughter Interaction (*)	Academic Performance	
	Neighbourhood	
	Authority Contact (+)	
	Antisocial Attitudes	
	Antisocial Behaviour	
	Coping Ability	
	Sexual Development (*)	

Note: (+) Item specific to the EARL-20B; (*) Item specific to the EARL-21G.

Research on the EARL-20B

In moving the EARL-20B from Version 1 to Version 2, it was necessary to evolve the tool within a research context so that basic psychometric properties such as reliability could be established. To do this, our first study of the EARL-20B, Version 1 measured the basic inter-rater reliability through a prospective study of twenty-one boys and their families admitted into the SNAP® Under 12 Outreach Project (ORP; more fully described below). Results showed moderate-to-good inter-rater agreement based on the total score (Hrynkiw-Augimeri, 1998). Qualitative findings further suggested that the tool was especially helpful in providing clinicians 'with a thorough assessment procedure, a guide to gear the treatment interventions, and a barometer to evaluate whether a child was still considered high-risk at post intervention' (Hrynkiw-Augimeri, 1998, p. 31).

As part of a more stringent evaluation, we tested the reliability and predictive validity of the EARL-20B through a follow-up of a large sample of ORP-treated children (Hrynkiw-Augimeri, 2005). Files of 379 boys who received the ORP between 1985 and 1999 were retrospectively coded using Version 1 of the EARL-20B (120 of which were common files to assess reliability). Results from this study revealed a highly acceptable level of correspondence between the three raters with intra-class correlation coefficients ranging from .79 to .97. To assess validity, a search of official police records was used to determine whether each study child had subsequently committed criminal acts. Using a median-split based on the distribution of total scores, chi-squared analyses revealed that boys scoring high on the EARL-20B were statistically more likely to have accumulated one or more criminal convictions than those who had a low EARL-20B score over the eight-year follow-up study period.

External evaluations of the EARL-20B, Version 2, have yielded similarly encouraging findings using a variety of clinician-derived measures of disruptive behaviours. Researchers tested the inter-rater reliability of Version 2 with children referred to seven child and adolescent psychiatric units across Sweden (Enebrink et al., 2001). Kappa statistics indicated good agreement for most of the individual EARL-20B items (mean=.62, range=.30–.87), whereas intraclass correlation coefficients for Total, Child and Family subscale scores indicated excellent agreement (.90–.92). Enebrink, Långström Hultén and Gumpert (2006) extended the scope of this study to nine child psychiatric clinics in mid-Sweden. Again, good inter-rater reliability was achieved for most of the individual EARL-20B items (average=.62), and excellent inter-rater agreement for the EARL-20B total score (.92).

The predictive validity of the EARL-20B was also assessed prospectively by the same researchers for a sample of seventy-six clinic-referred children (Enebrink, Långström & Gumpert, 2006). An examination of baseline, six-month and thirty-month follow-up assessments of reactive and proactive aggression and disruptive behaviours (conduct problems and DSM-IV Conduct Disorder) revealed that the EARL-20B was more consistently and strongly associated with these outcomes compared to unstructured (non-EARL-20B) clinical evaluations, providing strong support for its use as a clinical decision-enhancing tool.

Research on the EARL-21G

To date, a number of studies have been completed on the EARL-21G – all of which have produced similar positive findings to the EARL-20B in terms of the clinical utility, reliability and validity of the tool. The first of these studies (Levene et al., 2004) was a retrospective examination of the reliability and validity of the EARL-21G. Like the previously mentioned retrospective study for boys, a search of criminal records was performed in order to determine long-term involvement in crime. Intra-class correlation coefficients were calculated for total scores derived from three coders who assessed thirty common files.

Encouragingly, moderate-to-high agreement between raters was found, with statistically significant positive Pearson correlations of .64, .65 and .84, and intra-class correlation coefficients of .67 (single measure) and .86 (average measure). In terms of official delinquency, total scores derived for sixty-seven files were used to divide the sample at the median to compare the prevalence of offending between the bottom and top ends of the distribution. Official conviction data showed that, overall, only eighteen out of sixty-seven (27%) of the girls were found guilty of committing an offence at follow-up, and although higher EARL-21G scores were related to more offending (34% versus 20%) the difference between the two groups failed to reach statistical significance.

We subsequently repeated the inter-rater reliability coding exercise prospectively using seven clinicians who rated twelve common case files (see Levene et al., 2004).

In this study, a higher rate of agreement was achieved with an average Pearson correlation of .81 and intra-class correlation coefficients of .80 (single measure) and .96 (average measure). All correlations were significant at or beyond the 0.01 level.

With at least some evidence to suggest that the EARL-21G is a reliable and valid index of risk, Child Development Institute researchers began to explore the relationship between individual and overall risk scores and responsiveness to treatment (Walsh et al., 2007; Yuile et al., 2007). For these studies, a team of researchers and clinicians generated pre-admission EARL-21G profiles for a total of 162 girls who received the SNAP® Girls Connection. Behaviour symptoms were assessed by teachers and parents (using the Child Behaviour Checklist and Teacher Report Form; Achenbach, 1991, 2001) at admission, post-treatment, and at six, twelve and eighteen-month follow-up intervals. Mixed model analyses were used to investigate the association between behavioural assessments and the EARL-21G total score and specific Child (for example, Abuse/Neglect/Trauma, Peer Socialization, Sexual Development) Family (for example, Stressors, Parenting style, Caregiver-Daughter Interaction) and Responsivity risk factors. This analysis showed that total EARL-21G scores predicted problem behaviours at admission and treatment outcomes. Girls with high total-risk scores tended to show lower levels of change during treatment than girls with low total-risk scores. Moreover, ten individual risk factors significantly predicted elevated problem behaviours at admission: Supports, Parenting Style, Caregiver-Daughter Interaction, Antisocial Values and Conduct, Abuse/Neglect/Trauma, Hyperactivity/Impulsivity/Attention Deficits, Peer Socialization, Academic Performance, Sexual Development and Coping Ability. Girls who scored high on the gender-specific EARL-21G factor, Sexual Development, displayed particularly complex constellations of risk and less responsiveness to treatment.

The SNAP® Under 12 Outreach Project for Boys & the SNAP® Girls Connection

The cornerstone of the clinical programmes at the Child Development Institute that are offered to children with conduct problems is SNAP® (Stop Now And Plan). This cognitive-behavioural, self-control and problem-solving programme was developed in the late 1970s by the former Earlscourt Child and Family Centre. Under the SNAP umbrella, the Child Development Institute (operating as the former Earlscourt Child and Family Centre) developed two gender-specific, multi-component programmes to respond to children under age 12 in conflict with the law: the SNAP® Under 12 Outreach Project (ORP) and the SNAP® Girls Connection (GC).

Established in 1985, the mandate of the ORP is to serve boys under age 12 who engage in delinquent acts, but do not legally fall under the purview of Canada's *Youth Criminal Justice Act*. Over its twenty years of operation, the ORP has come to be regarded as the most fully developed, longest sustained, empirically based intervention specifically for 'pre-offender' youth under age 12 (Howell, 2003).

The programme consists of five key components:

1. a SNAP Children's Group – a structured group that teaches boys impulse

control skills through the use of SNAP
2. a concurrent SNAP Parent Group that teaches parents effective child management strategies;
3. one-on-one Family Counselling based on 'Stop Now and Plan Parenting' or SNAPP;
4. Individual Befriending for boys who are not connected with positive structured activities in their community and require extra support, and
5. Academic Tutoring to assist boys who are not performing at their age-appropriate grade level at school.

Other components of the programme that are deployed where appropriate include school advocacy and teacher consultation, victim restitution, and a Monday Night Club for high-risk boys who have completed the SNAP Children's Group but still require support. In addition, a Leaders-In-Training (LIT) programme is available to boys over 12 who still require support as they enter into their teenage years. Based on an assessment of their unique treatment needs, ORP children and families can access a range of these components. However, the two core components that are offered to all children and their families are the twelve-week child and parent SNAP groups.

The sister programme of the ORP, the SNAP Girls Connection (GC), began in 1996 when preliminary assessments of the then co-ed ORP groups revealed that the programme was not producing the same strong, positive outcomes for girls as it was for boys. Over its relatively short history, the GC has established itself as the most advanced gender-specific intervention for girls under age 12 who are in conflict with the law (Pepler, Walsh & Levene, 2004). Like the ORP, two core components of the GC are the SNAP Children's Group, and a concurrent SNAP Parent Group. Upon completion of these components, girls over 8 years of age and their mothers may also participate in a third core component: Girls Growing up Healthy (GGUH). This group for mothers and daughters focuses on relationship building and includes such topics as physical and sexual health, puberty, female role models and girls in the media, and intimate relationships. Other program components such as Individual Befriending, Academic Tutoring, one-on-one Family Counselling and the LIT programme are also made available, as needed.

Both the ORP and the GC were created with reference to the scientific literature on what works with children displaying clinical levels of problem behaviours. The programmes are fully manualised (Levene, 2003; Earlscourt Child and Family Centre, 2001a; 2001b), with complete logic models, and are in various stages of replication in Canada, the US and several countries in Europe. The target population served by these programmes is children who, according to clinical assessments, engage in above average levels of aggressive, destructive, and/or other disruptive behaviours. All admitted children have problem behaviours that place them in the top 2% of all children of similar age and gender, and/or have had recent contact with the police resulting from their own misbehaviour. Typical referral behaviours include stealing, lying, mischief and vandalism, aggression, assault, bullying and truancy. A significant proportion of these children also experience academic difficulties which place them at risk of school problem behaviours or early school dropout. Primary referral sources to both programmes include the police, schools, child protection agencies, parents and other medical professionals.

Since the establishment of these interventions, the ORP and the GC have been subject to ongoing evaluations, in addition to discrete research projects aimed at measuring their effectiveness. The following sections present some of the key findings from research studies conducted at Child Development Institute. For more detailed accounts, readers are referred to the original studies cited below.

Research on the SNAP® Under 12 Outreach Project (ORP)

Hrynkiw-Augimeri, Pepler and Goldberg (1993) first established programme effectiveness by gathering data on ORP children at admission, discharge, and at six- and twelve-month follow-up intervals using the Child Behaviour Checklist (CBCL; Achenbach & Edelbrock, 1983). The study was based on an initial sample of 104 children (88 boys and 16 girls) who were admitted to the ORP between 1985 and 1988. Comparisons between admission and discharge T-scores on Internalising, Externalising, Social Competence and Total CBCL scales revealed statistically significant improvements, and these treatment gains were maintained over the two follow-up periods. There was a fair degree of attrition from admission to the follow-up assessments. However, analysis of CBCL admission scores comparing study participants to drop-outs revealed no significant differences between the two groups suggesting that the attrition was not selective. Results also indicated that, after being discharged from the ORP, only one in five of the children had further contact with the police. Although encouraging, the overall positive results of this preliminary study could not necessarily be attributed to the programme due to the absence of comparable data for an untreated control group.

To overcome this limitation, a more stringent evaluation of the ORP was undertaken using a randomised controlled trial (see Augimeri, Farrington, Koegl & Day, 2007; Day & Hrynkiw-Augimeri, 1996). Sixteen pairs of children were matched on age, sex and severity of delinquency at admission and then randomly assigned to receive the ORP programme (the immediate treatment group or ITG) or to a group consisting of a non-clinical, recreation programme called the Cool Runners Club (the delayed treatment group, or DTG). At the end of three months, the groups were counterbalanced so that the DTG received the ORP programme and vice versa. Measures were administered pre-admission, at three months (that is, before the groups switched over), at six months (after both groups received the ORP and Cool Runners Club), at twelve months (first follow-up) and at eighteen months (second follow-up) post-admission.

Overall, the results of the study provided excellent support for the effectiveness of the ORP. Compared to the DTG, the ITG showed significant improvements on child problem behaviours as measured by the CBCL from pre- to post-intervention (that is, after three months). Moreover, these treatment gains were maintained over the duration of the study as nearly 60% of the ITG children who had scored in the clinical range of the Externalising problem behaviour subscale of CBCL pre-intervention scored in the normal range at second follow-up (in comparison, only one-third of the DTG children scored in the normal range at this time). In terms of the Aggression and Delinquency subscales, for those differences that were statistically significant, effect sizes were large, ranging from 0.79 to 1.19. Significant decreases were also observed for the ITG in children's self-reported delinquency, and parenting attitudes, parenting self-efficacy and parental stress.

When the ORP intervention was applied to the DTG children, it was not found to yield comparable positive changes on the self-report and parent-rated measures. It was suspected at that time that families of children in the DTG (who did not immediately receive clinical treatment) became frustrated at their children's lack of improvement and therefore became less willing to engage in treatment when the ORP programme was offered during the second session. Unfortunately, the programme also underwent concurrent staffing changes, which led to the delivery of a less intensive version of the ORP to the DTG. When we assessed treatment intensity through a secondary analysis of the data (Augimeri et al., 2007), we found that DTG children and their families participated in significantly fewer of the SNAP Children's and Parent Groups, individual family counselling, and academic tutoring sessions. Receiving less intensive, delayed treatment, therefore, appeared to produce a 'too little too late' effect, which limited the overall impact of the intervention for the DTG. While undesirable in one sense, this finding helped us to better grasp the importance of providing treatment in a timely fashion, and in an amount sufficient to produce both short-term and sustained changes.

Results from this study encouraged us to continue looking at treatment intensity in relation to the ORP, but we were also curious to understand whether client characteristics such as the age and sex of participating children were important to consider when assessing the program's overall effectiveness (Koegl, Farrington, Augimeri & Day 2008). Building upon the dataset created during the previous randomised controlled trial, we added a further fifty children who had received the ORP between 1986 and 1994. This group was similarly matched on age, sex and severity of delinquency at admission to be comparable to the ITG and DTG. Analysis of other demographic variables (that is, number of presenting problems, prior police contact and family composition) did not reveal differences between the three groups at admission. To examine the long-term effectiveness of the program, we performed a national search of criminal records for the entire sample up to each child's eighteenth birthday to see whether there were differences between the three groups in terms of their official involvement in crime.

For this analysis, only pre-to-post changes on raw score CBCL derived measures of Delinquency (based on ten items), Major Aggression (ten items) and Minor Aggression (nine items) were assessed (see Koegl et al., 2008). Accordingly, the DTG functioned as a pure control group (in that they did not receive the ORP between the two measurement intervals) against which two other treated groups could be compared. In examining pre-to-post changes, we found strong evidence in support of the effectiveness of the ORP. Specifically, the matched group showed significant decreases on all outcome measures, while the ITG decreased significantly in terms of Delinquency and Major Aggression, but showed a non-significant decrease in terms of Minor Aggression (P=0.10). No treatment gains were observed for the control group.

We also found evidence that the effects of the ORP treatment varied by age, sex and treatment intensity. Older children (aged 10–11) showed slightly larger decreases in delinquent behaviour compared to younger children (aged 6–9). Girls also showed larger decreases in Delinquency subscale of the CBCL compared to boys (who also decreased significantly), but the girls did not exhibit any changes in terms of either measure of Aggression, in contrast to the boys who demonstrated statistically significant improvements. To examine the role of treatment intensity, we correlated change scores for the CBCL outcome measures with the number of sessions received for each of five ORP service components (that is, SNAP Children's Groups, SNAP Parent Groups, Individual Befriending, Academic Tutoring and Individual Family Counselling Sessions). Results indicated that decreases in Delinquency were significantly related to the number of SNAP Children's Group and Family Counselling sessions received (r=.25 and .19, respectively; p<0.05), while reductions in Minor Aggression were associated with greater involvement in SNAP Children's Group sessions (r=.30, p<0.01). We also found that participation in SNAP Children's Group sessions was negatively related to long-term involvement in delinquency. Of those children who attended nine or more of these sessions, 36.1% were found guilty of at least one crime by their eighteenth birthday compared to 68.4% of children who attended eight or less sessions. Thus, as the central component of the ORP program, it appears that greater participation in the SNAP Children's Group may have played a role in preventing some children from becoming involved in delinquency during adolescence.

The influence of treatment intensity as a moderator of ORP outcomes was further explored in a recent study by Augimeri and colleagues (2006). This analysis was based on a large sample of 379 boys who had gone through the ORP programme during the period 1985–99 and who were eligible for youth court contact at the time of the study (for a description of the sample, see Augimeri, 2005). Outcome variables included T-scores on the Delinquency subscale of the CBCL obtained prior to admission to the ORP, post-treatment (three months following admission) and six months post-treatment, in addition to a dichotomous variable that was coded to indicate the presence or absence of a finding of guilt for one or more offences during the follow-up period. Retrospectively rated EARL-20B scores were also available for the 379 cases, making it possible to explore how risk might be related to treatment intensity and the two outcome variables. Our plan was to first examine the overall effect of the programme and then compare boys who had received an 'enhanced' version of the ORP (defined as receiving one or more Individual Befriending sessions) to boys who received a 'standard' version of the programme (that is, no Individual Befriending sessions). A growth-mixture model approach was employed to statistically classify boys, based on their CBCL scores, into high-, medium- and low-risk delinquency classes.

Overall, analyses indicated that the ORP was an effective program. Parent-reported levels of delinquency decreased significantly from clinical to non-clinical levels following treatment. Although there were further decreases for all three groups of boys at follow-up, the programme appeared to work best for boys with moderate levels of delinquency. The results also show that EARL-20B risk factors significantly predicted initial delinquency levels, suggesting that the tool could be used to make clinical decisions about the type and amount of services offered to children with conduct problems. This investigation also revealed that the enhanced ORP yielded an additional positive treatment effect, which was particularly important for boys with high levels of delinquency. In fact, high-delinquency boys who did not receive an enhanced version of the ORP got slightly, but not significantly, worse following treatment.

The findings from the series of studies summarised above and replication site studies (for example, Lipman et al., 2008) provide strong support for the effectiveness of the SNAP Under 12 Outreach Project. In general, we can be confident that the programme lowers aggression and delinquent behaviours in the short term, with evidence that these effects can be sustained over the intermediate future. There is also some indication that the programme may produce long-term changes, such as preventing delinquency during adolescence and adulthood, although more work is clearly needed to isolate the ORP as the key factor preventing this type of negative outcome.

Research on the SNAP® Girls Connection (GC)

The first evaluation of the SNAP® Girls Connection was initiated almost immediately after the programme was established in 1996. Using a qualitative design, sixteen girls and their families who received treatment between 1997 and 1999 participated in the study (Levene, Madsen & Pepler, 2005). The purpose of the research was to better understand the lives of young girls with pronounced disruptive behaviour to ensure that the treatment programme was addressing key clinical issues. A series of semi-structured interviews were completed with the girls and their caregivers, which were then transcribed and coded to uncover prominent themes. Most commonly identified across the sample were six potential risk factors: early childhood difficulties, strained family relationships, abuse, academic and behavioural difficulties at school, peer rejection and negative community experience. Early difficulties, including risk factors such as physical, temperamental and constitutional problems characterised all of the girls participating in the study. Complex family relationships, most often characterised by conflicted mother-daughter interactions and the longing for relationships with absent fathers also emerged as salient themes. Taken together, the findings from this study helped us to better understand the complexity of issues young girls face as they contend with early childhood adversity, and the importance of attending to strained caregiver-daughter interactions during the clinical process.

A more traditional evaluation of the GC programme was conducted for 98 of the 250 girls who were admitted during the period 1996–2000 – the first four years of the programme's operation (Walsh, Pepler & Levene, 2002). The analysis examined behavioural change comparing admission and six-month (N=72) and twelve-month (N=58) externalising problem behaviour scores using the Standardized Client Information System, a measure based on the CBCL (Offord & Boyle, 1996). At both follow-up periods, girls showed significant improvement in terms of externalising problem behaviours, which is an aggregation of conduct and oppositional behaviours. The girls also displayed an increase in social skills: statistically significant improvements from admission to the six-month follow-up were found, and these improvements were maintained at twelve months. Effect sizes for the change in externalising problem behaviours were in the small to medium range (*d*=0.42–0.49), whereas improvement in social relations emerged as a large effect (*d*=0.72).

Using the same retrospective sample, a further exploration of the effectiveness of the GC was subsequently completed by examining the effect of the programme on a wider range of problem behaviours (Pepler, Walsh & Levene, 2004). In this analysis, significant improvements over the two follow-up periods were found on parent ratings of the girls' anger regulation, including angry and resentful behaviours, temper tantrums, and cranky dispositions. There were also significant decreases in aggressive behaviours such as cruelty, bullying and the frequency of physical attacks on others. The frequency of defiant attitudes and behaviours (for example, talking back) over the six-month interval also significantly decreased. Stealing outside the home was the only behaviour in the delinquency and vandalism category which improved from admission to follow-up, although it is worth noting that the baseline prevalence of delinquent behaviour was very low. Girls' prosocial skills, encompassing their relations with both peers and adults, also improved. There were significant improvements over both time intervals in ratings of girls' abilities to wait their turn, avoid fights and get along with friends. Girls also showed improvements in getting along with teachers from admission to six months, getting along with parents from admission to twelve months, and in getting along with family members at both follow-up intervals.

The most recent evaluation of the SNAP Girls Connection was a prospective study of girls referred to the programme between 2002 and 2004 (Pepler et al., 2008). A quasi-experimental design was used to randomly assign referred girls either to immediate treatment in the programme (N=45), or to a wait-list control group (N=35). Both groups were stratified in terms of the severity of girls' problem behaviours at intake. Externalising problem behaviours were assessed at admission, post-treatment, and at six-, twelve- and eighteen-month follow-up intervals using the Child Behaviour Checklist (CBCL; Achenbach & Rescorla, 2001). Prior to the analyses, we tested age, cognitive ability and academic performance, and found that they were not significantly related to problem behaviours prior to or following the treatment phase. Therefore, these variables were dropped as covariates for future analyses. Mixed model analysis was used to assess change in behaviours after treatment and differences between treatment and control groups.

Results indicated a significant treatment effect of the program. In comparing the immediate treatment group to the control group, problem behaviours (for example, aggression, rule breaking, conduct disorder, oppositional defiant disorder and social problems) decreased significantly after girls received the GC intervention. There was also a significant decrease in parental reports of girls' externalising problem behaviours from pre- to post-programme (*d*=0.51), and significantly more of the immediate treatment girls (43%) moved into the non-clinical range on externalising problem behaviours post-treatment compared to controls (17%). We also found that the girls in the immediate treatment group significantly improved in terms of their self-control and cooperation skills. Based on both parent- and child-reported measures, there was also evidence of improved parenting practices and relationship quality in families receiving immediate treatment.

The evaluation period of this study has since been extended in order to obtain additional follow-up information about the girls' behaviour and functioning at home, school and the community. Preliminary analysis of these data suggests stable, sustained treatment effects attributable to the GC. In the future, we hope to learn more about girls' relationships with friends, families and dating partners during adolescence.

In summary, these findings provide an important step forward in our understanding of how to respond clinically to young girls with disruptive behaviours. Moreover, these data are among the first to demonstrate the effectiveness of a gender-sensitive treatment for young girls' aggression and relationship problems that place them in conflict with the law.

Community Implementation of the SNAP® ORP and GC Programme Models

Since the development of the ORP and GC in 1985 and 1996 respectively, these programmes have been replicated within various organisations across North America and Europe. As is the case with any programme, successful replication requires strong commitment by the target organisation to ensure fidelity and sustainability of the programme over the long term. Although not exhaustive, the following is a list of recommendations that address implementation issues encountered over the years as we have worked with organisations to replicate these two models. Specifically:

1. *Replication sites must enter into a formal licensing agreement* – to maximise integrity and fidelity and ensure that the model is being implemented and represented as intended. Furthermore, the license creates a mechanism through which programme updates and related materials can be communicated and transferred.
2. *The organisation's treatment philosophy should be consistent with that of the host organisation* – in order to minimise retraining of staff and facilitate a faster implementation of the model.
3. *The replication site must have a strong track record of collaboration with social service and other relevant stakeholders* (for example, child welfare, police, and schools) – given that these children and their families have complex and diverse needs that require access to a wide range of community resources.
4. *Agencies should allocate full-time staff to operate programmes* – otherwise we have found that it is difficult-to-impossible to sustain a model with high fidelity over time.
5. *Ongoing training and consultation should be built into the implementation plan* – so that staff are thoroughly trained in the model, and are using programme manuals correctly. Ongoing follow-up and consultation is recommended in order to address implementation issues, or to take into account unforeseen clinical realities that may be specific to an organisation's community (for

example, cultural diversity).

6. *Research must be an integral part of the replication* – in order to assess treatment effectiveness, and especially in those cases where there have been local modifications to the model.

Other than initial costs associated with intensive staff training, neither of these programmes require specialised physical space or equipment and can be implemented in most clinical, school, or community settings. In terms of operating the programme, the average cost-per-case varies depending on the number, intensity and duration of service components received, although all children and their parents receive SNAP Child and Parent Groups components. For example, a low-risk child would normally cost around $1,000 (CAD) and would not typically access additional ORP/GC service components over their three-month tenure in the program. A moderate-risk case, enrolled in the programme for approximately six months, would cost roughly $2,500 (CAD) but would also receive family counselling, individual befriending, school advocacy and the benefits of participating in a homework club. A high-risk child would cost $4,500 (CAD) on average, and would receive a higher intensity of the components offered to a moderate-risk child, over a longer period of time (that is, over one year), in addition to continued care groups (offered to the child and their parents) and specialised psychiatric assessment and consultation where indicated.

The typical programme cycle for either one of these programmes is twelve weeks, during which time children and their parents are enrolled in concurrent SNAP Child and Parent Groups. Additional components may be offered over this interval, but usually begin once families have completed the initial groups. The maximum number of children allowed in each group is seven, and there are usually three groups offered during the course of a week (children are assigned to groups based on their age and developmental needs). Accordingly, the programme serves approximately twenty-one families per programme cycle, assuming a staffing constellation that includes a programme manager/coordinator, one full-time family worker, a full-time child worker/group leader, a full-time researcher and one part-time child group leader. Up to three programme cycles can be offered per year, depending on the volume of referrals, the intensity of additional components offered, and the number of families continuing in service after the SNAP Child and Parent Groups have finished.

Summary and Conclusions

In this appendix we have outlined a multi-component approach to respond to children under age 12 in conflict with the law. We described these components – referral, assessment and gender-specific programmes – and their supporting research, which continues to grow and evolve. The importance of establishing reliable, straightforward referral mechanisms cannot be overstated. Navigating disruptive children and their families to the doors of appropriate service providers in the shortest possible time is a crucial step that has been historically overlooked with this particular population of young people. It is hoped that police-community referral protocols can help to minimise the delay in connecting children to evidence-based services. Moreover, it has become increasingly clear that once at-risk children and their families arrive at the doors of service providers, staff must gain a good understanding of their unique histories before effective clinical work can unfold. The Early Assessment Risk Lists are intended to assist clinicians with this task in a scientifically valid way. Lastly, once reliably assessed, it is imperative that children receive empirically sound treatment interventions that address their identified risks and needs. The two model programmes described in this appendix – the SNAP Girls Connection and the SNAP Under 12 Outreach Project - have been shown to reduce disruptive and delinquent behaviours and increase prosocial skills in children under age 12.

As the field increasingly moves toward a more systematic adoption of evidence-based crime prevention approaches, we can no longer respond to at-risk children and their families in a haphazard manner. It should be clear from this chapter that there are effective treatment options available for this important but often forgotten group of children within our communities and formal systems of care.

Bibliography

Achenbach, T. M. (1991). *Manual for the Child Behavior Checklist/4–18 and 1991 Profile*. Burlington, VT: University of Vermont, Department of Psychiatry.

Achenbach, T. M. (1993). *Empirically Based Taxonomy: How to Use Syndromes and Profile Types Derived from the CBCL/4–18, TRF, and YSR (CBCL)*. Burlington: University of Vermont, Department of Psychiatry.

Achenbach, T. M., & Edelbrock, C. (1983). *Manual for the Child Behavior Checklist and Revised Behavior Profile*. Burlington, VT: University Associates in Psychiatry.

Achenbach, T. M., & Rescorla, L.A. (2001). *Manual for the ASEBA School Age Forms and Profile*. Burlington: University of Vermont, Research Center for Children, Youth and Families.

Ackerman, P. T., Newton, J. E. O., McPherson, W. B., Jones, J. G., & Dykman, R. A. (1998). Prevalence of post traumatic stress disorder in three groups of abused children (sexual, physical, and both). *Child Abuse & Neglect*, *22*, 759–74.

Aguilar, B., Sroufe, L. A., Egeland, B., & Carlson, E. (2000). Distinguishing the early-onset/persistent and adolescence-onset antisocial behaviour types: From birth to 16 years. *Development and Psychopathology, 12*, 109–32.

Allen, R. (1993). Responding to youth crime in Norway: Suggestions for England and Wales. *The Howard Journal*, *32*, 99–113.

Allen, R. (1996). *Children and Crime: Taking Responsibility*. London: Institute for Public Policy Research.

Allen, R. (2006). *From Punishment to Problem Solving: A New Approach to Children in Trouble*. London: Centre for Crime and Justice Studies, King's College.

Allport, G. W. (1948). *ABC's of Scapegoating*. New York: Anti-Defamation League of B'nai B'rith.

American Psychiatric Association (1994). *Diagnostic and Statistical Manual of Mental Disorders*. Washington, DC: American Psychiatric Association.

American Psychological Association (1993). *Violence and Youth: Psychology's Response*. Washington, DC: Author.

Anderson, K. E., Lytton, H., & Romney, D. M. (1986). Mothers' interactions with normal and conduct-disordered boys: Who affects whom? *Developmental Psychology*, *22*, 604–609.

Andrews, D. A. (1995). The psychology of criminal conduct and effective treatment. In J. M. McGuire (ed.), *What Works: Reducing Reoffending. Guidelines from Research and Practice* (pp. 35–62). Chichester: Wiley.

Andrews, D. A., & Bonta, J. (2003). *The Psychology of Criminal Conduct*. Cincinnati, OH: Anderson (3rd edn).

Andrews, D. A., I. Zinger, I., R. I. Hoge, R. I., Bonta, J., Gendreau, P., & Cullen, F. T. (1990). Does correctional treatment work? A clinically relevant and psychologically informed meta-analysis. *Criminology*, *28*, 369–417.

Aos, S., Lieb, R., Mayfield, J., Miller, M., & Pennucci, A. (2004). *Benefits and Costs of Prevention and Early Intervention Programs for Youth* (Rep. No. 04-07-3901). Olympia: Washington State Institute for Public Policy.

Aos, S., Phipps, P., Barnoski, R., & Lieb, R. (2001). *The Comparative Costs and Benefits of Programs to Reduce Crime* (Rep. No. 01-05-1201). Olympia: Washington State Institute for Public Policy.

Appel, A.E., & Holden, G.W. (1998). The co-occurrence of spouse and physical child abuse: A review and appraisal. *Journal of Family Psychology*, *12*, 578–99.

Arbeitsgruppe Schulforschung (1980). *Leistung und Versagen* [Success and failure]. München, Germany: Juventa.

Archer, J., & Côté, S. (2005). Sex differences in aggressive behavior: A developmental and evolutionary perspective. In R. E. Tremblay, W. W. Hartup, & J. Archer (eds), *Developmental Origins of Aggression* (pp. 425–43). New York: Guilford Press.

Arseneault, L., Tremblay, R. E., Boulerice, B., & Saucier, J. F. (2002). Obstetrical complications and violent delinquency: Testing two developmental pathways. *Child Development*, *73*, 496–508.

Arseneault, L., Tremblay, R. E., Boulerice, B., Seguin, J. R., & Saucier, J. F. (2000). Minor physical anomalies and family adversity as risk factors for violent delinquency in adolescence. *American Journal of Psychiatry*, *157*, 917–23.

Arthur, M. W., Hawkins, J. D., Pollard, J. A., Catalano, R. F., & Baglioni Jr., A. J. (2002). Measuring risk and protective factors for substance use, delinquency, and other adolescent problem behaviors; the Communities That Care youth survey. *Evaluation Review*, *26*, 575–601.

Asher, S. A., Rose, A. J., & Gabriel, S. W. (2001). Peer rejection in everyday life. In M. R. Leary (ed.), *Interpersonal Rejection* (pp. 105–42). New York: Oxford University Press.

Atzaba-Poria, N., Pike, A., & Barrett, M. (2004). Internalising and externalising problems in middle childhood: A study of Indian (ethnic minority) and English (ethnic majority) children living in Britain. *International Journal of Behavioral Development*, *28*, 449–60.

Augimeri, L. K, Farrington, D. P., Koegl, C. J., & Day, D. M. (2007). The SNAP™ Under 12 Outreach Project: Effects of a community based program for children with conduct problems. *Journal of Child and Family Studies*, 16, 799–807.

Augimeri, L. K., Goldberg, K., & Koegl, C. J. (1999). *Canadian Children Under 12 Committing Offences: Police Protocols*. Toronto: Earlscourt Child and Family Centre.

Augimeri, L. K., Jiang, D., Koegl, C. J., & Carey, J. (2006). *Differential effects of the Under 12 Outreach Project (ORP) associated with client risk & treatment intensity*. Program Evaluation Report. Submitted to the Centre of Excellence for Child and Youth Mental Health at CHEO. Toronto: Earlscourt Child and Family Centre.

Augimeri, L. K., Koegl, C. J., & Goldberg, K. (2001). Children under age 12 years who commit offenses: Canadian legal and treatment approaches. In R. Loeber &

D. P. Farrington (eds), *Child Delinquents: Development, Intervention and Service Needs* (pp. 405–14). Thousand Oaks, CA: Sage.

Augimeri, L. K., Koegl, C. J., Webster, C. D., & Levene, K. S. (2001). *Early Assessment Risk List for Boys. Version 2.* Toronto: Earlscourt Child and Family Centre.

Augimeri, L., & Levene, K. (1994, revised 1997). *Outreach Programme: Risk Factors Associated with Possible Conduct Disorders and Non-Responders.* Toronto: Earlscourt Child and Family Centre.

Augimeri, L. K., Webster, C. D., Koegl, C. J., & Levene, K. S. (1998). *Early Assessment Risk List for Boys, Version 1 Consultation Edition.* Toronto: Earlscourt Child and Family Centre.

Austin, J. (1986). Using early release to relieve prison crowding: a dilemma in public policy. *Crime and Delinquency*, *32*, 404–502.

Baardewijk, Y., Stegge, G. T. M., Andershed, H., Thomaes, S. C. E., Scholte, E. M., & Vermeiren, R. (2007). Measuring psychopathic traits in children through self-report; Initial tests of the Youth Psychopathic Traits Inventory – Child Version.

Babinski, L. M., Hartsough, C. S., & Lambert, N. M. (2001). A comparison of self-report of criminal involvement and official arrest records. *Aggressive Behavior*, *27*, 44–54.

Bachman, J. G., O'Malley, P. M., & Johnston, J. (1978). *Youth in Transition, Volume 6.* Ann Arbor: University of Michigan Institute for Social Research.

Baerveldt, C. (1990). *De school: Broedplaats of Broeinest? Een vergelijkend onderzoek naar de rol van de school bij de bestrijding en verspreiding van kleine criminaliteit van leerlingen* [The school: breeding ground or hotbed? A comparative study of schools and their influence on the delinquency of pupils]. The Hague: Gouda Quint.

Bailey, S (2002). Violent children: a framework for assessment. *Advances in Psychiatric Treatment*, *8*, 97–106.

Baldry, A. C., & Farrington, D. P. (2007). Effectiveness of programs to prevent school bullying. *Victims and Offenders*, *2*, 183–204.

Banaschewski, T., Hollis, C., Oosterlaan, J., Roeyers, H., Rubia, K., Willcutt, E., & Taylor, E. (2005). Towards an understanding of unique and shared pathways in the psychopathophysiology of ADHD. *Developmental Science*, *8*, 132–40.

Bancroft, L., & Silverman, J. G. (2002). *The Batterer as Parent: Addressing the Impact of Domestic Violence on Family Dynamics.* Thousand Oaks, CA: Sage.

Bank, L., Forgatch, M. S., Patterson, G. S. & Fetrow, R. A. (1993). Parenting practices of single mothers: Mediators of negative contextual factors. *Journal of Marriage and the Family*, *55*, 371–84.

Bardone, A. M., Moffitt, T. E., Caspi, A., Dickson, N., Stanton, W. R., & Silva, P. A. (1998). Adult physical health outcomes of adolescent girls with conduct disorder, depression, and anxiety. *Journal of the American Academy of Child and Adolescent Psychiatry*, *37*, 594–601.

Barkley, R. A. (1997). Behavioural inhibition, sustained attention, and executive functions: Constructing a unifying theory of ADHD. *Psychological Bulletin*, *121*, 65–94.

Barling, J., MacEwen, K. E., & Nolte, M. L. (1993). Homemaker role experiences affect toddler behaviors via maternal well-being and parenting behavior. *Journal of Abnormal Child Psychology*, *21*, 213–29.

Barrish, H. H., Saunders, M., & Wolfe, M. D. (1969). Good Behavior Game: effects of individual contingencies for group consequences and disruptive behavior in the classroom. *Journal of Applied Behavioral Analysis*, *2*, 119–24.

Bartels, M., van den Oord, E. J., Hudziak, J. J., Rietveld, M. J., van Beijsterveldt, C. E., & Boomsma, D. I. (2004). Genetic and environmental mechanisms underlying stability and change in problem behaviors at ages 3, 7, 10, and 12. *Developmental Psychology*, *40*, 852–67.

Bastiaansen, D., Koot, H. M., Ferdinand, R. F., & Verhulst, F. C. (2004). Quality of life in children with psychiatric disorders: Self, parent, and clinician report. *Journal of the American Academy of Child and Adolescent Psychiatry*, *43*, 221–30.

Battin-Pearson, S. R., Thornberry, T. P., Hawkins, J. D., & Krohn, M. D. (1998). *Gang Membership, Delinquent Peers, and Delinquent Behavior*. Washington, DC: Department of Justice, Office of Justice Programs, Office of Juvenile Justice and Delinquency Prevention.

Baumrind, D. (1971). Current patterns of parental authority. *Developmental Psychology*, *4*, 1–103.

Beauchaine, T. P., Katkin, E. S., Strassberg, Z., & Snarr, J. (2001). Disinhibitory psychopathology in male adolescents: Discriminating conduct disorder from attention-deficit/hyperactivity disorder through concurrent assessment of multiple autonomic states. *Journal of Abnormal Psychology*, *110*, 610–24.

Behan, J., & Carr, A. (2000). Oppositional defiant disorder. In A. Carr (ed.), *What Works with Children and Adolescents? A Critical Review of Psychological Interventions with Children, Adolescents and their Families* (pp. 102–30). London & New York: Routledge.

Beirn, R., Kinsey, D. C., & McGinn, N. F. (1972). Antecedents and consequences of early school leaving. *Educational Documentation and Information*, *46*, 1–116.

Beitchman, J., Zucker, K., Hood, J., Da Costa, G., & Akman, D. (1991). A review of the short-term effects of child sexual abuse. *Child Abuse & Neglect*, *15*, 537–56.

Beke, B. M. W. A., & Kleiman, W. M. (1993). *De harde kern in beeld. Jongeren en geweldscriminaliteit* [Chronic offenders: Juveniles and violence]. Utrecht: SWP.

Bell, R. G., & Chapman, M. (1986). Child effects in studies using experimental or brief longitudinal approaches to socialization. *Developmental Psychology*, *22*, 595–603.

Bell, R. Q. (1968). A reinterpretation of the direction of effects in studies of socialization. *Psychological Review*, *75*, 81–95.

Belsky, J. (1984). The determinants of parenting: A process model. *Child Development*, *55*, 83–96.

Belsky, J. (1997). Variation in the susceptibility to environmental influence: An evolutionary argument. *Psychological Inquiry*, *8*, 182–6.

Belsky, J., & Barends, N. (2002). Personality and parenting. In M. H. Bornstein (ed.), *Handbook of Parenting:* Vol. 3. *Being and Becoming a Parent* (2nd edn, pp. 415–38). Mahwah, NJ: Erlbaum.

Belsky, J., Crnic, K., & Woodworth, S. (1995). Personality and parenting: Exploring the mediating role of transient mood and daily hassles. *Journal of Personality*, *63*, 905–29.

Bengi-Arslan, L., Verhulst, F. C., van der Ende, J., & Erol, N. (1997). Understanding childhood (problem) behaviors from a cultural perspective: comparison of problem behaviors and competencies in Turkish immigrant, Turkish and Dutch children. *Social Psychiatry and Psychiatric Epidemiology*, *32*, 477–84.

Bennathan, M., & Boxall, M. (1996). *Effective Intervention in Primary Schools. Nurture Groups.* London: David Fulton.

Bennet, D. S., & Gibbons, T. A. (2000). Efficacy of child cognitive-behavioral interventions for antisocial behanvior: a meta-analysis. *Child & Family Behavior Therapy*, *22*, 1–15.

Berger, M. (ed.) (2006). *IOG-Erger Voorkomen, de Methodiekhandleiding* [IOG – Prevention of bad outcomes, Methods manual]. Utrecht/Lichtenvoorde: NIZW & Forum.

Bernburg, J. G., Krohn, M. D., & Rivera, C. J. (2006). Official labeling, criminal embeddedness, and subsequent delinquency: a longitudinal test of labeling theory. *Journal of Research in Crime and Delinquency*, *43*, 67–88.

Bhabra, S., Hill, E., & Ghate, D. (2004). *Safer School Partnerships: National Evaluation of the Safer School Partnerships Programme.* London: Youth Justice Board for England and Wales/DfES.

Biederman, J., Milberger, S., Faraone, S. V., Kiely, K., Guite, J., Mick, E., Ablon, S., Warburton, R., & Reed, E. (1995). Family environment risk factors for attention-deficit hyperactivity disorder: A test of Rutter's indicators of adversity. *Archives of General Psychiatry*, *52*, 464–70.

Bierman, K. L., Coie, J. D., Dodge, K. A., Greenberg, M. T., Lochman, J. E., McMahon, R. J., & Pinderhughes, E. E. (2002). Using the Fast Track randomized prevention trial to test the early-starter model of the development of serious conduct problems. *Development and Psychopathology*, *14*, 925–43.

Blair, R. J. R. (2001). Neurocognitive models of aggression, the antisocial personality disorders, and psychopathy. *Journal of Neurology Neurosurgery and Psychiatry*, *71*, 727–31.

Blair, R. J. R., Colledge, E., & Mitchell, D. G. V. (2001). Somatic markers and response reversal: Is there orbitofrontal cortex dysfunction in boys with psychopathic tendencies? *Journal of Abnormal Child Psychology*, *29*, 499–511.

Bleichrodt, N., Resing, W. C. M., & Zaal, J. N. (1994). *Schoolgedrag Beoordelingslijst A en B (Revised)* [School behaviour assessment list A and B (Revised)]. Lisse: Swets & Zeitlinger.

Blokland, A., & Nieuwbeerta, P. (eds), *Developmental and life course studies in delinquency and crime.* The Hague: Boom Juridische Uitgevers.

Blokland, A., Nagin, D., & Nieuwbeerta, P. (2005). Life span offending trajectories of a Dutch conviction cohort. *Criminology*, *43*, 919–54.

Blumenfeld, Ph., Fishman, B. J., Krajcik, J., Marx, R. W., & Soloway, E. (2000). Creating usable innovations in systemic reform: Scaling up technology-embedded project-based science in urban schools. *Educational Psychologist*, *35*, 149–64.

Bogenschneider, K. (2002). *Family Policy Matters. How Policymaking Affects Families and What Professionals Can Do.* Mahwah, NJ: Lawrence Erlbaum.

Boivin, M., & Vitaro, F. (1995). The impact of peer relationships on aggression in childhood: Inhibition through coercion or promotion through peer support. In J. McCord (ed.), *Coercion and Punishment in Long-Term Perspectives* (pp. 183–197). New York, NY: Cambridge University Press.

Boivin, M., Vitaro, F., & Poulin, F. (2005). Peer relationships and the development of aggressive behavior in early childhood. In R. E. Tremblay, W. W. Hartup, & J. Archer (eds), *Developmental Origins of Aggression* (pp. 376–97). New York: Guilford Press.

Bol, M. W. (1991). *Leeftijdsgrenzen in het Strafrecht* [Age limits in penal law]. Arnhem: Gouda Quint.

Bongers, I. L., Koot, H. M., van der Ende, J., & Verhulst, F. C. (2003). The normative development of child and adolescent problem behavior. *Journal of Abnormal Psychology*, *112*, 179–92.

Bongers, I. L., Koot, H. M., van der Ende, J., & Verhulst, F. C. (2004). Developmental trajectories of externalizing behaviors in childhood and adolescence. *Child Development*, *75*, 1523–37.

Book, A. S., Starzyk, K. B., & Quinsey, V. L. (2001). The relationship between testosterone and aggression a meta-analysis. *Aggression and Violent Behaviour*, *6*, 579–99.

Boomsma, D. I., & Plomin, R. (1986). Heart rate and behaviour of twins. *Merrill Palmer Quarterly*, *32*, 141–51.

Boomsma, D. I., Vink, J. M., van Beijsterveld, C. E. M., de Geus, E. J. C., Beem, A. L., Mulder, E. J. C. M., Derks, E. M., Riese, H., Willemsen, G. A., Bartels, M., van den Berg, M., Kupper, N. H., Polderman, T. J., Posthuma, D., Rietveld, M. J., Stubbe, J. H., Knol, L. I., Stroet, T., & van Baal, G. C. (2002). Netherlands twin register: A focus on longitudinal research. *Twin Research*, *5*, 1–6.

Bor, W., Sanders, M. R., & Markie-Dadds, C. (in press). The effects of Triple P Positive Parenting Program in preschool children with co-occurring disruptive behaviour and attention/hyperactive difficulties. *Journal of Abnormal Child Psychology*.

Bouchard, T. J., & McGue, M. (2003). Genetic and environmental influences on human psychological differences. *Journal of Neurobiology*, *54*, 4–45.

Boutellier, H. (2005). *The Safety Utopia: Contemporary Discontent and Desire as to Crime and Punishment.* Dordrecht: Kluwer Academic.

Bowlby, J. (1969). Disruption of affectional bonds and its effects on behavior. *Journal of Contemporary Psychotherapy*, *2*, 75–86.

Boxer, P., Guerra, N. G., Huesmann, L. R., & Morales, J. (2005). Proximal peer-level effects of a small-group selected prevention on aggression in elementary school children: An investigation of the peer contagion hypothesis. *Journal of Abnormal Child Psychology*, *33*, 325–38.

Brame, B., Nagin, D. S., & Tremblay, R. E. (2001). Developmental trajectories of physical aggression from school entry to late adolescence. *Journal of Child Psychology and Psychiatry*, *42*, 503–12.

Brendgen, M., Vitaro, F., Bukowski, W. M., Doyle, A. B., & Markiewicz, D. (2001). Developmental profiles of peer social preference over the course of elementary school: Associations with trajectories of externalizing and internalizing behavior. *Developmental Psychology*, *37*, 308–20.

Brennan, P. A., Grekin, E. R., Mortensen, E. L., & Mednick, S. A. (2002). Relationship of maternal smoking during pregnancy with criminal arrest and hospitalization for substance abuse in male and female adult offspring. *American Journal of Psychiatry*, *159*, 48–54.

Brestan, E. V., & Eyberg, S. M. (1998). Effective psychosocial treatments of conduct-disordered children and adolescents: 29 years, 82 studies and 5272 kids. *Journal of Clinical Child Psychology*, *27*, 180–89.

Brezinka, V. (2002). Effectonderzoek naar preventieprogramma's voor kinderen met gedragsproblemen. *Kind en Adolescent*, *23*, 4–23.

Broidy, L. M., Nagin, D. S., Tremblay, R. E., Bates, J. E., Brame, B., Dodge, K. A., Fergusson, D., Horwood, J. L., Loeber, R., Laird, R., Lynam, D. R., Moffitt, T. E., & Pettit, G. S. (2003). Developmental trajectories of childhood disruptive behavior and adolescent delinquency: A six-site, cross-national study. *Developmental Psychology*, *39*, 222–45.

Brook, J. S., Whiteman, M., & Zheng, L. (2002). Intergenerational transmission of risk for problem behavior. *Journal of Abnormal Child Psychology*, *30*, 65–76.

Brosnan, R., & Carr, A. (2000). Adolescent conduct problems. In A. Carr (ed.), *What Works with Children and Adolescents? A Critical Review of Psychological Interventions with Children, Adolescents and their Families* (pp. 102–30). London & New York: Routledge.

Bruinsma, F. (1996). *De Jeugdige Zeden Delinquent* (The young sexual perpetrator). Utrecht: SWP.

Bry, B. H., McKeon, P., & Pandina, R. J. (1982). Extent of drug use as a function of number of risk factors. *Journal of Abnormal Psychology*, *91*, 273–9.

Buckland, G., & Stevens, A. (2001). *Review of Effective Practice with Young Offenders in Mainland Europe*. London: Youth Justice Board.

Buckner, J. C., Mezzacappa, E., & Beardslee, W. R. (2003). Characteristics of resilient youths living in poverty: The role of self-regulatory processes. *Development and Psychopathology*, *15*, 139–62.

Bullock, B. M., Deater-Deckard, K., & Leve, L. D. (2006). Deviant peer affiliation and problem behavior: A test of genetic and environmental influences. *Journal of Abnormal Child Psychology*, *34*, 29–41.

Burns, B. J., Howell, J. C., Wiig, J. K., Augimeri, L. K., Welsh, B. C., Loeber, R., & Petechuk, D. (March, 2003). Child delinquency intervention and services. *Child Delinquency Bulletin Series*. Washington DC: Office of Juvenile Justice and Delinquency Prevention.

Burton, V. S., Jr., Cullen, F. T., Evans, T. D., et al. (1995). The impact of parental controls on delinquency. *Journal of Criminal Justice*, *23*, 111–26.

Bushway, S. D., Thornberry, T. P., & Krohn, M. S. (2003). Desistance as a developmental process: A comparison of static and dynamic approaches. *Journal of Quantitative Criminology*, *19*, 129–53.

Buskop-Kobussen, M. P. M. H., & Cox, K. (2003). Jeugdgezondheidszorg, effectiviteit van de verpleegkundige voorlichting [Youth health care, effectiveness of nursing information]. In Y. Heijnen-Kaales (ed.), *State of the Art Study van Verzorging en Verpleging*. Eindrapportage, 382–425. Maarssen/Utrecht: Elsevier/LEVV.

Button, T. M., Scourfield, J., Martin, N., Purcell, S., & McGuffin, P. (2005). Family dysfunctioning interacts with genes in the causation of antisocial symptoms. *Behavior Genetics*, *35*, 115–20.

Cadoret, R. J., Yates, W. R., Troughton, E., Woodworth, G., & Stewart, M. A. (1995). Genetic-environmental interaction in the genesis of aggressivity and conduct disorders. *Archives of General Psychiatry*, *52*, 916–24.

Campbell, S. B., Pierce, E. W., March, C. L., Ewing, L. J., & Szumowski, E. K. (1994). Hard-to-manage preschool boys: Symptomatic behavior across contexts and time. *Child Development*, *65*, 836–51.

Carrey, N. J., Butter, J. H. ., Persinger, M.A., & Bailak, R. J. (1995). Physiological and cognitive correlates of child abuse. *Journal of the American Academy of Child and Adolescent Psychiatry*, *34*, 1067–975.

Casey. R. J. (1996). Emotional competence in children with externalizing and internalizing disorders. In M. Lewis, & M. Sullivan (eds), *Emotional Development in Atypical Children* (pp.161–83). Mahwah, NJ: Lawrence Erlbaum Associates.

Caspi, A. (1998). Personality development across the life course. In W. Damon (series ed.) & N. Eisenberg (vol. ed.), *Handbook of Child Psychology:* Vol. 3. *Social, Emotional and Personality Development* (5th edn, pp. 311–88). New York: Wiley.

Caspi, A., McClay, J., Moffitt, T. E., Mill, J., Martin, J., Craig, I. W., Taylor, A., & Poulton, R. (2002). Role of genotype in the cycle of violence in maltreated children. *Science*, *297*, 851–4.

Caspi, A., Moffitt, T. E., Cannon, M., McClay, J., Murray, R., Harrington, H., Taylor, A., Arsenault, L., Williams, B., Braithwaite, A., Poulton, R., & Craig, I. W. (2005). Moderation of the effect of adolescent-onset cannabis use on adult psychosis by a functional polymorphism in the catechol-O-methyltransferase gene: Longitudinal evidence of a gene X environment interaction. *Biological Psychiatry*, *57*, 1117–27.

Caspi, A., Moffitt, T. E., Newman, D. L., & Silva, P. A. (1996). Behavioral observations at age 3 predict adult psychiatric disorders: Longitudinal evidence from a birth cohort. *Archives of General Psychiatry*, *53*, 1033–9.

Caspi, A., Moffitt, T. E., Silva, P. A., Stouthamer-Loeber, M., Krueger, R. F., & Schmutte, P. S. (1994). Are some people crime prone? Replications of the personality-crime relationship across countries, genders, races, and methods. *Criminology*, *32*, 163–95.

Caspi, A., Sugden, K., Moffitt, T. E., Taylor, A., Craig, I. W., Harrington, H., McClay, J., Mill, J., Martin, J., Braithwaite, A., & Poulton, R. (2003). Influence of life stress on depression: Moderation by a polymorphism in the 5-HTT gene. *Science*, *301*, 386–9.

Cassidy, B., Zoccolillo, M., & Hughes, S. (1996). Psychopathology in adolescent mothers and its effects on mother-infant interactions: A pilot study. *Canadian Journal of Psychiatry*, *41*, 379–84.

Catalano, R. F., & Hawkins, J. D. (1996).The social development model: a theory of antisocial behaviour: In J. D. Hawkins (ed.), *Delinquency and Crime: Current Theories* (pp. 149–97). New York: Cambridge University Press.

Center for Substance Abuse Treatment. (1997). *Substance Abuse Treatment and Domestic Violence* (Volume 25). Washington, DC: Government Printing Office.

Cernkovich, S. A., & Giordano, P. C. (1987). Family relationships and delinquency. *Criminology*, *25*, 295–321.

Chambers, W. J., Puig-Antich, J., Hirsch, M., Paez, P., Ambrosini, P., Tabrizi, M. A., & Davies, M. (1985). The assessment of affective disorders in children and adolescents by semistructured interview. *Archives of General Psychiatry*, *42*, 696–702.

Charlebois, P., & LeBlanc, M. (1994). Methodological issues in multiple-gating screening procedures for antisocial behaviors in elementary students. *Remedial and Special Education*, *15*, 44–55.

Cicchetti, D., Rogosh, F., Maughan, A., Toth, S., & Bruce, J. (2003). False belief understanding in maltreated children. *Development and Psychopathology*, *15*, 1967–91.

Cho, H., Hallfors, D. D., & Sanchez, V. (2005). Evaluation of a high school peer group intervention for at-risk youth. *Journal of Abnormal Child Psychology*, *33*, 363–74.

Clark, C., Prior, M., & Kinsella, G. J. (2000). Do executive function deficits differentiate between adolescents with ADHD and oppositional defiant/conduct disorder? A neuropsychological study using the Six Elements Test and Hayling Sentence Completion Test. *Journal of Abnormal Child Psychology*, *28*, 403–14.

Cohen, M. A. (1988). Pain, suffering, and jury awards: a study of the cost of crime to victims. *Law and Society Review*, *22*, 537–55.

Cohen, M. A. (1998). The monetary value of saving a high-risk youth. *Journal of Quantitative Criminology*, *14*, 5–33.

Cohen, M. A., Swaray, R. B., & McDougall, C. (2002). *Cost Benefit Validity Scale* <www.york.ac.uk/criminaljustice>.

Coie, J. D., & Dodge, K. A. (1998). Aggression and antisocial behavior. In N. Eisenberg, & W. Damon (eds), *Handbook of Child Psychology, Social, Emotional, and Personality Development* (pp. 779–862). New York: Wiley.

Coie, J. D., & Kupersmidt, J. D. (1983). A behavioral analysis of emerging social status in boys' groups. *Child Development*, *54*, 1400–1416.

Coie, J., Terry, R., Lenox, K., Lochman, J., & Hyman, C. (1995b). Childhood peer rejection as predictors of stable patterns of adolescent disorder. *Development and Psychopathology*, *7*, 697–713.

Augimeri, L., & Levene, K. (1994, revised 1997). *Outreach Programme: Risk factors Associated with Possible Conduct Disorders and Non-Responders*. Toronto: Earlscourt Child and Family Centre.

Cole, P. M., Teti, L. O., & Zahn-Waxler, C. (2003). Mutual emotion regulation and the stability of conduct problems between preschool and early school age. *Development and Psychopathology*, *15*, 1–18.

Collier, G. (1994). *Social Origins of Mental Ability.* New York: Wiley.

Collin-Vezina, D., & Hebert, M. (2005). Comparing dissociation and PTSD in sexually abused school-aged girls. *Journal of Nervous and Mental Disease*, *193*, 47–52.

Collins, W. A., Maccoby, E. E., Steinberg, L., Hetherington, E. M., & Bornstein, M. H. (2000). Contemporary research on parenting: The case for nature and nurture. *American Psychologist*, *55*, 218–32.

Society for Prevention Research (2004). *Community Monitoring Systems* <www.preventionresearch.org/commlmon.php#CMS>.

Communities That Care (2005). *Findings from the Safer London Youth Survey 2004* <www.communitiesthatcare.org.uk/news.html#201>.

Conduct Problems Prevention Research Group. (1992). A developmental and clinical model for the prevention of conduct disorders: The Fast Track program. *Development and Psychopathology*, *4*, 509–527.

Conger, R. D., Ge, X., Elder, G. H., Lorenz, F. O., & Simons, R. (1994). Economic stress, coercive family process, and developmental problems of adolescents. *Child Development*, *65*, 541–61.

Conger, R. D., Patterson, G. R., & Ge, X. (1995). It takes two to replicate: A mediational model for the impact of parents' stress on adolescent adjustment. *Child Development*, *66*, 80–97.

Connor, D. F. (2002). *Aggression and Antisocial Behavior in Children and Adolescents. Research and Treatment*. New York: The Guilford Press.

Conseur, A., Rivara, F., Barnoski, R., & Emanuel, I. (1997). Maternal and perinatal risk factors for later delinquency. *Pediatrics*, *99*, 785–90.

Conway, A. (2005). Girls, aggression, and emotion regulation. *American Journal of Orthopsychiatry*, *75*, 334–9.

Cooper, M. L., Shaver, P. R., & Collins, N. L. (1998). Attachment styles, emotion regulation and adjustment in adolescence. *Journal of Personality and Social Psychology*, *74*, 1380–97.

Côté, S., Vaillancourt, T., Le Blanc, J. C., Nagin, D. S., & Tremblay, R. E. (2006). The development of physical aggression from toddlerhood to pre-adolescence: A nationwide longitudinal study of Canadian children. *Journal of Abnormal Child Psychology*, *34*, 71–85.

Cottle, C. C., Lee, R. J., & Heilbrun, K. (2001). The prediction of criminal recidivism in juveniles: A meta-analysis. *Criminal Justice and Behavior*, *28*, 367–94.

Council of Europe (2003). *Recommendation (2003)20 of the Committee of Ministers to Member States Concerning New Ways of Dealing with Juvenile Delinquency and the Role of Juvenile Justice*. Strasbourg: Council of Europe.

Craig, I. W. (2005). The role of monoamine oxidase A, MAOA, in the aetiology of antisocial behavior: The importance of gene-environment interactions. *Novartis Foundation Symposium*, *268*, 227–37.

Crick, N. R. (1997). Engagement in gender normative versus nonnormative forms of aggression: Links to social-psychological adjustment. *Developmental Psychology*, *33*, 610–17.

Crick, N. R., Casas, J. F., & Mosher, M. (1997). Relational and overt aggression in preschool. *Developmental Psychology*, *33*, 579–88.

Crick, N. R., & Dodge, K. A. (1994). A review and reformulation of social information processing mechanisms in children's social adjustment. *Psychological Bulletin, 115*, 74–101.

Crijnen, A. A. M., Achenbach, T. M., & Verhulst, F. C. (1997). Comparisons of problems reported by parents of children in 12 cultures: Total problems, externalizing, and internalizing. *Journal of the American Academy of Child and Adolescent Psychiatry, 36*, 1269–77.

Crijnen, A. A. M., Achenbach, T. M., & Verhulst, F. C. (1999). Problems reported by parents of children in multiple cultures: The Child Behavior Checklist syndrome constructs. *American Journal of Psychiatry, 156*, 569–74.

Crijnen, A. A. M., Bengi Arslan, L., & Verhulst, F. C. (2000). Teacher-reported problem behaviour in Turkish immigrant and Dutch children: A cross-cultural comparison. *Acta Psychiatrica Scandinavica, 102*, 439–44.

Cronbach, L. J. (1983). *Designing Evaluations of Educational and Social Programs.* San Francisco, CA: Jossey-Bass.

Crowell, S. E., Beauchaine, T. P., Gatzke-Kopp, L., Sylvers, P., Mead, H., & Chipman-Chacon, J. (2006). Autonomic correlates of attention-deficit/hyperactivity disorder and oppositional defiant disorder in preschool children. *Journal of Abnormal Psychology, 115*, 174–8.

Cunningham, C. E., Cunningham, L. J., Martorelli, V., Tran, A., Young, J., & Zacharias, R. (1998). The effects of primary diversion, and student-mediated conflict resolution programs on playground aggression. *Journal of Child Psychology and Psychiatry, 39*, 653–62.

Dadds, M. R., & Salmon, K. (2003). Punishment insensitivity and parenting: Temperament and learning as interacting risks for antisocial behavior. *Clinical Child and Family Psychology Review, 6*, 69–86.

Damon, W. (1990). *The Moral Child. Nurturing Children's Natural Moral Growth.* New York: Free Press.

Damon, W. (1997). *The Youth Charter. How Communities can Work Together to Raise Standards for All Our Children.* New York: Free Press.

Das, J., Domburgh, L. van, Ruiter, C. De, & Hildebrand, M. (2003). Antisocial Process Screening Device – Dutch Version. Maastricht: Maastricht University

Daugherty, T. K., & Quay, H. C. (1991). Response perseveration and delayed responding in childhood behavior disorders. *Journal of Child Psychology and Psychiatry and Allied Disciplines, 32*, 453–61.

Day, D. M. (1998). Risk for court contact and predictors of an early age for a first court contact among a sample of high risk youths: A survival analysis approach. *Canadian Journal of Criminology, 40*, 421–43.

Day, D. M., & Hrynkiw-Augimeri, L. A. (1996). *Serving Children at Risk for Juvenile Delinquency: An Evaluation of the Earlscourt Under 12 Outreach Project (ORP).* Submitted to the Department of Justice. Canada, Toronto: Earlscourt Child and Family Centre.

Day, D. M., & Hunt, A. C. (1996). A multivariate assessment of a risk model for juvenile delinquency with an under 12 offender sample. *Journal of Emotional and Behavioural Disorders, 4*, 66–72.

Deater-Deckard, K., Dodge, K. A., Bates, J. E., & Pettit, G. S. (1998). Multiple risk factors in the development of externalizing behavior problems: Group and individual differences. *Developmental Psychopathology*, *10*, 469–93.

De Bellis, M. D. (1997). Posttraumatic stress disorder and acute stress disorder. In R. T. Ammerman, & M. Hersen (eds), *Handbook of Prevention and Treatment with Children and Adolescents* (pp. 455–94). New York: John Wiley & Sons, Inc.

De Bellis, M. D. (2001). Developmental traumatology: The psychobiological development of maltreated children and its implications for research, treatment, and policy. *Development and Psychopathology*, *13*, 539–64.

De Bellis, M. D., Baum, A. S., Birmaher, B., Keshavan, M. S., Eccard, C. H., Boring, A. M., Jenkins, F. J., & Ryan, N. D. (1999). Developmental traumatology. Part I: Biological stress systems. *Society of Biological Psychiatry*, *45*, 1259–70.

Deblinger, E., Lippman, J., & Steer, R. (1996). Sexually abused children suffering posttraumatic stress symptoms: Initial treatment outcome findings. *Child Maltreatment*, *1*, 310–21.

De Jonge, G., & Linden, A.P. van der (2004). *Jeugd & Strafrecht*. Deventer: Kluwer.

Dekker, M. C., Koot, H. M., van der Ende, J., & Verhulst, F. C. (2002). Emotional and behavioral problems in children and adolescents with and without intellectual disability. *Journal of Child Psychology and Psychiatry*, *43*, 1087–98.

Deković, M. (1999). Risk and protective factors in the development of problem behavior during adolescence. *Journal of Youth and Adolescence*, *28*, 667–85.

Deković, M., Janssens, J. M. A. M., & van As, N. M. C. (2001). Gezinsfactoren en het gebruik van ernstig geweld [Family factors and the perpetration of serious violence]. In R. Loeber, M. W. Slot, & J. A. Sergeant, (eds), *Ernstige en Gewelddadige Jeugddelinquentie* (pp. 225–44). Houten/Diegem: Bohn Stafleu Van Loghum.

Deković, M., Janssens, J. M. A. M., & van As, N. M. C. (2003). Family predictors of antisocial behavior in adolescence. *Family Process*, *42*, 223–35.

Deković, M., & Meeus, W. (1997). Peer relations in adolescents: Effects of parenting and adolescents' self-concept. *Journal of Adolescence*, *20*, 163–76.

Deković, M., Wissink, I. B., & Meijer, A. M. (2004). The role of family and peer relations in adolescent antisocial behavior: Comparison of four ethnic groups. *Journal of Adolescence*, *27*, 497–514.

Dembo, R. (1994). *Use of the Problem Oriented Screening Instrument for Teenagers (POSIT) in the Juvenile Justice System*. Tampa: University of South Florida.

De Mey, W., Messiaen, V., van Hulle, N., Merlevede, E., & Winters, S. (2005). *Samen sterker Terug Op Pad (STOP 4–7). Een Vroege Interventie voor jonge Kinderen met Gedragsproblemen*. Amsterdam: SWP.

Department for Education and Skills (2006). *Parenting Support Guidance for Local Authorities in England*. London: Her Majesty's Stationary Office.

De Ruiter, K. P., Dekker, M. C., Verhulst, F. C., & Koot, H. M. (2007). Developmental course of psychopathology in youths with and without intellectual disabilities. *Journal of Child Psychology and Psychiatry*, *48*, 498–507.

De Vogel, V., de Ruiter, C., Hildebrand, M., Bos, B., & van de Ven, P. (2004). Type of discharge and risk of recidivism measured by the HCR-20: A retrospective study in a Dutch sample of treated forensic psychiatric patients. *International Journal of Forensic Mental Health*, *3*, 149–65.

Dishion, T. J. (2000). Cross-setting consistency in early adolescent psychopathology: Deviant friendships and problem behavior sequelae. *Journal of Personality*, *68*, 1109–25.

Dishion, T. J., Andrews, D. W., & Crosby, L. (1995). Antisocial boys and their friends in early adolescence: Relationship characteristics, quality, and interactional process. *Child Development*, *66*, 139–51.

Dishion, T. J., Capaldi, D., Spracklen, K. M., & Li, F. (1995). Peer ecology of male adolescent drug use. *Development and Psychopathology*, *7*, 803–24.

Dishion, T. J., & Dodge, K. A. (2005). Peer contagion in interventions for children and adolescents: Moving towards an understanding of the ecology and dynamics of change. *Journal of Abnormal Child Psychology*, *33*, 395–400.

Dishion, T. J., French, D. C., & Patterson, G. R. (1995). The development and ecology of antisocial behavior. In D. Cicchetti, & D. J. Cohen (eds), *Developmental Psychopathology:* Vol. 2. *Risk, Disorder, and Adaptation* (pp. 421–71). New York: Wiley.

Dishion, T. J., McCord, J., & Poulin, F. (1999). When interventions harm: Peer groups and problem behavior. *American Psychologis*t, *54*, 755–64.

Dishion, T. J., & Patterson, G. R. (1997). The timing and severity of antisocial behavior: Three hypotheses within an ecological framework. In D. Stoff, J. Breiling, & J. Maser (eds), *Handbook of Antisocial Behavior* (pp. 205–17). New York: John Wiley & Sons.

Dishion, T. J., Poulin, F., & Burraston, B. (2001). Peer group dynamics associated with iatrogenic effects in group interventions with high-risk young adolescents. *New Directions for Child and Adolescent Development*, 79–92.

Dishion, T. J., Spracklen, K. M., Andrews, D. W., & Patterson, G. R. (1996). Deviancy training in male adolescents friendships. *Behavior Therapy*, *27*, 373–90.

Dodge, K. A. (1983). Behavioral antecedents of peer social status. *Child Development*, *54*, 1386–99.

Dodge, K. A. (1986). A social information processing model of social competence in children. In M. Perlmutter (ed.), *Minnesota Symposia on Child Psychology* (pp. 77–125). Hillsdale, NJ: Erlbaum.

Dodge, K. A. (1993). Social-cognitive mechanisms in the development of conduct disorder and depression. *Annual Review of Psychology*, *44*, 559–84.

Dodge, K A., & Coie, J. D. (1987). Social information processing factors in reactive and proactive aggression in children's peer groups. *Journal of Personality and Social Psychology*, *53*, 1146–58.

Dodge, K. A., Dishion, T. J., & Lansford, J. E. (2006). *Deviant Peer Influences in Intervention and Public Policy for Youth*. Social Report. Ann Arbor, MI: Society for Research in Child Development.

Dodge, K. A., Lansford, J. E., Burks, V. S., Bates, J. E., Pettit, G. S., Fontaine, R., & Price, J. (2003). Peer rejection and social information-processing factors in the development of aggressive behavior problems in children. *Child Development*, *74*, 374–93.

Dodge, K. A., Pettit, G. S., & Bates, J. E. (1994). Socialization mediators of the relation between socioeconomic status and child conduct problems. *Child Development*, *65*, 649–65.

Dolan, L. J., Jaylan, T., Werthamer, L., & Kellam, S. (1989). *The Good Behavior Game Manual*. Baltimore, MD: The Johns Hopkins Prevention Research Center.

Dolan, L. J., Kellam, S. G., Brown, C. H., Werthamer-Larsson L., Rebok, L. W., Mayer, L. S., Laudolf, J., Turkkan, J. S., Ford, C., & Wheeler, L. (1993). The short-term impact of two classroom-based preventive interventions on aggressive and shy behaviours and poor achievement. *Journal of Applied Developmental Psychology*, *14*, 317–45.

Domburgh, L., & Popma, A. (2003). *Reactive and Proactive Questionnaire – Dutch Version*. Duivendrecht: De Bascule.

Donker, A. G., Smeenk, W. H., van der Laan, P. H., & Verhulst, F. C. (2003). Individual stability of antisocial behavior from childhood to adulthood: Testing the stability postulate of Moffitt's developmental theory. *Criminology*, *41*, 593–610.

Donker, A. G., Smeenk, W., van der Laan, P. H., & Verhulst, F. C. (2004). Wie ziet wat? Docent- en ouderrapportage gecombineerd en vergeleken [Who sees what? Teacher and parent reports combined and compared]. *Tijdschrift voor Criminologie*, *46*, 382–94.

Doreleijers, T. A. H. (2004). Developments in youth care and the justice system in the Netherlands. In S. Bailey, & M. Dolan (eds), *Adolescent Forensic Psychiatry*. London: Arnold.

Doreleijers, T. A. H., Bijl., B, Veldt, M. C. van der, & Loosbroek, E. (1999). *BARO, Standaardisatie en protocollering basisonderzoek strafzaken Raad voor de Kinderbescherming* [BARO, Standardization and protocol basic examination of penal cases. Council for Child Care and Protection]. Amsterdam/Utrecht: Vrije Universiteit/NIZW.

Doreleijers, T. A. H., & Spaander, M. (2002). The development and implementation of the BARO: a new device to detect psychopathology in minors with first police contacts. In R. R. Corrado, R. Roesch, S. D. Hart, & J. K. Gierowski (eds), *Multi-Problem Violent Youth. A Foundation for Comparative Research on Needs, Interventions and Outcomes*. Washington, DC: IOS Press.

Douglas, K. S., & Kropp, P. R. (2002). A prevention-based paradigm for violence risk assessment. *Criminal Justice and Behavior*, *29*, 617–58.

Drieschner, K. H., Lammers, S. M. M., & van der Staak, C. P. F. (2004). Treatment motivation: An attempt for clarification of an ambiguous concept. *Clinical Psychology Review*, *23*, 1115–37.

Dryfoos, J. G. (1990). *Adolescence at Risk: Prevalence and Prevention*. London: Oxford University Press.

Dryfoos, J. G. (1998). *Safe Passage, Making it through Adolescence in a Risky Society. What Parents, Schools and Communities Can Do*. Oxford/New York: Oxford University Press.

Durlak, J. A. (1995). *School-based Prevention Programs for Children and Adolescents*. London: Sage.

Durlak, J. A. (1997). *Successful Prevention Programs for Children and Adolescents*. New York/London: Springer.

Dutton, M. A. (1992). *Empowering and Healing the Battered Woman: A Model for Assessment & Intervention*. New York: Springer.

Earlscourt Child and Family Centre. (2001a). *SNAP™ children's group manual*. Toronto: Earlscourt Child and Family Centre.

Earlscourt Child and Family Centre. (2001b). *SNAP™ parent group manual*. Toronto: Earlscourt Child and Family Centre.

Eckenrode, J., Laird, M., & Doris, J. (1993). Academic performance and disciplinary problems among abused and neglected children. *Developmental Psychology*, *29*, 53–62.

Eddy, J. M., Leve, L. D., & Fagot, B. I. (2001). Coercive family processes: A replication and extension of Patterson's coercion model. *Aggressive Behavior*, *27*, 14–25.

Eggen, A. T. J., & Heide, W. van der (2006). *Criminaliteit en Rechtshandhaving 2005* [Crime and Law Enforcement 2005]. The Hague: Boom Juridische Uitgevers.

Eigsti, I.-M., & Cicchetti, D. (2004). The impact of child maltreatment on expressive syntax at 60 months. *Developmental Science*, *7*, 88–102.

Eisenberg, N., & Fabes, R. A. (1992). Emotion, emotion-regulated regulation, and quality of socioemotional functioning. In L. Balter (ed.), *Child Psychology: A Handbook of Contemporary Issues* (pp. 318–35). Philadelphia, PA: Psychology Press/Taylor & Francis.

Eisenberg, N., Zhou, Q., Losoya, S. H., Fabes, R. A., Shepard, S. A., Murphy, B. C., Reiser, M., Guthrie, I. K., & Cumberland, A. (2003). The relations of parenting, effortful control, and ego control to children's emotional expressivity. *Child Development*, *74*, 875–95.

Eley, T. C., Lichtenstein, P., & Moffitt, T. E. (2003). A longitudinal behavioral genetic analysis of the etiology of aggressive and nonaggressive antisocial behavior. *Development and Psychopathology*, *15*, 383–402.

Elliott, D. S. (1994). Longitudinal research in criminology: Promise and practice. In E. G. M. Weitekamp, & H. J. Kerner (eds), *Cross-National Longitudinal Research on Human Development and Criminal Behaviour* (pp. 189–201). Dordrecht: Kluwer Academic Publishers.

Elliott, D. S. (ed.) (1997). *Blueprints for Violence Prevention* (vols 1–11). Boulder: Centre for the Study and Prevention of Violence, Institute of Behavioural Science, University of Colorado.

Elliott, D. S., Huizinga, D., & Ageton, S. S. (1985). *Explaining Delinquency and Drug Use*. Beverly Hills, CA: Sage.

Elliot, D. S., Huizinga, D., & Menard, S. (1989). *Multiple Problem Youth: Delinquency, Substance Use, and Mental Health Problems*. New York: Springer-Verlag.

Elliott, D. S., & Tolan, P. H. (1999). Youth violence, prevention, intervention and social policy: An overview. In D. J. Flannery, & C. R. Huff (eds), *Youth Violence, Prevention, Intervention and Social Policy* (pp. 2–47). Washington, DC/London: Clinical practice.

Elmund, A., Melin, L., von Knorring, A. L., Proos, L., & Tuvemo, T. (2004). Cognitive and neuropsychological functioning in transnationally adopted juvenile delinquents. *Acta Paediatrica*, *93*, 1507–13.

Enebrink, P., Långström, N., & Gumpert, C. H. (2006). *Predicting aggressive and disruptive behaviour in referred 6–12 year-old boys: Prospective validation of the EARL-20B risk/needs checklist*. Manuscript in preparation.

Enebrink, P., Långström, N., Hultén, A., & Gumpert, C.H. (2006). Swedish validation of the Early Assessment Risk List for Boys (EARL-20B), a decision-aid for use with children presenting with conduct-disordered behaviour. *Nordic Journal of Psychiatry, 60*(6), 438–446.

Enebrink, P., Långström, N., Neij, J., Grann, M., & Gumpert, C. H. (2001). *Brief report: Interrater reliability of the early assessment risk list: EARL-20B: A new guide for clinical evaluation of conduct-disordered boys*. Huddinge, Sweden: Karolinska Institutet.

Ernst, M., Grant, S. J., London, E. D., Contoreggi, C. S., Kimes, A. S., & Spurgeon, L. (2003). Decision making in adolescents with behavior disorders and adults with substance abuse. *American Journal of Psychiatry*, *160*, 33–40.

Eslinger, P. J. (1996). Conceptualizing, describing, and measuring components of executive function. In G. R. Lyon, & N. A. Krasnegor (eds), *Attention, Memory, and Executive Function* (pp. 367–95). Baltimore, MD: Paul H. Brookes.

Estell, D. B., Cairns, R. B., Farmer, T. W., & Cairns, B. D. (2002). Aggression in inner-city early elementary classrooms: Individual and peer-group configurations. *Merrill-Palmer Quarterly*, *48*, 52–76.

Faber, S. E. K., & Steensma, H. Y. (1995). *Wat doen we eraan? Gedragsproblemen en sociale ontwikkeling bij 4- tot 12-jarigen* [What do we do about it? Behaviour problems and social development among 4 to 12-year-olds]. Baarn: Intro.

Farrington, D. P. (1986). Age and Crime. In M. Tonry & N. Morris (eds), *Crime and Justice* (pp. 29–90). Chicago, IL: University of Chicago Press.

Farrington, D. P. (1991). Childhood aggression and adult violence: early precursors and later-life outcomes. In D. J. Pepler, & K. H. Rubin (eds), *The Development and Treatment of Childhood Aggression* (pp. 5–29). Hillsdale, NJ: Lawrence Erlbaum.

Farrington, D. P. (1994). Interactions between individual and contextual factors in the development of offending. In R. K. Silbereisen, & E. Todt (eds), *Adolescence in Context: The Interplay of Family, School, Peers and Work in Adjustment* (pp. 366–89). New York: Springer-Verlag.

Farrington, D. P. (1996). Individual, family and peer factors in the development of delinquency. In C. R. Hollin, & K. Howells (eds), *Clinical Approaches to Working with Young Offenders* (pp. 21–56). Chichester: Wiley.

Farrington, D. P. (1997). Early prediction of violent and non-violent youthful offending. *European Journal on Criminal Policy and Research*, *5*, 51–66.

Farrington, D. P. (2003a). Developmental and life-course criminology: Key theoretical and empirical issues. *Criminology*, *41*, 221–55.

Farrington, D. P. (2003b). Methodological quality standards for evaluation research. *Annals of the American Academy of Political and Social Science*, *587*, 49–68.

Farrington, D. P. (2004). Conduct disorder, aggression, and delinquency. In R. Lerner, & L. Steinberg (eds), *Handbook of Adolescent Psychology* (2nd edn) (pp. 627–64). Hoboken, NJ: Wiley.

Farrington, D. P. (2005). *Integrated Developmental and Life-Course Theories of Offending*. New Brunswick, NJ: Transaction.

Farrington, D. P., Jolliffe, D., Loeber, R., & Homish, D. L. (2007), How many offenses are really committed per juvenile court offender? *Victims and Offenders*, *2*, 227–49.

Farrington, D. P., Loeber, R., & Stallings, R. (November 2007). Effects of convictions on self-reported delinquency. Paper presented at the meeting of the American Society of Criminology, Atlanta, GA.

Farrington, D. P., Osborn, S. G., & West, D. J. (1978). The persistence of labelling effects. *British Journal of Criminology*, *18*, 277-84.

Farrington, D. P., & Welsh, B. C. (2003). Family-based prevention of offending: A meta-analysis. *The Australian and New Zealand Journal of Criminology*, *36*, 127–51.

Farrington, D. P., & Welsh, B. C. (2005). Randomized experiments in criminology: What have we learned in the last two decades. *Journal of Experimental Criminology*, *1*, 9–38.

Farrington, D. P., & Welsh, B. C. (2007). *Saving Children from a Life of Crime: Early Risk Factors and Effective Interventions*. Oxford: Oxford University Press

Farver, J. A. M. (1996). Aggressive behavior in preschoolers' social networks: Do birds of a feather flock together? *Early Childhood Research Quarterly*, *11*, 333–50.

Feehan, M., McGee, R., Stanton, W. R., & Silva, P. A. (1991). Strict and inconsistent discipline in childhood: Consequences for adolescent mental health. *British Journal of Clinical Psychology*, *30*, 325–31.

Feil, E. G., Severson, H., & Walker, H. M. (1995). Identification of critical factors in the assessment of preschool behaviour problems. *Education and Treatment of Children*, *18*, 261–71.

Feil, E. G., Severson, H., & Walker, H. M. (1998). Screening for emotional and behavioral delays: The Early Screening Project. *Journal of Early Intervention*, *21*, 252–66.

Fekkes, M. (2005). *Bullying Among Elementary School Children*. Leiden: University of Leiden.

Fergusson, D. M., Horwood, L. J., & Lynskey, M. (1997). The childhoods of multiple problem adolescents – A 15-year longitudinal study. *Journal of Child Psychology and Psychiatry and Allied Disciplines*, *35*, 1123–45.

Fergusson, D. M., Horwood, L. J., & Ridder, E. M. (2005a). Show me the child at seven: the consequences of conduct problems in childhood for psychosocial functioning in adulthood. Journal of Child Psychology and Psychiatry, 46, 837–49.

Fergusson, D. M., Horwood, L. J., & Ridder, E. M. (2005b). Show me the child at seven II: childhood intelligence and later outcomes in adolescence and young adulthood. Journal of Child Psychology and Psychiatry, 46, 850–58.

Fergusson, D. M., & Woodward, L. J. (2000). Educational, psychosocial, and sexual outcomes of girls with conduct problems in early adolescence. *Journal of Child Psychology and Psychiatry and Allied Disciplines*, *41*, 779–92.

Fergusson, D. M., Woodward, L. J., & Horwood, L. J. (1998). Maternal smoking during pregnancy and psychiatric adjustment in late adolescence. *Archives of General Psychiatry*, *55*, 721–7.

Ferrer-Wreder, L., Stattin, H., Lorente, C. C., Tubman, J. G., & Adamson, L. (2004). *Successful Prevention and Youth Development Programs, Across Borders*. New York: Kluwer Academic Plenum Publishers.

Ferwerda, H. B. (1992). *Watjes en ratjes. Een longitudinaal onderzoek naar het verband tussen maatschappelijke kwetsbaarheid en jeugdcriminaliteit* [Wallies and rats: A longitudinal study of the relationship between social vulnerability and juvenile crime]. Groningen: Wolters-Noordhoff.

Ferwerda, H. B., Jakobs, J. P., & Beke, B. M. W. A. (1996). *Signalen voor Toekomstig Crimineel Gedrag* [Markers for future criminal behaviour]. The Hague: Ministerie van Justitie.

Fine, S. E., Trentacosta, C. J., Izard, C. E., Mostow, A. J., & Campbell, J. L. (2004). Anger perception, caregivers' use of physical discipline, and aggression in children at risk. *Social Development*, *13*, 213–28.

Finn-Stevenson, M., & Stern, B. M. (1997). Integrating early-childhood and family-support services with a school improvement process: The Comer-Zigler initiative. *The Elementary School Journal*, *98*, 51–66.

Fonseca, A. C., & Yule, W. (1995). Personality and antisocial-behavior in children and adolescents – an inquiry into Eysenck's and Gray's theories. *Journal of Abnormal Child Psychology*, *23*, 767–81.

Forgatch, M. S., Patterson, G. R., & Skinner, M. L. (1988). A mediational model for the effect of divorce on antisocial behavior in boys. In E. M. Hetherington, & J. D. Arasteh (eds), *Impact of Divorce, Single Parenting and Stepparenting on Children* (pp. 135–54). Hillsdale, NJ: Erlbaum.

Förrer, M., Kenter, B., & Veenman, S. (2000). *Coöperatief Leren in het Basisonderwijs* [Cooperative learning in primary education]. Amersfoort: CPS.

Fossen, D. (1998). Hulpverlening aan seksueel misbruikte kinderen: een onderzoek naar de hulpverlening aan seksueel misbruikte kinderen in Nederland [Care for sexually abused children: a study of care provides to sexually abused children in the Netherlands]. Unpublished doctoral thesis. Amsterdam: Vrije Universiteit.

Foster, E. M., Jones, D. E., & Conduct Problems Prevention Research Group (2005). The high cost of aggression: Public expenditures resulting from Conduct Disorder. *American Journal of Public Health*, *95*, 1767–72.

Frick, P. J., & Hare, R. D. (2001). *Antisocial Process Screening Device*. Toronto: Multi-Heath Systems.

Frick, P. J., Juper, K., Silverthorn, P., & Cotter, M. (1995). Antisocial behavior, somatization, and sensation-seeking behavior in mothers of clinic-referred children. *Journal of the American Academy of Child and Adolescent Psychiatry*, *34*, 805–12.

Fried, P. A. (1996). Behavioral outcomes in preschool and school-age children exposed prenatally to marijuana: A review and speculative interpretation. *NIDA Research Monograph*, *164*, 242–60.

Fried, P. A., Watkinson, B., & Gray, R. (1998). Differential effects on cognitive functioning in 9- to 12-year olds prenatally exposed to cigarettes and marihuana. *Neurotoxicology and Teratology*, *20*, 293–306.

Fried, P. A., Watkinson, B., & Gray, R. (2003). Differential effects on cognitive functioning in 13- to 16-year-olds prenatally exposed to cigarettes and marihuana. *Neurotoxicology and Teratology*, *25*, 427–36.

Friedich, W. N. (1997). Parents Report of Traumatic Impact. Unpublished text. Rochester, MN: Mayo Clinic.

Fulker D. W., DeFries J. C., & Plomin R. (1988). Genetic influence on general mental ability increases between infancy and middle childhood. *Nature*, *336*, 767–9.

Furstenberg, F. F. (1999). *Managing to Make It. Urban Families and Adolescent Success*. Chicago, IL/London: University of Chicago Press.

Galambos, N. L., Barker, E. T., & Almeida, D. M. (2003). Parents do matter: Trajectories of change in externalizing and internalizing problems in early adolescence. *Child Development*, *74*, 578–94.

Galvan, A., Hare, T. A., Parra, C. E., Penn, J., Voss, H., Glover, G., & Casey, B. J. (2006). Earlier development of the accumbens relative to orbitofrontal cortex might underlie risk-taking behavior in adolescents. *Journal of Neuroscience*, *26*, 6885–92.

Garland, D. (2001). *The Culture of Control: Crime and Social Order in Contemporary Society*. Chicago, IL: University of Chicago Press.

Gatti, U., & Tremblay, R. E. (2005). Social capital and physical violence. In R. Tremblay, W. Hartup, & J. Archer (eds), *Developmental Origins of Aggression* (pp. 398–423). New York: Guilford Press.

Gatti, U., Tremblay, R. E., Vitaro, F., & McDuff, P. (2005). Youth gangs, delinquency and drug use: A test of the selection, facilitation, and enhancement hypotheses. *Journal of Child Psychology and Psychiatry*, *46*, 1178–90.

Ge, X., Conger, R. D., Cadoret, R. J.; Neiderhiser, J. M., Yates, W., Troughton, E., & Stewart, M. A. (1996). The developmental interface between nature and nurture: A mutual influence model of child antisocial behavior and parent behaviors. *Developmental Psychology*, *32*, 574–89.

Gendreau, P., Little, T., & Goggin, C. (1996). A meta-analysis of the predictors of adult offender recidivism: What works! *Criminology*, *34*, 575–607.

Geraghty, T. F. (1997). Justice for children: How do we get there? *Journal of Criminal Law and Criminology*, *88*, 190–241.

Gerard, J. M., & Buehler, C. (2004). Cumulative environmental risk and youth maladjustment: The role of youth attributes. *Child Development*, *75*, 1832–49.

Gershoff, E. T. (2002). Corporal punishment by parents and associated child behaviors and experiences: A meta-analytic and theoretical review. *Psychological Bulletin*, *128*, 539–79.

Giancola, P. R., & Mezzich, A. C. (2000). Executive cognitive functioning mediates the relation between language competence and antisocial behavior in conduct-disordered adolescent females. *Aggressive Behavior*, *26*, 359–75.

Gilsing, R., & Keuzenkamp, S. (2004). *Naar een Stelsel van Sociale Indicatoren voor het Integraal Toezicht Jeugdzaken. Advies in Opdracht van de Inspectie voor de Gezondheidszorg, de Inspectie Jeugdzorg, de Inspectie Openbare*

Orde en Veiligheid en de Inspectie van het Onderwijs. Werkdocument nr. 108 [Towards a system of social indicators for the integral inspection youth cases. Advice commissioned by the Health Inspectorate, the Youth Care Inspectorate, the Inspectorate of Public Order and Safety and the Education Inspectorate. Work document No. 108]. The Hague: Sociaal en Cultureel Planbureau.

Gilsing, R., Roes, T., Veldheer, V., & Vorthoren, M. (2000). *Knelpunten in het stedlijk jeugdbeleid.* The Hague: Sociaal en Cultureel Planbureau.

Gispen-de Wied, C. C., Jansen, L. M., Wynne, H. J., Matthys, W., van der Gaag, R. J., Thijssen, J. H., & van Engeland, H. (1998). Differential effects of hydrocortisone and dexamethasone on cortisol suppression in a child psychiatric population. *Psychoneuroendocrinology*, *23*, 295–306.

Glueck, S., & Glueck, E. (1950). *Unraveling Juvenile Delinquency*. Cambridge, MA: Harvard University Press.

Goderie, M. (2005). Motiveren en helpen. Het Gezins Gedrag Interventieproject [Motivating and supporting. The Family Behaviour Intervention project]. *Secondant, Tijdschrift van het Centrum voor Criminaliteitspreventie en Veiligheid, 19*, 19–21.

Goldsmith, H. H., Losoya, S. H., Bradshaw, D. L., & Campos, J. J. (1994). Genetics of personality: A twin study of the five factor model and parental-offspring analyses. In C. Halverson, R. Martin, & G. Kohnstamm (eds), *The Developing Structure of Temperament and Personality from Infancy to Adulthood* (pp. 241–65). Hillsdale, NJ: Erlbaum.

Goldstein, H. (1995). *Multilevel Statistical Models.* London: Arnold.

Goleman, D. (1995). *Emotional Intelligence.* New York: Bantam Books.

Goodman, R. (1997). The strengths and difficulties questionnaire: A research note. *Journal of Child Psychology and Psychiatry*, *38*, 581–6.

Gorman-Smith, D., & Loeber, R. (2005). Are developmental pathways in disruptive behaviors the same for girls and boys? *Journal of Child and Family Studies*, *14*, 15–27.

Gottfredson, M. R., & Hirschi, T. (1990). *A General Theory of Crime*. Stanford, CA: Stanford University Press.

Graaf, I. de, Onrust, S., & Janssens, J. (2007). *Eerste resultaten van het Effectonderzoek naar Niveau 3 en 4 van Triple P* [First results of the effectiveness study of Level 3 and 4 of Triple P]. Utrecht: Trimbos Instituut.

Grapendaal, M., van der Veer, P., & Essers, A. (1996). *Over Criminaliteit en Kattekwaad bij 7- t/m 11-jarigen* [Crime and mischief among 7 to 11-year-olds]. The Hague: WODC.

Gray, J. A. (1987). *The Psychology of Fear and Stress* (2nd edn). Cambridge: Cambridge University Press.

Greenberg, M. T., Weissberg, R. P., O'Brien, M. N., Zins, J. E., Fredericks, L., Resnik, H., & Elias, M. J. (2003). Enhancing school-based prevention and youth development through coordinated social, emotional and academic learning. *American Psychologist*, *58*, 466–75.

Greenwood, P. W. (2006). *Changing Lives. Delinquency Prevention As Crime-Control Policy.* Chicago, IL: Chicago University Press.

Greenwood, P. W., Model, K. E., Rydell, C. P., & Chiesa, J. (1996). *Diverting Children from a Life of Crime: Measuring Costs and Benefits*. Santa Monica, CA: RAND Corporation.

Grisso, T., Vincent, G., & Seagrave, D. (2005). *Mental Health Screening and Assessment in Juvenile Justice*. New York: Guilford Press.

Grisso, T., & Zimring, F. E. (2004). *Double Jeopardy: Adolescent Offenders with Mental Disorders*. Chicago, IL: University of Chicago Press.

Gross, J. J., (1998). The emerging field of emotion regulation: An integrative review. *Review of General Psychology*, *2*, 271–99.

Gunthert, K. C., Cohen, L. H., & Armeli, S. (1999). Role of neuroticism in daily stress and coping. *Journal of Personality and Social Psychology*, *77*, 1087–100.

Gutschner, D., & Doreleijers, T. A. H. (2004). Das Screeningsinstrument BARO. ch zur Beurteilung van jugendlichen Starftätern [The Baro-child screening for adolescent offenders]. *Nervenheilkunde*, *23*, 326–31.

Gutschner, D., Kobel, B., Hug, C., Doreleijers, T. A. H., Schmeck, K., & Fegert, J. (2006). BARO – Screeningsinstrument zur Erstbeurteilung von jugendlichen Straftätern [The BARO-screening device for juvenile offenders]. *Zeitschrift für Jugendkriminalrecht und Jugendhilfe*, *2*, 133–9.

Haagse Ondersteunings Functie (1994). *Crips & Bloods in Nederland. Tussen Mode en Menens* [Crips and Bloods in the Netherlands. Between fashion and getting serious]. 's-Gravenhage: Auteur.

Hahn, R., Faqua-Whitley, D., Wethington, H., Lowy, J., Crosby, A., Fullilove, M., Johnson, R., Liberman, A., Moscicki, E., Price, L., Snyder, S., Tuma, F., Cory, S., Stone, G., Mukhopadhaya, K., Chattopadhyay, S., Dahlberg, L., & Task Force on Community Prevention Services (2007). Effectiveness of universal school-based programs to prevent violent and aggressive behavior. A systematic review. *American Journal of Preventive Medicine*, *33*, S114–S129,

Hanish, L. D., Martin, C. L., Fabes, R. A., Leonard, S., & Herzog, M. (2005). Exposure to externalizing peers in early childhood: Homophily and peer contagion processes. *Journal of Abnormal Child Psychology*, *33*, 267–81.

Hare, R. D. (1991). *Manual for the Hare Psychopathy Checklist—Revised*. Toronto: Multi-Health Systems.

Hartup, W. W. (2005). Peer interaction: What causes what? *Journal of Abnormal Child Psychology*, *33*, 387–94.

Haselager, G. J. T., & van Lieshout, C. F. M. (1992). Inventarisatie van sociaal-emotionele problemen in het basisonderwijs [Inventory of social-emotional problems in primary education]. In C. F. M. van Lieshout (ed.), *Basisschoolleerlingen met Sociaal-emotionele Problemen. Diagnostiek en Begeleiding*. Nijmegen: Katholieke Universiteit, Vakgroep Ontwikkelingspsychologie.

Hawkins, J. D., Catalano, R. F., & Miller, J. Y. (1992). Risk and protective factors for alcohol and other drug problems in adolescence and early adulthood. Implications for substance abuse prevention. *Psychological Bulletin*, *112*, 64–105.

Hawkins, J. D., Herrenkohl, T., Farrington, D. P., Brewer, D., Catalano, R. F., & Harachi, T. W. (1998). A review of predictors of youth violence. In R. Loeber, & D. P. Farrington (eds), *Serious and Violent Juvenile Offenders: Risk Factors and Successful Interventions* (pp. 106–146). Thousand Oaks, CA: Sage Publications.

Hawkins, J. D., Smith, B. H., Hill, K. G., Kosterman, R., Catalano, R. F., & Abbott, R. D. (2003). Understanding and preventing crime and violence findings from the Seattle Social Development Project. In T. P. Thornberry, & M. D. Krohn (eds), *Taking Stock Of Delinquency: An Overview Of Findings From Contemporary Longitudinal Studies* (pp. 255–312). New York: Kluwer Academic/Plenum Publishers.

Hawley, P. H. (1999). The ontogenesis of social dominance: A strategy-based evolutionary perspective. *Developmental Review*, *19*, 97–132.

Heim, C., & Nemeroff, C. B. (2001). The role of childhood trauma in the neurobiology of mood and anxiety: Preclincial and clinical studies. *Biological Psychiatry*, *49*, 1023–39.

Hendriks, J., & Bijleveld, C. (1999). Jeugdige zedendelinquenten: verschillen tussen groeps-en alleen plegers. *Delikt en Delinkwent*, *29*, 722–36.

Henggeler, S. W., Schoenwald, S. K., Borduin, C. M., Rowland, M. D., & Cunningham, P. B. (1998). *Multisystemic Treatment of Antisocial Behavior in Children and Adolescents*. New York: Guilford Press.

Hepler, J. B. (1998). Social integration of children with emotional disabilities and nonhandicapped peers in a school setting. *Early Child Development and Care*, *147*, 99–115.

Hermanns, J. (1979). Het ontstaan van schoolproblemen. Een longitudinaal onderzoek in kleuter- en lagere school [The emergence of school problems: A longitudinal study in kindergarten and primary school]. *Pedagogische Studiën*, *56*, 348–57.

Hermanns, J. (1980). Het ontstaan van schoolproblemen (II). Gedragsobservatie door kleuterleidsters [The emergence of school problems (II). Observation of behaviour by kindergarten teachers]. *Pedagogische Studiën*, *57*, 11–21.

Hermanns, J. M. A., Öry, F., & Schrijvers, G. (2005). *Helpen bij Opgroeien en Opvoeden: Eerder, Sneller En Beter* [Supporting growing up and parenting: Earlier, faster and better]. Utrecht: Julius Centrum, Rijksuniversiteit Utrecht.

Hermanns, J. M. A., & Vergeer, M. M. (2002). *Opvoedingsondersteuning en Ontwikkelingsstimulering in Nederlandse Gemeenten. Stand van Zaken* [Parenting support and stimulating development in Dutch municipalities. State of the art]. Amsterdam: SCO-Kohnstamm Instituut.

Herpertz, S. C., Mueller, B., Wenning, B., Qunaibi, M., Lichterfeld, C., & Herpertz-Dahlmann, B. (2003). Autonomic responses in boys with externalizing disorders. *Journal of Neural Transmission*, *110*, 1181–95.

Herpertz, S. C., Wenning, B., Mueller, B., Qunaibi, M., Sass, H., & Herpertz-Dahlmann, B. (2001). Psychophysiological responses in ADHD boys with and without conduct disorder: Implications for adult antisocial behavior. *Journal of the American Academy of Child and Adolescent Psychiatry*, *40*, 1222–30.

Herrenkohl, T. L., Hawkins, J. D., Chung, I., Hill, K. G., & Battin-Pearson, S. (2001). School and community risk factors and interventions. In R. Loeber & D. P. Farrington (eds), *Child Delinquents: Development, Intervention, and Service Needs* (pp. 211–46). Thousand Oaks, CA: Sage Publications.

Herrenkohl, R. C., & Russo, M. J. (2001). Abusive early child rearing and early childhood aggression. *Child Maltreatment*, *6*, 3–16.

Herwaarden, Y. van (2004). Het Basis Raads Onderzoek (BARO) in de praktijk: een kwaliteitsslag [The use of the BARO screening instrument in daily practice: A step forward]. *Tijdschrift voor Orthopedagogiek, Kinderpsychiatrie en Klinische Kinderpsychologie*, *29*, 18–29.

Higgins, D. J., & McCabe, M.P. (2000). Multi-type maltreatment and the long-term adjustment of adults. *Child Abuse Review*, *9*, 6–18.

Hill, J. (2002). Biological, psychological and social processes in the conduct disorders. *Journal of Child Psychology and Psychiatry and Allied Disciplines*, *43*, 133–64.

Hinshaw, S. P., Lahey, B. B., & Hart, E. L. (1993). Issues of taxonomy and comorbidity in the development of conduct disorder. *Development and Psychopathology*, *5*, 31–49.

Hipwell, A. E., & Loeber R. (2006). Do we know which interventions are effective for disruptive and delinquent girls? *Clinical Child and Family Psychology Review*, *9*, 221–55.

Hipwell, A. E., White, H. R., Loeber, R., Stouthamer Loeber, M., Chung, T., & Sembower, M. A. (2005). Young girls' expectancies about the effects of alcohol, future intentions and patterns of use. *Journal on Studies of Alcohol*, *66*, 630–39.

Hirschi, T. (1969). *Causes of Delinquency*. Berkeley: University of California Press.

Hoeve, M., Dubas, J. S., Eichelsheim, V. I., van der Laan, P. H., Smeenk, W. H., & Gerris, J. R. M. (submitted). The relationship between parenting and delinquency: A meta-analysis.

Hoffenaar, P. J. (2004). The assessment and development of oppositionality. Unpublished dissertation, Amsterdam: Vrije Universiteit.

Hoffenaar, P. J., & Hoeksma, J. B. (2002). The structure of oppositionality: Response dispositions and situational aspects. *Journal of Child Psychology and Psychiatry*, *43*, 375–85.

Hofstra, M. B., van der Ende, J., & Verhulst, F. C. (2000). Continuity and change of psychopathology from childhood into adulthood: A 14-year follow-up study. *Journal of the American Academy of Child and Adolescent Psychiatry*, *39*, 850–58.

Hogan, A. E. (1999). Cognitive functioning in children with oppositional defiant disorder and conduct disorder. In H. C. Quay, & A. E. Hogan (eds), *Handbook of Disruptive Behavior* (pp. 317–35). New York: Kluwer Academic/Plenum Press.

Holden, G., & Ritchie, K. (1991). Linking extreme marital discord, child rearing, and child behavior problems: Evidence from battered women. *Child Development*, *62*, 311–27.

Holden, G. W., Stein, J. D., Ritchie, K. L., Harris, S. D., & Jouriles, E. N. (1998). Parenting behaviors and beliefs of battered women. In G. W. Holden, R. G. Geffner, & E. N. Jouriles (eds), *Children Exposed to Marital Violence* (pp. 289–334). Washington, DC: American Psychological Association.

Holmbeck, G. N. (1997). Toward terminological, conceptual, and statistical clarity in the study of mediators and moderators: examples from the child-clinical and pediatric psychology literatures. *Journal of Consulting and Clinical Psychology*, 65, 599–610.

Horizon Jeugdzorg (2006). *Methodiekbeschrijving Besloten Groep* [Method manual for closed groups] . Rotterdam: Horizon Jeugdzorg en Onderwijs.

Howe, G. W., Reiss, D., & Yuh, J. (2002). Can prevention trials test theories of etiology? *Development and Psychopathology*, *14*, 673–694.

Howell, J. C. (2001). Juvenile justice programs and strategies. In R. Loeber, & D. P. Farrington (eds), *Child Delinquents: Development, Interventions, and Service Needs* (pp. 305–22). Thousand Oaks, CA: Sage Publications.

Howell, J .C. (2003). Diffusing research into practice using the comprehensive strategy for serious, violent, and chronic juvenile offenders. *Youth Violence and Juvenile Justice*, *1*, 219–45.

Howell, J. C. (2003). *Preventing and Reducing Juvenile Delinquency, a Comprehensive Framework*. Thousand Oaks, CA: Sage Publications.

Huang, Y. Y., Cate, S. P., Battustuzzi, C., Oquendo, M. A., Brent, D., & Mann, J. J. (2004). An association between a functional polymorphism in the monoamine oxidase a gene promoter, impulsive traits and early abuse experiences. *Neuropsychopharmacology*, *29*, 1498–505.

Huey, S. J., Jr., & Weisz, J. R. (1997). Ego control, ego resiliency, and the Five-Factor Model as predictors of behavioral and emotional problems in clinic-referred children and adolescents. *Journal of Abnormal Psychology*, *106*, 404–15.

Hughes, J. N., Cavell, T. A., & Grossman, P. B. (1997). A positive view of self: Risk or protection of aggressive children? *Development and Psychopathology*, *9*, 75–94.

Huizinga, D., Thornberry, T. P., Knight, K. E., Lovegrove, P. J., Loeber, R., Hill, K., & Farrington, D. P. (2006). Disproportionate minority contact in the juvenile justice system: A study of differential minority arrest/referral to court in three cities. Report to the Office of Juvenile Justice and Delinquency Prevention <www.ncjrs.gov/pdffiles1/ojjdp/grants/219743.pdf>.

Huizink, A. C., Mulder, E. J., & Buitelaar, J. K. (2004). Prenatal stress and risk for psychopathology: Specific effects or induction of general susceptibility? *Psychological Bulletin*, *130*, 115–42.

Huizink, A. C., Robles de Medina, P. G., Mulder, E. J., Visser, G. H., & Buitelaar, J. K. (2003). Stress during pregnancy is associated with developmental outcome in infancy. *Journal of Child Psychology and Psychiatry*, *44*, 810–18.

Hrynkiw-Augimeri, L. K. (1998). Assessing risk for violence in boys: A preliminary risk assessment study using the Early Assessment Risk List for Boys *(EARL-20B)*. Unpublished Master's thesis, Ontario Institute for Studies in Education, University of Toronto, Ontario, Canada.

Hrynkiw-Augimeri, L. K. (2005). Aggressive and antisocial young children: Risk assessment and management utilizing the Early Assessment Risk List for Boys *(EARL-20B)*. Unpublished Ph.D Dissertation, Ontario Institute for Studies in Education, University of Toronto, Ontario, Canada.

Hrynkiw-Augimeri, L., Pepler, D., & Goldberg, K. (1993). An outreach program for children having police contact. *Canada's Mental Health*, *41*, 7–12.

Ince, D., Beumer, M., Jonkman, H., & Vergeer, M. (2004). *Veelbelovend en effectief. Overzicht van preventieve projecten en programma's in de domeinen gezin, school, jeugd, wijk* [Promising and effective. Overview of prevention projects and programmes in the domains of family, youth, and neighbourhood]. Utrecht: Netherlands Institute for Care and Welfare.

Jaarbericht – 2006 [Annual report 2006] (2007). Utrecht: Raad voor de Kinderbescherming.

Jaarbericht Halt-sector – 2006 [Annual report Halt-sector 2006]. Leiden: Halt.

Jackson, P. W. (1968). *Life in Classrooms*. New York: Holt, Rinehart and Winston.

Jaffee, S. R., Caspi, A., Moffitt, T. E., Dodge, K. A., Rutter, M., Taylor, A., & Tully, L. A. (2005). Nature x nurture: Genetic vulnerabilities interact with physical maltreatment to promote conduct problems. *Development and Psychopathology*, *17*, 67–84.

Jang, K. L., McCrae, R. R., Angleitner, A., Riemann, R., & Livesly, J. W. (1998). Heritability of facet-level traits in a cross-cultural twin sample: Support for a hierarchical model of personality. *Journal of Personality and Social Psychology*, *74*, 1556–65.

Jansen, L. M., Gispen-de Wied, C. C., Jansen, M. A., van der Gaag, R. J., Matthys, W., & van Engeland, H. (1999). Pituitary-adrenal reactivity in a child psychiatric population: Salivary cortisol response to stressors. *European Neuropsychopharmacology*, *9*, 67–75.

Jansen, W., van Berkel, A., & Veelen-Dieleman, N. (2003). *Rotterdamse Jeugdmonitor groep 6* [Rotterdam Youth Monitor group 6]. Rotterdam: GGD Rotterdam en Omstreken.

Japel, C., Tremblay, R. E., Vitaro, F., & Boulerice, B. (1999). Early parental separation and the psychosocial development of daughters 6–9 years old. *American Journal of Criminology*, *35*, 13–47.

Jeglum-Bartusch, D., Lynam, D., Moffitt, T. E., & Silva, P. (1997). Is age important: Testing general versus developmental theories of antisocial behavior. *Orthopsychiatry*, *69*, 49–60.

Jensen-Campbell, L. A., & Graziano, W. G. (2001). Agreeableness as a moderator of interpersonal conflict. *Journal of Personality*, *69*, 323–62.

Jessor, R. (1998). *New Perspectives on Adolescent Risk Behaviour*. Cambridge: Cambridge University Press.

John, O. P., Caspi, A., Robins, R. W., Moffitt, T. E., & Stouthamer-Loeber, M. (1994). The 'little five': Exploring the nomological network of the five-factor model of personality in adolescent boys. *Child Development*, *65*, 160–78.

John, O. P., & Gross, J. J. (2004). Healthy and unhealthy emotion regulation: Personality processes, individual differences, and life span development. *Journal of Personality*, *72*, 1301–33.

Johnson, R. J., Ross, M. W., Taylor, W. C., Williams, M. L., Carvajal, R. I., & Peters, R. J. (2006). Prevalence of childhood sexual abuse among incarcerated males in county jail. *Child Abuse & Neglect*, *30*, 75–86.

Johnson, J. H., & Sheeber, L. B. (1999). Developmental assessment. In W. K. Silverman, & T. H. Ollendick (eds), *Developmental Issues in the Clinical Treatment of Children* (pp. 44–59). Boston, MA: Allyn and Bacon.

Jones, I., Gullo, D. F., Burton-Maxwell, C., & Stoiber, K. (1998). Social and academic effects of varying types of early schooling experiences. *Early Child Development and Care*, *146*, 1–11.

Jonkman, H., Junger-Tas, J., & van Dijk, B. (2005). Communities That Care behind dikes and dunes. *Children and Society*, *19*, 105–17.

Junger, M., Feder, L., & Côté, S. M. (2007a). Policy implications of present knowledge on the development of prevention of physical aggression. *European Journal of Criminal Policy and Research, 13, 301–26*

Junger, M., Feder, L., Clay, J., Côté, S. M., Farrington, D. P., Freiberg, K., Genovés, V. G., Homel, R., Lösel, F., Manning, M., Mazerolle, P., Santos, R., Schmucker, M., Sullivan, C., Sutton, C., van Yperen, T., & Tremblay, R. E. (2007b). Preventing violence in seven countries: Global convergence in politics. *European Journal of Criminal Policy and Research*, 13, 327–56.

Junger, M., Wittebrood, K., & Timman, R. (2001). Ethniciteit en ernstige en geweldadig crimineel gedrag [Ethnicity and serious and violent offending]. In R. Loeber, N. W. Slot, & J. A. Sergeant (eds), *Ernstige en Geweldadige Jeugddelinquentie, Omvang, Oorzakeen en Interventies* (pp. 97–127). Houten/ Diegem: Bohn Stafleu Van Loghem.

Junger-Tas, J. (1996). *Jeugd en Gezin* [Youth and family]. The Hague: Ministerie van Justitie.

Junger-Tas, J. (2001). Beleid en preventie van jeugdcriminaliteit [Policy and prevention of juvenile crime]. In D. Ince, M. Beumer, H. Jonkman, & M. Pannebakker (eds), *Veelbelovend en Effectief* (pp. 13–26). Eerste editie CtC-gids [1st edn CtC-guide], NIZW: Utrecht.

Junger-Tas, J., & Haen-Marshall, I. (1999). The self-report methodology in crime research. In M. Tonry (ed.), *Crime and Justice. A Review of Research* (pp. 291–367). Chicago, IL: University of Chicago Press.

Junger-Tas, J., & Slot, N. W. (2001). Preventie van ernstig delinquent en gewelddadig gedrag [Prevention of serious delinquent and violent behaviour]. In R. Loeber, N. W. Slot & J. A. Sergeant (eds), *Ernstige en Geweldadige Jeugddelinquentie, Omvang, Oorzakeen en Interventies* (pp. 265–89). Houten/Diegem: Bohn Stafleu Van Loghem.

Kalb, L. M., Farrington, D. P., & Loeber, R. (2001). Leading longitudinal studies on delinquency, substance use, sexual behaviour, and mental health problems with childhood samples. In R. Loeber & D. P. Farrington (eds), *Child Delinquents: Development, Intervention, and Service Needs* (pp. 415–23). Thousand Oaks, CA/London/New Delhi: Sage.

Kalsbeek, E. (2002). Astounded en effectief. Nota jeugdcriminaliteit. The Hague: Ministerie van Justitie (26 March) < www.justitie.nl>.

Kandel, E., Mednick, S. A., Kirkegaard-Sorensen, L., Hutchings, B., Knop, J., Rosenberg, R., & Schulsinger, F. (1988). IQ as a protective factor for subjects at high risk for antisocial behavior. *Journal of Consulting and Clinical Psychology*, *56*, 224–6.

Kaplan, A., Gheen, M., & Midgley, C. (2002). Classroom goal structure and student disruptive behaviour. *British Journal of Educational Psychology*, *72*, 191–211.

Kaufman, J., & Zigler, E. (1987). Do abused children become abusive parents? *American Journal of Orthopsychiatry*, *57*, 186–92.

Kazdin, A. E. (1997). Practitioner review: Psychosocial treatments for conduct disorders in children. *Journal of Child Psychology and Psychiatry*, *62*, 161–82.

Kazdin, A. E. (2001). Progression of therapy research and clinical application of treatment require better understanding of the change process. *Clinical Psychology: Science and Practice*, *8*, 143–51.

Keating, D. P., & Hertzman, C. (eds) (1999). *Developmental Health and the Wealth of Nations. Social, Biological and Educational Dynamics.* New York/London: Guilford Press.

Keenan, K. (2001). Uncovering preschool precursors to problem behaviour. In R. Loeber, & D. P. Farrington (eds), *Child Delinquents: Development, Intervention, and Service Needs* (pp. 117–34). Thousand Oaks, CA: Sage.

Keenan, K., & Shaw, D. D. (2003). Development of conduct problems during the preschool years. In B. B. Lahey, T. E. Moffitt, & A. Caspi (eds), *Causes of Conduct Disorder and Juvenile Delinquency* (pp. 153–81). New York: Guilford Press.

Keiley, M. K., Bates, J. E., Dodge, K. A., & Pettit, G. S. (2000). A cross-domain growth analysis: Externalizing and internalizing behaviors during 8 years of childhood. *Journal of Abnormal Child Psychology*, *28*, 161–79.

Kellam, S. G., Ling, X., Merisca, R., Brown, C. H., & Ialongo, N. (1998). The effect of the level of aggression in the first grade classroom on the course and malleability of aggressive behavior into middle school. *Development and Psychopathology*, *10*, 165–85.

Kellam, S. G, Rebok, G.W., Ialongo, N., & Mayer, L.S. (1994). The course and malleability of aggressive behaviour from early first grade into middle school: Results of a developmental epidemiologically-based preventive trial. *Journal of Child Psychology and Psychiatry*, *35*, 259–81.

Kelley, B. T., Loeber, R., Keenan, K., & DeLamatre, M. (1997). *Developmental Pathways in Boys Disruptive and Delinquent Behavior.* Washington, DC: OJJDP Juvenile Justice Bulletin.

Kendall-Tackett, K. E., Williams, L. M., & Finkelhor, D. (1993). The impact of sexual abuse on children: A review and synthesis of recent empirical studies. *Psychological Bulletin*, *113*, 164–80.

Kendler, K. S., & Eaves, L. J. (2004). Models for the joint effect of genotype and environment on liability to psychiatric illness. *American Journal of Psychiatry*, *143*, 279–89.

Kendler, K. S., Jacobson, K. C., Gardner, C. O., Gillespie, N., Aggen, S. A., & Prescott, C. A. (2007). Creating a social world: a developmental twin study of peer-group deviance. *Archives of General Psychiatry*, *64*, 958–65.

Killingsworth Rini, C., Dunkel-Scheter, C., Wadhwa, P. D., & Sandman, C. A. (1999). Psychological adaptation and birth outcomes: The role of personal resources, stress, and sociocultural context in pregnancy. *Health Psychology*, *18*, 333–45.

Kipke, M. D. (ed.) (1999). *Risks and Opportunities, Syntheses of Studies on Risk and Opportunities.* National Research Council/Institute of Medicine/Board on children, youth and families. Washington, DC: National Academy Press.

Kirschner, G. (1997). *Die Kinder Stark Machen. Aggressionsabbau Durch Persönlichkeitsaufbau.* Lichtenau: AOL-Verlag.

Klasse (1994). Leraars kunnen pestkoppen stoppen. *Klasse, Mandblad voor Onderwijs in Vlaanderen*, *49*, 24–5.

Klooster, E., Slump, G.-J., Nauta, O., & Bürmann, A. (2002). *Stopreactie, Redenen van Niet Bereik*. Amsterdam: DSP Groep.

Knutson, J. F., DeGarmo, D., Koeppl, G., & Reid, J. B. (2005). Care neglect, supervisory neglect, and harsh parenting in the development of children's aggression: A replication and extension. *Child Maltreatment*, *10*, 92–107.

Kochanska, G., Clark, L. A., & Goldman, M. S. (1997). Implications of mothers' personality for their parenting and their young children's development outcomes. *Journal of Personality*, *65*, 387–420.

Koegl, C. J., Farrington, D. P., & Augimeri, L. K., & Day, D. M. (2008). Evaluation of a targeted cognitive-behavioural programme for children with conduct problems – The SNAP® Under 12 Outreach Project: Service intensity, age and gender effects on short- and long-term outcomes. *Clinical Child Psychology and Psychiatry, 13*(3), 419–434.

Koegl, C. J., Webster, C. D., & Levens, K. S. (2001). *Early Assessment Risk List for Boys: EARL-20B, Version 2*. Toronto: Earlscourt Child and Family Centre.

Kolko, D. (1992). Characteristics of child victims of physical violence: Research findings and clinical implications. *Journal of Interpersonal Violence*, *7*, 244–76.

Kolko, D. J. (1996). Individual cognitive behavioural treatment and family therapy for physically abused children and their offending parents: A comparison of clinical outcomes. *Child Maltreatment*, *1*, 322–42.

Kooijman, K., & Wolzak, A. (2004). *Verkennende Studie Preventie Kindermishandeling* [Explorative study of preventing child abuse]. The Hague: Ministerie van Justitie.

Korte, J. (1992). *Faustrecht auf dem Schulhof.* Weinheim: Beltz.

Kounin, J. S. (1970). *Discipline and Group Management in Classrooms.* New York: Holt, Rinehart and Winston.

Kroon, K. (2005). 12-. Een onderzoek naar de (gezins)kenmerken van kinderen in de leeftijd van nul tot twaalf jaar die meerdere malen met de politie in aanraking zijn geweest in Amsterdam [12-. A study of family characteristics of children aged 0 to 12 who have been in contact with the police in Amsterdam more than once]. Unpublished doctoral thesis. Amsterdam: Vrije Universiteit.

Krueger, R. F., Caspi, A., Moffitt, T. E., Silva, P. A., & McGee, R. (1996). Personality traits are differentially linked to mental disorders: A multitrait–multidiagnosis study of an adolescent birth cohort. *Journal of Abnormal Psychology*, *105*, 299–312.

Krueger, R. F., Caspi, A., Moffitt, T. E., White, J., & Stouthamer-Loeber, M. (1996). Delay of gratification, psychopathology, and personality: Is low self-control specific to externalizing problems? *Journal of Personality*, *64*, 107–29.

Kuire, R. (2003). Finland. In A. Stevens, & B. Gladstone (eds), *Learning not Offending Diversion of Young People from Crime in Europe.* Brasted: RPS Rainer.

Kumpfer, K. L., & Alvarado, R. (2003). Family strengthening approaches for the prevention of youth problem behaviours. *American Psychologist*, *58*, 457–66.

Kyvsgaard, B. (2004). Youth justice in Denmark. In M. Tonry, & A. N. Doob (eds), *Youth Crime and Youth Justice* (pp. 349–90). Chicago. IL/London: University of Chicago Press.

Lacourse, E., Dupéré, V., & Loeber, R. (2008). Developmental trajectories of violence and theft. In R. Loeber, D. P. Farrington, M. Stouthamer-Loeber, & H. R. White (eds), *Violence and Serious Theft: Development and Prediction from Childhood to Adulthood*. New York: Routledge.

Lacourse, E., Nagin, D., Tremblay, R. E., Vitaro, F., & Claes, M. (2003). Developmental trajectories of boys' delinquent group membership and facilitation of violent behaviors during adolescence. *Development and Psychopathology*, *15*, 183–97.

Lahey, B. B., Loeber, R., Burke, J. D., & Applegate, B. (2005). Predicting future antisocial personality disorder in males from a clinical assessment in childhood. *Journal of Consulting and Clinical Psychology*, *73*, 389–99.

Lahey, B. B., Moffitt, T. E., & Caspi, A. (eds) (2003). *Causes of Conduct Disorder and Juvenile Delinquency*. New York: Guilford.

Laird, R. D., Jordan, K. Y., Dodge, K. A., Pettit, G. S., & Bates, J. E. (2001). Peer rejection in childhood, involvement with antisocial peers in early adolescence, and the development of externalizing behavior problems. *Development and Psychopathology*, *13*, 337–54.

Lamers-Winkelman, F. (2004). *Als alle kleine beetjes helpen ... Effecten van het programma Let op de Kleintjes in de provincie Overijssel* [When all small bits help ... Effects of the programme Mind the little ones in the province of Overijssel]. Amsterdam: Vrije Universiteit.

Lamers-Wilkelman, F. (in preparation). *Victimized Children*. Amsterdam: Vrije Universiteit.

Lamers-Winkelman, F., Slot, N. W., Bijl, B., & Vijlbrief, A. C. (2007). *Scholieren over mishandeling: resultaten van een landelijk onderzoek naar de omvang van kindermishandeling onder leerlingen van het voortgezet onderwijs* [Students about abuse: Results of a national study on the magnitude of child abuse among students in secondary education]. Amsterdam/Duivendrecht: Vrije Universiteit/PI Research.

Lane, D. A. (1989). Violent histories: Bullying and criminality. In D. P. Tattum, & D. A. Lane (eds), *Bullying in Schools* (pp. 95–104). Stoke-on-Trent: Trentham Books.

Lansford, J. E., Miller-Johnson, S., Berlin, L. J., Dodge, K. A., Bates, J. E., & Pettit, G. S. (2007). Early physical abuse and later violent delinquency: A prospective longitudinal study. *Child Maltreatment*, *12*, 233–45.

Larsson, A. <www.rikoksentorjunta.fi/uploads/u7fw7yhpp.doc>.

Laub, J. H., & Sampson, R. J. (2003). *Shared Beginnings, Divergent Lives: Delinquent Boys up to Age 70*. Cambridge, MA: Harvard University Press.

Lavallee, K. L., Bierman, K. L., & Nix, R. L. (2005). The impact of first-grade 'friendship group' experiences on child social outcomes in the fast track program. *Journal of Abnormal Child Psychology*, *33*, 307–24.

Le Blanc, M. (1998). Screening of serious and violent juvenile offenders: Identification, classification and prediction. In R. Loeber, & D. P. Farrington (eds), *Serious and Violent Juvenile Offenders* (pp. 167–96). Thousand Oakes, CA: Sage.

Le Blanc, M. (2000). Review of screening, decision-making, and clinical assessments strategies and instruments for adolescent offenders 1. Paper presented at Multi-problem violent Youth: A foundation for comparative research on needs, intervention, and outcomes. NATO Advanced Research Workshop.

Le Blanc, M. (2002). The offending cycle, escalation and de-escalation in delinquent behavior: A challenge for criminology. *International Journal of Comparative and Applied Criminal Justice*, *26*, 53–83.

Le Blanc, M., Côté, G., & Loeber, R. (1991). Temporal paths in delinquency: Stability, regression, and progression analyzed with panel data from an adolescent and a delinquent male sample. *Canadian Journal of Criminology*, *33*, 23–44.

Le Blanc, M., & Fréchette, M. (1989). *Male Criminal Activity from Childhood Through Youth. Multilevel and Developmental Perspectives*. New York: Springer-Verlag.

Lemerize, E. A., & Dodge, K. A. (1993). The development of anger and hostile interactions. In M. Lewis, & J. M. Haviland (eds). *Handbook of Emotions* (pp. 537–46). New York: Guilford Press.

Lengua, L. J. (2002). The contribution of emotionality and self-regulation to the understanding of children's responses to multiple risks. *Child Development*, *73*, 144–61.

Lengua, L. J., Wolchik, S. A., Sandler, I. N., & West, S. G. (2000). The additive and interactive effects of parenting and temperament in predicting problems of children of divorce. *Journal of Clinical Child Psychology*, *29*, 232–44.

Lerner, R. M., & Castellino, D. R. (2002). Contemporary, developmental theory and adolescence: Developmental systems and applied developmental science. *Journal of Adolescent Health*, *31*, 122–35.

Levene, K. S. (2003). *SNAP™ Girls Group Manual: The Girls Club*. Toronto: Earlscourt Child and Family Centre.

Levene, K. S., Augimeri, L. K., Pepler, D. J., Walsh, M. M., Webster, C. D., & Koegl, C.J. (2001). *Early Assessment Risk List for Girls. Version 1: Consultation version.* Toronto: Earlscourt Child and Family Centre.

Levene, K. S., Madsen, K. C., & Pepler, D. J. (2005). Girls growing up angry: A qualitative study. In D. J. Pepler, K. C. Madsen, C. Webster, & K. S. Levene (eds), *The Development and Treatment of Girlhood Aggression.* Mahwah, NJ: Lawrence Erlbaum.

Levene, K. S., Walsh, M. M., Augimeri, L. K., & Pepler, D. J. (2004). Linking identification and treatment of early risk factors for female delinquency. In M. M. Moretti, C. L. Odgers, & M. A. Jackson (eds), *Girls and Aggression: Contributing Factors and Intervention Principles* (pp. 41–56). New York: Kluwer Academic/Plenum.

Lewin, K., Lippitt, R., & White, R. K. (1939). Patterns of aggressive behavior in experimentally created social climates. *Journal of Social Psychology*, *10*, 271–99.

Lieshout, C. F. M. van, Scholte, R. H. J., Haselager, G. J. T., & Cillessen, A. H. N. (2001).Ontwikkeling van relaties en delinquentie [Development of relationships and delinquency]. In R. Loeber, N. W. Slot, & J. A. Sergeant (eds), *Ernstige enGewelddadige Jeugddelinquentie* (pp. 185–204). Houten/Diegem: Bohn Stafleu Van Loghum.

Liefaard, T., *Toegang tot de beginselenwet justitiele jeugdinrichtingen* [Access to the legislation concern institutions for juveniles]. Amsterdam: SWP Uitgeverij, 2005.

Lieverse, G., Heineke, D., & Hoffman, E. (2002). *Handleiding JPP, een Handleiding voor Jeugdpreventiewerkers* [Manual JJP: a manual for youth prevention workers]. Utrecht: NIZW.

Ligthart, L., Bartels, M., Hoekstra, R. A., Hudziak, J. J., & Boomsma, D. I. (2005). Genetic contributions to subtypes of aggression. *Twin Research and Human Genetics*, *8*, 483–91.

Lipman, E. L., Kenny, M., Sniderman, C., O'Grady, S., Augimeri, L., Khayutin, S., & Boyle, M. H. (2008). Evaluation of a community-based program for young boys at-risk of antisocial behaviour: Results and issues. *Journal of the Canadian Academy of Child and Adolescent Psychiatry, 17*(1), 12–19.

Lipsey, M. W. (1995). What do we learn from 400 research studies on the effectiveness off treatment with juvenile delinquents? In J. McGuire (ed.), *What Works: Reducing Reoffending, Guidelines from Research and Practice* (pp. 63–78). Chichester: John Wiley & Sons.

Lipsey, M. W., & Derzon, J. H. (1998). Predictors of violent or serious delinquency in adolescence and early adulthood: A synthesis of longitudinal research. In R. Loeber, & D. P. Farrington (eds), *Serious and Violent Juvenile Offenders: Risk Factors and Successful Interventions* (pp. 86–105). Thousands Oaks, CA: Sage Publications.

Lipsey, M. W., & Wilson, D. (1998). Effective intervention for serious juvenile offenders: A synthesis of research. In R. Loeber, & D. P. Farrington (eds), *Serious and Violent Juvenile offenders: Risk Factors and Successful Interventions* (pp. 313–45). Newbury Park, CA: Sage.

Littell, J. H., Popa, M., & Forsythe, B. (2005). *Multisystemic Therapy for Social, Emotional, and Behavioral Problems in Youth Aged 10-17* (Review). The Cochrane Collaboration.

Lodewijks, H., de Ruiter, C., & Doreleijers, T. A. H. (2003). Risicotaxatie en risicohantering van geweldadig gedrag bij adolescenten [Risk assessment and risk management of adolescents' violent behaviour]. *Directieve Therapie*, *23*, 25–42.

Loeber, R. (1982). The stability of antisocial and delinquent child behavior: A review. *Child Development*, *53*, 1431–46.

Loeber, R. (1985). Patterns and development of antisocial child behavior. In G. J. Whitehurst (ed.), *Annals of Child Development* (pp. 77–116). Greenwich, CT: JAI Press.

Loeber, R. (1988). Natural histories of conduct problems, delinquency, and associated substance use: Evidence for developmental progressions. In B. B. Lahey, & A. E. Kazdin (eds), *Advances in Clinical Child Psychology* (pp. 73–124). New York, NY: Plenum.

Loeber, R. (1990). Development and risk factors of juvenile antisocial behavior and delinquency. *Clinical Psychology Review*, *10*, 1–41.

Loeber, R. (1991). Antisocial behavior: More enduring than changeable? *Journal of the American Academy of Child and Adolescent Psychiatry*, *30*, 393–7.

Loeber, R. (1996). Developmental continuity, change, and pathways in male juvenile problem behaviors and delinquency. In J. D. Hawkins (ed.), *Delinquency and Crime: Current Theories* (pp. 1–27). New York: Cambridge University Press.

Loeber, R., Burke, J. D., & Lahey, B. B. (2002). What are adolescent antecedents to antisocial personality disorder? *Criminal Behaviour and Mental Health*, *12*, 24–36.

Loeber, R., Burke, J. D., Lahey, B. B., Winters, A., & Zera, M. (1993). Oppositional Defiant and Conduct Disorder: A Review of the Past 10 Years, Part I. *Journal of the American Academy of Child and Adolescent Psychiatry*, *39*, 1468–84.

Loeber, R., DeLamatre, M., Keenan, K., & Zhang, Q. (1998). A prospective replication of developmental pathways in disruptive and delinquent behavior. In R. Cairns, L. Bergman, & J. Kagan (eds), *Methods and Models for Studying the Individual* (pp. 185–215). Thousand Oaks, CA: Sage.

Loeber, R., & Dishion, T. J. (1983). Early predictors of male delinquency: A review. *Psychological Bulletin*, *94*, 68–99.

Loeber, R., Dishion, T. J., & Patterson, G. R. (1984). Multiple gating: A multistage assessment procedure for identifying youths at risk for delinquency. *Journal of Research on Crime and Delinquency*, *21*, 7–32.

Loeber, R., Drinkwater, M., Yin, Y., Anderson, S.J., Schmidt, L.C.,, & Crawford, A. (2000). Stability of family interactions from ages 6 to 18. *Journal of Abnormal Child Psychology*, *28*, 353–69.

Loeber, R., & Farrington, D. P. (1997). Strategies and yields of longitudinal studies on antisocial behavior. In D. M. Stoff, J. Breiling, & J. D. Maser (eds), *Handbook of Antisocial Behavior* (pp. 125–39). New York: John Wiley & Sons, Inc.

Loeber, R., & Farrington, D. F. (1998). *Serious and Violent Juvenile Offenders: Risk Factors and Successful Interventions.* Thousand Oaks, CA: Sage.

Loeber, R., & Farrington, D. P. (2000). Young children who commit crime: epidemiology, development origins, risk factors, early interventions, and policy implications. *Development and Psychopathology*, *12*, 737–62.

Loeber, R., & Farrington, D. P. (2001). *Child Delinquents: Development, Intervention and Service Needs.* Thousand Oaks, CA: Sage.

Loeber, R., & Farrington, D. P. (2004). Verschillende oorzaken van delinquentie tussen etnische en nationale groepen? Longitudinale analyses van criminaliteit onder jonge mannen in Pittsburgh en Londen [Different causes of delinquency for ethnic and national groups? Longitudinal analysis of crime among young men in Pittsburgh and London]. *Tijdschrift voor Criminologie*, *46*, 330–46.

Loeber, R., Farrington, D. P., & Petechuk, D. (2003, May). Child delinquency: Early intervention and prevention. *Child Delinquency Bulletin Series*. Washington, DC: Office of Juvenile Justice and Delinquency Prevention.

Loeber, R., Farrington, D. P., Stouthamer-Loeber, M., & White, H. R. (2008). *Violence and Serious Theft: Development and Prediction from Childhood to Adulthood.* New York: Routledge.

Loeber, R., Homish, D. L., Wei, E. H., Pardini, D., Crawford, A. M., Farrington, D. P., Stouthamer-Loeber, M., Creemers, J., Koehler, S. A., & Rosenfeld, R. (2005).

The prediction of violence and homicide in young males. *Journal of Consulting and Clinical Psychology, 73, 1074–88.*

Loeber, R., & Keenan, K. (1994). Interaction between Conduct Disorder and its comorbid conditions: Effects of age and gender. *Clinical Psychology Review, 14*, 497–523.

Loeber, R., Keenan, K., Lahey, B. B., Green, S. M., & Thomas, C. (1993). Evidence for developmentally based diagnoses of Oppositional Defiant Disorder and Conduct Disorder. *Journal of Abnormal Child Psychology*, *21*, 377–410.

Loeber, R., Keenan, K., & Zhang, Q. (1997). Boys' experimentation and persistence in developmental pathways toward serious delinquency. *Journal of Child and Family Studies*, *6*, 321–57.

Loeber, R., Pardini, D. A., Stouthamer-Loeber, M., & Raine, A. (2007). Do cognitive, physiological and psycho-social risk and promotive factors predict desistance from delinquency in males? *Development and Psychopathology*, *19*, 867–87.

Loeber, R., & Slot, W. (2007). Serious and violent juvenile delinquency: An update. In M. Tonry, & C. Bijleveld (eds), *Crime and Justice in the Netherlands* (vol. 35, pp. 503–92). Chicago, IL: University of Chicago Press.

Loeber, R., Slot, N. W., & Sergeant, J. A. (2001). *Ernstige en Gewelddadige Jeugddelinquentie, Omvang, Oorzaken en Interventies*. Houten/Diegum: Bohn Stafleu Van Loghum.

Loeber, R., Slot, N. W., & Stouthamer-Loeber, M. (2006). A three-dimensional, cumulative developmental model of serious delinquency. In P.-O. H. Wikström, & R. Sampson (eds), *The Explanation of Crime: Contexts and Mechanisms* (pp. 153–94). Cambridge: Cambridge University Press.

Loeber, R., & Stouthamer-Loeber, M. (1986). Family factors as correlates and predictors of juvenile conduct problems and delinquency. In M. Tonry, & N. Morris (eds), *Crime and Justice: An Annual Review of Research* (Vol. 7, pp. 29–149). Chicago, IL: University of Chicago Press.

Loeber, R., & Stouthamer-Loeber, M. (1998). Development of juvenile aggression and behavior: Some common misconceptions and controversies. *American Psychologist*, *53*, 242–59.

Loeber, R., Stouthamer Loeber, M., & Green, S. M. (1991). Age at onset of problem behaviour in boys, and later disruptive and delinquent behaviours. *Criminal Behaviour and Mental Health*, *1*, 229–46.

Loeber, R., Wei, E., Stouthamer-Loeber, M., Huizinga, D., & Thornberry, T. (1999). Behavioral antecedents to serious and violent juvenile offending: Joint analyses from the Denver Youth Survey, Pittsburgh Youth Study, and the Rochester Development Study. *Studies in Crime and Crime Prevention*, *8*, 245–63.

Loeber, R., & Wikström, P.-O. (1993). Individual pathways to crime in different types of neighborhood. In D. P. Farrington, R. J. Sampson, & P.-O. Wikström (eds), *Integrating Individual and Ecological Aspects of Crime* (pp. 169–204). Stockholm, Sweden: Liber Forlag.

Loeber, R., Wung, P., Keenan, K., Giroux, B., Stouthamer-Loeber, M., van Kammen, W.B., & Maughan, B. (1993). Developmental pathways in disruptive child behavior. *Development and Psychopathology*, *5*, 101–32.

Loehlin, J. C., & Horn, J. M. (2000). Stoolmiller on restriction of range in adoption studies: A comment. *Behavior Genetics*, *30*, 245–7.

Lorber, M. F. (2004). Psychophysiology of aggression, psychopathy, and conduct problems: A meta-analysis. *Psychological Bulletin*, *130*, 531–52.

Lösel, F., & Bender, D. (2003). Protective factors and resilence. In D. P. Farrington, & J. Coid (eds), *Early Prevention of Adult Anti-social Behaviour*. Cambridge: Cambridge University Press.

Lynam, D. R., Caspi, A., Moffitt, T. E., Wikström, P.-O., Loeber, R., & Novak, S. (2000). The interaction between impulsivity and neighborhood context on offending: The effects of impulsivity are stronger in poorer neighborhoods. *Journal of Abnormal Psychology*, *109*, 563–74.

Lynam, D. R., & Henry, B. (2001). The role of neuropsychological deficits in conduct disorders. In J. Hill, & B. Maughan (eds), *Conduct Disorders in Childhood and Adolescence* (pp 235–63). New York: Cambridge University Press.

Lyons, M. J., True, W. R., Eisen, S. A., Goldberg, J., Meyer, J. M., Faraone, S. V., Eaves, L. J., & Tsuang, M. T. (1995). Differential heritability of adult and juvenile antisocial traits. *Archives of General Psychiatry*, *52*, 906–15.

Lyons-Ruth, K. (1991). Rapprochement of approchement: Mahler's theory reconsidered from the vantage point of recent research in early attachment relationships. *Psychoanalytic Psychology*, *8*, 1–23.

Lytton, H. (1990). Child and parent effects in boys' conduct disorder: A reinterpretation. *Developmental Psychology*, *26*, 683–97.

Lytton, H., & Romney, D. M. (1991). Parents' differential socialization of boys and girls: A meta-analysis. *Psychological Bulletin*, *109*, 267–96.

Maccoby, E. E. (1992). The role of parents in the socialization of children: A historical overview. *Developmental Psychology*, *28*, 1006–17.

Maccoby, E. E. (1998). *The Two Sexes: Growing up Apart, Coming Together*. Cambridge, MA: Belknap Press/Harvard University Press.

Maccoby, E. E., & Martin, J. A. (1983). Socialization in the context of the family: Parent–child interaction. In P. H. Mussen, & E. M. Hetherington (eds), *Handbook of Child Psychology: Vol. 4. Socialization, Personality, and Social Development* (4th edn, pp. 1–101). New York: Wiley.

Mager, W., Milich, R., Harris, M. J., & Howard, A. (2005). Intervention groups for adolescents with conduct problems: Is aggregation harmful or helpful? *Journal of Abnormal Child Psychology*, *33*, 349–62.

Maguin, E., & Loeber, R. (1996). Academic performance and its relationship to delinquency. In S. C. Cramer, & W. Ellis (eds), *Learning Disabilities: Lifelong Issues* (pp. 235–40). Baltimore, MD: Paul H. Brooks.

Mahoney, J. L., Stattin, H., & Magnusson, D. (2001). Youth recreation centre participation and criminal offending: A 20-year longitudinal study of Swedish boys. *International Journal of Behavioral Development*, *25*, 509–20.

Mangione, P. K., & Speth, T. (1998). The transition to elementary school: A framework for creating early childhood continuity through home, school, and community partnerships. *The Elementary School Journal*, *98*, 381–97.

Manke, B., McGuire, S., Reiss, D., Hetherington, E. M., & Plomin, R. (1995). Genetic contributions to adolescents' extrafamilial social interactions: Teachers, best friends, and peers. *Social Development*, *4*, 238–56.

Mann, M. (2003). Searching for the Key to the Self. Evaluation of the 'I Am The Key' program for Mental Heath Promotion. Unpublished doctoral thesis. Maastricht: University of Maastricht.

Marsh, P., Rosser, E., & Harré, R. (1978). *The Rules of Disorder.* London: Routledge & Kegan Paul.

Matthys, W., van Goozen, S. H. M., De Vries, H., Cohen-Kettenis, P. T., & van Engeland, H. (1998). The dominance of behavioural activation over behavioural inhibition in conduct disordered boys with or without attention deficit hyperactivity disorder. *Journal of Child Psychology and Psychiatry and Allied Disciplines*, *39*, 643–51.

Matthys, W. C. H. J. (2005). Het effect van een oudertraining en een sociaal probleemoplossende training voor kinderen met gedragsstoornissen in de alledaagse klinische praktijk [The effects of parent training and social problem solving training for children with conduct disorder in everyday clinical practice]. Paper presented at the Congres Jeugdzorg in Onderzoek, Amsterdam, January 2005.

Maughan, B., Pickles, A., Rowe, R., Costello, E. Jane, & Angold, A. (2000). Developmental trajectories of aggressive and non-aggressive conduct problems. *Journal of Quantitative Criminology*, *16*, 137–99.

Maughan, B., Taylor, A., Caspi, A., & Moffitt, T. E. (2004). Prenatal smoking and early childhood conduct problems: Testing genetic and environmental explanations of the association. *Archives of General Psychiatry*, *61*, 836–43.

Maxfield, M. G., Weiler, B. L., & Widom, C. S. (2000). Comparing self-reports and official records of arrests. *Journal of Quantitative Criminology*, *16*, 87-110.

McAlonan, G. M., Cheung, V., Cheung, C., Chua, S. E., Murphy, D. G., Suckling, J., Tai, K. S., Yip, L.K., Leung, P., & Ho, T. P (2007). Mapping brain structure in attention deficit-hyperactivity disorder: A voxel-based MRI study of regional grey and white matter volume. *Psychiatry Research*, *154*, 171–80.

McBurnett, K., Lahey, B. B., Rathouz, P. J., & Loeber, R. (2000). Low salivary cortisol and persistent aggression in boys referred for disruptive behavior. *Archives of General Psychiatry*, *57*, 38–43.

McBurnett, K., Raine, A., Stouthamer-Loeber, M., Loeber, R., Kumar, A. M., Kumar, M., & Lahey, B. B. (2005). Mood and hormone responses to psychological challenge in adolescent males with conduct problems. *Biological Psychiatry*, *57*, 1109–16.

McCord, J. (ed.) (1997). *Violence and Childhood in the Inner City.* Cambridge: Cambridge University Press.

McCrae, R. R., & Costa, P. T., Jr. (1996). Toward a new generation of personality theories: Theoretical contexts for the five-factor model. In J. S. Wiggins (ed.), *The Five-Factor Model of Personality: Theoretical Perspectives* (pp. 51–87). New York: Guilford Press.

McDougal, P., Hymel, S., Vaillancourt, T., & Mercer, L. (2001). The consequences of childhood peer rejection. In M.R. Lerner (ed.), *Interpersonal Rejection* (pp. 213–47). New York, NY: Oxford University Press.

McDougall, C., Cohen, M. A., Swaray, R., & Perry, A. (2003). The costs and benefits of sentencing: A systematic review. *The Annals of the American Academy, 587*, 160–77.

McEwen, B., & Lasley, E. N. (2003). Allostatic load: When protection gives way to damage. *Advances in Mind and Body Medicine, 19*, 28–33.

McFarlane, A. C., & van der Kolk, B. A. (1996). Trauma and its challenge to society. In B.A. van der Kolk, A.C. McFarlane, & L. Weisath (eds), *Traumatic Stress: The Effects of Overwhelming Experience on Mind, Body, and Society* (pp. 24–46). New York: Guilford Press.

Meeus, W., de la Rie, S., Luijpers, E., & de Wilde, E-J. (2001). De harde kern; ernstige, gewelddadige en persistente jeugdcriminaliteit in Nederland [Chronic offenders: serious, violent, and persistent juvenile delinquency in the Netherlands]. In R. Loeber, N. W. Slot, & J. A. Sergeant (eds), *Ernstige en Gewelddadige Jeugddelinquentie, Omvang, Oorzaken en Interventies* (pp. 51–71). Houten/Diegum: Bohn Stafleu Van Loghum.

Meeus, W., Oosterwegel, A., & Vollebergh, W. (2002). Parental and peer attachment and identity development in adolescence. *Journal of Adolescence, 25*, 93–106.

Melief, W., Verkuyl, L., & Flikweert, M. (2000). *Services Available in the Netherlands for Young Persons who have Experienced Sexual Abuse and Sexual Violence*. Utrecht: Verwey-Jonker Instituut.

Merry, S. N., Franzcp, C. B., & Andrews, L. K. (1994). Psychiatric status of sexually abused children 12 months after disclosure of abuse. *Journal of the American Academy of Child and Adolescent Psychiatry, 33*, 939–44.

Metselaar, J., Tönis, I., & van Lakerveld, J. (2000). *Initiatieven Rond Twaalfminners*. Leiden: PLATO/Universiteit Leiden.

Miles, D. R., & Carey, G. (1997). Genetic and environmental architecture of human aggression. *Journal of Personality and Social Psychology, 72*, 207–17.

Miller-Johnson, S., Coie, J. D., Maumary-Gremaud, A., & Bierman, K. (2002). Peer rejection and aggression and early starter models of conduct disorder. *Journal of Abnormal Child Psychology, 30*, 217–30.

Miller-Johnson, S., Coie, J. D., Maumary-Gremoud, A., Lochman, J. E., & Terry, R. (1999). Relationship between childhood peer rejection and aggression and adolescent delinquency severity and type among African American youth. *Journal of Emotional and Behavioral Disorders, 7*, 137–46.

Moffitt, T. E. (1993). Adolescence-limited and life-course-persistent and adolescence-limited antisocial behavior: A developmental taxonomy. *Psychological Review, 100*, 674–701.

Moffitt, T. E. (1997). Neuropsychology, antisocial behaviour and neighbourhood context. In J. McCord (ed.), *Violence and Childhood in the Inner City* (pp. 116–71). Cambridge: Cambridge University Press.

Moffitt, T. E. (2005). The new look of behavioral genetics in developmental psychopathology: Gene environment interplay in antisocial behaviors. *Psychological Bulletin, 131*, 533–54.

Moffitt, T. E., Arseneault, L., Jaffee, S. R., Kim-Cohen, J., Koenen, K. C., Odgers, C. L., Slutske, W. S., & Viding, E. (in press). Research reviews: DSM-V conduct disorder: Research needs for an evidence base. *Journal of Child Psychology and Psychiatry*.

Moffitt, T. E., & Caspi, A. (2001). Childhood predictors differentiate life-course persistent and adolescence-limited antisocial pathways among males and females. *Development and Psychopathology*, *13*, 355–75.

Moffitt, T. E., Caspi, A., Rutter, M., & Silva, P. A. (2001). *Sex Differences in Antisocial Behavior: Conduct Disorder, Delinquency and Violence in the Dunedin Longitudinal Study*. New York: Cambridge University Press.

Moffitt, T. E., Lynam, D. R., & Silva, P. A. (1994). Neuropsychological tests predicting persistent male delinquency. *Criminology*, *32*, 277–300.

Molenaar, D. E. G. (2006). Uitgaven aan criminaliteit. In W. Van der Heide, & A. T. J. Eggen (eds), *Criminaliteit en rechtshandhaving 2006* [Crimality and Justice 2006] (pp. 251–77). The Hague: Boom Juridische Uitgevers.

Mooij, T. (1980). Schoolproblemen en uitval in het voortgezet onderwijs. *Pedagogische Studiën*, *57*, 369-82.

Mooij, T. (1982). Onderwijsleersituatie en lesondergravend gedrag van ltoleerlingen. In E. Diekerhof (ed.), *Leren, wat moet je ermee?* (pp. 39-52). Muiderberg: Coutinho.

Mooij, T. (1987). *Interactional Multi-level Investigation into Pupil Behaviour, Achievement, Competence, and Orientation in Educational Situations*. The Hague: SVO.

Mooij, T. (1992). *Pesten in het Onderwijs* [Bullying in schools]. Nijmegen: University of Nijmegen, ITS.

Mooij, T. (1994). *Leerlinggeweld in het Voortgezet Onderwijs* [Student violence in secondary education]. Nijmegen: University of Nijmegen, ITS.

Mooij, T. (1999a). Preventing antisocial behaviour of young children at risk. *Risk Management: An International Journal*, *1*, 49–61.

Mooij, T. (1999b). Integrating gifted children into kindergarten by improving educational processes. *Gifted Child Quarterly*, *43*, 63–74.

Mooij, T. (2000). Screening children's entry characteristics in kindergarten. *Early Child Development and Care*, *165*, 23–40.

Mooij, T. (2001). *Veilige Scholen en (Pro)sociaal Gedrag* [Safe schools and prosocial behaviour]. Nijmegen: University of Nijmegen, ITS.

Mooij, T. (2002). Designing a digital instructional management system to optimize early education. *Educational Technology Research & Development*, *50*, 11–23.

Mooij, T. (2004). Optimising ICT effectiveness in instruction and learning: Multilevel transformation theory and a pilot project in secondary education. *Computers & Education*, *42*, 25–44.

Mooij, T. (2005). National campaign effects on secondary pupils' bullying and violence. *British Journal of Educational Psychology*, *75*, 489–511.

Mooij, T. (2007). Design of educational and ICT conditions to integrate differences in learning: Contextual learning theory and a first transformation step in early education. *Computers in Human Behavior*, *23*, 1499–530.

Mooij, T., Sijbers, R., & Sperber, M. (2006). *Rapportage Veiligheidsmonitor V(S)O* [Report Safety Monitor V(S)O]. Nijmegen: Radboud Universiteit, ITS.

Mooij, T., & Smeets, E. (2006). Design, development and implementation of inclusive education. *European Educational Research Journal*, *5*, 94–109 <www.wwwords.co.uk/EERJ>.

Moors, H., Pardoel, K., & Bruinsma, M. (2005). Lastpakken in groepsverband [Troublemakers in a group context]. *Secondant, Tijdschrift van het Centrum voor Criminaliteitspreventie en Veiligheid*, *19*, 14–8.

Morgan, A. B., & Lilienfeld, S. O. (2000). A meta-analytic review of the relation between antisocial behavior and neuropsychological measures of executive function. *Clinical Psychology Review*, *20*, 113–36.

Morris, A. S., Silk, J. S., Steinberg, L., Sessa, F. M., Avenevoli, S., & Essex, M. J. (2002). Temperamental vulnerability and negative parenting as interacting predictors of child adjustment. *Journal of Marriage and the Family*, *64*, 461–71.

Mrazek, P. J & Haggerty, R. J. (eds) (1994). *Reducing Risks for Mental Disorders: Frontiers for Preventive Intervention Research.* Washington, DC: National Academy Press.

Mulder, M. (1977). *Omgaan met Macht* [Dealing with power]. Amsterdam: Elsevier.

Muris, P., Meesters, C., Vincken, M., & Eijkelenboom, A. (2005). Reducing children's aggressive and oppositional behaviors in the schools: Preliminary results on the effectiveness of a social-cognitive group intervention program. *Child & Family Behaviour Therapy*, *27*, 17–32.

Nagin, D. S., & Tremblay, R. E. (2001). Developmental trajectories of physical aggression from school entry to late adolescence. *Journal for Child Psychology and Psychiatry*, *42*, 503–12.

Nagin, D., & Tremblay, R. E. (2005). What has been learned from group-based trajectory modeling? Examples from physical aggression and other problem behaviors. *Annals of the American Academy of Political and Social Science*, *602*, 82–117.

Neumann, P. J. (2005). *Using Cost-effectiveness Analysis in Health Care*. New York: Oxford University Press.

Newman, J. P., & Wallace, J. F. (1993). Diverse pathways to deficient self-regulation – implications for disinhibitory psychopathology in children. *Clinical Psychology Review*, *13*, 699–720.

NICHD Early Child Care Research Network (2004). Trajectories of physical aggression from toddlerhood to middle childhood. *SRCD Monographs*, *69* (4, 278), 1–146.

Nigg, J. T., & Hinshaw, S. P. (1998). Parent personality traits and psychopathology associated with antisocial behaviors in childhood attention deficit hyperactivity disorder. *Journal of Child Psychology and Psychiatry and Allied Disciplines*, *39*, 145–59.

Nigg, J. T., & Huang-Pollock, C. L. (2003). An early onset model of the role of executive functions and intelligence in conduct disorder/delinquency. In B. B. Lahey, T. E. Moffitt, & A. Caspi (eds), *Causes of Conduct Disorder and Juvenile Delinquency* (pp. 227–53). New York: Guilford Press.

NOVA (Norsk Institutt for Forskning om Oppvekst, Velferd og Aldring) (2007). Personal communication.

Nye, F. I. (1958). *Family Relationships and Delinquent Behavior*. New York: Wiley.

O'Brien, B. S., & Frick, P. J. (1996). Reward dominance: Associations with anxiety, conduct problems, and psychopathy in children. *Journal of Abnormal Child Psychology*, *24*, 223–40.

O'Connor, T. G., Caspi, A., Defries, J. C., & Plomin, R. (2003). Genotype-environment interaction in children's adjustment to parental separation. *Journal of Child Psychology and Psychiatry*, *44*, 849–56.

O'Connor, T. G., Deater-Deckard, K., Fulker, D., Rutter, M., & Plomin, R. (1998). Genotype-environment correlations in late childhood and early adolescence: Antisocial behavioral problems and coercive parenting. *Developmental Psychology*, *34*, 970–81.

Offord, D., & Boyle, M. (1996). *Standard Client Information System*. Toronto: Ontario Association of Children's Mental Health Centres.

Offord, D., & Kraemer, H. C. (2000). Risk factors and prevention. *Evidence Based Mental Health*, *3*, 70–71.

Offord, D. R., Kraemer, H. C., Kazdin, A. E., Jensen, P. S., Harrington, R., & Gardner, J. S. (1999). Lowering the burdening of suffering: Monitoring the benefits of clinical, targeted and universal approaches. In D. P. Keating, & C. Hertzman, (eds), *Developmental Health and the Wealth of Nations. Social, Biological and Educational Dynamics* (pp. 293–311) New York: Guilford Press.

Offord, D. R., Lipman, E. L., & Duku, E. K. (2001). Epidemiology of problem behavior up to age 12 years. In R. Loeber, & D. P. Farrington (eds), *Child Delinquents: Development, Intervention and Service Needs* (pp. 95–116). Thousand Oaks, CA: Sage.

Ogden, T., & Halliday-Boykins, C.A. (2004). Multi-systemic treatment of antisocial adolescents in Norway: Replication of clinical outcomes outside of the U.S. *Child and Adolescent Mental Health*, *9*, 77–83.

O'Keefe, M. (1995). Predictors of child abuse in maritally violent families. *Journal of Interpersonal Violence*, *10*, 3–25.

Oldehinkel, A. J., Hartman, C. A., De Winter, A. F., Veenstra, R., & Ormel, J. (2004). Temperament profiles associated with internalizing and externalizing problems in preadolescence. *Development and Psychopathology*, *16*, 421–40.

Olds, D. L. (1998). *Prenatal and Infancy Home Visitation by Nurses, Book Seven*. Blueprints for Violence Prevention Series. Boulder, CO: Center for the Study and Prevention of Violence, Institute of Behavioral Science, University of Colorado.

Olds, D. L., Kitzman, H., Cole, R., Robinson, J., Sidora, K., Luckey, D. W., Henderson, C. R., Hanks, C., Bondy, J., & Holmberg, J. (2004a). Effects of Nurse Home-Visiting on maternal life course and child development: Age 6 follow-up results of a randomized trial. *Pediatrics*, *114*, 1550–59.

Olds, D. L., Robinson, J., Petitt, L. M., Luckey, D. W., Holmberg, J., Ng, R. K., Isacks, K., Sheff, K. L., & Henderson, C. R. (2004b). Effects of home visits by paraprofessionals and by nurses: Age 4 follow-up results of a randomized trial. *Pediatrics*, *114*, 1560–68.

Olson, H. C., Streissguth, A. P., Sampson, P. D., Barr, H. M., Bookstein, F. L., & Thiede, K. (1997). Association of prenatal alcohol exposure with behavioral and learning problems in early adolescence. *Journal of the American Academy of Child & Adolescent Psychiatry*, *36*, 1187–94.

Olson, S. L., Bates, J. E., Sandy, J. M., & Lanthier, R. (2000). Early developmental precursors of externalizing behavior in middle childhood and adolescence. *Journal of Abnormal Child Psychology*, *28*, 119-133.

Olweus, D. (1980). Familial and temperamental determinants of aggressive behavior in adolescent boys: A causal analysis. *Developmental Psychology*, *16*, 644–60.

Olweus, D. (1984). Aggressors and their victims: Bullying at school. In N. Frude, & H. Gault (eds), *Disruptive Behavior in Schools* (pp. 57–76). New York: Wiley.

Olweus, D. (1987). Bully/victim problems among school children in Scandinavia. In J. P. Myklebust, & R. Ommundsen (eds), *Psykologprofesjonen mot ar 2000* (pp. 395–413). Oslo: Universitetsforlaget.

Olweus, D. (1991). Bully/victim problems among schoolchildren: Basic facts and effects of a school based intervention program. In D. J. Pepler, & K. H. Rubin (eds), *The Development and Treatment of Childhood Aggression* (pp. 411–48). Hillsdale, NJ: Erlbaum.

Olweus, D. (1993). *Bullying at School: What We Know and What We Can Do*. Oxford: Blackwell.

Olweus, D. (1995). *Gewalt in der Schule. Was Lehrer und Eltern wissen sollten – und tun können*. Bern: Huber.

Olweus, D., Limber, S., & Mihalic, S. F. (1999). *Bullying Prevention Program: Blueprints for Violence Prevention, Book Nine*. Blueprints for Violence Prevention Series. Boulder, CO: Center for the Study and Prevention of Violence, Institute of Behavioral Science, University of Colorado.

Oosterlaan, J., Logan, G. D., & Sergeant, J. A. (1998). Response inhibition in AD/HD, CD, comorbid AD/HD+CD, anxious, and control children: A meta-analysis of studies with the stop task. *Journal of Child Psychology and Psychiatry*, *39*, 411–25.

Oosterlaan, J., Scheres, A., & Sergeant, J. A. (2005). Which executive functioning deficits are associated with AD/HD, ODD/CD and comorbid AD/HD plus ODD/CD? *Journal of Abnormal Child Psychology*, *33*, 69–85.

Oosterlaan, J., Scheres, A., & Sergeant, J. A. (2007). Which executive functioning deficits are associated with AD/HD, ODD/CD and comorbid AD/HD+ODD/CD? *Journal of Abnormal Child Psychology*, *33*, 69–85.

Orobio de Castro, B. (1999). Opzet Screeningslijst Risicofactoren [Development of a screen for risk factors]. Interne notitie. Duivendrecht: PI Research.

Orobio de Castro, B., Veerman, J.W., Bond, E., & De Beer, L. (2002). *Kansen gekeerd? Criminaliteitspreventie door gezinsondersteuning* [Crime prevention through family support]. Utrecht: PI-research BV & Capaciteitsgroep Ontwikkelingspsychologie, Universiteit Utrecht.

Ortiz, J., & Raine, A. (2004). Heart rate level and antisocial behavior in children and adolescents: A meta-analysis. *Journal of the American Academy of Child and Adolescent Psychiatry*, *43*, 154–62.

Paterson, G., & Sanson, A. (1999). The association of behavioral adjustment to temperament, parenting, and family characteristics among 5-year-old children. *Social Development*, *8*, 293–309.

Patterson, C. J., DeBaryshe, B. D., & Ramsey, E. (1989). A developmental perspective on antisocial behavior. *American Psychologist*, *44*, 329–35.

Patterson, G. R. (1982). *Coercive Family Process*. Eugene, OR: Castalia.

Patterson, G. R. (2002). The early developmental of coercive family process. In J. B. Reid, G. R. Patterson, & J. Snyder (eds), *Antisocial Behavior in Children and Adolescents: Developmental Theories and Models for Intervention* (pp. 25–44). Washington, DC: American Psychological Association.

Patterson, G. R. (2005). The next generation of PMTO models. *Behavior Therapist*, *28*, 25–32.

Patterson, G. R., & Dishion, T. J. (1988). Multilevel family process models: Traits, interactions, and relationships. In R. Hinde, & S. J. Hinde (eds), *Relationships Within Families: Mutual Influences* (pp. 283–310). Oxford: Clarendon Press.

Patterson, G. R., Dishion, T. J., & Yoerger, K. (2000). Adolescent growth in new forms of problem behavior: Macro- and micro-peer dynamics. *Prevention Science*, *1*, 3–13.

Patterson, G. R., & Fisher, P. A. (2002). Recent developments in our understanding of parenting: Bidirectional effects, causal models, and the search for parsimony. In M. Bornstein (ed.), *Handbook of Parenting: Practical and Applied Parenting* (2nd edn, Vol. 5, pp. 59–88). Mahwah, NJ: Erlbaum.

Patterson, G. R., Reid, J. B., & Dishion, T. J. (1992). *Antisocial Boys*. Eugene, OR: Castalia.

Patterson, G. R., & Yoerger, K. (2002). A developmental model for early- and late-onset delinquency. In J. B. Reid, G. R. Patterson, & J. Snyder (eds), *Antisocial Behavior in Children and Adolescents: A Developmental Analysis and Model for Intervention* (pp. 147–72). Washington, DC: American Psychological Association.

Patterson, G. R., & Yoerger, K. (1997). A developmental model for late-onset delinquency. In D. W. Osgood (ed.), *Motivation and delinquency. Nebraska Symposium on Motivation* (pp. 119–77). Lincoln, NE: University of Nebraska Press.

Paulussen-Hoogeboom, M. C., Stams, G. J. J. M., Hermanns, J. M. A., & Peetsma, T. D. (2007). Child negative emotionality and parenting from infancy to preschool: A meta-analytic review. *Developmental Psychology 43*, 438–53.

Paulussen-Hoogeboom, M. C., Stams, G. J. J. M., Hermanns, J. M. A., & Peetsma, T. D. (2008). Relations among child negative emotionality, parenting stress, and maternal sensitive responsiveness in early childhood. *Parenting: Science and Practice*, *8*, 1–16

Paulussen-Hoogeboom, M. C., Stams, G. J. J. M., Hermanns, J. M. A., Peetsma, T. D., & Hoffenaar, P. J. (2007). Parent's perceived control as a mediator of the relation between child negative emotionality and parenting style: A multilevel perspective. Manuscript submitted for publication.

Paulussen-Hoogeboom, M. C., Stams, G. J. J. M., Hermanns, J. M. A., Peetsma, T. D., & van den Wittenboer, G. L. H. (in press). Parenting style as a mediator between children's negative emotionality and problematic behavior in early childhood. *Journal of Genetic Psychology*.

Pellegrini, A. D., & Long, J. D. (2002). A longitudinal study of bullying, dominance, and victimization during the transition from primary school through secondary school. *British Journal of Developmental Psychology*, *20*, 259–80.

Pennington, B. F., & Ozonoff, S. (1996). Executive functions and developmental psychopathology. *Journal of Child Psychology and Psychiatry*, *37*, 51–87.

Pepler, D. J., Walsh, M. M., & Levene, K. S. (2004). Interventions for aggressive girls: Tailoring and measuring the fit. In M. M. Moretti, C. L. Odgers, & M. A. Jackson (eds), *Girls and Aggression: Contributing Factors and Intervention Principles,* Perspectives in Law & Psychology Series, Volume 19 (pp. 41–56). New York: Kluwer Academic/Plenum.

Pepler, D., Walsh, M., Yuile, A., Levene, K., Webber, J., Vaughan, A., & Jiang D. (2008). *Bridging the Gender Gap: Understanding and Treating Girls' Aggression*. Manuscript in preparation.

Perkins-Dock, R. (2001). Family interventions with incarcerated youth: A review of the literature. *International Journal of Offender Therapy and Comparative Criminology*, *45*, 606–25.

Pérusse, D., & Gendrau, P.L. (2005). Genetics and the development of aggression. In R.E. Tremblay, W. W. Hartup, & J. Archer (eds), *Developmental Origins of Aggression* (pp. 223–41). New York, NY: Guilford Press.

Petrosino, A. (2000). Mediators and moderators in the evaluation of programs for children. Current practice and agenda for improvement. *Evaluation Review*, *24*, 47–72.

Pijnacker Hordijk, Y., & Verwoerd, M. L. (2005). *Basis Dataset JGZ* [Basic dataset JGZ]. Leidschendam: Nationaal ICT Instituut in de Zorg.

Pike, A., Manke, B., Reiss, D., & Plomin, R. (2000). A genetic analysis of differential experiences of adolescent siblings across three years. *Social Development*, *9*, 96–114.

Piquero, A. R. (2007). Taking stock of developmental trajectories of criminal activity over the life course. In A. Liberman (ed.), *The Yield Of Recent Longitudinal Research On Crime And Delinquency*. New York: Springer.

Piquero, A. R., Farrington, D. P., & Blumstein, A. (2007). *Key Issues in Criminal Career Research*. Cambridge: Cambridge University Press.

Piquero, A. R., & White, N. A. (2003). On the relationship between cognitive abilities and life-course-persistent offending among a sample of African Americans: A longitudinal test of Moffitt's hypothesis. *Journal of Criminal Justice*, *31*, 399–409.

PI Research (2002). *Tweede Voortgangsrapportage over het SPRINT Project.* Duivendrecht: PI Research.

Ploeg, J.D. van der, & Scholte, E.M. (1997*). Hulpvraag en hulpaanbod in de regio Rotterdam e.o.* [Care needs and available care in the Rotterdam region]. Rotterdam: GGD.

Plomin, R., & Asbury, K. (2005). Nature and nurture: Genetic and environmental influences on behavior. *Annals of the American Academy of Political and Social Science*, *600*, 86–98.

Plomin, R., & Crabbe, J. (2000). DNA. *Psychological Bulletin*, *126*, 806–28.

Plomin, R., & DeFries, J.C. (1985). *Origins of Individual Differences in Infancy: The Colorado Adoption Project.* Orlando, FL: Academic Press

Plomin, R., Emde, R., Braungart, J., Campos, J., Corley, R., Fulker, D., Kagan, J., Reznick, J., Robinson, J., Zahn-Waxler, C., & DeFries, J. (1993). Genetic change and continuity from fourteen to twenty months: The MacArthur Longitudinal Twin Study. *Child Development*, *64*, 1354–76.

Pollard, J. A., Hawkins, J. D., & Arthur, M. W. (1999). Risk and protection: Are both necessary to understand diverse behavioral outcomes in adolescence? *Social Work Research*, *23*, 145–58.

Pope, A. W., & Bierman, K. L. (1999). Predicting adolescent peer problems and antisocial activities: The relative roles of aggression and dysregulation. *Developmental Psychology*, *35*, 335–46.

Popma, A., Doreleijers, T. A. H., Jansen, L. M. C., van Goozen, S. H. M., van Engeland, H., & Vermeiren, R. (2007). The diurnal cortisol cycle in delinquent male adolescents and normal controls. *Neuropsychopharmacology*, *32*, 1622–8.

Popma, A., Jansen, L. M., Vermeiren, R., Steiner, H., Raine, A., van Goozen, S. H., van Engeland, H., & Doreleijers, T. A. (2006). Hypothalamus pituitary adrenal axis and autonomic activity during stress in delinquent male adolescents and controls. *Psychoneuroendocrinology*, *31*, 948–57

Popma, A., & Raine, A. (2006). Will future forensic assessment be neurobiologic? *Child and Adolescent Psychiatric Clinics of North America*, *15*, 429–44.

Popma, A., Vermeiren, R., Geluk, C. A., Rinne, T., van den, B. W., Knol, D. L., Jansen, L. M., van Engeland, H., & Doreleijers, T. A. (2007). Cortisol moderates the relationship between testosterone and aggression in delinquent male adolescents. *Biological Psychiatry*, *61*, 405–11.

Poulin, F., & Boivin, M. (2000). The role of proactive and reactive aggression in the formation and development of boys' friendships. *Developmental Psychology*, *36*, 223–40.

Prasad, M. R., Kramer, L. A., & Ewing-Bobbs, L. (2005). Cognitive and neuroimaging findings in physically abused preschoolers. *Archives of Disease in Childhood*, *90*, 82–5.

Prinsen, B., & Ligtermoet, I. (2006). Dat gaat werken. Veelbelovende en effectieve interventies voor opvoedingsondersteuning in de JGZ [This is going to work: Promising and effective interventions for family support in Youth Health Care]. Utrecht: NIZW.

Prinzie, P. (2002). Coercive family processes, parent and child personality characteristics as predictors of antisocial behavior in 4-to-9-year-old children. Unpublished doctoral dissertation. Leuven: Katholieke Universiteit Leuven.

Prinzie, P., Onghena, P., & Hellinckx, W. (2006). A cohort-sequential multivariate latent growth curve analysis of normative CBCL aggressive and delinquent problem behavior: associations with harsh discipline and gender. *International Journal of Behavioral Development*, *30*, 444–59.

Prinzie, P., Onghena, P., Hellinckx, W., Grietens, H., Ghesquière, P., & Colpin, H. (2003). The additive and interactive effects of parenting and children's personality on externalising behaviour. *European Journal of Personality*, *17*, 95–117.

Prinzie, P., Onghena, P., Hellinckx, W., Grietens, H., Ghesquière, P., & Colpin, H. (2004). Parent and child personality characteristics as predictors of negative discipline and externalizing problem behavior in children. *European Journal of Personality*, *18*, 73–102.

Prinzie, P., Onghena, P., Hellinckx, W., Grietens, H., Ghesquière, P., & Colpin, H. (2005). Direct and indirect relationships between parental personality and externalising behaviour: The role of negative parenting. *Psychologica Belgica*, *45*, 123–45.

Quay, H. C. (1993). The psychobiology of undersocialized aggressive conduct disorder – A theoretical perspective. *Development and Psychopathology*, *5*, 165–80.

Queloz, N. (2007). Personal Communication.

Rabiner, D., & Coie, J. (1989). Effect of expectancy inductions on rejected children's acceptance by unfamiliar peers. *Developmental Psychology*, *25*, 450–57.

Rae-Grant, N., Thomas, B. H., Offord, D. R., & Boyle, M. H. (1989). Risk, protective factors, and the prevalence of behavioral and emotional disorders in children and adolescents. *Journal of the American Academy of Child and Adolescent Psychiatry*, *28*, 262–8.

Raine, A. (1993). *The Psychopathology of Crime: Criminal Behavior as a Clinical Disorder*. San Diego, CA: Academic Press.

Raine, A., Dodge, K., Loeber, R., Gatze-Kopp, L., Lynam, D., Reynolds, C., Stouthamer-Loeber, M., & Liu, J. (2006). The reactive-proactive aggression questionnaire: Differential correlates of reactive and proactive aggression in adolescent boys. *Aggressive Behaviour*, *32*, 159–71.

Raine, A., Venables, P. H., & Mednick, S. A. (1997). Low resting heart rate at age 3 years predisposes to aggression at age 11 years: Evidence from the Mauritius Child Health Project. *Journal of the American Academy of Child and Adolescent Psychiatry*, *36*, 1457–64.

Ramsden, S. R., & Hubbard, J. A. (2002). Family expressiveness and parental emotion coaching: Their role in children's emotion regulation and aggression. *Journal of Abnormal Child Psychology*, *30*, 657–67.

Rand, A. (1987). Transitional life events and desistance from delinquency and crime. In M. E. Wolfgang, T. P. Thornberry, & R. M. Figlio (eds), *From Boy to Man: From Delinquency to Crime* (pp. 134–62). London: University of Chicago Press.

Rankin, J. H., & Wells, L. E. (1990). The effect of parental attachments and direct controls on delinquency. *Journal of Research in Crime and Delinquency*, *27*, 140–65.

Raver, C. C., & Zigler, E. F. (1997). Social competence: An untapped dimension in evaluating head start's success. *Early Childhood Research Quarterly*, *12*, 363–85.

Reich, C., & Young, V. (1975). Patterns of dropping out. *Interchange*, *6*, 6–15.

Reich, W., & Welner, Z. (1988). *Diagnostic Interview for Children, Adolescents, and Parents*. St. Louis, MO: Washington University.

Reid, J. B., & Patterson, G. R. (1989). The development of antisocial behavior patterns in childhood and adolescence. *European Journal of Personality*, *3*, 107–19.

Reid, J. B., Patterson, G. R., & Loeber, R. (1982). The abused child: Victim, instigator, or innocent bystander? *Nebraska Symposium on Motivation*, *29*, 47–68.

Reid, J. B., Patterson, G. R., & Snyder, J. (2002). *Antisocial Behavior in Children and Adolescents. A Developmental Analysis and Model for Intervention*. Washington, DC: American Psychological Association.

Reis, H. T., Collins, W. A., & Berscheid, E. (2000). The relationship context of human behavior and development. *Psychological Bulletin*, *126*, 844–72.

Reiss, A. J. Jr. (1988). Co-offending and criminal careers. In M. Tonry, & N. Morris (eds), *Crime and Justice: A Review of Research* (Vol. 10, pp. 117–70). Chicago, IL: University of Chicago Press.

Reiss, A. J., & Farrington, D. F. (1991). Advancing knowledge about co-offending: Results from a prospective longitudinal survey of London males. *Journal of Criminal Law and Criminology*, *82*, 360–65.

Rhee, S. H., & Waldman, I. D. (2002). Genetic and environmental influences on antisocial behavior: A meta-analysis of twin and adoption studies. *Psychological Bulletin*, *128*, 490–529.

Richman, M., Stevenson, J., & Graham, P. J. (1982). *Preschool to School: A Behavioral Study*. London: Academic Press.

Riggins-Caspers, K.M., Cadoret, R. J., Knutson, J. F., & Langbehn, D. (2003). Biology-environment interaction and evocative biology-environment correlation: Contributions of harsh discipline and parental psychopathology to problem adolescent behaviors. *Behavior Genetics*, *33*, 205–20.

Robertson, A. A., Grimes, P. W., & Rogers, K. E. (2001). A short-run cost-benefit analysis of community-based interventions for juvenile offenders. *Crime and Delinquency*, *47*, 265–85.

Robins, L. N. (1966). *Deviant Children Grown Up: A Sociological and Psychiatric Study of Sociopathic Personality*. Baltimore, MD: Williams & Wilkins.

Robins, R. W., John, O. P., & Caspi, A. (1994). Major dimensions of personality in early adolescence: The Big Five and beyond. In C. F. Halverson, J. A. Kohnstamn, & R. P. Martin (eds), *The Developing Structure of Temperament and Personality from Infancy to Adulthood* (pp. 267–91). Hillsdale, NJ: Erlbaum.

Rock, P. (2002). Sociological theories of crime. In M. Maguire, R. Morgan, & R. Reiner (eds), *The Oxford Handbook of Criminology.* Oxford: Oxford University Press.

Roland, E. (1989). Bullying: The Scandinavian research tradition. In D. P. Tattum, & D. A. Lane (eds), *Bullying in Schools* (pp. 21–32). Stoke-on-Trent, UK: Trentham Books.

Rose, R. J. (2002). How do adolescents select their friends? A behavior-genetic perspective. In L. Pulkkinen & A. Caspi (eds), *Paths to Successful Development: Personality in the Life Course* (pp. 106–25). New York: Cambridge University Press.

Rosen, L. (1985). Family and delinquency: Structure or function? *Criminology*, *23*, 553–73.

Rossi, P. H., Lipsey, M. W., & Freeman, H. E. (2004). *Evaluation. A Systematic Approach.* Thousand Oaks, CA: Sage.

Rothbart, M. K., & Bates, J. E. (1998). Temperament. In W. Damon, & N. Eisenberg (eds), *Social, Emotional and Personality Development* (Vol. 3, pp. 105–76). New York: Wiley.

Rothbaum, F., & Weisz, J. R. (1994). Parental caregiving and child externalising behavior in non-clinical samples: A meta-analysis. *Psychological Bulletin, 116*, 55–74.

Rowe, R., Maughan, B., Worthman, C. M., Costello, E. J., & Angold, A. (2004). Testosterone, antisocial behavior, and social dominance in boys: Pubertal development and biosocial interaction. *Biological Psychiatry*, *55*, 546–52.

Rubin, K. H., Bukowski, W., & Parker, J. G. (1998). Peer interactions, relationships, and groups. In W. Damon, & N. Eisenberg (eds), *Handbook of Child Psychology: Social Emotional and Personality Development* (pp. 619–700). New York: Wiley.

Rubin, K. H., Stewart, S. L., & Chen, X. (1995). Parents of aggressive and withdrawn children. In M. H. Bornstein (ed.), *Handbook of Parenting. Vol. 1. Children and Parenting* (pp. 255–84). Mahwah, NJ: Erlbaum.

Ruiter, C. de (2005). Risicosignalering, risicotaxatie en risicohantering: Naar een effectieve aanpak in het jeugdbeleid [Identification, assessment and management of risk: Towards an effective policy on juveniles]. In J. Hermanns, F. Öry, & G. Schrijvers (eds), *Helpen Opgroeien en Opvoeden: Eerder, Sneller en Beter.* The Hague: Operatie Jong.

Rushton, J. P., & Bons, T. A. (2005). Mate choice and friendship in twins. *Psychology Science*, *16*, 555–559.

Rutter, M. (1979). Protective factors in children's responses to stress and disadvantage. In J.E. Rolf (ed.), *Primary Prevention of Psychopathology* (pp. 49–74). Hanover, NH: University Press of New England.

Rutter, M. (1985). Resilience in the face of adversity. *British Journal of Psychiatry*, *147*, 589–611.

Rutter, M. (1990). Psychosocial resilience and protective mechanisms. In J. E. Rolf, A. S. Masten, D. Cicchetti, K. H. Nuechterlein, & S. Weintraub (eds), *Risk and Protective Factors in the Development of Psychopathology* (pp. 181–214). New York: Cambridge University Press.

Rutter, M. (2002). Nature, nurture and development: From evangelism through science toward police and practice. *Child Development*, *73*, 1–21.

Rutter, M., Giller, H., & Hagell, A. (1998). *Antisocial Behaviour by Young People.* Cambridge: Cambridge University Press.

Rutter, M., Pickles, A., Murray, R., & Eaves, L. (2001). Testing hypotheses on specific environmental causal effects on behavior. *Psychological Bulletin, 127*, 291–324.

Rutter, M., & Taylor, M. (2004). *Child and Adolescent Psychiatry.* 4th edn. Oxford: Blackwell Science.

Rutter, M., Tizard, J., & Whitmore, K. (1970). *Education, Health, and Behavior*. New York: Wiley.

Saarni, C. (1993). The socialization of emotion. In M. Lewis, & J. Haviland (eds), *Handbook of Emotions* (pp. 435–46). New York: Guilford Press.

Sameroff, A. J. (2000). Developmental systems and psychopathology. *Development and Psychopathology*, *13*, 297–312.

Sameroff, A. J., Bartko, W. T., Baldwin, A., Baldwin, C., & Seifer, R. (1998). Family and social influences on the development of child competence. In M. Lewis, & C. Feiring (eds), *Families, Risk, and Competence* (pp. 161–85). Mahwah, NJ: Lawrence Erlbaum Associates.

Sameroff, A. J., Seifer, R., Baldwin, A., & Baldwin, C. (1993). Stability of intelligence from preschool to adolescence: The influence of social and family risk factors. *Child Development*, *64*, 80–97.

Sampson, R. J., & Laub, J. H. (1990). Crime and deviance over the life course: The salience of adult social bonds. *American Sociological Review*, *55*, 609–27.

Sampson, R. J., & Laub, J. H. (1993). *Crime in the Making: Pathways and Turning Points Through Life*. Cambridge, MA: Harvard University Press.

Sampson, R. J., Raudenbusch, S. W., & Earls, F. (1997). Neighbourhoods and violent crime: a multilevel study of collective efficacy, *Science*, *277*, 918-224.

Sanders, M. R., Dadds, C. M., & Turner, K. M. T. (2003). Theoretical, scientific and clinical foundations of the Triple P Positive Parenting Program: A population approach to the promotion of parenting competence. *Parenting research and practice* monograph, 1, pp. 1–21. Brisbane: The Parenting & Family Support Centre, University of Queensland.

Sanders, M. R., Markie-Dadds C., Turner K. M. T., & Brechman-Toussaint, M. (2002). *Triple P Positive Parenting Program: A guide to the system*. Brisbane: Triple P International.

Sanders M. R., Ralph, A. Thompson, R., Sofronoff, K., Gardiner, P., Bidwell, K., & Dwyer, S. (2005). *Every Family: A Public Health Approach to Promoting Children's Wellbeing* (brief report). Brisbane: University of Queensland.

Sanders, M. R., Turner, K. M. T., & Markie-Dadds, C. (2002a). The development and dissemination of the Triple P Positive Parenting Program: A multilevel, evidence-based system of parenting and family support. *Prevention Science*, *3*, 173–89.

Sanson, A., Hemphill, S. A., & Smart, D. (2004). Connections between temperament and social development: A review. *Social Development*, *8*, 293–309.

Sanson, A., & Prior, M. (1999). Temperament and behavioral precursors to oppositional defiant disorder and conduct disorder. In H. C. Quay, & A. E. Hogan (eds), *Handbook of Disruptive Behavior Disorders* (pp. 397–417). New York: Kluwer Academic.

Sandstrom, M. J., & Coie, J. D. (1999). A developmental perspective on peer rejection: Mechanisms of stability and change. *Child Development*, *70*, 955–66.

Sawyer, M.G., Baghurst, P., and Mathias, J. (1992). Differences between informants' reports describing emotional and behavioral problems in community and clinic-referred children: A research note. *Journal of Child Psychology and Psychiatry*, *33*, 441–9.

Schäfer, H. (2004). Combating criminal behaviour among children under 14 year of age – the responsibility of the educational system. In Centre for Prevention of Youth Crime (ed.), *Prevention of Youth Crime in Germany: Educational Strategies – Trends, Experiences and Approaches*. Munich: German Youth Institute.

Schippers, G. M., & De Jonge, J. (2002). Motiverende gespreksvoering [Motivational discussion techniques]. *Maandblad Geestelijke Volksgezondheid*, *57*, 250–65.

Scholte, E. M. (1995). Longitudinal studies on the effectiveness of care services for juveniles. In M. Colton, W. Hellinckx, M. Williams, & P. Ghesquire (eds), *The Art and Science of Caring* (pp. 103–30). Aldershot: Arena.

Scholte, E. M. (1998). School en jeugdzorg [School and youth care]. In J. D. van der Ploeg, & T. Mooij (eds), *Geweld op School. Achtergronden, Omvang, Oorzaak, Preventie en Aanpak* (pp. 119–38). Rotterdam: Lemniscaat.

Schweinhart, L. J. (2003). *Benefits, Costs, and Explanation of the High/Scope Perry Preschool* Program. Paper presented at the Meeting of the Society for Research in Child Development, Tampa, FL.

Schweinhart, L. J. (2007). Crime prevention by the High/Scope Perry Preschool Program. *Victims and Offenders*, *2*, 141–60.

Schweinhart, L. J., Montie, J., Xiang, Z., Barnett, W. S., Belfield, C. R., & Nores, M. (2005). *Life Time Effects: The High/Scope Perry Preschool Study Through Age 40*. Ypsilanti, MI: High/Scope Press.

Sedlak, A. J., & Broadhurst, D. D. (1996). *Third National Incidence Study of Child Abuse and Neglect: Final Report.* Washington, DC: US Department of Health and Human Services, Administration on Children and Youth, And Families, National Center On Child Abuse And Neglect.

Seelye, K. Q. (1999). Clinton's new gun proposal, include charging parents of children who commit gun crimes. *New York Times* (27 April).

Seguin, J., Nagin, D., Assaad, J. M., & Tremblay, R. E. (2004). Cognitive-neuropsychological function in chronic physical aggression and hyperactivity. *Journal of Abnormal Psychology*, *113*, 603–13.

Seguin, J. R., Pihl, R. O., Harden, P. W., Tremblay, R. E., & Boulrice, B. (1995). Cognitive and psychological characteristics of physically aggressive boys. *Journal of Abnormal Psychology*, *104*, 614–24.

Sergeant, J. A., Geurts, H., & Oosterlaan, J. (2002). How specific is a deficit of executive functioning for Attention-Deficit/Hyperactivity Disorder? *Behavioural Brain Research*, *130*, 3–28.

Serketich, W.J., & Dumas, J. E. (1996). The effectiveness of behavioural parent training to modify antisocial behavior in children: A meta-analysis. *Behavior Therapy*, *27*, 171–86.

Shapiro, S. K., Quay, H. C., Hogan, A. E., & Schwartz, K. P. (1988). Response perseveration and delayed responding in undersocialized aggressive conduct disorder. *Journal of Abnormal Psychology*, *97*, 371–3.

Sharp, S., & Smith, P. K. (1993). Tackling bullying: The Sheffield project. In D. Tattum (ed.), *Understanding and Managing Bullying* (pp. 45–56). Oxford: Heinemann.

Shaw, D. S., Bell, R. Q., & Gilliom, M. (2000). A truly early starter model of antisocial behavior revisited. *Clinical Child and Family Psychology Review*, *3*, 155–72.

Shaw, D. S., & Emery, R. E. (1988). Chronic family adversity and school age children's adjustment. *Journal of the American Academy of Child and Adolescent Psychiatry*, *27*, 200–206.

Shaw, D. S., Gilliom, M., Ingoldsby, E. M., & Nagin, D. S. (2003). Trajectories leading to school-age conduct problems. *Developmental Psychology*, *39*, 189–200.

Shaw, D. S., Lacourse, E., & Nagin, D. S. (2005). Developmental trajectories of conduct problems and hyperactivity from ages 2 to 10. *Journal of Child Psychology and Psychiatry*, *46*, 931–42.

Sheeber, L. B., & McDevitt, S. C. (1998). Temperament-focused parent training. In J. M. Briesmeister & C. E. Schaefer (eds), *Handbook of Parent Training: Parents as Co-therapists for Children's Behavior Problems* (2nd edn, pp. 479–507). New York: Wiley.

Sherman, L. (2003). Misleading evidence and evidence-led policy. Making science more experimental. *Annals of the American Academy of Political and Social Science*, *589*, 6–19.

Sherman, L. W., Gottfredson, D., MacKenzie, D., Eck, J., Reuter, P., & Bushway, S. (1996). *Preventing Crime: What Works, What Doesn't, What is Promising. A Report to the United States Congress*. College Park: University of Maryland at College Park Department of Criminology and Criminal Justice.

Shiner, R. L., & Caspi, A. (2003). Personality differences in childhood and adolescence: Measurement, development, and consequences. *Journal of Child Psychology and Psychiatry*, *44*, 2–32.

Shirk, S. R., & Karver, M. (2003). Prediction of treatment outcome from relationship variables in child and adolescent therapy: A meta-analytic review. *Journal of Consulting and Clinical Psychology*, *71*, 452–64.

Shirtcliff, E. A., Granger, D. A., Booth, A., & Johnson, D. (2005). Low salivary cortisol levels and externalizing behavior problems in youth. *Development and Psychopathology*, *17*, 167–84.

Silk, J. S., Steinberg, L., & Morris, A. S. (2003). Adolescents' emotion regulation in daily life: Links to depressive symptoms and problem behavior. *Child Development*, *74*, 1869–80.

Skinner, D., Bryant, D., Coffman, J., & Campbell, F. (1998). Creating risk and promise children's and teachers' coconstructions in the cultural world of kindergarten. *The Elementary School Journal*, *98*, 297–310.

Slot, N. W. (1995). Competency-based treatment for antisocial youth. In H. P. J. G. van Bilsen, P. C. Kendall, & J. H. Slavenburg (eds), *Behavioral Approaches for Children and Adolescents* (pp. 77–87). New York: Plenum Press.

Slot, W., Orobio de Castro, B., & Duivenvoorden, Y. (2000). WAS-instrument, first measurement, version 1.0. WAS-Lijst, eerste afname, versie 1.0. Duivendrecht: Peadologisch Instituut.

Slump, G. J., Dijk, E. van, Klooster, E., & Rietveld, M. (2000). *Stop-reactie. Bereik, ervaringen en effecten tijdens het experimentele jaar* ['Stop-reactie': Reach, experience and effects during the pilot year]. The Hague: Ministerie van Justitie.

Smith, B. D., & Testa, M. F. (2002). The risk of subsequent maltreatment allegations in families with substance-exposed infants. *Child Abuse and Neglect*, *26*, 97–114.

Smith, C., Lizotte, A. J., Thornberry, T. P., & Krohn, M. D. (1995). Resilient youth: Identifying factors that prevent high-risk youth from engaging in delinquency and drug use. In J. Hagan (ed.), *Delinquency in the Life Course* (pp. 217–47). Greenwich, CT: JAI Press.

Smith, C.A., Ireland, T.O., & Thornberry, T. P. (2005). Adolescent maltreatment and its impact on young adult antisocial behaviour. *Child Abuse and Neglect*, *29*, 1099–119.

Smith, P. K., & Sharp, S. (eds) (1994). *School Bullying: Insights and Perspectives.* London: Routledge.

Smith, P. K., Singer, M., Hoel, H., & Cooper, C. L. (2003). Victimization in the school and the workplace: are there any links? *British Journal of Psychology*, *94*, 175–88.

Snyder, H. N. (2001). Epidemiology of official offending. In R. Loeber, & D. P. Farrington (eds), *Child delinquents: Development Intervention and Service Needs* (pp. 25–66). Thousand Oaks, CA: Sage.

Snyder, H. N., Espiritu, R. C., Huizinga, D., Loeber, R., & Petechuk, D. (March 2003). Epidemiology and development of child delinquency. *Child Delinquency Bulletin Series.* Washington, DC: Office of Juvenile Justice and Delinquency Prevention.

Snyder, J., Cramer, A., Afrank, J., & Patterson, G. R. (2005). The contributions of ineffective discipline and parental hostile attributions of child misbehavior to the development of conduct problems at home and school. *Developmental Psychology*, *41*, 30–41.

Snyder, J., Horsch, E., & Childs, J. (1997). Peer relationships of young children: Afflictive choices and the shaping of aggressive behavior. *Journal of Clinical Child Psychology*, *26*, 145–56.

Snyder, J., Prichard, J., Schrepferman, L., Patrick, M. R., & Stoolmiller, M. (2004). Child impulsiveness-inattention, early peer experiences, and the development of early onset conduct problems. *Journal of Abnormal Child Psychology*, *32*, 579–94.

Snyder, J. J. (1995). Coercion: A two-level theory of antisocial behavior. In W. T. O'Donohue (ed.), *Theories of Behavior Therapy: Exploring Behavior Change* (pp. 313–48). Washington, DC: American Psychological Association.

Soepboer, G., Veenstra, R., & Verhulst, F. C. (2006). *Ben Ik te Min: Aard, Omvang en Achtergronden van Antisociaal Gedrag aan het Einde van de Basisschool en het Begin van het Voortgezet Onderwijs* [Am I 'below': Type, prevalence and backgrounds of antisocial behaviour at the end of primary education and the beginning of secondary education]. Groningen: Rijksuniversiteit Groningen.

Southam-Gerow, M. A., & Kendall, P. (2001). Emotion regulation and understanding implications for child psychopathology and therapy. *Clinical Psychology Review*, *22*, 189–222.

Stams, G. J. M., Juffer, F., & van IJzendoorn, M. H. (2001). Attachment-based intervention in adoptive families in infancy and children's development at age 7: Two follow-up studies. *British Journal of Developmental Psychology*, *19*, 159–80.

Stams, G. J. M., Juffer, F., & van IJzendoorn, M. H. (2002). Maternal sensitivity, infant attachment, and temperament in early childhood predict adjustment in middle childhood: The case of adopted children and their biologically unrelated parents. *Developmental Psychology*, *38*, 806–21.

Stanger, C., Achenbach, T. M., & Verhulst, F. C. (1997). Accelerated longitudinal comparisons of aggressive versus delinquent syndromes. *Development and Psychopathology*, *9*, 43–58.

Statistisch Jaarboek 2007. The Hague: Centraal Bureau voor de Statistiek.

Steinberg, L., Lamborn, S. D., Darling, N., Mounts, N. S., & Dornbusch, S. M. (1994). Over-time changes in adjustment and competence among adolescents from authoritative, authoritarian, indulgent, and neglectful families. *Child Development*, *65*, 754–70.

Stevens, V., Bourdeaudhuij, I. de, & van Oost, P. (2000). Bullying in Flemish schools: An evaluation of ant bullying intervention in primary and secondary schools. *British Journal of Educational Psychology*, *70*, 195–210.

Stevens, A., Kessler, I., & Gladstone, B. (2006). *Review of Good Practices in Preventing Juvenile Crime in the European Union*. European Crime Prevention Network.

Stevens, G. W. J. M., Pels, T., Bengi Arslan, L., Verhulst, F. C., Vollebergh, W. A. M., & Crijnen, A. A. M. (2003). Parent, teacher and self-reported problem behaviour in The Netherlands: Comparing Moroccan immigrant with Dutch and with Turkish immigrant children and adolescents. *Social Psychiatry and Psychiatric Epidemiology*, *38*, 576–85.

Stevens, G. W. J. M., Pels, T. V. M., Vollebergh, W. A. M., Bengi Arslan, L., Verhulst, F. C., & Crijnen, A. A. M. (2005). Emotionele problemen en gedragsproblemen bij Marokkaanse, Turkse en Nederlandse 4- tot 18-jarigen in Nederland [Emotional and behavioural problems of Moroccan, Turkish and Dutch 4- to 18-year-olds in the Netherlands]. *Tijdschrift voor Psychiatrie*, *47*, 779–86.

Stewart, A., Dennison, S., & Hurren, E. (2005). *Juvenile Offending Trajectories: Pathways from Child Maltreatment to Juvenile Offending, and Police Cautioning in Queensland*. Queensland, Australia: Griffith University School of Criminology and Criminal Justice.

Stoolmiller, M. (1999). Implications of the restricted range of family environments for estimates of heritability and nonshared environment in behavior-genetic adoption studies. *Psychological Bulletin*, *125*, 392–409.

Stoolmiller, M. (2001). Synergistic interaction of child manageability problems and parent-discipline tactics in predicting future growth in externalizing behavior for boys. *Developmental Psychology*, *37*, 814–25.

Stouthamer-Loeber, M., Loeber, R., Farrington D. P., Zhang, Q., van Kammen, W. B., & Maguin, E. (1993). The double edge of protective and risk factors for delinquency: Inter-relations and developmental patterns. *Development and Psychopathology*, *5*, 683–70.

Stouthamer-Loeber, M., Loeber, R., Wei, E., Farrington, D. P., & Wikström, P.-O. (2002). Risk and promotive effects in the explanation of persistent serious delinquency in boys. *Journal of Consulting and Clinical Psychology*, *70*, 11–23.

Stouthamer-Loeber, M, Wei, E, Loeber, R, & Masten, A. F. (2004). Desistance from persistent serious delinquency in the transition to adulthood. *Development and Psychopathology*, *16*, 897–918.

Sultana, C., Matthews, J., De Bortoli, D., & Cann, W. (2000). Outcome evaluation of the primary care level of the Positive Parenting Program implemented in a community setting primary care practitioners. Paper presented at the 3rd Annual Helping Families Change Conference. Brisbane, Queensland.

Sunseri, P. A. (2004). Family functioning and residential treatment outcomes. *Residential Treatment for Children and Youth*, *22*, 33–53.

Supplee, L. H., & Shaw, D. S., Hailstones, K., & Hartman, K. (2003). Family and child influences on early academic and emotion regulatory behaviors. *Journal of School Psychology*, *42*, 221–42.

Swanborn, P. G. (1999). *Evalueren. Het Ontwerpen, Begeleiden en Evalueren van Interventies: een Methodische Basis voor Evaluatie-onderzoek* [Evaluation: Designing, guiding and evaluating interventions: A methodological basis for evaluation research]. Amsterdam: Boom.

Swaray, R. B., Bowles, R., & Pradiptyo, R. (2005). The application of economic analysis to criminal justice interventions: A review of the literature. *Criminal Justice Policy Review*, *16*, 141–63.

Sylwander, L. (2001). *Children as Participants. Swedish Experience of Child Participation in Society's Decisionmaking Processes*. Stockholm: Ministry of Foreign Affairs and Ministry of Health and Social Affairs, Swedish Government.

Sytema, S., Gunther, N., Reelick, F., Drukker, M., Pijl, B., & van't Land, H. (2006). *Verkenningen in de Kinder- en Jeugdpsychiatrie: Een Bijdrage uit de Psychiatrische Casusregisters* [Explorations in child and youth psychiatry]. Utrecht: Trimbos-Instituut.

Tattum, D. (1993). *Understanding and Managing Bullying*. Oxford: Heinemann.

Taylor, A., & Kim-Cohen, J. (2007). Meta-analysis of gene-environment interactions in developmental psychopathology. *Development and Psychopathology*, *19*, 1029–37.

Taylor, J., Iacono, W. G., & McGue, M. (2000). Evidence for a genetic etiology of early-onset delinquency. *Journal of Abnormal Psychology*, *109*, 634–43.

Taylor, T. K., & Biglan, A. (1998). Behavioral family interventions for improving child-rearing: A review of the literature for clinicians and policy makers. *Clinical Child and Family Psychology Review*, *1*, 41–60.

Thomas, A., & Chess, S. (1977). *Temperament and Development*. New York: Brunner/Mazel.

Thomas, M. (1993). *Every Mother's Nightmare. The Killing of James Bulger*. London: Pan Books.

Thornberry, T. P. (1997). *Developmental Theories of Crime and Delinquency*. New Brunswick, NJ: Transaction Publishers.

Thornberry, T. P., Ireland, T.O., & Smith, C.A. (2001). The importance of timing: The varying impact of childhood and adolescence maltreatment on multiple problem outcomes. *Development and Psychopathology*, *13*, 957–79.

Thornberry, T. P., & Krohn, M. D. (2003). *Taking Stock of Delinquency: An Overview of Findings from Contemporary Longitudinal Studies*. New York: Kluwer.

Teichner, G., & Golden, C. J. (2000). The relationship of neuropsychological impairment to conduct disorder in adolescence: A conceptual review. *Aggression and Violent Behavior*, *5*, 509–28.

Tick, N. T. (2007). Time trends in Dutch children's mental health. PhD dissertation, Erasmus University, Rotterdam.

Tolan, P. H., & Gorman Smith, D. (1998). Development of serious and violent offending careers. In R. Loeber, & D. P. Farrington (eds), *Serious and Violent Juvenile Offenders: Risk Factors and Successful Interventions* (pp. 68–85). Thousand Oaks, CA: Sage.

Tolan, P. H., Gorman-Smith, D., & Loeber, R. (2000). Developmental timing of onsets of disruptive behaviors and later delinquency of inner-city youth. *Journal of Child and Family Studies*, *9*, 203–30.

Tonry, M., & Bijleveld, C. (eds) (2007a). *Crime and Justice in the Netherlands. (Crime and Justice*, vol. 35) Chicago, IL: University of Chicago Press.

Tonry, M., & Bijleveld, C. (2007b). Crime, criminal justice, and criminology in the Netherlands. In M. Tonry, & C. Bijleveld (eds), *Crime and Justice in the Netherlands* (vol. 35, pp. 1–30). Chicago, IL: University of Chicago Press.

Toupin, J., Dery, M., Pauze, R., Mercier, H., & Fortin, L. (2000). Cognitive and familial contributions to conduct disorder in children. *Journal of Child Psychology and Psychiatry and Allied Disciplines*, *41*, 333–44.

Tremblay, R. E. (2001). The development of physical aggression during childhood and the prediction of later dangerousness. In L. Pagani, & G. F. Pinard (eds), *Clinical Assessment of Dangerousness: Empirical Contributions* (pp. 47–65). New York: Cambridge University Press.

Tremblay, R. E., & Craigg, W. M. (1995). Developmental crime prevention. In M. Tonry & D. P. Farrington (eds), *Building a Safer Society. Strategic Approaches to Crime Prevention* (Vol. 19, pp. 151–236). Chicago, IL: University of Chicago Press.

Tremblay, R. E., & LeMarquand, D. (2001). Individual risk and protective factors. In R. Loeber, & D. P. Farrington (eds), *Child delinquents: Development, Intervention, and Service Needs* (pp. 137–64). Thousand Oaks, CA: Sage.

Tremblay, R. E., McCord, J., Boileau, H., Charlebois, P., Gagnon, C., Le Blanc, M., & Larivée, S. (1991). Can disruptive boys be helped to become competent? *Psychiatry*, *54*, 148–61.

Tremblay, R. E., & Nagin, D. S. (2005). The developmental origins of physical aggression in humans. In R. E. Tremblay, W. H. Hartup, & J. Archer (eds), *Developmental Origins of Aggression*. (pp. 83–106). New York: Guilford Press.

Tremblay, R. E., Nagin, D. S., Seguin, J. R., Zoccolillo, M., Zelazo, P. D., Boivin, M., Pérusse, D., & Japel, C. (2004). Physical aggression during early childhood: Trajectories and predictors. *Pediatrics*, *114*, e43–e50.

Tremblay, R. E., Pihl, R. O., Vitaro, F., & Dobkin, P. L. (1994). Predicting early onset of male antisocial behavior from preschool behavior. *Archives of General Psychiatry*, *51*, 732–9.

Trickett, P. K. (1998). Multiple maltreatment and the development of self and emotion regulation. *Journal of Aggression, Maltreatment, & Trauma*, *2*, 171–87.

Tricket, P. K., McBride-Chang, C., & Putnam, F. W. (1994). The classroom performance and behavior of sexually abused girls. *Development and Psychopathology*, *6*, 183–94.

Tsjebanova, V., Harland, P., & Versteegh, P. (2006). Criminaliteitsbeeldanalyse Jeugd 2005 Regio Haaglanden [Analysis of Youth Crime 2005, Region Haaglanden]. The Hague: Politie Haaglanden.

Tuijl, C. van (2001). *Effecten van Opstap Opnieuw. Effecten van een Gezinsgericht Stimuleringsprogramma bij Turkse en Marokkaanse Gezinnen* [The effects of 'Opstap Opnieuw': Effectiveness of a family-oriented encouraging programme for Turkish and Moroccan families]. Alkmaar: Extern Print.

Tuijl, C. van (2002). *Effecten van Opstap Opnieuw bij follow-up. Effecten van een Gezinsgericht Stimuleringsprogramma bij Turkse en Marokkaanse Leerlingen op Middellange termijn* [The effects of 'Opstap Opnieuw' at follow-up: The middle-term effects of a family-oriented encouraging program for Turkisch and Moroccan pupils]. Alkmaar: Extern Print.

Tuijl, C. van & Siebe, R. (2006). *Het rendement van Opstap in de Basisschoolperiode. Een longitudinaal Onderzoek naar Effecten van een Gezinsgericht Stimuleringsprogramma bij Turkse en Marokkaanse Gezinnen* [The effectiveness of 'Opstap' during primary school: A longitudinal study on the effects of a family-oriented encouraging program for Turkish and Moroccan families]. Alkmaar: Extern Print.

US Department of Health, Education and Welfare (1973). *Positive Approaches to Dropout Prevention.* Washington, DC: US Government Printing Office.

US Public Health Service (2001). *Youth Violence: A Report of the Surgeon General,* Washington DC: US Government Printing Office.

Utting, D., Monteiro, H., & Ghate, D. (2007). *Interventions for Children at Risk of Developing Antisocial Personality Disorder.* London: Policy Research Bureau.

Van Beers, H., Invernizzi, A., & Milne, B. (2006). *Beyond Article 12. Essential Readings in Child's Participation*. Bangkok: Knowing Children.

Van Bokhoven, I., Matthys, W., Van Goozen, S. H. M., & Van Engeland, H. (2005). Prediction of adolescent outcome in children with disruptive behaviour disorders – A study of neurobiological, psychological and family factors. *European Child & Adolescent Psychiatry*, *14*, 153–63.

Van den Boom, D. C. (1995). Do first-year intervention effects endure? Follow-up during toddlerhood of a sample of Dutch irritable infants. *Child Development*, *66*, 1798–816.

Van den Hoogen-Saleh (2000). *Hoe eerder hoe beter. Evaluatierapport van het pilotjaar van het Twaalfmin-project in Haaglanden 1999* [The sooner the better: Evaluation report of the pilot study on the 'Twaalfmin' project in Haaglanden 1999]. The Hague: Politie Haaglanden.

Van den Oord, E. J., & Rispens, J. (1999). Differences between school classes in preschoolers' psychosocial adjustment: Evidence for the importance of children's interpersonal relations. *Journal of Child Psychology Psychiatry*, *40*, 417–30.

Van der Kolk, B. A. (1996). The body keeps the score: approaches to the psychobiology of posttraumatic stress disorder. In B. A. van der Kolk, A. C. McFarlane, & L. Weiseth, (eds), *Traumatic Stress: The Overwhelming Experience on Mind, Body, and Society* (pp. 214–41). New York: Guilford Press.

Van der Laan, A. M., & Blom, M. (2006). *Jeugddelinquentie: Risico's en bescherming* [Juvenile delinquency: Risks and protection] (WODC reeks Onderzoek en Beleid, No. 245). The Hague: Boom Juridische Uitgevers.

Van der Laan, P. H. (2004). Over straffen, effectiviteit en erkenning [Punishment, efficacy and identification]. *Justitiële Verkenningen*, *30*, 31–48.

Van der Laan, P. H. (2005). Jeugdcriminaliteit [Juvenile crime]. In J. Hermanns, C. van Nijnatten, M. Smit, F. Verwey, & M. Reuling (eds), *Handboek Jeugdzorg*. Houten: Bohn Stafleu Van Loghum.

Van der Laan, P. H., Spaans, E. C., Essers, A. A. M., & Essers, J. J. A. (1997). *Jeugdcriminaliteit en jeugdbescherming. Ontwikkelingen in de periode 1980–1994* [Youth crime and youth protection: Trends during 1980–1994]. The Hague: WODC.

Van der Meer, B. (1988). *De Zondebok in de Klas* [The scapegoat in classrooms]. Den Bosch / Nijmegen: KPC/Berkhout.

Van der Ploeg, J. D. (2000). *Gedragsproblemen: Ontwikkelingen en Risico's* [Behaviour problems: Developments and risk]. Rotterdam: Lemniscaat.

Van der Ploeg, J. D., & Scholte, E. M. (1997). *Homeless Youth*. Thousand Oaks, CA: Sage.

Van der Ploeg, J. D., & Scholte, E. M. (2000). *Interventies bij Zeer Problematische jeugdigen* [Interventions for very problematic youth]. Amsterdam: NIPPO.

Van der Valk, J. C., van den Oord, E. J., Verhulst, F. C., & Boomsma, D. I. (2003). Using shared and unique parental views to study the etiology of 7-year-old twins' internalizing and externalizing problems. *Behavior Genetics*, *33*, 409–20.

Van der Valk, J. C., Verhulst, F. C., Stroet, T. M., & Boomsma, D. I. (1998). Quantitative genetic analysis of internalising and externalising problems in a large sample of 3-year-old twins. *Twin Research*, *1*, 25–33.

Van de Wiel, N (2002). *The effect of manualized behaviour therapy with disruptive behaviour disordered children in everyday clinical practice: A randomised clinical trial.* PhD Dissertation. Utrecht: Universiteit Utrecht

Van de Wiel, N., Matthys, W., Cohen-Kettenis, P., Maassen, G. H., Lochman, J. E., & van Engeland, H. (2007). The effectiveness of an experimental treatment when compared with care as usual depends on the type of care as usual. *Behavior Modification*, 31, 298–312.

Van de Wiel, N. M., van Goozen, S. H., Matthys, W., Snoek, H., & van Engeland, H. (2004). Cortisol and treatment effect in children with disruptive behavior disorders: A preliminary study. *Journal of the American Academy of Child and Adolescent Psychiatry*, *43*, 1011–18.

Van Domburgh, L. (2006). Neighbourhood and Socio-demographic Characteristics of First Offending Child Delinquents. Unpublished doctoral thesis. Amsterdam, University of Amsterdam.

Van Domburgh, L., Vermeiren, R., van der Laan, P. H., Loeber, R., & Doreleijers, T.A.H. (submitted). Neighbourhood and socio-demographic characteristics of first-time child delinquents.

Van Goozen, S. H. M. (2005). Hormones and the developmental origins of aggression. In R. Tremblay, W. Hartup, & J. Archer, *Developmental Origins of Aggression* (pp. 281–306). New York: Guilford Press.

Van Goozen, S. H., van den Ban, B. E., Matthys, W., Cohen-Kettenis, P. T., Thijssen, J. H., & van Engeland, H. (2000). Increased adrenal androgen functioning in children with oppositional defiant disorder: A comparison with psychiatric and normal controls. *Journal of the American Academy of Child and Adolescent Psychiatry*, *39*, 1446–51.

Van Haeringen, H. (1977). *Macht en Onmacht van het Individualiserend (Beroeps)Onderwijs* [Power and powerlessness of individualised vocational education]. Burgh-Haamstede: author.

Van't Hoff, C. A., van Overbeeke, R. W., van der Sprong, C. J. M., & Hilhorst, N. C. (1995). *Het jeugdpreventieproject Eindhoven. Evaluatie van een Samenwerkingsproject van Politie en Jeugdhulpverlening* [The youth prevention project Eindhoven: Evaluation of a cooperation project of police and youth care]. Amsterdam: DSP Groep BV.

Van Leeuwen, E., & Bijl, B. (2003a) *De Validiteit van het SPRINT Instrumentarium; Eerste Deelrapport van het Evaluatieonderzoek, Peildatum 1-12-2003* [The validity of the assessment instrument 'SPRINT': The first report of the evaluation study, reference date 12-1-2003]. Duivendrecht: PI-research.

Van Leeuwen, E., & Bijl, B.(2003b). *SPRINT Resultaten; Tweede Deelrapport van het Evaluatieonderzoek, over de Uitkomsten van de Interventie* ['SPRINT' results: Second report on the intervention outcomes]. Duivendrecht: PI-research.

Van Lier, P. A. C. (2002). *Preventing Disruptive behaviour in Early Elementary Schoolchildren.* Rotterdam: Doctoral dissertation at Erasmus University.

Van Lier, P. A. C., Boivin, M., Vitaro, F., Brendgen, M., Koot, H. M., Dionne, G., Koot, H., Tremblay, R., & Perusse, D. (2006). Kindergarten children's genetic vulnerabilities interact with friends' aggression to promote physical aggression. *Journal of the American Academy of Child and Adolescent Psychiatry*, *46*, 1080–87.

Van Lier, P. A. C., & Crijnen, A. A. M. (2004). Preventie van gedragsproblemen bij kinderen in Nederland Richting een bewezen effectief preventief jeugdbeleid [Prevention of behavioural problems in Dutch children: Towards an effective preventive youth policy]. In J. R. M. Gerris (ed.), *Jeugdzorg en Probleemgedrag: Opvoedingswaarden en Vernieuwingen in aanpak* (Vol. 18, pp. 77–94). Assen: Van Gorcum.

Van Lier, P. A. C., & Crijnen, A. A. M. (2005). Trajectories of peer-nominated aggression: Risk status, predictors and outcomes. *Journal of Abnormal Child Psychology*, *33*, 99–112.

Van Lier, P. A. C., Verhulst, F. C., van der Ende, J., & Crijnen, A. A. M. (2003). Classes of disruptive behaviour in a sample of young elementary school children. *Journal of Child Psychology and Psychiatry*, *44*, 377–87.

Van Lier, P. A. C., Vitaro, F., Wanner, B., Vuijk, P., & Crijnen, A. A. M. (2005). Gender differences in the developmental links between antisocial behavior, friends' antisocial behavior and peer rejection in childhood: Results from two cultures. *Child Development*, *76*, 841–55.

Van Lier, P. A. C., Vuijk, P., & Crijnen, A. A. M. (2005). Understanding mechanisms of change in the development of antisocial behavior: The impact of a universal intervention. *Journal of Abnormal Child Psychology*, *33*, 521–35.

Van Lier, P. A. C., Wanner, B., & Vitaro, F. (2007). Onset of antisocial behavior, affiliation with deviant friends, and childhood maladjustment: A test of the childhood- and adolescent-onset models. *Development and Psychopathology*, *19*, 167–85.

Van Lieshout, C. F. M., Haselager, G. J. T., & Liebrand, J. M. (1992). Begeleiding van de sociaal-emotionele ontwikkeling. Conclusies en aanbevelingen [Guiding social-emotional development: Conclusions and recommendations]. In C. F. M. van Lieshout (ed.), *Basisschoolleerlingen met Sociaal-emotionele Problemen. Diagnostiek en Begeleiding.* Nijmegen: Katholieke Universiteit, Vakgroep Ontwikkelingspsychologie.

Van Lieshout, C. F. M., Scholte, R. H. J., Haselager, G. J.,T., & Cillessen, A. H. N. (2001). Ontwikkeling van relaties met leeftijdgenoten en delinquentie [Development of peer relations and delinquency]. In R. Loeber, N. W. Slot, & J. A. Sergeant (eds), *Ernstige en Gewelddadige Jeugddelinquentie. Omvang, Oorzaken en Interventies* (pp. 185–203). Houten: Bohn, Stafleu Van Loghum.

Van Lieshout, C. F. M., Verhoeven, M., Güroglu, B., Haselager, G. J. T., & Scholte, R. H. J. (2004). Vriendschappen en antipathieën. Relatienetwerken van kinderen en adolescenten in klasgroepen [Friendships and antipathies: Relationship networks of children and adolescents in classrooms]. *Kind en Adolescent*, *25*, 113–31.

Van Manen, T. (2001). *Zelfcontrole, een Sociaal-cognitief Interventieprogramma voor Kinderen met Agressief en oppositioneel gedrag* [Self-control: A social-cognitive intervention program for children with aggressive and oppositional behaviour]. Houten/Diegem: Bohn Stafleu Van Loghum.

Van Manen, T. G., Prins, P. J. M., & Emmelkamp, P. M. G. (2004). Reducing aggressive behavior in boys with a social-cognitive group treatment: Results of a randomized control trial. *Journal of the American Academy of Child and Adolescent Psychiatry*, *43*, 1478–87.

Van Montfrans Committee (1994). *Met de Neus op de Feiten.* The Hague: Ministerie van Justitie.

Van Veluw, N. (2006). *Programma Ouders van Tegendraadse Jeugd* ['Parents of Oppositional Youths' programme]. Gouda: JSO Expertisecentrum voor Jeugd, Samenleving en Opvoeding.

Van Voorhis, P., Cullen, F. T., Mathers, R. A., & Garner, C. C. (1988). The impact of family structure and quality on delinquency: A comparative assessment of structural and functional factors. *Criminology*, *26*, 235–61.

Van Widenfelt, B. M., Goedhart, A. W., Treffers, P. D. A., & Goodman, R. (2003). Dutch version of the Strengths and Difficulties Questionnaire (SDQ). *European Child and Adolescent Psychiatry*, *12*, 281–9.

Van Wijk, A. Ph., Doreleijers, T. A. H., Bullens, R. A. R., & Ferwerda, H. B. (2001). Kenmerken en achtergronden van jeugdige zedendelinquenten [Characteristics and background of juvenile sex offenders]. In R. Loeber, N.W. Slot, & J. A. Sergeant (eds), *Ernstige en Geweldadige Jeugddelinquentie: Omvang, Oorzaken en Interventies* (pp. 73–95). Houten/Diegem: Bohn Stafleu Van Loghem.

Van Yperen, T. A. (2001). Antisociaal gedrag en jeugddelinquentie: Valt er wat te keren? [Antisocial behaviour and juvenile delinquency: Can they be changed?] *Kind en Adolescent*, *22*, 326–41.

Van Yperen, T. A., Booy, Y., & van der Veldt, M. C. (2003). *Vraaggerichte Hulp, Motivatie en Effectiviteit Jeugdzorg* [Needs-directed help, motivation and effectiveness of youth care]. Utrecht: NIZW.

Vanyukov, M. M., Moss, H. B., Plail, J. A., Blackson, T., Mezzich, A. C., & Tarter, R. E. (1993). Antisocial symptoms in preadolescent boys and in their parents: Associations with cortisol. *Psychiatry Research*, *46*, 9–17.

Van Zeijl, J., Mesman, J., van Zeijl, J., Stolk, M. N., Alink, L. R. A., van IJzendoorn, M. H., Bakermans-Kranenburg, M. J., Juffer, F., & Koot, H. M. (2006). Terrible ones? Assessment of externalizing behaviors in infancy with the Child Behavior Checklist. *Journal of Child Psychology and Psychiatry*, *47*, 801–10.

Veenstra, R., Lindenberg, S., Oldehinkel, A. J., De Winter, A. F., Verhulst, F. C., & Ormel, J. (2005). Bullying and victimization in elementary schools: A comparison of bullies, victims, bully/victims, and uninvolved preadolescents. *Developmental Psychology*, *41*, 672–82.

Veerman, J. W., Janssens, J. M. A. M., & Delicat, J. W. (2004). *Opvoeden in Onmacht, of ... ? Een Meta-analyse van 17 Methodieken voor Intensieve Pedagogische Thuishulp bij Normovertredend Gedrag* [Parenting without power, or ... ? A meta-analysis on 17 methods for intensive pedagogical help at home for norm-violating behaviour]. Nijmegen: Radboud Universiteit Nijmegen, ACSW/Praktikon.

Verdurmen, J. M., van Oort, M., Meeuwissen, J., Ketelaars, T., de Graaf, I., Cuijpers, P., de Ruiter, C., & Vollebergh, W. (2003). *Effectiviteit van Preventieve Interventies Gericht op Jeugdigen: De Stand van Zaken* [Effectiveness of prevention programmes aimed at juveniles: The state of the art]. Utrecht: Trimbos Instituut.

Verhoeven, W. (2002). Kinderen die niet vragen worden overgeslagen: Onderzoek naar hulp aan kinderen die mishandeld of misbruikt zijn [Children who do not ask, will be forgotten: A study of the help that physically or sexually abused children receive]. Tilburg: Provinciaal Incest Team Noord Brabant.

Verhulst, F. C., Koot, H. M., & Berden, G. F. M. G. (1990). Four-year follow-up of an epidemiological sample. *Journal of the American Academy of Child and Adolescent Psychiatry*, *29*, 440–48.

Verhulst, F. C., Koot, H. M., & van der Ende, J. (1994). Differential predictive value of parents' and teachers' reports of children's problem behaviors: A longitudinal study. *Journal of Abnormal Child Psychology*, *22*, 531–46.

Verhulst, F. C., & van der Ende, J. (1992). Six-year stability of parent-reported problem behavior in an epidemiological sample. *Journal of Abnormal Child Psychology*, *20*, 595–610.

Verhulst, F. C., & van der Ende, J. (1993). 'Comorbidity' in an epidemiological sample: A longitudinal perspective. *Journal of Child Psychology and Psychiatry*, *34*, 767–83.

Verhulst, F. C., van der Ende, J., & Koot, H. M. (1996). *Handleiding voor de CBCL/4-18* [Manual for the CBCL/4-18]. Rotterdam: Afdeling Kinder- en jeugdpsychiatrie, Sophia Kinderziekenhuis/Academisch Ziekenhuis Rotterdam/Erasmus Universiteit Rotterdam.

Verhulst, F. C., van der Ende, J., & Koot, H. M. (1997). *Handleiding voor de Teacher's Report Form (TRF)* [Manual for the TRF]. Rotterdam: Afdeling

Kinder- en jeugdpsychiatrie, Sophia Kinderziekenhuis/Academisch Ziekenhuis Rotterdam/Erasmus Universiteit Rotterdam.

Verhulst, F. C., van der Ende, J., & Rietbergen, A. (1997). Ten-year time trends of psychopathology in Dutch children and adolescents: No evidence for strong trends. *Acta Psychiatrica Scandinavica*, *96*, 7–13.

Vermaas, J., & van der Pluijm, J. (2004). *Brede evaluatie WSNS, LGF en OAB. Samenvattend Overzicht van de Onderzoeksrapporten en Reviews* [Broad evaluation of WSNS, LGF and OAB: Overview of the research reports and reviews]. The Hague: Ministerie van Onderwijs, Cultuur en Wetenschap.

Vermeiren, R., Jespers, I., & Moffitt, T. (2006). Mental health problems in juvenile justice populations. *Child and Adolescent Psychiatric Clinics of North America*, *15*, 333–51.

Versantvoort, M. C., Verster, A. C. M., Jannink, J., Broek van den, L. G., Zutphen van, F., & Donker van Heel, P. A. (2005). *Kosten en Baten van Justitiële Interventies: Ontwikkeling van een Analyse- en Rekenmodel* [Costs and benefits of judicial interventions: Development of an analysis and calculation model]. Rotterdam: Ecorys.

Verwers, C., & van der Laan, A. (2006). *Startnotities Evaluatie STOP Reactie* [Evaluation of the 'STOP Reactie']. The Hague: WODC.

Vitaro, F., & Brendgen, M. (2005). Proactive and reactive aggression: A developmental perspective. In: R. Tremblay, W. Hartup, & J. Archer (eds), *Developmental Origins of Aggression* (pp. 179–201). New York: Guilford Press.

Vitaro, F., Brendgen, M., Pagani, L., Tremblay, R. E., & McDuff, P. (1999). Disruptive behavior, peer association, and conduct disorder: Testing the developmental links through early intervention. *Development and Psychopathology*, *11*, 287–304.

Vitaro, F., Brendgen, M., & Tremblay, R. E. (2001). Preventive intervention: Assessing its effects on the trajectories of delinquency and testing for mediational processes. *Applied Developmental Science*, *5*, 201–13.

Vitaro, F., Pedersen, S., & Brendgen, M. (2007). Children's disruptiveness, peer rejection, friends' deviancy, and delinquent behaviors: A process-oriented approach. *Development and Psychopathology*, *19*, 433–53.

Vitaro, F., Tremblay, R. E., Kerr, M., Pagani, L., & Bukowski, W. M. (1997). Disruptiveness, friends' characteristics, and delinquency in early adolescence: A test of two competing models of development. *Child Development*, *68*, 676–89.

Vreugdenhil, C., van den Brink, W., Ferdinand, R., Wouters, L., & Doreleijers, T. A. H. (2006). The ability of YSR scales to predict DSM/DISC-C psychiatric disorders among incarcerated male adolescents, *European Journal of Child Adolescent Psychiatry*, *15*, 88–96.

Wakschlag, L. S., Leventhal, B. L., Thomas, J., & Pine, D. S. (2007). Disruptive behaviour disorders and ADHD in preschool children. In W. E. Narrow, M. B. First, P. J. Sirovatka, & D. A. Regier (eds), *Age and Gender Considerations in Psychiatric Diagnosis* (pp. 243–57). Arlington, VA: American Psychiatric Association.

Walker, H. M., Kavanagh, K., Stiller, B., Golly, A., Severson, H. H., & Feil, E. G. (1998). First step to success: An early intervention approach for preventing school antisocial behavior. *Journal of Emotional and Behavioral Disorders*, *6*, 66–80.

Waller, I. (2006). *Less Law, More Order. The Truth About Reducing Crime.* Westport, CT: Praeger.

Walsh, C., MacMillan, H., & Jamieson, E. (2002). The relationship between parental psychiatric disorder and child physical and sexual abuse: Findings from the Ontario Health Supplement. *Child Abuse & Neglect*, *26*, 11–22.

Walsh, M. M., Pepler, D. J., & Levene, K. S. (2002). A model intervention for girls with disruptive behaviour problems: The Earlscourt Girls Connection. *Canadian Journal of Counselling*, *36*, 297–311.

Walsh, M., Yuile, A., Jiang, D., Augimeri, L. K., Pepler, D. (2007). Early assessment risk list for girls (EARL-21G): Predicting antisocial behaviours and clinical implications. Manuscript in preparation.

Wandersman, A., & Florin, P. (2003). Community interventions and effective prevention. *American Psychologist*, *5*, 441–8.

Warr, M. (1996). Organization and instigation in delinquent groups. *Criminology*, *34*, 11–37.

Warren, A. R., & McGough, L. S. (1996). Research on children's suggestibility. In B. L. Bottoms, & G. S. Goodman (eds), *International Perspectives on Child Abuse and Children's Testimony* (pp. 12–44). Thousand Oaks, CA: Sage.

Warren, K., Schoppelrey, S., Moberg, D. P., & McDonald, M. (2005). A model of contagion through competition in the aggressive behaviors of elementary school students. *Journal of Abnormal Child Psychology*, *33*, 283–92.

Wasserman, G. A., Keenan, K., Tremblay, R. E., Coie, J., Herrenkohl, T. I., Loeber, R., & Petechuk, D. (2003). Risk and protective factors of child delinquency. *Child Delinquency Bulletin Series* (April). Washington, DC: Office of Juvenile Justice and Delinquency Prevention.

Wasserman, G. A., & Seracini, A. M. (2001). Family risk factors and interventions. In R. Loeber, & D. P. Farrington (eds), *Child delinquents: Development, Intervention and Service Needs* (pp. 165–89). Thousand Oaks, CA: Sage.

Webster, C. D., Douglas, K. S., & Eaves, D., & Hart, S. D. (1997). *HCR-20: Assessing Risk for Violence – Version 2.* Burnaby, BC: Mental Health, Law, and Policy Institute, Simon Fraser University.

Webster-Stratton, C., & Mihalic, S. F. (2001). *The Incredible Years: Parent, Teacher, and Child Training Series*. Boulder, CO: University of Colorado.

Webster-Stratton, C., Reid, J., & Hammond, M. (2001). Social skills and problem-solving training for children with early-onset conduct problems: who benefits? *Journal of Child Psychology and Psychiatry*, *42*, 943–52.

Weeks, R., & Widom, C. S. (1998). Early childhood victimization among incarcerated adult male felons. *Journal of Interpersonal Violence*, *13*, 346–61.

Weersing, V. R., & Weisz, J. R. (2002). Mechanisms of action in youth psychotherapy. *Journal of Child Psychology and Psychiatry*, *43*, 3–29.

Weijers, I. (2000). *Schuld en Schaamte* [Guilt and shame]. Houten/Diegem: Bohn Stafleu Van Loghum.

Weisz, J. R., Donenberg, G. R., Han, S. S., & Kauneckis, D. (1995). Child and adolescent psychotherapy outcomes in experiments versus clinics: why the disparity? *Journal of Abnormal Child Psychology*, *23*, 83–106.

Weisz, J. R., Weiss, B., Han, S. S., Granger, D. A., & Morton, T. (1995). Effects of psychotherapy with children and adolescents revisited: A meta-analysis of treatment outcome studies. *Psychological Bulletin*, *117*, 450–68.

Wells, L. E., & Rankin, J. H. (1988). Direct parental controls and delinquency. *Criminology*, *26*, 263–85.

Welsh, B.C. (2001). Economic costs and benefits of early developmental prevention. In R. Loeber, & D. P. Farrington. *Child delinquents: Development, Intervention and Service Needs* (pp. 339–55). Thousand Oaks, CA: Sage Publications.

Welsh, B. C., & Farrington, D. P. (2000). Correctional intervention programs and cost-benefit analysis. *Criminal Justice and Behavior*, *27*, 115–33.

Welsh, B. C., Farrington, D. P., & Sherman, L. W. (eds) (2000). *Costs and Benefits of Preventing Crime*. Oxford: Westview Press.

Welsh, B.C., Loeber, R., Stevens, B. R., Stouthamer-Loeber, M., Cohen, M. A., & Farrington, D. P. (2008). Costs of juvenile crime in urban areas. *Youth Violence and Juvenile Justice*, *6*, 3–27.

Werner, E. E. (2005). What can we learn about resilience from large-scale longitudinal studies? In S. Goldstein, & R. B. Brooks (eds), *Handbook of Resilience in Children* (pp. 91–106). New York: Kluwer Academic/Plenum Publishers.

West, K. A. (1987). Juvenile delinquency and adolescent alcohol abuse: the predictive power of family factors. MS thesis. Michigan State University. School of Criminal Justice.

White, H. R., Bates, M. E., & Buyske, S. (2001). Adolescence-limited versus persistent delinquency: Extending Moffitt's hypothesis into adulthood. *Journal of Abnormal Psychology*, *110*, 600–609.

White, J. L., Moffitt, T. E., Caspi, A., Bartusch, D. J., Needles, D. J., & Stouthamer-Loeber, M. (1994). Measuring impulsivity and examining its relationship to delinquency. *Journal of Abnormal Psychology*, *103*, 192–205.

Wilson, S. J., & Lipsey, M. W. (2007). School-based intervention for aggressive and disruptive behavior. Update of a meta-analysis. *American Journal of Preventive Medicine*, *33*, S130–S143.

World Health Organization (2002). *World Report On Violence And Health.* Geneva: World Health Organization.

Wibord, G., & Hamewinkel, R. (2005). Eigenstaendig warden: Sucht-und Gewalpraevention in der Schule durch Persoenlichct. (Becoming Autonomous – Prevention of Addiction and Violence in School by Supporting the Development of Personality) Evaluation Sergebnisse der ersten Klassenstufe <www.edu_butler.at/Rotary/docs/EW-Merzer.pdf>.

Widom, C. S. (1992). The cycle of violence. In *Research in brief.* Washington, DC: National Institute of Justice.

Widom, C. S., & Maxfield, M. G. (2001). A prospective examination of risk for violence among abused and neglected children. *Annals of the New York Academy of Sciences*, *794*, 224–37.

Wikström, P.-O. (2005). The social origins of pathways in crime. In D. P. Farrington (ed.), *Integrated Developmental and Life Course Theories of Offending: Advances in Criminological Theory* (pp. 1–49). New Brunswick, NJ: Transaction Publishers.

Wikström, P.-O., & Loeber, R. (2000). Do disadvantaged neighborhoods cause well-adjusted children to become adolescent delinquents? A study of male juvenile serious offending, risk and protective factors, and neighborhood context. *Criminology*, *38*, 1109–41.

Wilson, J. Q., & Hernstein, R. J. (1985). *Crime and Human Nature*. New York: Simon and Schuster.

Wilson, W. J. (1987). *The Truly Disadvantaged. The Inner-city, the Underclass and Public Policy*. Chicago, IL: Chicago University Press.

Winslow, E. B., & Shaw, D. S. (2007). Impact of neighborhood disadvantage on overt behaviour problems during early childhood. *Aggressive Behavior*, *33*, 207–19.

Wissink, I. B. (2006). Parenting, Friendship Relations and Adolescent Functioning in Different Ethnic Groups. Unpublished dissertation. Amsterdam: University of Amsterdam.

Wissink, I. B., Deković, M., & Meijer, A. M. (2006). Parenting behavior, quality of the parent-adolescent relationship, and adolescent functioning in four ethnic groups. *Journal of Early Adolescence*, *26*, 133–59.

Wolfgang, M. E., Figlio, R. M., & Sellin, T. (1972). *Delinquency in a Birth Cohort*. Chicago, IL: University of Chicago Press.

Wolke, D., Woods, S., Stanford, K., & Schulz, H. (2001). Bullying and victimization of primary school children in England and Germany: Prevalence and school factors. *British Journal of Psychology*, *92*, 673–96.

Wolzak, A. (2005). *Adviezen en meldingen over kindermishandeling in 2005: registratiegegevens van de Advies en Meldpunten Kindermishandeling* [Advice and reports on child maltreatment in 2005: registration data of the Advice and Reporting Centres for Child Abuse and Neglect]. Utrecht: NIZW Jeugd.

Wright, B. R. E., Caspi, A., Moffitt, T. E., & Silva, P. A. (2001). The effects of social ties on crime vary by criminal propensity: A life-course model of interdependence. *Criminology*, *39*, 321–51.

YJB (Youth Justice Board) (2004). *National Evaluation of the Restorative Justice in Schools Programme*. London: Youth Justice Board .

YJB (Youth Justice Board) website <www.yjb.gov.uk/en-gb/yjs/Prevention/YISP>.

Yoneyama, S., & Naito, A. (2003). Problems with the paradigm: The school as a factor in understanding bullying (with special reference to Japan). *British Journal of Sociology of Education*, *24*, 315–30.

Young, S. E., Smolen, A., Corley, R. P., Krauter, K. S., Defries, J. C., Crowley, T. J., Hewitt, J. K. (2002). Dopamine transporter polymorphism associated with externalizing behaviour problems in children. *American Journal of Medical Genetics*, *114*, 144–9.

Yuile, A., Walsh, M., Jiang, D., Pepler, D., & Levene, K. (2007). Risk factors and intervention outcomes for aggressive girls in the SNAP™ Girls Connection: A prospective replication. Manuscript in preparation.

Zeijl, E., Crone, M., Wiefferink, K., Keuzenkamp, S., & Reijneveld, M. (2005). *Kinderen in Nederland* [Children in the Netherlands]. The Hague: Sociaal Cultureel Planbureau.

Zeijl, E., Keuzenkamp, S., & Beker, M. (2003). *Voorstel voor de Toekomstige Ontwikkeling van de Landelijke Jeugdmonitor. Werkdocument 95* [Proposal for the development of the National Youth Survey]. The Hague: Sociaal en Cultureel Planbureau.

Zimmer, E. (2000). Systemische Arbeit mit Kindern und deren Familien – Integrative Familienhilfe [Systematic work with children and their families – Integrative family support]. In DJI (ed.), *Wider die Ratlosigkeit im Umgang mit Kinderdelinquenz: Präventive Ansätze und Konzepte*, pp. 73–85.

Zonnevylle-Bender, M. J. S., Matthys, W., van de Wiel, M. H., & Lochman, J. (2007). Preventive effects of treatment of DBD in middle childhood on substance use and delinquent behavior. *Journal of the American Academy of Child and Adolescent Psychiatry*, 46, 33–39.

Zwaanswijk, M., Verhaak, P. F. M., van der Ende, J., Bensing, J. M., & Verhulst, F. C. (2005). Consultation for and identification of child and adolescent psychological problems in Dutch general practice. *Family Practice*, *22*, 498–506.

Zwaanswijk, M., Verhaak, P. F. M., van der Ende, J., Bensing, J. M., & Verhulst, F. C. (2006). Change in children's emotional and behavioural problems over a one-year period: Associations with parental problem recognition and service use. *European Child and Adolescent Psychiatry*, *15*, 127–31.

Zuckerman, M. (1979). *Sensation Seeking: Beyond the Optimal Level of Arousal.* Hillsdale, NJ: Erlbaum.

Zuckerman, M. (1991). *Psychobiology of Personality*. Cambridge: Cambridge University Press.

Zwirs, B. W. C., Burger, H., Buitelaar, J. K., & Schulpen, T. W. J. (2006). Ethnic differences in parental detection of externalizing disorders. *European Child and Adolescent Psychiatry*, *15*, 418–26.

Zwirs, B. W. C., Burger, H., Schulpen, T. W. J., Wiznitzer, M., Fedder, H., & Buitelaar, J. K. (2007). Prevalence of psychiatric disorders among children of different ethnic origin. *Journal of Abnormal Child Psychology*, *35*, 556–66.

Index